Apache HTTP Server 2.4 Reference Manual 1/3

A catalogue record for this book is available from the Hong Kong Public Libraries.

Published in Hong Kong by Samurai Media Limited.

Email: info@samuraimedia.org

ISBN 978-988-8381-79-1

Contents

Chapter 1

Release Notes

1.1 Upgrading to 2.4 from 2.2

In order to assist folks upgrading, we maintain a document describing information critical to existing Apache HTTP Server users. These are intended to be brief notes, and you should be able to find more information in either the New Features (p. 7) document, or in the `src/CHANGES` file. Application and module developers can find a summary of API changes in the API updates (p. 959) overview.

This document describes changes in server behavior that might require you to change your configuration or how you use the server in order to continue using 2.4 as you are currently using 2.2. To take advantage of new features in 2.4, see the New Features document.

This document describes only the changes from 2.2 to 2.4. If you are upgrading from version 2.0, you should also consult the 2.0 to 2.2 upgrading document.[1]

See also

- Overview of new features in Apache HTTP Server 2.4 (p. 7)

Compile-Time Configuration Changes

The compilation process is very similar to the one used in version 2.2. Your old `configure` command line (as found in `build/config.nice` in the installed server directory) can be used in most cases. There are some changes in the default settings. Some details of changes:

- These modules have been removed: mod_authn_default, mod_authz_default, mod_mem_cache. If you were using mod_mem_cache in 2.2, look at MOD_CACHE_DISK in 2.4.
- All load balancing implementations have been moved to individual, self-contained mod_proxy submodules, e.g. MOD_LBMETHOD_BYBUSYNESS. You might need to build and load any of these that your configuration uses.
- Platform support has been removed for BeOS, TPF, and even older platforms such as A/UX, Next, and Tandem. These were believed to be broken anyway.
- configure: dynamic modules (DSO) are built by default
- configure: By default, only a basic set of modules is loaded. The other LOADMODULE directives are commented out in the configuration file.
- configure: the "most" module set gets built by default
- configure: the "reallyall" module set adds developer modules to the "all" set

Run-Time Configuration Changes

There have been significant changes in authorization configuration, and other minor configuration changes, that could require changes to your 2.2 configuration files before using them for 2.4.

Authorization

Any configuration file that uses authorization will likely need changes.

You should review the Authentication, Authorization and Access Control Howto (p. 217) , especially the section Beyond just authorization (p. 217) which explains the new mechanisms for controlling the order in which the authorization directives are applied.

[1] http://httpd.apache.org/docs/2.2/upgrading.html

Directives that control how authorization modules respond when they don't match the authenticated user have been removed: This includes AuthzLDAPAuthoritative, AuthzDBDAuthoritative, AuthzDBMAuthoritative, AuthzGroupFileAuthoritative, AuthzUserAuthoritative, and AuthzOwnerAuthoritative. These directives have been replaced by the more expressive REQUIREANY, REQUIRENONE, and REQUIREALL.

If you use MOD_AUTHZ_DBM, you must port your configuration to use `Require dbm-group ...` in place of `Require group ...`.

Access control

In 2.2, access control based on client hostname, IP address, and other characteristics of client requests was done using the directives ORDER, ALLOW, DENY, and SATISFY.

In 2.4, such access control is done in the same way as other authorization checks, using the new module MOD_AUTHZ_HOST. The old access control idioms should be replaced by the new authentication mechanisms, although for compatibility with old configurations, the new module MOD_ACCESS_COMPAT is provided.

Here are some examples of old and new ways to do the same access control.

In this example, all requests are denied.

2.2 configuration:

```
Order deny,allow
Deny from all
```

2.4 configuration:

```
Require all denied
```

In this example, all requests are allowed.

2.2 configuration:

```
Order allow,deny
Allow from all
```

2.4 configuration:

```
Require all granted
```

In the following example, all hosts in the example.org domain are allowed access; all other hosts are denied access.

2.2 configuration:

```
Order Deny,Allow
Deny from all
Allow from example.org
```

2.4 configuration:

```
Require host example.org
```

Other configuration changes

Some other small adjustments may be necessary for particular configurations as discussed below.

- MAXREQUESTSPERCHILD has been renamed to MAXCONNECTIONSPERCHILD, describes more accurately what it does. The old name is still supported.
- MAXCLIENTS has been renamed to MAXREQUESTWORKERS, which describes more accurately what it does. For async MPMs, like EVENT, the maximum number of clients is not equivalent than the number of worker threads. The old name is still supported.
- The DEFAULTTYPE directive no longer has any effect, other than to emit a warning if it's used with any value other than `none`. You need to use other configuration settings to replace it in 2.4.
- ALLOWOVERRIDE now defaults to `None`.
- ENABLESENDFILE now defaults to Off.
- FILEETAG now defaults to "MTime Size" (without INode).
- MOD_DAV_FS: The format of the DAVLOCKDB file has changed for systems with inodes. The old DAVLOCKDB file must be deleted on upgrade.
- KEEPALIVE only accepts values of `On` or `Off`. Previously, any value other than "Off" or "0" was treated as "On".
- Directives AcceptMutex, LockFile, RewriteLock, SSLMutex, SSLStaplingMutex, and WatchdogMutexPath have been replaced with a single MUTEX directive. You will need to evaluate any use of these removed directives in your 2.2 configuration to determine if they can just be deleted or will need to be replaced using MUTEX.
- MOD_CACHE: CACHEIGNOREURLSESSIONIDENTIFIERS now does an exact match against the query string instead of a partial match. If your configuration was using partial strings, e.g. using `sessionid` to match `/someapplication/image.gif;jsessionid=123456789`, then you will need to change to the full string `jsessionid`.
- MOD_CACHE: The second parameter to CACHEENABLE only matches forward proxy content if it begins with the correct protocol. In 2.2 and earlier, a parameter of '/' matched all content.
- MOD_LDAP: LDAPTRUSTEDCLIENTCERT is now consistently a per-directory setting only. If you use this directive, review your configuration to make sure it is present in all the necessary directory contexts.
- MOD_FILTER: FILTERPROVIDER syntax has changed and now uses a boolean expression to determine if a filter is applied.
- MOD_INCLUDE:
  - The `#if expr` element now uses the new expression parser (p. 89) . The old syntax can be restored with the new directive SSILEGACYEXPRPARSER.
  - An SSI* config directive in directory scope no longer causes all other per-directory SSI* directives to be reset to their default values.
- MOD_CHARSET_LITE: The `DebugLevel` option has been removed in favour of per-module LOGLEVEL configuration.
- MOD_EXT_FILTER: The `DebugLevel` option has been removed in favour of per-module LOGLEVEL configuration.
- MOD_PROXY_SCGI: The default setting for `PATH_INFO` has changed from httpd 2.2, and some web applications will no longer operate properly with the new `PATH_INFO` setting. The previous setting can be restored by configuring the `proxy-scgi-pathinfo` variable.
- MOD_SSL: CRL based revocation checking now needs to be explicitly configured through SSLCAREVOCATIONCHECK.

- MOD_SUBSTITUTE: The maximum line length is now limited to 1MB.
- MOD_REQTIMEOUT: If the module is loaded, it will now set some default timeouts.
- MOD_DUMPIO: DUMPIOLOGLEVEL is no longer supported. Data is always logged at LOGLEVEL `trace7`.
- On Unix platforms, piped logging commands configured using either ERRORLOG or CUSTOMLOG were invoked using `/bin/sh -c` in 2.2 and earlier. In 2.4 and later, piped logging commands are executed directly. To restore the old behaviour, see the piped logging documentation (p. 53) .

Misc Changes

- MOD_AUTOINDEX: will now extract titles and display descriptions for .xhtml files, which were previously ignored.
- MOD_SSL: The default format of the `*_DN` variables has changed. The old format can still be used with the new `LegacyDNStringFormat` argument to SSLOPTIONS. The SSLv2 protocol is no longer supported. SSLPROXYCHECKPEERCN and SSLPROXYCHECKPEEREXPIRE now default to On, causing proxy requests to HTTPS hosts with bad or outdated certificates to fail with a 502 status code (Bad gateway)
- `htpasswd` now uses MD5 hash by default on all platforms.
- The NAMEVIRTUALHOST directive no longer has any effect, other than to emit a warning. Any address/port combination appearing in multiple virtual hosts is implicitly treated as a name-based virtual host.
- MOD_DEFLATE will now skip compression if it knows that the size overhead added by the compression is larger than the data to be compressed.
- Multi-language error documents from 2.2.x may not work unless they are adjusted to the new syntax of MOD_INCLUDE's `#if expr=` element or the directive SSILEGACYEXPRPARSER is enabled for the directory containing the error documents.
- The functionality provided by `mod_authn_alias` in previous versions (i.e., the AUTHNPROVIDERALIAS directive) has been moved into MOD_AUTHN_CORE.
- The RewriteLog and RewriteLogLevel directives have been removed. This functionality is now provided by configuring the appropriate level of logging for the MOD_REWRITE module using the LOGLEVEL directive. See also the mod_rewrite logging (p. 804) section.

Third Party Modules

All modules must be recompiled for 2.4 before being loaded.

Many third-party modules designed for version 2.2 will otherwise work unchanged with the Apache HTTP Server version 2.4. Some will require changes; see the API update (p. 959) overview.

Common problems when upgrading

- Startup errors:
  - `Invalid command 'User', perhaps misspelled or defined by a module not included in the server configuration` - load module MOD_UNIXD
  - `Invalid command 'Require', perhaps misspelled or defined by a module not included in the server configuration`, or `Invalid command 'Order', perhaps misspelled or defined by a module not included in the server configuration` - load module MOD_ACCESS_COMPAT, or update configuration to 2.4 authorization directives.

  - `Ignoring deprecated use of DefaultType in line NN of /path/to/httpd.conf` - remove DefaultType and replace with other configuration settings.
  - `Invalid command 'AddOutputFilterByType', perhaps misspelled or defined by a module not included in the server configuration` - AddOutputFilterByType has moved from the core to mod_filter, which must be loaded.

- Errors serving requests:
  - `configuration error: couldn't check user: /path` - load module mod_authn_core.
  - `.htaccess` files aren't being processed - Check for an appropriate AllowOverride directive; the default changed to `None` in 2.4.

1.2 Overview of new features in Apache HTTP Server 2.4

This document describes some of the major changes between the 2.2 and 2.4 versions of the Apache HTTP Server. For new features since version 2.0, see the 2.2 new features (p. 11) document.

Core Enhancements

Run-time Loadable MPMs Multiple MPMs can now be built as loadable modules (p. 80) at compile time. The MPM of choice can be configured at run time via LOADMODULE directive.

Event MPM The Event MPM (p. 928) is no longer experimental but is now fully supported.

Asynchronous support Better support for asynchronous read/write for supporting MPMs and platforms.

Per-module and per-directory LogLevel configuration The LOGLEVEL can now be configured per module and per directory. New levels `trace1` to `trace8` have been added above the `debug` log level.

Per-request configuration sections <IF>, <ELSEIF>, and <ELSE> sections can be used to set the configuration based on per-request criteria.

General-purpose expression parser A new expression parser allows to specify complex conditions (p. 89) using a common syntax in directives like SETENVIFEXPR, REWRITECOND, HEADER, <IF>, and others.

KeepAliveTimeout in milliseconds It is now possible to specify KEEPALIVETIMEOUT in milliseconds.

NameVirtualHost directive No longer needed and is now deprecated.

Override Configuration The new ALLOWOVERRIDELIST directive allows more fine grained control which directives are allowed in `.htaccess` files.

Config file variables It is now possible to DEFINE variables in the configuration, allowing a clearer representation if the same value is used at many places in the configuration.

Reduced memory usage Despite many new features, 2.4.x tends to use less memory than 2.2.x.

New Modules

MOD_PROXY_FCGI FastCGI Protocol backend for MOD_PROXY

MOD_PROXY_SCGI SCGI Protocol backend for MOD_PROXY

MOD_PROXY_EXPRESS Provides dynamically configured mass reverse proxies for MOD_PROXY

MOD_REMOTEIP Replaces the apparent client remote IP address and hostname for the request with the IP address list presented by a proxies or a load balancer via the request headers.

MOD_HEARTMONITOR, MOD_LBMETHOD_HEARTBEAT Allow MOD_PROXY_BALANCER to base loadbalancing decisions on the number of active connections on the backend servers.

MOD_PROXY_HTML Formerly a third-party module, this supports fixing of HTML links in a reverse proxy situation, where the backend generates URLs that are not valid for the proxy's clients.

MOD_SED An advanced replacement of MOD_SUBSTITUTE, allows to edit the response body with the full power of sed.

MOD_AUTH_FORM Enables form-based authentication.

MOD_SESSION Enables the use of session state for clients, using cookie or database storage.

MOD_ALLOWMETHODS New module to restrict certain HTTP methods without interfering with authentication or authorization.

MOD_LUA Embeds the Lua[2] language into httpd, for configuration and small business logic functions. (Experimental)

MOD_LOG_DEBUG Allows the addition of customizable debug logging at different phases of the request processing.

MOD_BUFFER Provides for buffering the input and output filter stacks

MOD_DATA Convert response body into an RFC2397 data URL

MOD_RATELIMIT Provides Bandwidth Rate Limiting for Clients

MOD_REQUEST Provides Filters to handle and make available HTTP request bodies

MOD_REFLECTOR Provides Reflection of a request body as a response via the output filter stack.

MOD_SLOTMEM_SHM Provides a Slot-based shared memory provider (ala the scoreboard).

MOD_XML2ENC Formerly a third-party module, this supports internationalisation in libxml2-based (markup-aware) filter modules.

MOD_MACRO (available since 2.4.5) Provide macros within configuration files.

MOD_PROXY_WSTUNNEL (available since 2.4.5) Support web-socket tunnels.

MOD_AUTHNZ_FCGI (available since 2.4.10) Enable FastCGI authorizer applications to authenticate and/or authorize clients.

Module Enhancements

MOD_SSL MOD_SSL can now be configured to use an OCSP server to check the validation status of a client certificate. The default responder is configurable, along with the decision on whether to prefer the responder designated in the client certificate itself.

MOD_SSL now also supports OCSP stapling, where the server pro-actively obtains an OCSP verification of its certificate and transmits that to the client during the handshake.

MOD_SSL can now be configured to share SSL Session data between servers through memcached

EC keys are now supported in addition to RSA and DSA.

Support for TLS-SRP (available in 2.4.4 and later).

MOD_PROXY The PROXYPASS directive is now most optimally configured within a LOCATION or LOCATIONMATCH block, and offers a significant performance advantage over the traditional two-parameter syntax when present in large numbers. The source address used for proxy requests is now configurable. Support for Unix domain sockets to the backend (available in 2.4.7 and later).

MOD_PROXY_BALANCER More runtime configuration changes for BalancerMembers via balancer-manager

Additional BalancerMembers can be added at runtime via balancer-manager

Runtime configuration of a subset of Balancer parameters

BalancerMembers can be set to 'Drain' so that they only respond to existing sticky sessions, allowing them to be taken gracefully offline.

Balancer settings can be persistent after restarts.

[2] http://www.lua.org/

MOD_CACHE The MOD_CACHE CACHE filter can be optionally inserted at a given point in the filter chain to provide fine control over caching.

MOD_CACHE can now cache HEAD requests.

Where possible, MOD_CACHE directives can now be set per directory, instead of per server.

The base URL of cached URLs can be customised, so that a cluster of caches can share the same endpoint URL prefix.

MOD_CACHE is now capable of serving stale cached data when a backend is unavailable (error 5xx).

MOD_CACHE can now insert HIT/MISS/REVALIDATE into an X-Cache header.

MOD_INCLUDE Support for the 'onerror' attribute within an 'include' element, allowing an error document to be served on error instead of the default error string.

MOD_CGI, MOD_INCLUDE, MOD_ISAPI, ... Translation of headers to environment variables is more strict than before to mitigate some possible cross-site-scripting attacks via header injection. Headers containing invalid characters (including underscores) are now silently dropped. Environment Variables in Apache (p. 82) has some pointers on how to work around broken legacy clients which require such headers. (This affects all modules which use these environment variables.)

MOD_AUTHZ_CORE Authorization Logic Containers Advanced authorization logic may now be specified using the REQUIRE directive and the related container directives, such as <REQUIREALL>.

MOD_REWRITE MOD_REWRITE adds the `[QSD]` (Query String Discard) and `[END]` flags for REWRITERULE to simplify common rewriting scenarios. Adds the possibility to use complex boolean expressions in REWRITECOND. Allows the use of SQL queries as REWRITEMAP functions.

MOD_LDAP, MOD_AUTHNZ_LDAP MOD_AUTHNZ_LDAP adds support for nested groups. MOD_LDAP adds LDAPCONNECTIONPOOLTTL, LDAPTIMEOUT, and other improvements in the handling of timeouts. This is especially useful for setups where a stateful firewall drops idle connections to the LDAP server. MOD_LDAP adds LDAPLIBRARYDEBUG to log debug information provided by the used LDAP toolkit.

MOD_INFO MOD_INFO can now dump the pre-parsed configuration to stdout during server startup.

MOD_AUTH_BASIC New generic mechanism to fake basic authentication (available in 2.4.5 and later).

Program Enhancements

`fcgistarter` New FastCGI deamon starter utility

`htcacheclean` Current cached URLs can now be listed, with optional metadata included. Allow explicit deletion of individual cached URLs from the cache. File sizes can now be rounded up to the given block size, making the size limits map more closely to the real size on disk. Cache size can now be limited by the number of inodes, instead of or in addition to being limited by the size of the files on disk.

`rotatelogs` May now create a link to the current log file. May now invoke a custom post-rotate script.

`htpasswd`, `htdbm` Support for the bcrypt algorithm (available in 2.4.4 and later).

Documentation

mod_rewrite The MOD_REWRITE documentation has been rearranged and almost completely rewritten, with a focus on examples and common usage, as well as on showing you when other solutions are more appropriate. The Rewrite Guide (p. 136) is now a top-level section with much more detail and better organization.

mod_ssl The MOD_SSL documentation has been greatly enhanced, with more examples at the getting started level, in addition to the previous focus on technical details.

Caching Guide The Caching Guide (p. 40) has been rewritten to properly distinguish between the RFC2616 HTTP/1.1 caching features provided by MOD_CACHE, and the generic key/value caching provided by the socache (p. 104) interface, as well as to cover specialised caching provided by mechanisms such as MOD_FILE_CACHE.

Module Developer Changes

Check Configuration Hook Added A new hook, `check_config`, has been added which runs between the `pre_config` and `open_logs` hooks. It also runs before the `test_config` hook when the `-t` option is passed to `httpd`. The `check_config` hook allows modules to review interdependent configuration directive values and adjust them while messages can still be logged to the console. The user can thus be alerted to misconfiguration problems before the core `open_logs` hook function redirects console output to the error log.

Expression Parser Added We now have a general-purpose expression parser, whose API is exposed in *ap_expr.h*. This is adapted from the expression parser previously implemented in MOD_SSL.

Authorization Logic Containers Authorization modules now register as a provider, via ap_register_auth_provider(), to support advanced authorization logic, such as <REQUIREALL>.

Small-Object Caching Interface The *ap_socache.h* header exposes a provider-based interface for caching small data objects, based on the previous implementation of the MOD_SSL session cache. Providers using a shared-memory cyclic buffer, disk-based dbm files, and a memcache distributed cache are currently supported.

Cache Status Hook Added The MOD_CACHE module now includes a new `cache_status` hook, which is called when the caching decision becomes known. A default implementation is provided which adds an optional `X-Cache` and `X-Cache-Detail` header to the response.

The developer documentation contains a detailed list of API changes (p. 959) .

1.3 Overview of new features in Apache HTTP Server 2.2

This document describes some of the major changes between the 2.0 and 2.2 versions of the Apache HTTP Server. For new features since version 1.3, see the 2.0 new features (p. 14) document.

Core Enhancements

Authn/Authz The bundled authentication and authorization modules have been refactored. The new mod_authn_alias(already removed from 2.3/2.4) module can greatly simplify certain authentication configurations. See module name changes, and the developer changes for more information about how these changes affects users and module writers.

Caching MOD_CACHE, MOD_CACHE_DISK, and mod_mem_cache(already removed from 2.3/2.4) have undergone a lot of changes, and are now considered production-quality. `htcacheclean` has been introduced to clean up MOD_CACHE_DISK setups.

Configuration The default configuration layout has been simplified and modularised. Configuration snippets which can be used to enable commonly-used features are now bundled with Apache, and can be easily added to the main server config.

Graceful stop The PREFORK, WORKER and EVENT MPMs now allow `httpd` to be shutdown gracefully via the `graceful-stop` (p. 27) signal. The GRACEFULSHUTDOWNTIMEOUT directive has been added to specify an optional timeout, after which `httpd` will terminate regardless of the status of any requests being served.

Proxying The new MOD_PROXY_BALANCER module provides load balancing services for MOD_PROXY. The new MOD_PROXY_AJP module adds support for the `Apache JServ Protocol version 1.3` used by Apache Tomcat[3].

Regular Expression Library Updated Version 5.0 of the Perl Compatible Regular Expression Library[4] (PCRE) is now included. `httpd` can be configured to use a system installation of PCRE by passing the `--with-pcre` flag to configure.

Smart Filtering MOD_FILTER introduces dynamic configuration to the output filter chain. It enables filters to be conditionally inserted, based on any Request or Response header or environment variable, and dispenses with the more problematic dependencies and ordering problems in the 2.0 architecture.

Large File Support `httpd` is now built with support for files larger than 2GB on modern 32-bit Unix systems. Support for handling >2GB request bodies has also been added.

Event MPM The EVENT MPM uses a separate thread to handle Keep Alive requests and accepting connections. Keep Alive requests have traditionally required httpd to dedicate a worker to handle it. This dedicated worker could not be used again until the Keep Alive timeout was reached.

SQL Database Support MOD_DBD, together with the `apr_dbd` framework, brings direct SQL support to modules that need it. Supports connection pooling in threaded MPMs.

Module Enhancements

Authn/Authz Modules in the aaa directory have been renamed and offer better support for digest authentication. For example, `mod_auth` is now split into MOD_AUTH_BASIC and MOD_AUTHN_FILE; `mod_auth_dbm` is now called MOD_AUTHN_DBM; `mod_access` has been renamed MOD_AUTHZ_HOST. There is also a new mod_authn_alias(already removed from 2.3/2.4) module for simplifying certain authentication configurations.

[3] http://tomcat.apache.org/

[4] http://www.pcre.org/

MOD_AUTHNZ_LDAP This module is a port of the 2.0 `mod_auth_ldap` module to the 2.2 `Authn/Authz` framework. New features include using LDAP attribute values and complicated search filters in the REQUIRE directive.

MOD_AUTHZ_OWNER A new module that authorizes access to files based on the owner of the file on the file system

MOD_VERSION A new module that allows configuration blocks to be enabled based on the version number of the running server.

MOD_INFO Added a new `?config` argument which will show the configuration directives as parsed by Apache, including their file name and line number. The module also shows the order of all request hooks and additional build information, similar to `httpd -V`.

MOD_SSL Added a support for RFC 2817[5], which allows connections to upgrade from clear text to TLS encryption.

MOD_IMAGEMAP `mod_imap` has been renamed to MOD_IMAGEMAP to avoid user confusion.

Program Enhancements

`httpd` A new command line option `-M` has been added that lists all modules that are loaded based on the current configuration. Unlike the `-l` option, this list includes DSOs loaded via MOD_SO.

`httxt2dbm` A new program used to generate dbm files from text input, for use in REWRITEMAP with the `dbm` map type.

Module Developer Changes

APR 1.0 API Apache 2.2 uses the APR 1.0 API. All deprecated functions and symbols have been removed from `APR` and `APR-Util`. For details, see the APR Website[6].

Authn/Authz The bundled authentication and authorization modules have been renamed along the following lines:

- `mod_auth_*` -> Modules that implement an HTTP authentication mechanism
- `mod_authn_*` -> Modules that provide a backend authentication provider
- `mod_authz_*` -> Modules that implement authorization (or access)
- `mod_authnz_*` -> Module that implements both authentication & authorization

There is a new authentication backend provider scheme which greatly eases the construction of new authentication backends.

Connection Error Logging A new function, `ap_log_cerror` has been added to log errors that occur with the client's connection. When logged, the message includes the client IP address.

Test Configuration Hook Added A new hook, `test_config` has been added to aid modules that want to execute special code only when the user passes `-t` to `httpd`.

Set Threaded MPM's Stacksize A new directive, THREADSTACKSIZE has been added to set the stack size on all threaded MPMs. This is required for some third-party modules on platforms with small default thread stack size.

Protocol handling for output filters In the past, every filter has been responsible for ensuring that it generates the correct response headers where it affects them. Filters can now delegate common protocol management to MOD_FILTER, using the `ap_register_output_filter_protocol` or `ap_filter_protocol` calls.

[5] http://www.ietf.org/rfc/rfc2817.txt
[6] http://apr.apache.org/

Monitor hook added Monitor hook enables modules to run regular/scheduled jobs in the parent (root) process.

Regular expression API changes The `pcreposix.h` header is no longer available; it is replaced by the new `ap_regex.h` header. The POSIX.2 `regex.h` implementation exposed by the old header is now available under the `ap_` namespace from `ap_regex.h`. Calls to `regcomp`, `regexec` and so on can be replaced by calls to `ap_regcomp`, `ap_regexec`.

DBD Framework (SQL Database API) With Apache 1.x and 2.0, modules requiring an SQL backend had to take responsibility for managing it themselves. Apart from reinventing the wheel, this can be very inefficient, for example when several modules each maintain their own connections.

Apache 2.1 and later provides the `ap_dbd` API for managing database connections (including optimised strategies for threaded and unthreaded MPMs), while APR 1.2 and later provides the `apr_dbd` API for interacting with the database.

New modules SHOULD now use these APIs for all SQL database operations. Existing applications SHOULD be upgraded to use it where feasible, either transparently or as a recommended option to their users.

1.4 Overview of new features in Apache HTTP Server 2.0

This document describes some of the major changes between the 1.3 and 2.0 versions of the Apache HTTP Server.

See also

- Upgrading to 2.0 from 1.3 (p. 2)

Core Enhancements

Unix Threading On Unix systems with POSIX threads support, Apache httpd can now run in a hybrid multiprocess, multithreaded mode. This improves scalability for many, but not all configurations.

New Build System The build system has been rewritten from scratch to be based on `autoconf` and `libtool`. This makes Apache httpd's configuration system more similar to that of other packages.

Multiprotocol Support Apache HTTP Server now has some of the infrastructure in place to support serving multiple protocols. MOD_ECHO has been written as an example.

Better support for non-Unix platforms Apache HTTP Server 2.0 is faster and more stable on non-Unix platforms such as BeOS, OS/2, and Windows. With the introduction of platform-specific multi-processing modules (p. 80) (MPMs) and the Apache Portable Runtime (APR), these platforms are now implemented in their native API, avoiding the often buggy and poorly performing POSIX-emulation layers.

New Apache httpd API The API for modules has changed significantly for 2.0. Many of the module-ordering/-priority problems from 1.3 should be gone. 2.0 does much of this automatically, and module ordering is now done per-hook to allow more flexibility. Also, new calls have been added that provide additional module capabilities without patching the core Apache HTTP Server.

IPv6 Support On systems where IPv6 is supported by the underlying Apache Portable Runtime library, Apache httpd gets IPv6 listening sockets by default. Additionally, the LISTEN, NAMEVIRTUALHOST, and VIRTUALHOST directives support IPv6 numeric address strings (e.g., `"Listen [2001:db8::1]:8080"`).

Filtering Apache httpd modules may now be written as filters which act on the stream of content as it is delivered to or from the server. This allows, for example, the output of CGI scripts to be parsed for Server Side Include directives using the `INCLUDES` filter in MOD_INCLUDE. The module MOD_EXT_FILTER allows external programs to act as filters in much the same way that CGI programs can act as handlers.

Multilanguage Error Responses Error response messages to the browser are now provided in several languages, using SSI documents. They may be customized by the administrator to achieve a consistent look and feel.

Simplified configuration Many confusing directives have been simplified. The often confusing `Port` and `BindAddress` directives are gone; only the LISTEN directive is used for IP address binding; the SERVERNAME directive specifies the server name and port number only for redirection and vhost recognition.

Native Windows NT Unicode Support Apache httpd 2.0 on Windows NT now uses utf-8 for all filename encodings. These directly translate to the underlying Unicode file system, providing multilanguage support for all Windows NT-based installations, including Windows 2000 and Windows XP. *This support does not extend to Windows 95, 98 or ME, which continue to use the machine's local codepage for filesystem access.*

Regular Expression Library Updated Apache httpd 2.0 includes the Perl Compatible Regular Expression Library[7] (PCRE). All regular expression evaluation now uses the more powerful Perl 5 syntax.

[7] http://www.pcre.org/

Module Enhancements

MOD_SSL New module in Apache httpd 2.0. This module is an interface to the SSL/TLS encryption protocols provided by OpenSSL.

MOD_DAV New module in Apache httpd 2.0. This module implements the HTTP Distributed Authoring and Versioning (DAV) specification for posting and maintaining web content.

MOD_DEFLATE New module in Apache httpd 2.0. This module allows supporting browsers to request that content be compressed before delivery, saving network bandwidth.

MOD_AUTH_LDAP New module in Apache httpd 2.0.41. This module allows an LDAP database to be used to store credentials for HTTP Basic Authentication. A companion module, MOD_LDAP provides connection pooling and results caching.

MOD_AUTH_DIGEST Includes additional support for session caching across processes using shared memory.

MOD_CHARSET_LITE New module in Apache httpd 2.0. This experimental module allows for character set translation or recoding.

MOD_FILE_CACHE New module in Apache httpd 2.0. This module includes the functionality of `mod_mmap_static` in Apache HTTP Server version 1.3, plus adds further caching abilities.

MOD_HEADERS This module is much more flexible in Apache httpd 2.0. It can now modify request headers used by MOD_PROXY, and it can conditionally set response headers.

MOD_PROXY The proxy module has been completely rewritten to take advantage of the new filter infrastructure and to implement a more reliable, HTTP/1.1 compliant proxy. In addition, new <PROXY> configuration sections provide more readable (and internally faster) control of proxied sites; overloaded `<Directory "proxy:...">` configuration are not supported. The module is now divided into specific protocol support modules including `proxy_connect`, `proxy_ftp` and `proxy_http`.

MOD_NEGOTIATION A new FORCELANGUAGEPRIORITY directive can be used to assure that the client receives a single document in all cases, rather than NOT ACCEPTABLE or MULTIPLE CHOICES responses. In addition, the negotiation and MultiViews algorithms have been cleaned up to provide more consistent results and a new form of type map that can include document content is provided.

MOD_AUTOINDEX Autoindex'ed directory listings can now be configured to use HTML tables for cleaner formatting, and allow finer-grained control of sorting, including version-sorting, and wildcard filtering of the directory listing.

MOD_INCLUDE New directives allow the default start and end tags for SSI elements to be changed and allow for error and time format configuration to take place in the main configuration file rather than in the SSI document. Results from regular expression parsing and grouping (now based on Perl's regular expression syntax) can be retrieved using MOD_INCLUDE's variables `$0` .. `$9`.

MOD_AUTH_DBM Now supports multiple types of DBM-like databases using the AUTHDBMTYPE directive.

1.5 The Apache License, Version 2.0

Apache License
Version 2.0, January 2004
http://www.apache.org/licenses/

TERMS AND CONDITIONS FOR USE, REPRODUCTION, AND DISTRIBUTION

1. **Definitions**

   "License" shall mean the terms and conditions for use, reproduction, and distribution as defined by Sections 1 through 9 of this document.

   "Licensor" shall mean the copyright owner or entity authorized by the copyright owner that is granting the License.

   "Legal Entity" shall mean the union of the acting entity and all other entities that control, are controlled by, or are under common control with that entity. For the purposes of this definition, "control" means (i) the power, direct or indirect, to cause the direction or management of such entity, whether by contract or otherwise, or (ii) ownership of fifty percent (50%) or more of the outstanding shares, or (iii) beneficial ownership of such entity.

   "You" (or "Your") shall mean an individual or Legal Entity exercising permissions granted by this License.

   "Source" form shall mean the preferred form for making modifications, including but not limited to software source code, documentation source, and configuration files.

   "Object" form shall mean any form resulting from mechanical transformation or translation of a Source form, including but not limited to compiled object code, generated documentation, and conversions to other media types.

   "Work" shall mean the work of authorship, whether in Source or Object form, made available under the License, as indicated by a copyright notice that is included in or attached to the work (an example is provided in the Appendix below).

   "Derivative Works" shall mean any work, whether in Source or Object form, that is based on (or derived from) the Work and for which the editorial revisions, annotations, elaborations, or other modifications represent, as a whole, an original work of authorship. For the purposes of this License, Derivative Works shall not include works that remain separable from, or merely link (or bind by name) to the interfaces of, the Work and Derivative Works thereof.

   "Contribution" shall mean any work of authorship, including the original version of the Work and any modifications or additions to that Work or Derivative Works thereof, that is intentionally submitted to Licensor for inclusion in the Work by the copyright owner or by an individual or Legal Entity authorized to submit on behalf of the copyright owner. For the purposes of this definition, "submitted" means any form of electronic, verbal, or written communication sent to the Licensor or its representatives, including but not limited to communication on electronic mailing lists, source code control systems, and issue tracking systems that are managed by, or on behalf of, the Licensor for the purpose of discussing and improving the Work, but excluding communication that is conspicuously marked or otherwise designated in writing by the copyright owner as "Not a Contribution."

   "Contributor" shall mean Licensor and any individual or Legal Entity on behalf of whom a Contribution has been received by Licensor and subsequently incorporated within the Work.

2. **Grant of Copyright License.** Subject to the terms and conditions of this License, each Contributor hereby grants to You a perpetual, worldwide, non-exclusive, no-charge, royalty-free, irrevocable copyright license to reproduce, prepare Derivative Works of, publicly display, publicly perform, sublicense, and distribute the Work and such Derivative Works in Source or Object form.

3. **Grant of Patent License.** Subject to the terms and conditions of this License, each Contributor hereby grants to You a perpetual, worldwide, non-exclusive, no-charge, royalty-free, irrevocable (except as stated in this section)

patent license to make, have made, use, offer to sell, sell, import, and otherwise transfer the Work, where such license applies only to those patent claims licensable by such Contributor that are necessarily infringed by their Contribution(s) alone or by combination of their Contribution(s) with the Work to which such Contribution(s) was submitted. If You institute patent litigation against any entity (including a cross-claim or counterclaim in a lawsuit) alleging that the Work or a Contribution incorporated within the Work constitutes direct or contributory patent infringement, then any patent licenses granted to You under this License for that Work shall terminate as of the date such litigation is filed.

4. **Redistribution.** You may reproduce and distribute copies of the Work or Derivative Works thereof in any medium, with or without modifications, and in Source or Object form, provided that You meet the following conditions:

   (a) You must give any other recipients of the Work or Derivative Works a copy of this License; and

   (b) You must cause any modified files to carry prominent notices stating that You changed the files; and

   (c) You must retain, in the Source form of any Derivative Works that You distribute, all copyright, patent, trademark, and attribution notices from the Source form of the Work, excluding those notices that do not pertain to any part of the Derivative Works; and

   (d) If the Work includes a "NOTICE" text file as part of its distribution, then any Derivative Works that You distribute must include a readable copy of the attribution notices contained within such NOTICE file, excluding those notices that do not pertain to any part of the Derivative Works, in at least one of the following places: within a NOTICE text file distributed as part of the Derivative Works; within the Source form or documentation, if provided along with the Derivative Works; or, within a display generated by the Derivative Works, if and wherever such third-party notices normally appear. The contents of the NOTICE file are for informational purposes only and do not modify the License. You may add Your own attribution notices within Derivative Works that You distribute, alongside or as an addendum to the NOTICE text from the Work, provided that such additional attribution notices cannot be construed as modifying the License.

   You may add Your own copyright statement to Your modifications and may provide additional or different license terms and conditions for use, reproduction, or distribution of Your modifications, or for any such Derivative Works as a whole, provided Your use, reproduction, and distribution of the Work otherwise complies with the conditions stated in this License.

5. **Submission of Contributions.** Unless You explicitly state otherwise, any Contribution intentionally submitted for inclusion in the Work by You to the Licensor shall be under the terms and conditions of this License, without any additional terms or conditions. Notwithstanding the above, nothing herein shall supersede or modify the terms of any separate license agreement you may have executed with Licensor regarding such Contributions.

6. **Trademarks.** This License does not grant permission to use the trade names, trademarks, service marks, or product names of the Licensor, except as required for reasonable and customary use in describing the origin of the Work and reproducing the content of the NOTICE file.

7. **Disclaimer of Warranty.** Unless required by applicable law or agreed to in writing, Licensor provides the Work (and each Contributor provides its Contributions) on an "AS IS" BASIS, WITHOUT WARRANTIES OR CONDITIONS OF ANY KIND, either express or implied, including, without limitation, any warranties or conditions of TITLE, NON-INFRINGEMENT, MERCHANTABILITY, or FITNESS FOR A PARTICULAR PURPOSE. You are solely responsible for determining the appropriateness of using or redistributing the Work and assume any risks associated with Your exercise of permissions under this License.

8. **Limitation of Liability.** In no event and under no legal theory, whether in tort (including negligence), contract, or otherwise, unless required by applicable law (such as deliberate and grossly negligent acts) or agreed to in writing, shall any Contributor be liable to You for damages, including any direct, indirect, special, incidental, or consequential damages of any character arising as a result of this License or out of the use or inability to use the Work (including but not limited to damages for loss of goodwill, work stoppage, computer failure or malfunction, or any and all other commercial damages or losses), even if such Contributor has been advised of the possibility of such damages.

9. **Accepting Warranty or Additional Liability.** While redistributing the Work or Derivative Works thereof, You may choose to offer, and charge a fee for, acceptance of support, warranty, indemnity, or other liability obligations and/or rights consistent with this License. However, in accepting such obligations, You may act only on Your own behalf and on Your sole responsibility, not on behalf of any other Contributor, and only if You agree to indemnify, defend, and hold each Contributor harmless for any liability incurred by, or claims asserted against, such Contributor by reason of your accepting any such warranty or additional liability.

END OF TERMS AND CONDITIONS

APPENDIX: How to apply the Apache License to your work.

To apply the Apache License to your work, attach the following boilerplate notice, with the fields enclosed by brackets "[]" replaced with your own identifying information. (Don't include the brackets!) The text should be enclosed in the appropriate comment syntax for the file format. We also recommend that a file or class name and description of purpose be included on the same "printed page" as the copyright notice for easier identification within third-party archives.

```
Copyright [yyyy] [name of copyright owner]

Licensed under the Apache License, Version 2.0 (the "License");
you may not use this file except in compliance with the License.
You may obtain a copy of the License at

    http://www.apache.org/licenses/LICENSE-2.0

Unless required by applicable law or agreed to in writing, software
distributed under the License is distributed on an "AS IS" BASIS,
WITHOUT WARRANTIES OR CONDITIONS OF ANY KIND, either express or implied.
See the License for the specific language governing permissions and
limitations under the License.
```

Chapter 2

Using the Apache HTTP Server

2.1 Compiling and Installing

This document covers compilation and installation of the Apache HTTP Server on Unix and Unix-like systems only. For compiling and installation on Windows, see Using Apache HTTP Server with Microsoft Windows (p. 251) and Compiling Apache for Microsoft Windows (p. 259) . For other platforms, see the platform (p. 250) documentation.

Apache httpd uses `libtool` and `autoconf` to create a build environment that looks like many other Open Source projects.

If you are upgrading from one minor version to the next (for example, 2.4.9 to 2.4.10), please skip down to the upgrading section.

See also

- Configure the source tree (p. 295)
- Starting Apache httpd (p. 25)
- Stopping and Restarting (p. 27)

Overview for the impatient

Download	`$ lynx http://httpd.apache.org/download.cgi`

Extract	`$ gzip -d httpd-NN.tar.gz`
	`$ tar xvf httpd-NN.tar`
	`$ cd httpd-NN`

Configure	`$ ./configure --prefix=PREFIX`
Compile	`$ make`
Install	`$ make install`
Customize	`$ vi PREFIX/conf/httpd.conf`
Test	`$ PREFIX/bin/apachectl -k start`

NN must be replaced with the current version number, and *PREFIX* must be replaced with the filesystem path under which the server should be installed. If *PREFIX* is not specified, it defaults to `/usr/local/apache2`.

Each section of the compilation and installation process is described in more detail below, beginning with the requirements for compiling and installing Apache httpd.

Requirements

The following requirements exist for building Apache httpd:

APR and APR-Util Make sure you have APR and APR-Util already installed on your system. If you don't, or prefer to not use the system-provided versions, download the latest versions of both APR and APR-Util from Apache APR[1], unpack them into `/httpd_source_tree_root/srclib/apr` and `/httpd_source_tree_root/srclib/apr-util` (be sure the directory names do not have version numbers; for example, the APR distribution must be under /httpd_source_tree_root/srclib/apr/) and use `./configure`'s `--with-included-apr` option. On some platforms, you may have to install the corresponding `-dev` packages to allow httpd to build against your installed copy of APR and APR-Util.

Perl-Compatible Regular Expressions Library (PCRE) This library is required but not longer bundled with httpd. Download the source code from http://www.pcre.org[2], or install a Port or Package. If your build system can't find the pcre-config script installed by the PCRE build, point to it using the `--with-pcre` parameter. On some platforms, you may have to install the corresponding `-dev` package to allow httpd to build against your installed copy of PCRE.

[1] http://apr.apache.org/
[2] http://www.pcre.org/

Disk Space Make sure you have at least 50 MB of temporary free disk space available. After installation the server occupies approximately 10 MB of disk space. The actual disk space requirements will vary considerably based on your chosen configuration options, any third-party modules, and, of course, the size of the web site or sites that you have on the server.

ANSI-C Compiler and Build System Make sure you have an ANSI-C compiler installed. The GNU C compiler (GCC)[3] from the Free Software Foundation (FSF)[4] is recommended. If you don't have GCC then at least make sure your vendor's compiler is ANSI compliant. In addition, your `PATH` must contain basic build tools such as `make`.

Accurate time keeping Elements of the HTTP protocol are expressed as the time of day. So, it's time to investigate setting some time synchronization facility on your system. Usually the `ntpdate` or `xntpd` programs are used for this purpose which are based on the Network Time Protocol (NTP). See the NTP homepage[5] for more details about NTP software and public time servers.

Perl 5[6] [OPTIONAL] For some of the support scripts like `apxs` or `dbmmanage` (which are written in Perl) the Perl 5 interpreter is required (versions 5.003 or newer are sufficient). If no Perl 5 interpreter is found by the `configure` script, you will not be able to use the affected support scripts. Of course, you will still be able to build and use Apache httpd.

Download

The Apache HTTP Server can be downloaded from the Apache HTTP Server download site[7], which lists several mirrors. Most users of Apache on unix-like systems will be better off downloading and compiling a source version. The build process (described below) is easy, and it allows you to customize your server to suit your needs. In addition, binary releases are often not up to date with the latest source releases. If you do download a binary, follow the instructions in the `INSTALL.bindist` file inside the distribution.

After downloading, it is important to verify that you have a complete and unmodified version of the Apache HTTP Server. This can be accomplished by testing the downloaded tarball against the PGP signature. Details on how to do this are available on the download page[8] and an extended example is available describing the use of PGP[9].

Extract

Extracting the source from the Apache HTTP Server tarball is a simple matter of uncompressing, and then untarring:

```
$ gzip -d httpd-NN.tar.gz
$ tar xvf httpd-NN.tar
```

This will create a new directory under the current directory containing the source code for the distribution. You should `cd` into that directory before proceeding with compiling the server.

Configuring the source tree

The next step is to configure the Apache source tree for your particular platform and personal requirements. This is done using the script `configure` included in the root directory of the distribution. (Developers downloading an

[3]http://gcc.gnu.org/
[4]http://www.gnu.org/
[5]http://www.ntp.org
[7]http://httpd.apache.org/download.cgi
[8]http://httpd.apache.org/download.cgi#verify
[9]http://httpd.apache.org/dev/verification.html

unreleased version of the Apache source tree will need to have `autoconf` and `libtool` installed and will need to run `buildconf` before proceeding with the next steps. This is not necessary for official releases.)

To configure the source tree using all the default options, simply type `./configure`. To change the default options, `configure` accepts a variety of variables and command line options.

The most important option is the location `--prefix` where Apache is to be installed later, because Apache has to be configured for this location to work correctly. More fine-tuned control of the location of files is possible with additional configure options (p. 295) .

Also at this point, you can specify which features (p. 295) you want included in Apache by enabling and disabling modules (p. 1025) . Apache comes with a wide range of modules included by default. They will be compiled as shared objects (DSOs) (p. 65) which can be loaded or unloaded at runtime. You can also choose to compile modules statically by using the option `--enable-`*module*`=static`.

Additional modules are enabled using the `--enable-`*module* option, where *module* is the name of the module with the `mod_` string removed and with any underscore converted to a dash. Similarly, you can disable modules with the `--disable-`*module* option. Be careful when using these options, since `configure` cannot warn you if the module you specify does not exist; it will simply ignore the option.

In addition, it is sometimes necessary to provide the `configure` script with extra information about the location of your compiler, libraries, or header files. This is done by passing either environment variables or command line options to `configure`. For more information, see the `configure` manual page. Or invoke `configure` using the `--help` option.

For a short impression of what possibilities you have, here is a typical example which compiles Apache for the installation tree `/sw/pkg/apache` with a particular compiler and flags plus the two additional modules MOD_LDAP and MOD_LUA:

```
$ CC="pgcc" CFLAGS="-O2" \
./configure --prefix=/sw/pkg/apache \
--enable-ldap=shared \
--enable-lua=shared
```

When `configure` is run it will take several minutes to test for the availability of features on your system and build Makefiles which will later be used to compile the server.

Details on all the different `configure` options are available on the `configure` manual page.

Build

Now you can build the various parts which form the Apache package by simply running the command:

```
$ make
```

Please be patient here, since a base configuration takes several minutes to compile and the time will vary widely depending on your hardware and the number of modules that you have enabled.

Install

Now it's time to install the package under the configured installation *PREFIX* (see `--prefix` option above) by running:

```
$ make install
```

This step will typically require root privileges, since *PREFIX* is usually a directory with restricted write permissions.

If you are upgrading, the installation will not overwrite your configuration files or documents.

Customize

Next, you can customize your Apache HTTP server by editing the configuration files (p. 30) under `PREFIX/conf/`.

```
$ vi PREFIX/conf/httpd.conf
```

Have a look at the Apache manual under `PREFIX/docs/manual/` or consult http://httpd.apache.org/docs/2.4/ for the most recent version of this manual and a complete reference of available configuration directives (p. 1030) .

Test

Now you can start (p. 25) your Apache HTTP server by immediately running:

```
$ PREFIX/bin/apachectl -k start
```

You should then be able to request your first document via the URL `http://localhost/`. The web page you see is located under the DOCUMENTROOT, which will usually be `PREFIX/htdocs/`. Then stop (p. 27) the server again by running:

```
$ PREFIX/bin/apachectl -k stop
```

Upgrading

The first step in upgrading is to read the release announcement and the file `CHANGES` in the source distribution to find any changes that may affect your site. When changing between major releases (for example, from 2.0 to 2.2 or from 2.2 to 2.4), there will likely be major differences in the compile-time and run-time configuration that will require manual adjustments. All modules will also need to be upgraded to accommodate changes in the module API.

Upgrading from one minor version to the next (for example, from 2.2.55 to 2.2.57) is easier. The `make install` process will not overwrite any of your existing documents, log files, or configuration files. In addition, the developers make every effort to avoid incompatible changes in the `configure` options, run-time configuration, or the module API between minor versions. In most cases you should be able to use an identical `configure` command line, an identical configuration file, and all of your modules should continue to work.

To upgrade across minor versions, start by finding the file `config.nice` in the `build` directory of your installed server or at the root of the source tree for your old install. This will contain the exact `configure` command line that you used to configure the source tree. Then to upgrade from one version to the next, you need only copy the `config.nice` file to the source tree of the new version, edit it to make any desired changes, and then run:

```
$ ./config.nice
$ make
$ make install
$ PREFIX/bin/apachectl -k graceful-stop
$ PREFIX/bin/apachectl -k start
```

You should always test any new version in your environment before putting it into production. For example, you can install and run the new version along side the old one by using a different `--prefix` and a different port (by adjusting the LISTEN directive) to test for any incompatibilities before doing the final upgrade.

You can pass additional arguments to `config.nice`, which will be appended to your original `configure` options:

```
$ ./config.nice --prefix=/home/test/apache --with-port=90
```

Third-party packages

A large number of third parties provide their own packaged distributions of the Apache HTTP Server for installation on particular platforms. This includes the various Linux distributions, various third-party Windows packages, Mac OS X, Solaris, and many more.

Our software license not only permits, but encourages, this kind of redistribution. However, it does result in a situation where the configuration layout and defaults on your installation of the server may differ from what is stated in the documentation. While unfortunate, this situation is not likely to change any time soon.

A description of these third-party distrubutions[10] is maintained in the HTTP Server wiki, and should reflect the current state of these third-party distributions. However, you will need to familiarize yourself with your particular platform's package management and installation procedures.

[10] http://wiki.apache.org/httpd/DistrosDefaultLayout

2.2 Starting Apache

On Windows, Apache is normally run as a service. For details, see Running Apache as a Service (p. 251) .

On Unix, the `httpd` program is run as a daemon that executes continuously in the background to handle requests. This document describes how to invoke `httpd`.

See also

- Stopping and Restarting (p. 27)
- `httpd`
- `apachectl`

How Apache Starts

If the LISTEN specified in the configuration file is default of 80 (or any other port below 1024), then it is necessary to have root privileges in order to start apache, so that it can bind to this privileged port. Once the server has started and performed a few preliminary activities such as opening its log files, it will launch several *child* processes which do the work of listening for and answering requests from clients. The main `httpd` process continues to run as the root user, but the child processes run as a less privileged user. This is controlled by the selected Multi-Processing Module (p. 80) .

The recommended method of invoking the `httpd` executable is to use the `apachectl` control script. This script sets certain environment variables that are necessary for `httpd` to function correctly under some operating systems, and then invokes the `httpd` binary. `apachectl` will pass through any command line arguments, so any `httpd` options may also be used with `apachectl`. You may also directly edit the `apachectl` script by changing the `HTTPD` variable near the top to specify the correct location of the `httpd` binary and any command-line arguments that you wish to be *always* present.

The first thing that `httpd` does when it is invoked is to locate and read the configuration file (p. 30) `httpd.conf`. The location of this file is set at compile-time, but it is possible to specify its location at run time using the `-f` command-line option as in

```
/usr/local/apache2/bin/apachectl -f
/usr/local/apache2/conf/httpd.conf
```

If all goes well during startup, the server will detach from the terminal and the command prompt will return almost immediately. This indicates that the server is up and running. You can then use your browser to connect to the server and view the test page in the DOCUMENTROOT directory.

Errors During Start-up

If Apache suffers a fatal problem during startup, it will write a message describing the problem either to the console or to the ERRORLOG before exiting. One of the most common error messages is `"Unable to bind to Port ..."`. This message is usually caused by either:

- Trying to start the server on a privileged port when not logged in as the root user; or
- Trying to start the server when there is another instance of Apache or some other web server already bound to the same Port.

For further trouble-shooting instructions, consult the Apache FAQ[11].

[11] http://wiki.apache.org/httpd/FAQ

Starting at Boot-Time

If you want your server to continue running after a system reboot, you should add a call to `apachectl` to your system startup files (typically `rc.local` or a file in an `rc.N` directory). This will start Apache as root. Before doing this ensure that your server is properly configured for security and access restrictions.

The `apachectl` script is designed to act like a standard SysV init script; it can take the arguments `start`, `restart`, and `stop` and translate them into the appropriate signals to `httpd`. So you can often simply link `apachectl` into the appropriate init directory. But be sure to check the exact requirements of your system.

Additional Information

Additional information about the command-line options of `httpd` and `apachectl` as well as other support programs included with the server is available on the Server and Supporting Programs (p. 282) page. There is also documentation on all the modules (p. 1025) included with the Apache distribution and the directives (p. 1030) that they provide.

2.3 Stopping and Restarting Apache HTTP Server

This document covers stopping and restarting Apache HTTP Server on Unix-like systems. Windows NT, 2000 and XP users should see Running httpd as a Service (p. 251) and Windows 9x and ME users should see Running httpd as a Console Application (p. 251) for information on how to control httpd on those platforms.

See also

- `httpd`
- `apachectl`
- Starting (p. 25)

Introduction

In order to stop or restart the Apache HTTP Server, you must send a signal to the running `httpd` processes. There are two ways to send the signals. First, you can use the unix `kill` command to directly send signals to the processes. You will notice many `httpd` executables running on your system, but you should not send signals to any of them except the parent, whose pid is in the PIDFILE. That is to say you shouldn't ever need to send signals to any process except the parent. There are four signals that you can send the parent: `TERM`, `USR1`, `HUP`, and `WINCH`, which will be described in a moment.

To send a signal to the parent you should issue a command such as:

```
kill -TERM `cat /usr/local/apache2/logs/httpd.pid`
```

The second method of signaling the `httpd` processes is to use the `-k` command line options: `stop`, `restart`, `graceful` and `graceful-stop`, as described below. These are arguments to the `httpd` binary, but we recommend that you send them using the `apachectl` control script, which will pass them through to `httpd`.

After you have signaled `httpd`, you can read about its progress by issuing:

```
tail -f /usr/local/apache2/logs/error_log
```

Modify those examples to match your SERVERROOT and PIDFILE settings.

Stop Now

Signal: TERM `apachectl -k stop`

Sending the `TERM` or `stop` signal to the parent causes it to immediately attempt to kill off all of its children. It may take it several seconds to complete killing off its children. Then the parent itself exits. Any requests in progress are terminated, and no further requests are served.

Graceful Restart

Signal: USR1 `apachectl -k graceful`

The USR1 or graceful signal causes the parent process to *advise* the children to exit after their current request (or to exit immediately if they're not serving anything). The parent re-reads its configuration files and re-opens its log files. As each child dies off the parent replaces it with a child from the new *generation* of the configuration, which begins serving new requests immediately.

This code is designed to always respect the process control directive of the MPMs, so the number of processes and threads available to serve clients will be maintained at the appropriate values throughout the restart process. Furthermore, it respects STARTSERVERS in the following manner: if after one second at least STARTSERVERS new children have not been created, then create enough to pick up the slack. Hence the code tries to maintain both the number of children appropriate for the current load on the server, and respect your wishes with the STARTSERVERS parameter.

Users of MOD_STATUS will notice that the server statistics are **not** set to zero when a USR1 is sent. The code was written to both minimize the time in which the server is unable to serve new requests (they will be queued up by the operating system, so they're not lost in any event) and to respect your tuning parameters. In order to do this it has to keep the *scoreboard* used to keep track of all children across generations.

The status module will also use a G to indicate those children which are still serving requests started before the graceful restart was given.

At present there is no way for a log rotation script using USR1 to know for certain that all children writing the pre-restart log have finished. We suggest that you use a suitable delay after sending the USR1 signal before you do anything with the old log. For example if most of your hits take less than 10 minutes to complete for users on low bandwidth links then you could wait 15 minutes before doing anything with the old log.

When you issue a restart, a syntax check is first run, to ensure that there are no errors in the configuration files. If your configuration file has errors in it, you will get an error message about that syntax error, and the server will refuse to restart. This avoids the situation where the server halts and then cannot restart, leaving you with a non-functioning server.
This still will not guarantee that the server will restart correctly. To check the semantics of the configuration files as well as the syntax, you can try starting httpd as a non-root user. If there are no errors it will attempt to open its sockets and logs and fail because it's not root (or because the currently running httpd already has those ports bound). If it fails for any other reason then it's probably a config file error and the error should be fixed before issuing the graceful restart.

Restart Now

Signal: HUP `apachectl -k restart`

Sending the HUP or restart signal to the parent causes it to kill off its children like in TERM, but the parent doesn't exit. It re-reads its configuration files, and re-opens any log files. Then it spawns a new set of children and continues serving hits.

Users of MOD_STATUS will notice that the server statistics are set to zero when a HUP is sent.

As with a graceful restart, a syntax check is run before the restart is attempted. If your configuration file has errors in it, the restart will not be attempted, and you will receive notification of the syntax error(s).

Graceful Stop

Signal: WINCH `apachectl -k graceful-stop`

The WINCH or graceful-stop signal causes the parent process to *advise* the children to exit after their current request (or to exit immediately if they're not serving anything). The parent will then remove its PIDFILE and cease listening on all ports. The parent will continue to run, and monitor children which are handling requests. Once all children have finalised and exited or the timeout specified by the GRACEFULSHUTDOWNTIMEOUT has been reached, the parent will also exit. If the timeout is reached, any remaining children will be sent the `TERM` signal to force them to exit.

A `TERM` signal will immediately terminate the parent process and all children when in the "graceful" state. However as the PIDFILE will have been removed, you will not be able to use `apachectl` or `httpd` to send this signal.

⟹ The `graceful-stop` signal allows you to run multiple identically configured instances of `httpd` at the same time. This is a powerful feature when performing graceful upgrades of httpd, however it can also cause deadlocks and race conditions with some configurations.
Care has been taken to ensure that on-disk files such as lock files (MUTEX) and Unix socket files (SCRIPTSOCK) contain the server PID, and should coexist without problem. However, if a configuration directive, third-party module or persistent CGI utilises any other on-disk lock or state files, care should be taken to ensure that multiple running instances of `httpd` do not clobber each other's files.
You should also be wary of other potential race conditions, such as using `rotatelogs` style piped logging. Multiple running instances of `rotatelogs` attempting to rotate the same logfiles at the same time may destroy each other's logfiles.

2.4 Configuration Files

This document describes the files used to configure Apache HTTP Server.

Main Configuration Files

Related Modules	Related Directives
MOD_MIME	<IfDefine> Include TypesConfig

Apache HTTP Server is configured by placing directives (p. 1030) in plain text configuration files. The main configuration file is usually called `httpd.conf`. The location of this file is set at compile-time, but may be overridden with the `-f` command line flag. In addition, other configuration files may be added using the Include directive, and wildcards can be used to include many configuration files. Any directive may be placed in any of these configuration files. Changes to the main configuration files are only recognized by httpd when it is started or restarted.

The server also reads a file containing mime document types; the filename is set by the TypesConfig directive, and is `mime.types` by default.

Syntax of the Configuration Files

httpd configuration files contain one directive per line. The backslash "\" may be used as the last character on a line to indicate that the directive continues onto the next line. There must be no other characters or white space between the backslash and the end of the line.

Arguments to directives are separated by whitespace. If an argument contains spaces, you must enclose that argument in quotes.

Directives in the configuration files are case-insensitive, but arguments to directives are often case sensitive. Lines that begin with the hash character "#" are considered comments, and are ignored. Comments may **not** be included on the same line as a configuration directive. White space occurring before a directive is ignored, so you may indent directives for clarity. Blank lines are also ignored.

The values of variables defined with the Define of or shell environment variables can be used in configuration file lines using the syntax `${VAR}`. If "VAR" is the name of a valid variable, the value of that variable is substituted into that spot in the configuration file line, and processing continues as if that text were found directly in the configuration file. Variables defined with Define take precedence over shell environment variables. If the "VAR" variable is not found, the characters `${VAR}` are left unchanged, and a warning is logged. Variable names may not contain colon ":" characters, to avoid clashes with RewriteMap's syntax.

Only shell environment variables defined before the server is started can be used in expansions. Environment variables defined in the configuration file itself, for example with SetEnv, take effect too late to be used for expansions in the configuration file.

The maximum length of a line in normal configuration files, after variable substitution and joining any continued lines, is approximately 16 MiB. In .htaccess files (p. 30) , the maximum length is 8190 characters.

You can check your configuration files for syntax errors without starting the server by using `apachectl configtest` or the `-t` command line option.

You can use MOD_INFO's `-DDUMP_CONFIG` to dump the configuration with all included files and environment variables resolved and all comments and non-matching <IfDefine> and <IfModule> sections removed. However, the output does not reflect the merging or overriding that may happen for repeated directives.

Modules

Related Modules	Related Directives
MOD_SO	<IFMODULE> LOADMODULE

httpd is a modular server. This implies that only the most basic functionality is included in the core server. Extended features are available through modules (p. 1025) which can be loaded into httpd. By default, a base (p. 350) set of modules is included in the server at compile-time. If the server is compiled to use dynamically loaded (p. 65) modules, then modules can be compiled separately and added at any time using the LOADMODULE directive. Otherwise, httpd must be recompiled to add or remove modules. Configuration directives may be included conditional on a presence of a particular module by enclosing them in an <IFMODULE> block. However, <IFMODULE> blocks are not required, and in some cases may mask the fact that you're missing an important module.

To see which modules are currently compiled into the server, you can use the `-l` command line option. You can also see what modules are loaded dynamically using the `-M` command line option.

Scope of Directives

Related Modules	Related Directives
	<DIRECTORY> <DIRECTORYMATCH> <FILES> <FILESMATCH> <LOCATION> <LOCATIONMATCH> <VIRTUALHOST>

Directives placed in the main configuration files apply to the entire server. If you wish to change the configuration for only a part of the server, you can scope your directives by placing them in <DIRECTORY>, <DIRECTORYMATCH>, <FILES>, <FILESMATCH>, <LOCATION>, and <LOCATIONMATCH> sections. These sections limit the application of the directives which they enclose to particular filesystem locations or URLs. They can also be nested, allowing for very fine grained configuration.

httpd has the capability to serve many different websites simultaneously. This is called Virtual Hosting (p. 114) . Directives can also be scoped by placing them inside <VIRTUALHOST> sections, so that they will only apply to requests for a particular website.

Although most directives can be placed in any of these sections, some directives do not make sense in some contexts. For example, directives controlling process creation can only be placed in the main server context. To find which directives can be placed in which sections, check the Context (p. 351) of the directive. For further information, we provide details on How Directory, Location and Files sections work (p. 33) .

.htaccess Files

Related Modules	Related Directives
	ACCESSFILENAME ALLOWOVERRIDE

httpd allows for decentralized management of configuration via special files placed inside the web tree. The special files are usually called `.htaccess`, but any name can be specified in the ACCESSFILENAME directive. Directives placed in `.htaccess` files apply to the directory where you place the file, and all sub-directories. The `.htaccess` files follow the same syntax as the main configuration files. Since `.htaccess` files are read on every request, changes made in these files take immediate effect.

To find which directives can be placed in `.htaccess` files, check the Context (p. 351) of the directive. The server administrator further controls what directives may be placed in `.htaccess` files by configuring the ALLOWOVERRIDE directive in the main configuration files.

For more information on `.htaccess` files, see the .htaccess tutorial (p. 239) .

2.5 Configuration Sections

Directives in the configuration files (p. 30) may apply to the entire server, or they may be restricted to apply only to particular directories, files, hosts, or URLs. This document describes how to use configuration section containers or `.htaccess` files to change the scope of other configuration directives.

Types of Configuration Section Containers

Related Modules	Related Directives
core	<Directory>
mod_version	<DirectoryMatch>
mod_proxy	<Files>
	<FilesMatch>
	<If>
	<IfDefine>
	<IfModule>
	<IfVersion>
	<Location>
	<LocationMatch>
	<Proxy>
	<ProxyMatch>
	<VirtualHost>

There are two basic types of containers. Most containers are evaluated for each request. The enclosed directives are applied only for those requests that match the containers. The <IfDefine>, <IfModule>, and <IfVersion> containers, on the other hand, are evaluated only at server startup and restart. If their conditions are true at startup, then the enclosed directives will apply to all requests. If the conditions are not true, the enclosed directives will be ignored.

The <IfDefine> directive encloses directives that will only be applied if an appropriate parameter is defined on the `httpd` command line. For example, with the following configuration, all requests will be redirected to another site only if the server is started using `httpd -DClosedForNow`:

```
<IfDefine ClosedForNow>
    Redirect "/" "http://otherserver.example.com/"
</IfDefine>
```

The <IfModule> directive is very similar, except it encloses directives that will only be applied if a particular module is available in the server. The module must either be statically compiled in the server, or it must be dynamically compiled and its LoadModule line must be earlier in the configuration file. This directive should only be used if you need your configuration file to work whether or not certain modules are installed. It should not be used to enclose directives that you want to work all the time, because it can suppress useful error messages about missing modules.

In the following example, the MimeMagicFile directive will be applied only if mod_mime_magic is available.

```
<IfModule mod_mime_magic.c>
    MimeMagicFile "conf/magic"
</IfModule>
```

The <IfVersion> directive is very similar to <IfDefine> and <IfModule>, except it encloses directives that will only be applied if a particular version of the server is executing. This module is designed for the use in test suites and large networks which have to deal with different httpd versions and different configurations.

```
<IfVersion >= 2.4>
    # this happens only in versions greater or
    # equal 2.4.0.
</IfVersion>
```

<IfDefine>, <IfModule>, and the <IfVersion> can apply negative conditions by preceding their test with `"!"`. Also, these sections can be nested to achieve more complex restrictions.

Filesystem, Webspace, and Boolean Expressions

The most commonly used configuration section containers are the ones that change the configuration of particular places in the filesystem or webspace. First, it is important to understand the difference between the two. The filesystem is the view of your disks as seen by your operating system. For example, in a default install, Apache httpd resides at `/usr/local/apache2` in the Unix filesystem or `"c:/Program Files/Apache Group/Apache2"` in the Windows filesystem. (Note that forward slashes should always be used as the path separator in Apache httpd configuration files, even for Windows.) In contrast, the webspace is the view of your site as delivered by the web server and seen by the client. So the path `/dir/` in the webspace corresponds to the path `/usr/local/apache2/htdocs/dir/` in the filesystem of a default Apache httpd install on Unix. The webspace need not map directly to the filesystem, since webpages may be generated dynamically from databases or other locations.

Filesystem Containers

The <Directory> and <Files> directives, along with their regex counterparts, apply directives to parts of the filesystem. Directives enclosed in a <Directory> section apply to the named filesystem directory and all subdirectories of that directory (as well as the files in those directories). The same effect can be obtained using .htaccess files (p. 239) . For example, in the following configuration, directory indexes will be enabled for the `/var/web/dir1` directory and all subdirectories.

```
<Directory "/var/web/dir1">
    Options +Indexes
</Directory>
```

Directives enclosed in a <Files> section apply to any file with the specified name, regardless of what directory it lies in. So for example, the following configuration directives will, when placed in the main section of the configuration file, deny access to any file named `private.html` regardless of where it is found.

```
<Files "private.html">
    Require all denied
</Files>
```

To address files found in a particular part of the filesystem, the <Files> and <Directory> sections can be combined. For example, the following configuration will deny access to `/var/web/dir1/private.html`, `/var/web/dir1/subdir2/private.html`, `/var/web/dir1/subdir3/private.html`, and any other instance of `private.html` found under the `/var/web/dir1/` directory.

```
<Directory "/var/web/dir1">
    <Files "private.html">
        Require all denied
    </Files>
</Directory>
```

Webspace Containers

The <LOCATION> directive and its regex counterpart, on the other hand, change the configuration for content in the webspace. For example, the following configuration prevents access to any URL-path that begins in /private. In particular, it will apply to requests for `http://yoursite.example.com/private`, `http://yoursite.example.com/private123`, and `http://yoursite.example.com/private/dir/file.html` as well as any other requests starting with the `/private` string.

```
<LocationMatch "^/private">
    Require all denied
</LocationMatch>
```

The <LOCATION> directive need not have anything to do with the filesystem. For example, the following example shows how to map a particular URL to an internal Apache HTTP Server handler provided by MOD_STATUS. No file called `server-status` needs to exist in the filesystem.

```
<Location "/server-status">
    SetHandler server-status
</Location>
```

Overlapping Webspace

In order to have two overlapping URLs one has to consider the order in which certain sections or directives are evaluated. For <LOCATION> this would be:

```
<Location "/foo">
</Location>
<Location "/foo/bar">
</Location>
```

<ALIAS>es on the other hand, are mapped vice-versa:

```
Alias "/foo/bar" "/srv/www/uncommon/bar"
Alias "/foo" "/srv/www/common/foo"
```

The same is true for the PROXYPASS directives:

```
ProxyPass "/special-area" "http://special.example.com" smax=5 max=10
ProxyPass "/" "balancer://mycluster/" stickysession=JSESSIONID|jsessionid nofailover=On
```

Wildcards and Regular Expressions

The <DIRECTORY>, <FILES>, and <LOCATION> directives can each use shell-style wildcard characters as in `fnmatch` from the C standard library. The character "*" matches any sequence of characters, "?" matches any single character, and "[*seq*]" matches any character in *seq*. The "/" character will not be matched by any wildcard; it must be specified explicitly.

If even more flexible matching is required, each container has a regular expression (regex) counterpart <DIRECTORYMATCH>, <FILESMATCH>, and <LOCATIONMATCH> that allow perl-compatible regular expressions to be used in choosing the matches. But see the section below on configuration merging to find out how using regex sections will change how directives are applied.

A non-regex wildcard section that changes the configuration of all user directories could look as follows:

```
<Directory "/home/*/public_html">
    Options Indexes
</Directory>
```

Using regex sections, we can deny access to many types of image files at once:

```
<FilesMatch "\.(?i:gif|jpe?g|png)$">
    Require all denied
</FilesMatch>
```

Regular expressions containing **named groups and backreferences** are added to the environment with the corresponding name in uppercase. This allows elements of filename paths and URLs to be referenced from within expressions (p. 89) and modules like MOD_REWRITE.

```
<DirectoryMatch "^/var/www/combined/(?<SITENAME>[^/]+)">
    require ldap-group "cn=%{env:MATCH_SITENAME},ou=combined,o=Example"
</DirectoryMatch>
```

Boolean expressions

The <IF> directive change the configuration depending on a condition which can be expressed by a boolean expression. For example, the following configuration denies access if the HTTP Referer header does not start with "http://www.example.com/".

```
<If "!(%{HTTP_REFERER} -strmatch 'http://www.example.com/*')">
    Require all denied
</If>
```

What to use When

Choosing between filesystem containers and webspace containers is actually quite easy. When applying directives to objects that reside in the filesystem always use <DIRECTORY> or <FILES>. When applying directives to objects that do not reside in the filesystem (such as a webpage generated from a database), use <LOCATION>.

It is important to never use <LOCATION> when trying to restrict access to objects in the filesystem. This is because many different webspace locations (URLs) could map to the same filesystem location, allowing your restrictions to be circumvented. For example, consider the following configuration:

```
<Location "/dir/">
    Require all denied
</Location>
```

This works fine if the request is for `http://yoursite.example.com/dir/`. But what if you are on a case-insensitive filesystem? Then your restriction could be easily circumvented by requesting `http://yoursite.example.com/DIR/`. The <DIRECTORY> directive, in contrast, will apply to any content served from that location, regardless of how it is called. (An exception is filesystem links. The same directory can be placed in more than one part of the filesystem using symbolic links. The <DIRECTORY> directive will follow the symbolic link without resetting the pathname. Therefore, for the highest level of security, symbolic links should be disabled with the appropriate OPTIONS directive.)

If you are, perhaps, thinking that none of this applies to you because you use a case-sensitive filesystem, remember that there are many other ways to map multiple webspace locations to the same filesystem location. Therefore you should always use the filesystem containers when you can. There is, however, one exception to this rule. Putting configuration restrictions in a `<Location "/">` section is perfectly safe because this section will apply to all requests regardless of the specific URL.

Nesting of sections

Some section types can be nested inside other section types. On the one hand, <Files> can be used inside <Directory>. On the other hand, <If> can be used inside <Directory>, <Location>, and <Files> sections. The regex counterparts of the named section behave identically.

Nested sections are merged after non-nested sections of the same type.

Virtual Hosts

The <VirtualHost> container encloses directives that apply to specific hosts. This is useful when serving multiple hosts from the same machine with a different configuration for each. For more information, see the Virtual Host Documentation (p. 114) .

Proxy

The <Proxy> and <ProxyMatch> containers apply enclosed configuration directives only to sites accessed through mod_proxy's proxy server that match the specified URL. For example, the following configuration will prevent the proxy server from being used to access the `www.example.com` website.

```
<Proxy "http://www.example.com/*">
    Require all granted
</Proxy>
```

What Directives are Allowed?

To find out what directives are allowed in what types of configuration sections, check the Context (p. 351) of the directive. Everything that is allowed in <Directory> sections is also syntactically allowed in <DirectoryMatch>, <Files>, <FilesMatch>, <Location>, <LocationMatch>, <Proxy>, and <ProxyMatch> sections. There are some exceptions, however:

- The AllowOverride directive works only in <Directory> sections.
- The `FollowSymLinks` and `SymLinksIfOwnerMatch` Options work only in <Directory> sections or `.htaccess` files.
- The Options directive cannot be used in <Files> and <FilesMatch> sections.

How the sections are merged

The configuration sections are applied in a very particular order. Since this can have important effects on how configuration directives are interpreted, it is important to understand how this works.

The order of merging is:

1. <Directory> (except regular expressions) and `.htaccess` done simultaneously (with `.htaccess`, if allowed, overriding <Directory>)

2. <DirectoryMatch> (and `<Directory "~">`)
3. <Files> and <FilesMatch> done simultaneously
4. <Location> and <LocationMatch> done simultaneously
5. <If>

Apart from <Directory>, each group is processed in the order that they appear in the configuration files. <Directory> (group 1 above) is processed in the order shortest directory component to longest. So for example, `<Directory "/var/web/dir">` will be processed before `<Directory "/var/web/dir/subdir">`. If multiple <Directory> sections apply to the same directory they are processed in the configuration file order. Configurations included via the Include directive will be treated as if they were inside the including file at the location of the Include directive.

Sections inside <VirtualHost> sections are applied *after* the corresponding sections outside the virtual host definition. This allows virtual hosts to override the main server configuration.

When the request is served by mod_proxy, the <Proxy> container takes the place of the <Directory> container in the processing order.

Later sections override earlier ones, however each module is responsible for interpreting what form this override takes. A later configuration section with directives from a given module might cause a conceptual "merge" of some directives, all directives, or a complete replacement of the modules configuration with the module defaults and directives explicitly listed in the later context.

Technical Note

There is actually a `<Location>`/`<LocationMatch>` sequence performed just before the name translation phase (where `Aliases` and `DocumentRoots` are used to map URLs to filenames). The results of this sequence are completely thrown away after the translation has completed.

Some Examples

Below is an artificial example to show the order of merging. Assuming they all apply to the request, the directives in this example will be applied in the order A > B > C > D > E.

```
<Location "/">
    E
</Location>

<Files "f.html">
    D
</Files>

<VirtualHost *>
<Directory "/a/b">
    B
</Directory>
</VirtualHost>

<DirectoryMatch "^.*b$">
    C
</DirectoryMatch>
```

```
<Directory "/a/b">
    A
</Directory>
```

For a more concrete example, consider the following. Regardless of any access restrictions placed in <DIRECTORY> sections, the <LOCATION> section will be evaluated last and will allow unrestricted access to the server. In other words, order of merging is important, so be careful!

```
<Location "/">
    Require all granted
</Location>

# Woops!  This <Directory> section will have no effect
<Directory "/">
    <RequireAll>
        Require all granted
        Require not host badguy.example.com
    </RequireAll>
</Directory>
```

2.6 Caching Guide

This document supplements the MOD_CACHE, MOD_CACHE_DISK, MOD_FILE_CACHE and htcacheclean (p. 306) reference documentation. It describes how to use the Apache HTTP Server's caching features to accelerate web and proxy serving, while avoiding common problems and misconfigurations.

Introduction

The Apache HTTP server offers a range of caching features that are designed to improve the performance of the server in various ways.

Three-state RFC2616 HTTP caching MOD_CACHE and its provider modules MOD_CACHE_DISK provide intelligent, HTTP-aware caching. The content itself is stored in the cache, and mod_cache aims to honor all of the various HTTP headers and options that control the cacheability of content as described in Section 13 of RFC2616[12]. MOD_CACHE is aimed at both simple and complex caching configurations, where you are dealing with proxied content, dynamic local content or have a need to speed up access to local files on a potentially slow disk.

Two-state key/value shared object caching The shared object cache API (p. 104) (socache) and its provider modules provide a server wide key/value based shared object cache. These modules are designed to cache low level data such as SSL sessions and authentication credentials. Backends allow the data to be stored server wide in shared memory, or datacenter wide in a cache such as memcache or distcache.

Specialized file caching MOD_FILE_CACHE offers the ability to pre-load files into memory on server startup, and can improve access times and save file handles on files that are accessed often, as there is no need to go to disk on each request.

To get the most from this document, you should be familiar with the basics of HTTP, and have read the Users' Guides to Mapping URLs to the Filesystem (p. 61) and Content negotiation (p. 68) .

Three-state RFC2616 HTTP caching

Related Modules	Related Directives
MOD_CACHE	CACHEENABLE
MOD_CACHE_DISK	CACHEDISABLE
	USECANONICALNAME
	CACHENEGOTIATEDDOCS

The HTTP protocol contains built in support for an in-line caching mechanism

described by section 13 of RFC2616[13], and the MOD_CACHE module can be used to take advantage of this.

Unlike a simple two state key/value cache where the content disappears completely when no longer fresh, an HTTP cache includes a mechanism to retain stale content, and to ask the origin server whether this stale content has changed and if not, make it fresh again.

An entry in an HTTP cache exists in one of three states:

Fresh If the content is new enough (younger than its **freshness lifetime**), it is considered **fresh**. An HTTP cache is free to serve fresh content without making any calls to the origin server at all.

[12] http://www.w3.org/Protocols/rfc2616/rfc2616-sec13.html
[13] http://www.w3.org/Protocols/rfc2616/rfc2616-sec13.html

Stale If the content is too old (older than its **freshness lifetime**), it is considered **stale**. An HTTP cache should contact the origin server and check whether the content is still fresh before serving stale content to a client. The origin server will either respond with replacement content if not still valid, or ideally, the origin server will respond with a code to tell the cache the content is still fresh, without the need to generate or send the content again. The content becomes fresh again and the cycle continues.

The HTTP protocol does allow the cache to serve stale data under certain circumstances, such as when an attempt to freshen the data with an origin server has failed with a 5xx error, or when another request is already in the process of freshening the given entry. In these cases a `Warning` header is added to the response.

Non Existent If the cache gets full, it reserves the option to delete content from the cache to make space. Content can be deleted at any time, and can be stale or fresh. The htcacheclean (p. 306) tool can be run on a once off basis, or deployed as a daemon to keep the size of the cache within the given size, or the given number of inodes. The tool attempts to delete stale content before attempting to delete fresh content.

Full details of how HTTP caching works can be found in

Section 13 of RFC2616[14].

Interaction with the Server

The MOD_CACHE module hooks into the server in two possible places depending on the value of the CACHEQUICKHANDLER directive:

Quick handler phase This phase happens very early on during the request processing, just after the request has been parsed. If the content is found within the cache, it is served immediately and almost all request processing is bypassed.

In this scenario, the cache behaves as if it has been "bolted on" to the front of the server.

This mode offers the best performance, as the majority of server processing is bypassed. This mode however also bypasses the authentication and authorization phases of server processing, so this mode should be chosen with care when this is important.

Requests with an "Authorization" header (for example, HTTP Basic Authentication) are neither cacheable nor served from the cache when MOD_CACHE is running in this phase.

Normal handler phase This phase happens late in the request processing, after all the request phases have completed.

In this scenario, the cache behaves as if it has been "bolted on" to the back of the server.

This mode offers the most flexibility, as the potential exists for caching to occur at a precisely controlled point in the filter chain, and cached content can be filtered or personalized before being sent to the client.

If the URL is not found within the cache, MOD_CACHE will add a filter (p. 100) to the filter stack in order to record the response to the cache, and then stand down, allowing normal request processing to continue. If the content is determined to be cacheable, the content will be saved to the cache for future serving, otherwise the content will be ignored.

If the content found within the cache is stale, the MOD_CACHE module converts the request into a **conditional request**. If the origin server responds with a normal response, the normal response is cached, replacing the content already cached. If the origin server responds with a 304 Not Modified response, the content is marked as fresh again, and the cached content is served by the filter instead of saving it.

[14] http://www.w3.org/Protocols/rfc2616/rfc2616-sec13.html

Improving Cache Hits

When a virtual host is known by one of many different server aliases, ensuring that USECANONICALNAME is set to On can dramatically improve the ratio of cache hits. This is because the hostname of the virtual-host serving the content is used within the cache key. With the setting set to On virtual-hosts with multiple server names or aliases will not produce differently cached entities, and instead content will be cached as per the canonical hostname.

Freshness Lifetime

Well formed content that is intended to be cached should declare an explicit freshness lifetime with the `Cache-Control` header's `max-age` or `s-maxage` fields, or by including an `Expires` header.

At the same time, the origin server defined freshness lifetime can be overridden by a client when the client presents their own `Cache-Control` header within the request. In this case, the lowest freshness lifetime between request and response wins.

When this freshness lifetime is missing from the request or the response, a default freshness lifetime is applied. The default freshness lifetime for cached entities is one hour, however this can be easily over-ridden by using the CACHEDEFAULTEXPIRE directive.

If a response does not include an `Expires` header but does include a `Last-Modified` header, MOD_CACHE can infer a freshness lifetime based on a heuristic, which can be controlled through the use of the CACHELASTMODIFIEDFACTOR directive.

For local content, or for remote content that does not define its own `Expires` header, MOD_EXPIRES may be used to fine-tune the freshness lifetime by adding `max-age` and `Expires`.

The maximum freshness lifetime may also be controlled by using the CACHEMAXEXPIRE.

A Brief Guide to Conditional Requests

When content expires from the cache and becomes stale, rather than pass on the original request, httpd will modify the request to make it conditional instead.

When an `ETag` header exists in the original cached response, MOD_CACHE will add an `If-None-Match` header to the request to the origin server. When a `Last-Modified` header exists in the original cached response, MOD_CACHE will add an `If-Modified-Since` header to the request to the origin server. Performing either of these actions makes the request **conditional**.

When a conditional request is received by an origin server, the origin server should check whether the ETag or the Last-Modified parameter has changed, as appropriate for the request. If not, the origin should respond with a terse "304 Not Modified" response. This signals to the cache that the stale content is still fresh should be used for subsequent requests until the content's new freshness lifetime is reached again.

If the content has changed, then the content is served as if the request were not conditional to begin with.

Conditional requests offer two benefits. Firstly, when making such a request to the origin server, if the content from the origin matches the content in the cache, this can be determined easily and without the overhead of transferring the entire resource.

Secondly, a well designed origin server will be designed in such a way that conditional requests will be significantly cheaper to produce than a full response. For static files, typically all that is involved is a call to `stat()` or similar system call, to see if the file has changed in size or modification time. As such, even local content may still be served faster from the cache if it has not changed.

Origin servers should make every effort to support conditional requests as is practical, however if conditional requests are not supported, the origin will respond as if the request was not conditional, and the cache will respond as if the content had changed and save the new content to the cache. In this case, the cache will behave like a simple two state cache, where content is effectively either fresh or deleted.

What Can be Cached?

The full definition of which responses can be cached by an HTTP cache is defined in

RFC2616 Section 13.4 Response Cacheability[15], and can be summed up as follows:

1. Caching must be enabled for this URL. See the CACHEENABLE and CACHEDISABLE directives.
2. The response must have a HTTP status code of 200, 203, 300, 301 or 410.
3. The request must be a HTTP GET request.
4. If the response contains an "Authorization:" header, it must also contain an "s-maxage", "must-revalidate" or "public" option in the "Cache-Control:" header, or it won't be cached.
5. If the URL included a query string (e.g. from a HTML form GET method) it will not be cached unless the response specifies an explicit expiration by including an "Expires:" header or the max-age or s-maxage directive of the "Cache-Control:" header, as per RFC2616 sections 13.9 and 13.2.1.
6. If the response has a status of 200 (OK), the response must also include at least one of the "Etag", "Last-Modified" or the "Expires" headers, or the max-age or s-maxage directive of the "Cache-Control:" header, unless the CACHEIGNORENOLASTMOD directive has been used to require otherwise.
7. If the response includes the "private" option in a "Cache-Control:" header, it will not be stored unless the CACHESTOREPRIVATE has been used to require otherwise.
8. Likewise, if the response includes the "no-store" option in a "Cache-Control:" header, it will not be stored unless the CACHESTORENOSTORE has been used.
9. A response will not be stored if it includes a "Vary:" header containing the match-all "*".

What Should Not be Cached?

It should be up to the client creating the request, or the origin server constructing the response to decide whether or not the content should be cacheable or not by correctly setting the `Cache-Control` header, and MOD_CACHE should be left alone to honor the wishes of the client or server as appropriate.

Content that is time sensitive, or which varies depending on the particulars of the request that are not covered by HTTP negotiation, should not be cached. This content should declare itself uncacheable using the `Cache-Control` header.

If content changes often, expressed by a freshness lifetime of minutes or seconds, the content can still be cached, however it is highly desirable that the origin server supports **conditional requests** correctly to ensure that full responses do not have to be generated on a regular basis.

Content that varies based on client provided request headers can be cached through intelligent use of the `Vary` response header.

[15] http://www.w3.org/Protocols/rfc2616/rfc2616-sec13.html#sec13.4

Variable/Negotiated Content

When the origin server is designed to respond with different content based on the value of headers in the request, for example to serve multiple languages at the same URL, HTTP's caching mechanism makes it possible to cache multiple variants of the same page at the same URL.

This is done by the origin server adding a `Vary` header to indicate which headers must be taken into account by a cache when determining whether two variants are different from one another.

If for example, a response is received with a vary header such as;

```
Vary:  negotiate,accept-language,accept-charset
```

MOD_CACHE will only serve the cached content to requesters with accept-language and accept-charset headers matching those of the original request.

Multiple variants of the content can be cached side by side, MOD_CACHE uses the `Vary` header and the corresponding values of the request headers listed by `Vary` to decide on which of many variants to return to the client.

Caching to Disk

The MOD_CACHE module relies on specific backend store implementations in order to manage the cache, and for caching to disk MOD_CACHE_DISK is provided to support this.

Typically the module will be configured as so;

```
CacheRoot    "/var/cache/apache/"
CacheEnable disk /
CacheDirLevels 2
CacheDirLength 1
```

Importantly, as the cached files are locally stored, operating system in-memory caching will typically be applied to their access also. So although the files are stored on disk, if they are frequently accessed it is likely the operating system will ensure that they are actually served from memory.

Understanding the Cache-Store

To store items in the cache, MOD_CACHE_DISK creates a 22 character hash of the URL being requested. This hash incorporates the hostname, protocol, port, path and any CGI arguments to the URL, as well as elements defined by the Vary header to ensure that multiple URLs do not collide with one another.

Each character may be any one of 64-different characters, which mean that overall there are 64^22 possible hashes. For example, a URL might be hashed to `xyTGxSMO2b68mBCykqkp1w`. This hash is used as a prefix for the naming of the files specific to that URL within the cache, however first it is split up into directories as per the CACHEDIRLEVELS and CACHEDIRLENGTH directives.

CACHEDIRLEVELS specifies how many levels of subdirectory there should be, and CACHEDIRLENGTH specifies how many characters should be in each directory. With the example settings given above, the hash would be turned into a filename prefix as `/var/cache/apache/x/y/TGxSMO2b68mBCykqkp1w`.

The overall aim of this technique is to reduce the number of subdirectories or files that may be in a particular directory, as most file-systems slow down as this number increases. With setting of "1" for CACHEDIRLENGTH there can at most be 64 subdirectories at any particular level. With a setting of 2 there can be 64 * 64 subdirectories, and so on. Unless you have a good reason not to, using a setting of "1" for CACHEDIRLENGTH is recommended.

Setting CACHEDIRLEVELS depends on how many files you anticipate to store in the cache. With the setting of "2" used in the above example, a grand total of 4096 subdirectories can ultimately be created. With 1 million files cached, this works out at roughly 245 cached URLs per directory.

Each URL uses at least two files in the cache-store. Typically there is a ".header" file, which includes meta-information about the URL, such as when it is due to expire and a ".data" file which is a verbatim copy of the content to be served.

In the case of a content negotiated via the "Vary" header, a ".vary" directory will be created for the URL in question. This directory will have multiple ".data" files corresponding to the differently negotiated content.

Maintaining the Disk Cache

The MOD_CACHE_DISK module makes no attempt to regulate the amount of disk space used by the cache, although it will gracefully stand down on any disk error and behave as if the cache was never present.

Instead, provided with httpd is the htcacheclean (p. 306) tool which allows you to clean the cache periodically. Determining how frequently to run htcacheclean (p. 306) and what target size to use for the cache is somewhat complex and trial and error may be needed to select optimal values.

htcacheclean (p. 306) has two modes of operation. It can be run as persistent daemon, or periodically from cron. htcacheclean (p. 306) can take up to an hour or more to process very large (tens of gigabytes) caches and if you are running it from cron it is recommended that you determine how long a typical run takes, to avoid running more than one instance at a time.

It is also recommended that an appropriate "nice" level is chosen for htcacheclean so that the tool does not cause excessive disk io while the server is running.

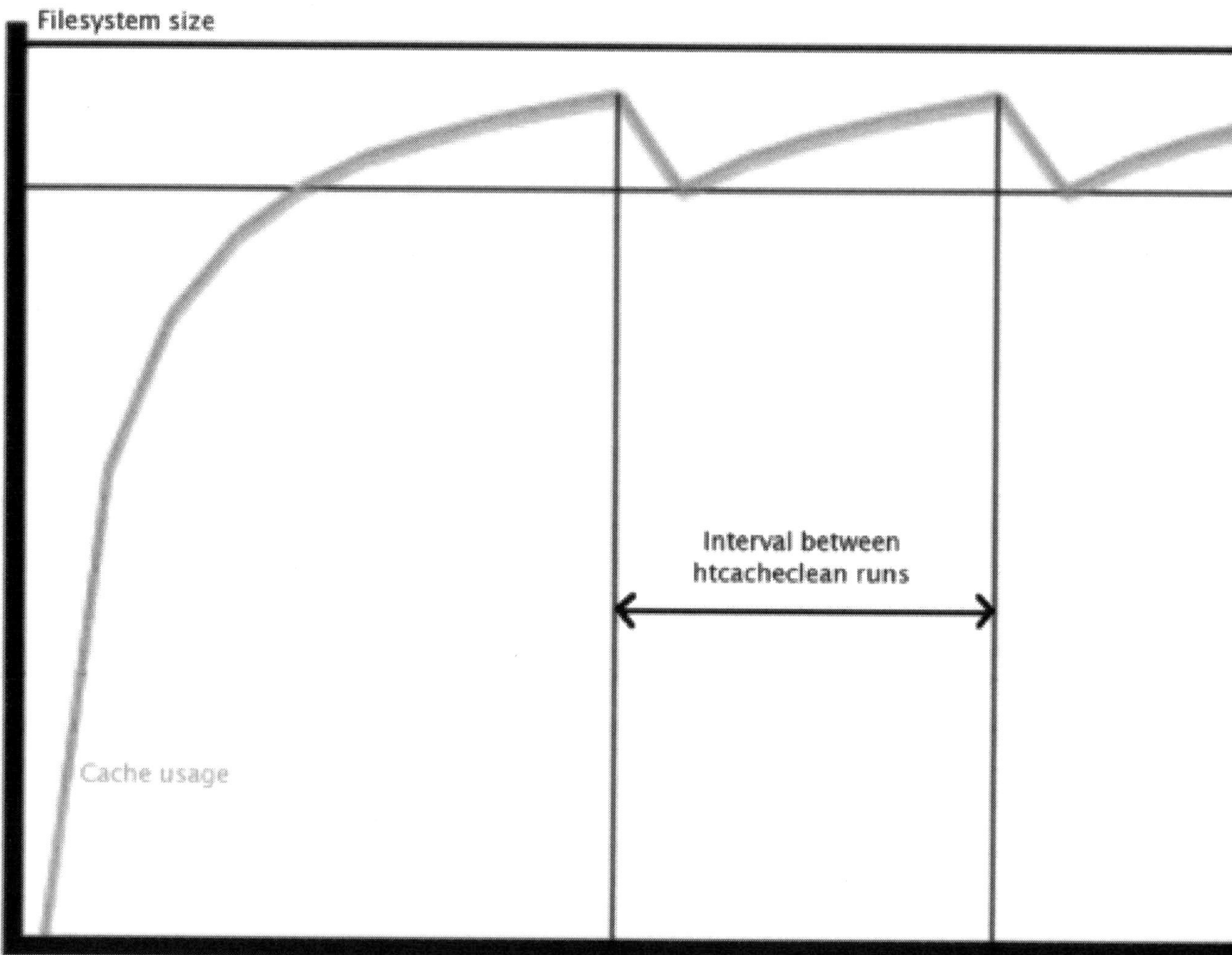

Figure 1: Typical cache growth / clean sequence.

Because MOD_CACHE_DISK does not itself pay attention to how much space is used you should ensure that htcacheclean (p. 306) is configured to leave enough "grow room" following a clean.

Two-state Key/Value Shared Object Caching

Related Modules	Related Directives
MOD_AUTHN_SOCACHE	AUTHNCACHESOCACHE
MOD_SOCACHE_DBM	SSLSESSIONCACHE
MOD_SOCACHE_DC	SSLSTAPLINGCACHE
MOD_SOCACHE_MEMCACHE	
MOD_SOCACHE_SHMCB	
MOD_SSL	

The Apache HTTP server offers a low level shared object cache for caching information such as SSL sessions, or authentication credentials, within the socache (p. 104) interface.

Additional modules are provided for each implementation, offering the following backends:

MOD_SOCACHE_DBM DBM based shared object cache.

MOD_SOCACHE_DC Distcache based shared object cache.

MOD_SOCACHE_MEMCACHE Memcache based shared object cache.

MOD_SOCACHE_SHMCB Shared memory based shared object cache.

Caching Authentication Credentials

Related Modules	Related Directives
MOD_AUTHN_SOCACHE	AUTHNCACHESOCACHE

The MOD_AUTHN_SOCACHE module allows the result of authentication to be cached, relieving load on authentication backends.

Caching SSL Sessions

Related Modules	Related Directives
MOD_SSL	SSLSESSIONCACHE SSLSTAPLINGCACHE

The MOD_SSL module uses the `socache` interface to provide a session cache and a stapling cache.

Specialized File Caching

Related Modules	Related Directives
MOD_FILE_CACHE	CACHEFILE MMAPFILE

On platforms where a filesystem might be slow, or where file handles are expensive, the option exists to pre-load files into memory on startup.

On systems where opening files is slow, the option exists to open the file on startup and cache the file handle. These options can help on systems where access to static files is slow.

File-Handle Caching

The act of opening a file can itself be a source of delay, particularly on network filesystems. By maintaining a cache of open file descriptors for commonly served files, httpd can avoid this delay. Currently httpd provides one implementation of File-Handle Caching.

CacheFile

The most basic form of caching present in httpd is the file-handle caching provided by MOD_FILE_CACHE. Rather than caching file-contents, this cache maintains a table of open file descriptors. Files to be cached in this manner are specified in the configuration file using the CACHEFILE directive.

The CACHEFILE directive instructs httpd to open the file when it is started and to re-use this file-handle for all subsequent access to this file.

```
CacheFile /usr/local/apache2/htdocs/index.html
```

If you intend to cache a large number of files in this manner, you must ensure that your operating system's limit for the number of open files is set appropriately.

Although using CACHEFILE does not cause the file-contents to be cached per-se, it does mean that if the file changes while httpd is running these changes will not be picked up. The file will be consistently served as it was when httpd was started.

If the file is removed while httpd is running, it will continue to maintain an open file descriptor and serve the file as it was when httpd was started. This usually also means that although the file will have been deleted, and not show up on the filesystem, extra free space will not be recovered until httpd is stopped and the file descriptor closed.

In-Memory Caching

Serving directly from system memory is universally the fastest method of serving content. Reading files from a disk controller or, even worse, from a remote network is orders of magnitude slower. Disk controllers usually involve physical processes, and network access is limited by your available bandwidth. Memory access on the other hand can take mere nano-seconds.

System memory isn't cheap though, byte for byte it's by far the most expensive type of storage and it's important to ensure that it is used efficiently. By caching files in memory you decrease the amount of memory available on the system. As we'll see, in the case of operating system caching, this is not so much of an issue, but when using httpd's own in-memory caching it is important to make sure that you do not allocate too much memory to a cache. Otherwise the system will be forced to swap out memory, which will likely degrade performance.

Operating System Caching

Almost all modern operating systems cache file-data in memory managed directly by the kernel. This is a powerful feature, and for the most part operating systems get it right. For example, on Linux, let's look at the difference in the time it takes to read a file for the first time and the second time;

```
colm@coroebus:~$ time cat testfile > /dev/null
real    0m0.065s
user    0m0.000s
sys     0m0.001s
colm@coroebus:~$ time cat testfile > /dev/null
real    0m0.003s
user    0m0.003s
sys     0m0.000s
```

Even for this small file, there is a huge difference in the amount of time it takes to read the file. This is because the kernel has cached the file contents in memory.

By ensuring there is "spare" memory on your system, you can ensure that more and more file-contents will be stored in this cache. This can be a very efficient means of in-memory caching, and involves no extra configuration of httpd at all.

Additionally, because the operating system knows when files are deleted or modified, it can automatically remove file contents from the cache when necessary. This is a big advantage over httpd's in-memory caching which has no way of knowing when a file has changed.

Despite the performance and advantages of automatic operating system caching there are some circumstances in which in-memory caching may be better performed by httpd.

MMapFile Caching

MOD_FILE_CACHE provides the MMAPFILE directive, which allows you to have httpd map a static file's contents into memory at start time (using the mmap system call). httpd will use the in-memory contents for all subsequent accesses to this file.

```
MMapFile /usr/local/apache2/htdocs/index.html
```

As with the CACHEFILE directive, any changes in these files will not be picked up by httpd after it has started.

The MMAPFILE directive does not keep track of how much memory it allocates, so you must ensure not to over-use the directive. Each httpd child process will replicate this memory, so it is critically important to ensure that the files mapped are not so large as to cause the system to swap memory.

Security Considerations

Authorization and Access Control

Using MOD_CACHE in its default state where CACHEQUICKHANDLER is set to `On` is very much like having a caching reverse-proxy bolted to the front of the server. Requests will be served by the caching module unless it determines that the origin server should be queried just as an external cache would, and this drastically changes the security model of httpd.

As traversing a filesystem hierarchy to examine potential `.htaccess` files would be a very expensive operation, partially defeating the point of caching (to speed up requests), MOD_CACHE makes no decision about whether a cached entity is authorised for serving. In other words; if MOD_CACHE has cached some content, it will be served from the cache as long as that content has not expired.

If, for example, your configuration permits access to a resource by IP address you should ensure that this content is not cached. You can do this by using the CACHEDISABLE directive, or MOD_EXPIRES. Left unchecked, MOD_CACHE - very much like a reverse proxy - would cache the content when served and then serve it to any client, on any IP address.

When the CACHEQUICKHANDLER directive is set to `Off`, the full set of request processing phases are executed and the security model remains unchanged.

Local exploits

As requests to end-users can be served from the cache, the cache itself can become a target for those wishing to deface or interfere with content. It is important to bear in mind that the cache must at all times be writable by the user which httpd is running as. This is in stark contrast to the usually recommended situation of maintaining all content unwritable by the Apache user.

If the Apache user is compromised, for example through a flaw in a CGI process, it is possible that the cache may be targeted. When using MOD_CACHE_DISK, it is relatively easy to insert or modify a cached entity.

This presents a somewhat elevated risk in comparison to the other types of attack it is possible to make as the Apache user. If you are using MOD_CACHE_DISK you should bear this in mind - ensure you upgrade httpd when security upgrades are announced and run CGI processes as a non-Apache user using suEXEC (p. 105) if possible.

Cache Poisoning

When running httpd as a caching proxy server, there is also the potential for so-called cache poisoning. Cache Poisoning is a broad term for attacks in which an attacker causes the proxy server to retrieve incorrect (and usually undesirable) content from the origin server.

For example if the DNS servers used by your system running httpd are vulnerable to DNS cache poisoning, an attacker may be able to control where httpd connects to when requesting content from the origin server. Another example is so-called HTTP request-smuggling attacks.

This document is not the correct place for an in-depth discussion of HTTP request smuggling (instead, try your favourite search engine) however it is important to be aware that it is possible to make a series of requests, and to exploit a vulnerability on an origin webserver such that the attacker can entirely control the content retrieved by the proxy.

Denial of Service / Cachebusting

The Vary mechanism allows multiple variants of the same URL to be cached side by side. Depending on header values provided by the client, the cache will select the correct variant to return to the client. This mechanism can become a problem when an attempt is made to vary on a header that is known to contain a wide range of possible values under normal use, for example the `User-Agent` header. Depending on the popularity of the particular web site thousands or millions of duplicate cache entries could be created for the same URL, crowding out other entries in the cache.

In other cases, there may be a need to change the URL of a particular resource on every request, usually by adding a "cachebuster" string to the URL. If this content is declared cacheable by a server for a significant freshness lifetime, these entries can crowd out legitimate entries in a cache. While MOD_CACHE provides a CACHEIGNOREURLSESSIONIDENTIFIERS directive, this directive should be used with care to ensure that downstream proxy or browser caches aren't subjected to the same denial of service issue.

2.7 Server-Wide Configuration

This document explains some of the directives provided by the CORE server which are used to configure the basic operations of the server.

Server Identification

Related Modules	Related Directives
	SERVERNAME SERVERADMIN SERVERSIGNATURE SERVERTOKENS USECANONICALNAME USECANONICALPHYSICALPORT

The SERVERADMIN and SERVERTOKENS directives control what information about the server will be presented in server-generated documents such as error messages. The SERVERTOKENS directive sets the value of the Server HTTP response header field.

The SERVERNAME, USECANONICALNAME and USECANONICALPHYSICALPORT directives are used by the server to determine how to construct self-referential URLs. For example, when a client requests a directory, but does not include the trailing slash in the directory name, httpd must redirect the client to the full name including the trailing slash so that the client will correctly resolve relative references in the document.

File Locations

Related Modules	Related Directives
	COREDUMPDIRECTORY DOCUMENTROOT ERRORLOG MUTEX PIDFILE SCOREBOARDFILE SERVERROOT

These directives control the locations of the various files that httpd needs for proper operation. When the pathname used does not begin with a slash (/), the files are located relative to the SERVERROOT. Be careful about locating files in paths which are writable by non-root users. See the security tips (p. 338) documentation for more details.

Limiting Resource Usage

Related Modules	Related Directives
	LimitRequestBody LimitRequestFields LimitRequestFieldsize LimitRequestLine RLimitCPU RLimitMEM RLimitNPROC ThreadStackSize

The LimitRequest* directives are used to place limits on the amount of resources httpd will use in reading requests from clients. By limiting these values, some kinds of denial of service attacks can be mitigated.

The RLimit* directives are used to limit the amount of resources which can be used by processes forked off from the httpd children. In particular, this will control resources used by CGI scripts and SSI exec commands.

The ThreadStackSize directive is used with some platforms to control the stack size.

Implementation Choices

Related Modules	Related Directives
	Mutex

The Mutex directive can be used to change the underlying implementation used for mutexes, in order to relieve functional or performance problems with APR's default choice.

2.8 Log Files

In order to effectively manage a web server, it is necessary to get feedback about the activity and performance of the server as well as any problems that may be occurring. The Apache HTTP Server provides very comprehensive and flexible logging capabilities. This document describes how to configure its logging capabilities, and how to understand what the logs contain.

Overview

Related Modules	Related Directives
MOD_LOG_CONFIG	
MOD_LOG_FORENSIC	
MOD_LOGIO	
MOD_CGI	

The Apache HTTP Server provides a variety of different mechanisms for logging everything that happens on your server, from the initial request, through the URL mapping process, to the final resolution of the connection, including any errors that may have occurred in the process. In addition to this, third-party modules may provide logging capabilities, or inject entries into the existing log files, and applications such as CGI programs, or PHP scripts, or other handlers, may send messages to the server error log.

In this document we discuss the logging modules that are a standard part of the http server.

Security Warning

Anyone who can write to the directory where Apache httpd is writing a log file can almost certainly gain access to the uid that the server is started as, which is normally root. Do *NOT* give people write access to the directory the logs are stored in without being aware of the consequences; see the security tips (p. 338) document for details.

In addition, log files may contain information supplied directly by the client, without escaping. Therefore, it is possible for malicious clients to insert control-characters in the log files, so care must be taken in dealing with raw logs.

Error Log

Related Modules	Related Directives
CORE	ERRORLOG
	ERRORLOGFORMAT
	LOGLEVEL

The server error log, whose name and location is set by the ERRORLOG directive, is the most important log file. This is the place where Apache httpd will send diagnostic information and record any errors that it encounters in processing requests. It is the first place to look when a problem occurs with starting the server or with the operation of the server, since it will often contain details of what went wrong and how to fix it.

The error log is usually written to a file (typically `error_log` on Unix systems and `error.log` on Windows and OS/2). On Unix systems it is also possible to have the server send errors to `syslog` or pipe them to a program.

The format of the error log is defined by the ERRORLOGFORMAT directive, with which you can customize what values are logged. A default is format defined if you don't specify one. A typical log message follows:

```
[Fri Sep 09 10:42:29.902022 2011] [core:error] [pid 35708:tid
4328636416] [client 72.15.99.187] File does not exist:
/usr/local/apache2/htdocs/favicon.ico
```

The first item in the log entry is the date and time of the message. The next is the module producing the message (core, in this case) and the severity level of that message. This is followed by the process ID and, if appropriate, the thread ID, of the process that experienced the condition. Next, we have the client address that made the request. And finally is the detailed error message, which in this case indicates a request for a file that did not exist.

A very wide variety of different messages can appear in the error log. Most look similar to the example above. The error log will also contain debugging output from CGI scripts. Any information written to `stderr` by a CGI script will be copied directly to the error log.

Putting a `%L` token in both the error log and the access log will produce a log entry ID with which you can correlate the entry in the error log with the entry in the access log. If MOD_UNIQUE_ID is loaded, its unique request ID will be used as the log entry ID, too.

During testing, it is often useful to continuously monitor the error log for any problems. On Unix systems, you can accomplish this using:

```
tail -f error_log
```

Per-module logging

The LogLevel directive allows you to specify a log severity level on a per-module basis. In this way, if you are troubleshooting a problem with just one particular module, you can turn up its logging volume without also getting the details of other modules that you're not interested in. This is particularly useful for modules such as MOD_PROXY or MOD_REWRITE where you want to know details about what it's trying to do.

Do this by specifying the name of the module in your LogLevel directive:

```
LogLevel info rewrite:trace5
```

This sets the main LogLevel to info, but turns it up to `trace5` for MOD_REWRITE.

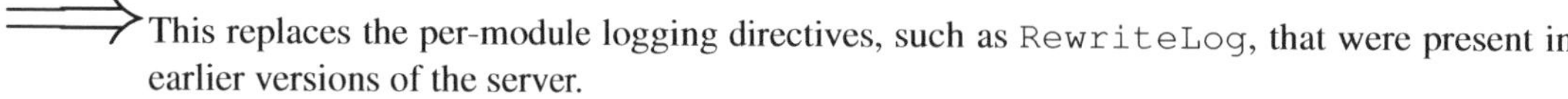

This replaces the per-module logging directives, such as `RewriteLog`, that were present in earlier versions of the server.

Access Log

Related Modules	Related Directives
MOD_LOG_CONFIG	CustomLog
MOD_SETENVIF	LogFormat
	SetEnvIf

The server access log records all requests processed by the server. The location and content of the access log are controlled by the CustomLog directive. The LogFormat directive can be used to simplify the selection of the contents of the logs. This section describes how to configure the server to record information in the access log.

Of course, storing the information in the access log is only the start of log management. The next step is to analyze this information to produce useful statistics. Log analysis in general is beyond the scope of this document, and not really part of the job of the web server itself. For more information about this topic, and for applications which perform log analysis, check the Open Directory[16] or Yahoo[17].

Various versions of Apache httpd have used other modules and directives to control access logging, including mod_log_referer, mod_log_agent, and the `TransferLog` directive. The CUSTOMLOG directive now subsumes the functionality of all the older directives.

The format of the access log is highly configurable. The format is specified using a format string that looks much like a C-style printf(1) format string. Some examples are presented in the next sections. For a complete list of the possible contents of the format string, see the MOD_LOG_CONFIG format strings (p. 661) .

Common Log Format

A typical configuration for the access log might look as follows.

```
LogFormat "%h %l %u %t \"%r\" %>s %b" common
CustomLog logs/access_log common
```

This defines the *nickname* `common` and associates it with a particular log format string. The format string consists of percent directives, each of which tell the server to log a particular piece of information. Literal characters may also be placed in the format string and will be copied directly into the log output. The quote character (`"`) must be escaped by placing a backslash before it to prevent it from being interpreted as the end of the format string. The format string may also contain the special control characters "`\n`" for new-line and "`\t`" for tab.

The CUSTOMLOG directive sets up a new log file using the defined *nickname*. The filename for the access log is relative to the SERVERROOT unless it begins with a slash.

The above configuration will write log entries in a format known as the Common Log Format (CLF). This standard format can be produced by many different web servers and read by many log analysis programs. The log file entries produced in CLF will look something like this:

```
127.0.0.1 - frank [10/Oct/2000:13:55:36 -0700] "GET /apache_pb.gif
HTTP/1.0" 200 2326
```

Each part of this log entry is described below.

`127.0.0.1` (`%h`) This is the IP address of the client (remote host) which made the request to the server. If HOSTNAMELOOKUPS is set to `On`, then the server will try to determine the hostname and log it in place of the IP address. However, this configuration is not recommended since it can significantly slow the server. Instead, it is best to use a log post-processor such as `logresolve` to determine the hostnames. The IP address reported here is not necessarily the address of the machine at which the user is sitting. If a proxy server exists between the user and the server, this address will be the address of the proxy, rather than the originating machine.

`-` (`%l`) The "hyphen" in the output indicates that the requested piece of information is not available. In this case, the information that is not available is the RFC 1413 identity of the client determined by `identd` on the clients machine. This information is highly unreliable and should almost never be used except on tightly controlled internal networks. Apache httpd will not even attempt to determine this information unless IDENTITYCHECK is set to `On`.

`frank` (`%u`) This is the userid of the person requesting the document as determined by HTTP authentication. The same value is typically provided to CGI scripts in the `REMOTE_USER` environment variable. If the status code for the request (see below) is 401, then this value should not be trusted because the user is not yet authenticated. If the document is not password protected, this part will be "`-`" just like the previous one.

[16] http://dmoz.org/Computers/Software/Internet/Site_Management/Log_analysis/
[17] http://dir.yahoo.com/Computers_and_Internet/Software/Internet/World_Wide_Web/Servers/Log_Analysis_Tools/

[10/Oct/2000:13:55:36 -0700] (%t) The time that the request was received. The format is:

```
[day/month/year:hour:minute:second zone]
day = 2*digit
month = 3*letter
year = 4*digit
hour = 2*digit
minute = 2*digit
second = 2*digit
zone = ('+' | '-') 4*digit
```

It is possible to have the time displayed in another format by specifying `%{format}t` in the log format string, where `format` is either as in `strftime(3)` from the C standard library, or one of the supported special tokens. For details see the MOD_LOG_CONFIG format strings (p. 661) .

"GET /apache_pb.gif HTTP/1.0" (\"%r\") The request line from the client is given in double quotes. The request line contains a great deal of useful information. First, the method used by the client is `GET`. Second, the client requested the resource `/apache_pb.gif`, and third, the client used the protocol `HTTP/1.0`. It is also possible to log one or more parts of the request line independently. For example, the format string `"%m %U%q %H"` will log the method, path, query-string, and protocol, resulting in exactly the same output as `"%r"`.

200 (%>s) This is the status code that the server sends back to the client. This information is very valuable, because it reveals whether the request resulted in a successful response (codes beginning in 2), a redirection (codes beginning in 3), an error caused by the client (codes beginning in 4), or an error in the server (codes beginning in 5). The full list of possible status codes can be found in the HTTP specification[18] (RFC2616 section 10).

2326 (%b) The last part indicates the size of the object returned to the client, not including the response headers. If no content was returned to the client, this value will be `"-"`. To log `"0"` for no content, use `%B` instead.

Combined Log Format

Another commonly used format string is called the Combined Log Format. It can be used as follows.

```
LogFormat "%h %l %u %t \"%r\" %>s %b \"%{Referer}i\" \"%{User-agent}i\"" combined
CustomLog log/access_log combined
```

This format is exactly the same as the Common Log Format, with the addition of two more fields. Each of the additional fields uses the percent-directive `%{`*header*`}i`, where *header* can be any HTTP request header. The access log under this format will look like:

```
127.0.0.1 - frank [10/Oct/2000:13:55:36 -0700] "GET /apache_pb.gif
HTTP/1.0" 200 2326 "http://www.example.com/start.html" "Mozilla/4.08
[en] (Win98; I ;Nav)"
```

The additional fields are:

"http://www.example.com/start.html" (\"%{Referer}i\") The "Referer" (sic) HTTP request header. This gives the site that the client reports having been referred from. (This should be the page that links to or includes `/apache_pb.gif`).

"Mozilla/4.08 [en] (Win98; I ;Nav)" (\"%{User-agent}i\") The User-Agent HTTP request header. This is the identifying information that the client browser reports about itself.

[18] http://www.w3.org/Protocols/rfc2616/rfc2616.txt

Multiple Access Logs

Multiple access logs can be created simply by specifying multiple CUSTOMLOG directives in the configuration file. For example, the following directives will create three access logs. The first contains the basic CLF information, while the second and third contain referer and browser information. The last two CUSTOMLOG lines show how to mimic the effects of the ReferLog and AgentLog directives.

```
LogFormat "%h %l %u %t \"%r\" %>s %b" common
CustomLog logs/access_log common
CustomLog logs/referer_log "%{Referer}i -> %U"
CustomLog logs/agent_log "%{User-agent}i"
```

This example also shows that it is not necessary to define a nickname with the LOGFORMAT directive. Instead, the log format can be specified directly in the CUSTOMLOG directive.

Conditional Logs

There are times when it is convenient to exclude certain entries from the access logs based on characteristics of the client request. This is easily accomplished with the help of environment variables (p. 82) . First, an environment variable must be set to indicate that the request meets certain conditions. This is usually accomplished with SETENVIF. Then the env= clause of the CUSTOMLOG directive is used to include or exclude requests where the environment variable is set. Some examples:

```
# Mark requests from the loop-back interface
SetEnvIf Remote_Addr "127\.0\.0\.1" dontlog
# Mark requests for the robots.txt file
SetEnvIf Request_URI "^/robots\.txt$" dontlog
# Log what remains
CustomLog logs/access_log common env=!dontlog
```

As another example, consider logging requests from english-speakers to one log file, and non-english speakers to a different log file.

```
SetEnvIf Accept-Language "en" english
CustomLog logs/english_log common env=english
CustomLog logs/non_english_log common env=!english
```

In a caching scenario one would want to know about the efficiency of the cache. A very simple method to find this out would be:

```
SetEnv CACHE_MISS 1
LogFormat "%h %l %u %t "%r " %>s %b %{CACHE_MISS}e" common-cache
CustomLog logs/access_log common-cache
```

MOD_CACHE will run before MOD_ENV and, when successful, will deliver the content without it. In that case a cache hit will log -, while a cache miss will log 1.

In addition to the env= syntax, LOGFORMAT supports logging values conditional upon the HTTP response code:

```
LogFormat "%400,501{User-agent}i" browserlog
LogFormat "%!200,304,302{Referer}i" refererlog
```

In the first example, the User-agent will be logged if the HTTP status code is 400 or 501. In other cases, a literal "-" will be logged instead. Likewise, in the second example, the Referer will be logged if the HTTP status code is **not** 200, 204, or 302. (Note the "!" before the status codes.

Although we have just shown that conditional logging is very powerful and flexible, it is not the only way to control the contents of the logs. Log files are more useful when they contain a complete record of server activity. It is often easier to simply post-process the log files to remove requests that you do not want to consider.

Log Rotation

On even a moderately busy server, the quantity of information stored in the log files is very large. The access log file typically grows 1 MB or more per 10,000 requests. It will consequently be necessary to periodically rotate the log files by moving or deleting the existing logs. This cannot be done while the server is running, because Apache httpd will continue writing to the old log file as long as it holds the file open. Instead, the server must be restarted (p. 27) after the log files are moved or deleted so that it will open new log files.

By using a *graceful* restart, the server can be instructed to open new log files without losing any existing or pending connections from clients. However, in order to accomplish this, the server must continue to write to the old log files while it finishes serving old requests. It is therefore necessary to wait for some time after the restart before doing any processing on the log files. A typical scenario that simply rotates the logs and compresses the old logs to save space is:

```
mv access_log access_log.old
mv error_log error_log.old
apachectl graceful
sleep 600
gzip access_log.old error_log.old
```

Another way to perform log rotation is using piped logs as discussed in the next section.

Piped Logs

Apache httpd is capable of writing error and access log files through a pipe to another process, rather than directly to a file. This capability dramatically increases the flexibility of logging, without adding code to the main server. In order to write logs to a pipe, simply replace the filename with the pipe character "|", followed by the name of the executable which should accept log entries on its standard input. The server will start the piped-log process when the server starts, and will restart it if it crashes while the server is running. (This last feature is why we can refer to this technique as "reliable piped logging".)

Piped log processes are spawned by the parent Apache httpd process, and inherit the userid of that process. This means that piped log programs usually run as root. It is therefore very important to keep the programs simple and secure.

One important use of piped logs is to allow log rotation without having to restart the server. The Apache HTTP Server includes a simple program called rotatelogs for this purpose. For example, to rotate the logs every 24 hours, you can use:

```
CustomLog "|/usr/local/apache/bin/rotatelogs /var/log/access_log 86400" common
```

Notice that quotes are used to enclose the entire command that will be called for the pipe. Although these examples are for the access log, the same technique can be used for the error log.

As with conditional logging, piped logs are a very powerful tool, but they should not be used where a simpler solution like off-line post-processing is available.

By default the piped log process is spawned without invoking a shell. Use "|$" instead of "|" to spawn using a shell (usually with /bin/sh -c):

```
# Invoke "rotatelogs" using a shell
CustomLog "|$/usr/local/apache/bin/rotatelogs   /var/log/access_log 86400" common
```

This was the default behaviour for Apache 2.2. Depending on the shell specifics this might lead to an additional shell process for the lifetime of the logging pipe program and signal handling problems during restart. For compatibility reasons with Apache 2.2 the notation "||" is also supported and equivalent to using "|".

Windows note
Note that on Windows, you may run into problems when running many piped logger processes, especially when HTTPD is running as a service. This is caused by running out of desktop heap space. The desktop heap space given to each service is specified by the third argument to the SharedSectionparameter in the HKEY_LOCAL_MACHINE\System\CurrentControlSet\Control\SessionManager\SubSystems\Windows registry value.**Change this value with care**; the normal caveats for changing the Windows registry apply, but you might also exhaust the desktop heap pool if the number is adjusted too high.

Virtual Hosts

When running a server with many virtual hosts (p. 114) , there are several options for dealing with log files. First, it is possible to use logs exactly as in a single-host server. Simply by placing the logging directives outside the <VIRTUALHOST> sections in the main server context, it is possible to log all requests in the same access log and error log. This technique does not allow for easy collection of statistics on individual virtual hosts.

If CUSTOMLOG or ERRORLOG directives are placed inside a <VIRTUALHOST> section, all requests or errors for that virtual host will be logged only to the specified file. Any virtual host which does not have logging directives will still have its requests sent to the main server logs. This technique is very useful for a small number of virtual hosts, but if the number of hosts is very large, it can be complicated to manage. In addition, it can often create problems with insufficient file descriptors (p. 134) .

For the access log, there is a very good compromise. By adding information on the virtual host to the log format string, it is possible to log all hosts to the same log, and later split the log into individual files. For example, consider the following directives.

```
LogFormat "%v %l %u %t \"%r\" %>s %b" comonvhost
CustomLog logs/access_log comonvhost
```

The %v is used to log the name of the virtual host that is serving the request. Then a program like split-logfile (p. 321) can be used to post-process the access log in order to split it into one file per virtual host.

Other Log Files

Related Modules	Related Directives
MOD_LOGIO	LOGFORMAT
MOD_LOG_CONFIG	BUFFEREDLOGS
MOD_LOG_FORENSIC	FORENSICLOG
MOD_CGI	PIDFILE
	SCRIPTLOG
	SCRIPTLOGBUFFER
	SCRIPTLOGLENGTH

Logging actual bytes sent and received

MOD_LOGIO adds in two additional LOGFORMAT fields (%I and %O) that log the actual number of bytes received and sent on the network.

Forensic Logging

MOD_LOG_FORENSIC provides for forensic logging of client requests. Logging is done before and after processing a request, so the forensic log contains two log lines for each request. The forensic logger is very strict with no customizations. It can be an invaluable debugging and security tool.

PID File

On startup, Apache httpd saves the process id of the parent httpd process to the file `logs/httpd.pid`. This filename can be changed with the PIDFILE directive. The process-id is for use by the administrator in restarting and terminating the daemon by sending signals to the parent process; on Windows, use the -k command line option instead. For more information see the Stopping and Restarting (p. 27) page.

Script Log

In order to aid in debugging, the SCRIPTLOG directive allows you to record the input to and output from CGI scripts. This should only be used in testing - not for live servers. More information is available in the mod_cgi (p. 549) documentation.

2.9 Mapping URLs to Filesystem Locations

This document explains how the Apache HTTP Server uses the URL of a request to determine the filesystem location from which to serve a file.

Related Modules and Directives

Related Modules	Related Directives
MOD_ACTIONS	ALIAS
MOD_ALIAS	ALIASMATCH
MOD_AUTOINDEX	CHECKSPELLING
MOD_DIR	DIRECTORYINDEX
MOD_IMAGEMAP	DOCUMENTROOT
MOD_NEGOTIATION	ERRORDOCUMENT
MOD_PROXY	OPTIONS
MOD_REWRITE	PROXYPASS
MOD_SPELING	PROXYPASSREVERSE
MOD_USERDIR	PROXYPASSREVERSECOOKIEDOMAIN
MOD_VHOST_ALIAS	PROXYPASSREVERSECOOKIEPATH
	REDIRECT
	REDIRECTMATCH
	REWRITECOND
	REWRITERULE
	SCRIPTALIAS
	SCRIPTALIASMATCH
	USERDIR

DocumentRoot

In deciding what file to serve for a given request, httpd's default behavior is to take the URL-Path for the request (the part of the URL following the hostname and port) and add it to the end of the DOCUMENTROOT specified in your configuration files. Therefore, the files and directories underneath the DOCUMENTROOT make up the basic document tree which will be visible from the web.

For example, if DOCUMENTROOT were set to `/var/www/html` then a request for `http://www.example.com/fish/guppies.html` would result in the file `/var/www/html/fish/guppies.html` being served to the requesting client.

If a directory is requested (i.e. a path ending with `/`), the file served from that directory is defined by the DIRECTORYINDEX directive. For example, if `DocumentRoot` were set as above, and you were to set:

```
DirectoryIndex index.html index.php
```

Then a request for `http://www.example.com/fish/` will cause httpd to attempt to serve the file `/var/www/html/fish/index.html`. In the event that that file does not exist, it will next attempt to serve the file `/var/www/html/fish/index.php`.

If neither of these files existed, the next step is to attempt to provide a directory index, if MOD_AUTOINDEX is loaded and configured to permit that.

httpd is also capable of Virtual Hosting (p. 114) , where the server receives requests for more than one host. In this case, a different DOCUMENTROOT can be specified for each virtual host, or alternatively, the directives provided by the module MOD_VHOST_ALIAS can be used to dynamically determine the appropriate place from which to serve content based on the requested IP address or hostname.

The DOCUMENTROOT directive is set in your main server configuration file (`httpd.conf`) and, possibly, once per additional Virtual Host (p. 114) you create.

Files Outside the DocumentRoot

There are frequently circumstances where it is necessary to allow web access to parts of the filesystem that are not strictly underneath the DOCUMENTROOT. httpd offers several different ways to accomplish this. On Unix systems, symbolic links can bring other parts of the filesystem under the DOCUMENTROOT. For security reasons, httpd will follow symbolic links only if the OPTIONS setting for the relevant directory includes `FollowSymLinks` or `SymLinksIfOwnerMatch`.

Alternatively, the ALIAS directive will map any part of the filesystem into the web space. For example, with

```
Alias "/docs" "/var/web"
```

the URL `http://www.example.com/docs/dir/file.html` will be served from `/var/web/dir/file.html`. The SCRIPTALIAS directive works the same way, with the additional effect that all content located at the target path is treated as CGI scripts.

For situations where you require additional flexibility, you can use the ALIASMATCH and SCRIPTALIASMATCH directives to do powerful regular expression based matching and substitution. For example,

```
ScriptAliasMatch "^/~([a-zA-Z0-9]+)/cgi-bin/(.+)"    "/home/$1/cgi-bin/$2"
```

will map a request to `http://example.com/~user/cgi-bin/script.cgi` to the path `/home/user/cgi-bin/script.cgi` and will treat the resulting file as a CGI script.

User Directories

Traditionally on Unix systems, the home directory of a particular *user* can be referred to as `~user/`. The module MOD_USERDIR extends this idea to the web by allowing files under each user's home directory to be accessed using URLs such as the following.

```
http://www.example.com/~user/file.html
```

For security reasons, it is inappropriate to give direct access to a user's home directory from the web. Therefore, the USERDIR directive specifies a directory underneath the user's home directory where web files are located. Using the default setting of `Userdir public_html`, the above URL maps to a file at a directory like `/home/user/public_html/file.html` where `/home/user/` is the user's home directory as specified in `/etc/passwd`.

There are also several other forms of the `Userdir` directive which you can use on systems where `/etc/passwd` does not contain the location of the home directory.

Some people find the "~" symbol (which is often encoded on the web as `%7e`) to be awkward and prefer to use an alternate string to represent user directories. This functionality is not supported by mod_userdir. However, if users' home directories are structured in a regular way, then it is possible to use the ALIASMATCH directive to achieve the desired effect. For example, to make `http://www.example.com/upages/user/file.html` map to `/home/user/public_html/file.html`, use the following `AliasMatch` directive:

```
AliasMatch "^/upages/([a-zA-Z0-9]+)(/(.*))?$"    "/home/$1/public_html/$3"
```

URL Redirection

The configuration directives discussed in the above sections tell httpd to get content from a specific place in the filesystem and return it to the client. Sometimes, it is desirable instead to inform the client that the requested content is located at a different URL, and instruct the client to make a new request with the new URL. This is called *redirection* and is implemented by the REDIRECT directive. For example, if the contents of the directory `/foo/` under the DOCUMENTROOT are moved to the new directory `/bar/`, you can instruct clients to request the content at the new location as follows:

```
Redirect permanent "/foo/"   "http://www.example.com/bar/"
```

This will redirect any URL-Path starting in `/foo/` to the same URL path on the `www.example.com` server with `/bar/` substituted for `/foo/`. You can redirect clients to any server, not only the origin server.

httpd also provides a REDIRECTMATCH directive for more complicated rewriting problems. For example, to redirect requests for the site home page to a different site, but leave all other requests alone, use the following configuration:

```
RedirectMatch permanent "^/$"    "http://www.example.com/startpage.html"
```

Alternatively, to temporarily redirect all pages on one site to a particular page on another site, use the following:

```
RedirectMatch temp ".*"  "http://othersite.example.com/startpage.html"
```

Reverse Proxy

httpd also allows you to bring remote documents into the URL space of the local server. This technique is called *reverse proxying* because the web server acts like a proxy server by fetching the documents from a remote server and returning them to the client. It is different from normal (forward) proxying because, to the client, it appears the documents originate at the reverse proxy server.

In the following example, when clients request documents under the `/foo/` directory, the server fetches those documents from the `/bar/` directory on `internal.example.com` and returns them to the client as if they were from the local server.

```
ProxyPass "/foo/" "http://internal.example.com/bar/"
ProxyPassReverse "/foo/" "http://internal.example.com/bar/"
ProxyPassReverseCookieDomain internal.example.com public.example.com
ProxyPassReverseCookiePath "/foo/" "/bar/"
```

The PROXYPASS configures the server to fetch the appropriate documents, while the PROXYPASSREVERSE directive rewrites redirects originating at `internal.example.com` so that they target the appropriate directory on the local server. Similarly, the PROXYPASSREVERSECOOKIEDOMAIN and PROXYPASSREVERSECOOKIEPATH rewrite cookies set by the backend server.

It is important to note, however, that links inside the documents will not be rewritten. So any absolute links on `internal.example.com` will result in the client breaking out of the proxy server and requesting directly from `internal.example.com`. You can modify these links (and other content) in a page as it is being served to the client using MOD_SUBSTITUTE.

```
Substitute "s/internal\.example\.com/www.example.com/i"
```

For more sophisticated rewriting of links in HTML and XHTML, the MOD_PROXY_HTML module is also available. It allows you to create maps of URLs that need to be rewritten, so that complex proxying scenarios can be handled.

Rewriting Engine

When even more powerful substitution is required, the rewriting engine provided by MOD_REWRITE can be useful. The directives provided by this module can use characteristics of the request such as browser type or source IP address in deciding from where to serve content. In addition, mod_rewrite can use external database files or programs to determine how to handle a request. The rewriting engine is capable of performing all three types of mappings discussed above: internal redirects (aliases), external redirects, and proxying. Many practical examples employing mod_rewrite are discussed in the detailed mod_rewrite documentation (p. 136) .

File Not Found

Inevitably, URLs will be requested for which no matching file can be found in the filesystem. This can happen for several reasons. In some cases, it can be a result of moving documents from one location to another. In this case, it is best to use URL redirection to inform clients of the new location of the resource. In this way, you can assure that old bookmarks and links will continue to work, even though the resource is at a new location.

Another common cause of "File Not Found" errors is accidental mistyping of URLs, either directly in the browser, or in HTML links. httpd provides the module MOD_SPELING (sic) to help with this problem. When this module is activated, it will intercept "File Not Found" errors and look for a resource with a similar filename. If one such file is found, mod_speling will send an HTTP redirect to the client informing it of the correct location. If several "close" files are found, a list of available alternatives will be presented to the client.

An especially useful feature of mod_speling, is that it will compare filenames without respect to case. This can help systems where users are unaware of the case-sensitive nature of URLs and the unix filesystem. But using mod_speling for anything more than the occasional URL correction can place additional load on the server, since each "incorrect" request is followed by a URL redirection and a new request from the client.

MOD_DIR provides FALLBACKRESOURCE, which can be used to map virtual URIs to a real resource, which then serves them. This is a very useful replacement for MOD_REWRITE when implementing a 'front controller'

If all attempts to locate the content fail, httpd returns an error page with HTTP status code 404 (file not found). The appearance of this page is controlled with the ERRORDOCUMENT directive and can be customized in a flexible manner as discussed in the Custom error responses (p. 75) document.

Other URL Mapping Modules

Other modules available for URL mapping include:

- MOD_ACTIONS - Maps a request to a CGI script based on the request method, or resource MIME type.
- MOD_DIR - Provides basic mapping of a trailing slash into an index file such as `index.html`.
- MOD_IMAGEMAP - Maps a request to a URL based on where a user clicks on an image embedded in a HTML document.
- MOD_NEGOTIATION - Selects an appropriate document based on client preferences such as language or content compression.

2.10 Dynamic Shared Object (DSO) Support

The Apache HTTP Server is a modular program where the administrator can choose the functionality to include in the server by selecting a set of modules. Modules will be compiled as Dynamic Shared Objects (DSOs) that exist separately from the main `httpd` binary file. DSO modules may be compiled at the time the server is built, or they may be compiled and added at a later time using the Apache Extension Tool (`apxs`).

Alternatively, the modules can be statically compiled into the `httpd` binary when the server is built.

This document describes how to use DSO modules as well as the theory behind their use.

Implementation

Related Modules	Related Directives
MOD_SO	LOADMODULE

The DSO support for loading individual Apache httpd modules is based on a module named MOD_SO which must be statically compiled into the Apache httpd core. It is the only module besides CORE which cannot be put into a DSO itself. Practically all other distributed Apache httpd modules will then be placed into a DSO. After a module is compiled into a DSO named `mod_foo.so` you can use MOD_SO's LOADMODULE directive in your `httpd.conf` file to load this module at server startup or restart.

The DSO builds for individual modules can be disabled via `configure`'s `--enable-mods-static` option as discussed in the install documentation (p. 20) .

To simplify this creation of DSO files for Apache httpd modules (especially for third-party modules) a support program named `apxs` (*APache eXtenSion*) is available. It can be used to build DSO based modules *outside of* the Apache httpd source tree. The idea is simple: When installing Apache HTTP Server the `configure`'s `make install` procedure installs the Apache httpd C header files and puts the platform-dependent compiler and linker flags for building DSO files into the `apxs` program. This way the user can use `apxs` to compile his Apache httpd module sources without the Apache httpd distribution source tree and without having to fiddle with the platform-dependent compiler and linker flags for DSO support.

Usage Summary

To give you an overview of the DSO features of Apache HTTP Server 2.x, here is a short and concise summary:

1. Build and install a *distributed* Apache httpd module, say `mod_foo.c`, into its own DSO `mod_foo.so`:

```
$ ./configure --prefix=/path/to/install --enable-foo
$ make install
```

2. Configure Apache HTTP Server with all modules enabled. Only a basic set will be loaded during server startup. You can change the set of loaded modules by activating or deactivating the LOADMODULE directives in `httpd.conf`.

```
$ ./configure --enable-mods-shared=all
$ make install
```

3. Some modules are only useful for developers and will not be build. when using the module set *all*. To build all available modules including developer modules use *reallyall*. In addition the LOADMODULE directives for all built modules can be activated via the configure option `--enable-load-all-modules`.

```
$ ./configure --enable-mods-shared=reallyall
--enable-load-all-modules
$ make install
```

4. Build and install a *third-party* Apache httpd module, say `mod_foo.c`, into its own DSO `mod_foo.so` *outside of* the Apache httpd source tree using `apxs`:

```
$ cd /path/to/3rdparty
$ apxs -cia mod_foo.c
```

In all cases, once the shared module is compiled, you must use a LOADMODULE directive in `httpd.conf` to tell Apache httpd to activate the module.

See the apxs documentation (p. 291) for more details.

Background

On modern Unix derivatives there exists a mechanism called dynamic linking/loading of *Dynamic Shared Objects* (DSO) which provides a way to build a piece of program code in a special format for loading it at run-time into the address space of an executable program.

This loading can usually be done in two ways: automatically by a system program called `ld.so` when an executable program is started or manually from within the executing program via a programmatic system interface to the Unix loader through the system calls `dlopen()/dlsym()`.

In the first way the DSO's are usually called *shared libraries* or *DSO libraries* and named `libfoo.so` or `libfoo.so.1.2`. They reside in a system directory (usually `/usr/lib`) and the link to the executable program is established at build-time by specifying `-lfoo` to the linker command. This hard-codes library references into the executable program file so that at start-time the Unix loader is able to locate `libfoo.so` in `/usr/lib`, in paths hard-coded via linker-options like `-R` or in paths configured via the environment variable `LD_LIBRARY_PATH`. It then resolves any (yet unresolved) symbols in the executable program which are available in the DSO.

Symbols in the executable program are usually not referenced by the DSO (because it's a reusable library of general code) and hence no further resolving has to be done. The executable program has no need to do anything on its own to use the symbols from the DSO because the complete resolving is done by the Unix loader. (In fact, the code to invoke `ld.so` is part of the run-time startup code which is linked into every executable program which has been bound non-static). The advantage of dynamic loading of common library code is obvious: the library code needs to be stored only once, in a system library like `libc.so`, saving disk space for every program.

In the second way the DSO's are usually called *shared objects* or *DSO files* and can be named with an arbitrary extension (although the canonical name is `foo.so`). These files usually stay inside a program-specific directory and there is no automatically established link to the executable program where they are used. Instead the executable program manually loads the DSO at run-time into its address space via `dlopen()`. At this time no resolving of symbols from the DSO for the executable program is done. But instead the Unix loader automatically resolves any (yet unresolved) symbols in the DSO from the set of symbols exported by the executable program and its already loaded DSO libraries (especially all symbols from the ubiquitous `libc.so`). This way the DSO gets knowledge of the executable program's symbol set as if it had been statically linked with it in the first place.

Finally, to take advantage of the DSO's API the executable program has to resolve particular symbols from the DSO via `dlsym()` for later use inside dispatch tables *etc.* In other words: The executable program has to manually resolve every symbol it needs to be able to use it. The advantage of such a mechanism is that optional program parts need not be loaded (and thus do not spend memory) until they are needed by the program in question. When required, these program parts can be loaded dynamically to extend the base program's functionality.

Although this DSO mechanism sounds straightforward there is at least one difficult step here: The resolving of symbols from the executable program for the DSO when using a DSO to extend a program (the second way). Why? Because "reverse resolving" DSO symbols from the executable program's symbol set is against the library design (where the library has no knowledge about the programs it is used by) and is neither available under all platforms nor standardized. In practice the executable program's global symbols are often not re-exported and thus not available for use in a DSO. Finding a way to force the linker to export all global symbols is the main problem one has to solve when using DSO for extending a program at run-time.

The shared library approach is the typical one, because it is what the DSO mechanism was designed for, hence it is used for nearly all types of libraries the operating system provides.

Advantages and Disadvantages

The above DSO based features have the following advantages:

- The server package is more flexible at run-time because the server process can be assembled at run-time via LOADMODULE `httpd.conf` configuration directives instead of `configure` options at build-time. For instance, this way one is able to run different server instances (standard & SSL version, minimalistic & dynamic version [mod_perl, mod_php], *etc.*) with only one Apache httpd installation.
- The server package can be easily extended with third-party modules even after installation. This is a great benefit for vendor package maintainers, who can create an Apache httpd core package and additional packages containing extensions like PHP, mod_perl, mod_security, *etc.*
- Easier Apache httpd module prototyping, because with the DSO/`apxs` pair you can both work outside the Apache httpd source tree and only need an `apxs -i` command followed by an `apachectl restart` to bring a new version of your currently developed module into the running Apache HTTP Server.

DSO has the following disadvantages:

- The server is approximately 20% slower at startup time because of the symbol resolving overhead the Unix loader now has to do.
- The server is approximately 5% slower at execution time under some platforms, because position independent code (PIC) sometimes needs complicated assembler tricks for relative addressing, which are not necessarily as fast as absolute addressing.
- Because DSO modules cannot be linked against other DSO-based libraries (`ld -lfoo`) on all platforms (for instance a.out-based platforms usually don't provide this functionality while ELF-based platforms do) you cannot use the DSO mechanism for all types of modules. Or in other words, modules compiled as DSO files are restricted to only use symbols from the Apache httpd core, from the C library (`libc`) and all other dynamic or static libraries used by the Apache httpd core, or from static library archives (`libfoo.a`) containing position independent code. The only chances to use other code is to either make sure the httpd core itself already contains a reference to it or loading the code yourself via `dlopen()`.

2.11 Content Negotiation

Apache HTTPD supports content negotiation as described in the HTTP/1.1 specification. It can choose the best representation of a resource based on the browser-supplied preferences for media type, languages, character set and encoding. It also implements a couple of features to give more intelligent handling of requests from browsers that send incomplete negotiation information.

Content negotiation is provided by the MOD_NEGOTIATION module, which is compiled in by default.

About Content Negotiation

A resource may be available in several different representations. For example, it might be available in different languages or different media types, or a combination. One way of selecting the most appropriate choice is to give the user an index page, and let them select. However it is often possible for the server to choose automatically. This works because browsers can send, as part of each request, information about what representations they prefer. For example, a browser could indicate that it would like to see information in French, if possible, else English will do. Browsers indicate their preferences by headers in the request. To request only French representations, the browser would send

```
Accept-Language: fr
```

Note that this preference will only be applied when there is a choice of representations and they vary by language.

As an example of a more complex request, this browser has been configured to accept French and English, but prefer French, and to accept various media types, preferring HTML over plain text or other text types, and preferring GIF or JPEG over other media types, but also allowing any other media type as a last resort:

```
Accept-Language: fr; q=1.0, en; q=0.5
Accept: text/html; q=1.0, text/*; q=0.8, image/gif; q=0.6,
image/jpeg; q=0.6, image/*; q=0.5, */*; q=0.1
```

httpd supports 'server driven' content negotiation, as defined in the HTTP/1.1 specification. It fully supports the `Accept`, `Accept-Language`, `Accept-Charset` and `Accept-Encoding` request headers. httpd also supports 'transparent' content negotiation, which is an experimental negotiation protocol defined in RFC 2295 and RFC 2296. It does not offer support for 'feature negotiation' as defined in these RFCs.

A **resource** is a conceptual entity identified by a URI (RFC 2396). An HTTP server like Apache HTTP Server provides access to **representations** of the resource(s) within its namespace, with each representation in the form of a sequence of bytes with a defined media type, character set, encoding, etc. Each resource may be associated with zero, one, or more than one representation at any given time. If multiple representations are available, the resource is referred to as **negotiable** and each of its representations is termed a **variant**. The ways in which the variants for a negotiable resource vary are called the **dimensions** of negotiation.

Negotiation in httpd

In order to negotiate a resource, the server needs to be given information about each of the variants. This is done in one of two ways:

- Using a type map (*i.e.*, a `*.var` file) which names the files containing the variants explicitly, or
- Using a 'MultiViews' search, where the server does an implicit filename pattern match and chooses from among the results.

Using a type-map file

A type map is a document which is associated with the handler named `type-map` (or, for backwards-compatibility with older httpd configurations, the MIME-type `application/x-type-map`). Note that to use this feature, you must have a handler set in the configuration that defines a file suffix as `type-map`; this is best done with

```
AddHandler type-map .var
```

in the server configuration file.

Type map files should have the same name as the resource which they are describing, followed by the extension `.var`. In the examples shown below, the resource is named `foo`, so the type map file is named `foo.var`.

This file should have an entry for each available variant; these entries consist of contiguous HTTP-format header lines. Entries for different variants are separated by blank lines. Blank lines are illegal within an entry. It is conventional to begin a map file with an entry for the combined entity as a whole (although this is not required, and if present will be ignored). An example map file is shown below.

URIs in this file are relative to the location of the type map file. Usually, these files will be located in the same directory as the type map file, but this is not required. You may provide absolute or relative URIs for any file located on the same server as the map file.

```
URI: foo

URI: foo.en.html
Content-type: text/html
Content-language: en

URI: foo.fr.de.html
Content-type: text/html;charset=iso-8859-2
Content-language: fr, de
```

Note also that a typemap file will take precedence over the filename's extension, even when Multiviews is on. If the variants have different source qualities, that may be indicated by the "qs" parameter to the media type, as in this picture (available as JPEG, GIF, or ASCII-art):

```
URI: foo

URI: foo.jpeg
Content-type: image/jpeg; qs=0.8

URI: foo.gif
Content-type: image/gif; qs=0.5

URI: foo.txt
Content-type: text/plain; qs=0.01
```

qs values can vary in the range 0.000 to 1.000. Note that any variant with a qs value of 0.000 will never be chosen. Variants with no 'qs' parameter value are given a qs factor of 1.0. The qs parameter indicates the relative 'quality' of this variant compared to the other available variants, independent of the client's capabilities. For example, a JPEG file is usually of higher source quality than an ASCII file if it is attempting to represent a photograph. However, if the resource being represented is an original ASCII art, then an ASCII representation would have a higher source quality than a JPEG representation. A qs value is therefore specific to a given variant depending on the nature of the resource it represents.

The full list of headers recognized is available in the mod_negotiation typemap (p. 721) documentation.

Multiviews

MultiViews is a per-directory option, meaning it can be set with an OPTIONS directive within a <DIRECTORY>, <LOCATION> or <FILES> section in httpd.conf, or (if ALLOWOVERRIDE is properly set) in .htaccess files. Note that Options All does not set MultiViews; you have to ask for it by name.

The effect of MultiViews is as follows: if the server receives a request for /some/dir/foo, if /some/dir has MultiViews enabled, and /some/dir/foo does *not* exist, then the server reads the directory looking for files named foo.*, and effectively fakes up a type map which names all those files, assigning them the same media types and content-encodings it would have if the client had asked for one of them by name. It then chooses the best match to the client's requirements.

MultiViews may also apply to searches for the file named by the DIRECTORYINDEX directive, if the server is trying to index a directory. If the configuration files specify

```
DirectoryIndex index
```

then the server will arbitrate between index.html and index.html3 if both are present. If neither are present, and index.cgi is there, the server will run it.

If one of the files found when reading the directory does not have an extension recognized by mod_mime to designate its Charset, Content-Type, Language, or Encoding, then the result depends on the setting of the MULTIVIEWSMATCH directive. This directive determines whether handlers, filters, and other extension types can participate in MultiViews negotiation.

The Negotiation Methods

After httpd has obtained a list of the variants for a given resource, either from a type-map file or from the filenames in the directory, it invokes one of two methods to decide on the 'best' variant to return, if any. It is not necessary to know any of the details of how negotiation actually takes place in order to use httpd's content negotiation features. However the rest of this document explains the methods used for those interested.

There are two negotiation methods:

1. **Server driven negotiation with the httpd algorithm** is used in the normal case. The httpd algorithm is explained in more detail below. When this algorithm is used, httpd can sometimes 'fiddle' the quality factor of a particular dimension to achieve a better result. The ways httpd can fiddle quality factors is explained in more detail below.

2. **Transparent content negotiation** is used when the browser specifically requests this through the mechanism defined in RFC 2295. This negotiation method gives the browser full control over deciding on the 'best' variant, the result is therefore dependent on the specific algorithms used by the browser. As part of the transparent negotiation process, the browser can ask httpd to run the 'remote variant selection algorithm' defined in RFC 2296.

Dimensions of Negotiation

Dimension	Notes
Media Type	Browser indicates preferences with the Accept header field. Each item can have an associated quality factor. Variant description can also have a quality factor (the "qs" parameter).
Language	Browser indicates preferences with the Accept-Language header field. Each item can have a quality factor. Variants can be associated with none, one or more than one language.
Encoding	Browser indicates preference with the Accept-Encoding header field. Each item can have a quality factor.
Charset	Browser indicates preference with the Accept-Charset header field. Each item can have a quality factor. Variants can indicate a charset as a parameter of the media type.

httpd Negotiation Algorithm

httpd can use the following algorithm to select the 'best' variant (if any) to return to the browser. This algorithm is not further configurable. It operates as follows:

1. First, for each dimension of the negotiation, check the appropriate *Accept** header field and assign a quality to each variant. If the *Accept** header for any dimension implies that this variant is not acceptable, eliminate it. If no variants remain, go to step 4.

2. Select the 'best' variant by a process of elimination. Each of the following tests is applied in order. Any variants not selected at each test are eliminated. After each test, if only one variant remains, select it as the best match and proceed to step 3. If more than one variant remains, move on to the next test.

   (a) Multiply the quality factor from the `Accept` header with the quality-of-source factor for this variants media type, and select the variants with the highest value.

   (b) Select the variants with the highest language quality factor.

   (c) Select the variants with the best language match, using either the order of languages in the `Accept-Language` header (if present), or else the order of languages in the `LanguagePriority` directive (if present).

   (d) Select the variants with the highest 'level' media parameter (used to give the version of text/html media types).

   (e) Select variants with the best charset media parameters, as given on the `Accept-Charset` header line. Charset ISO-8859-1 is acceptable unless explicitly excluded. Variants with a `text/*` media type but not explicitly associated with a particular charset are assumed to be in ISO-8859-1.

   (f) Select those variants which have associated charset media parameters that are *not* ISO-8859-1. If there are no such variants, select all variants instead.

   (g) Select the variants with the best encoding. If there are variants with an encoding that is acceptable to the user-agent, select only these variants. Otherwise if there is a mix of encoded and non-encoded variants, select only the unencoded variants. If either all variants are encoded or all variants are not encoded, select all variants.

   (h) Select the variants with the smallest content length.

   (i) Select the first variant of those remaining. This will be either the first listed in the type-map file, or when variants are read from the directory, the one whose file name comes first when sorted using ASCII code order.

3. The algorithm has now selected one 'best' variant, so return it as the response. The HTTP response header `Vary` is set to indicate the dimensions of negotiation (browsers and caches can use this information when caching the resource). End.

4. To get here means no variant was selected (because none are acceptable to the browser). Return a 406 status (meaning "No acceptable representation") with a response body consisting of an HTML document listing the available variants. Also set the HTTP `Vary` header to indicate the dimensions of variance.

Fiddling with Quality Values

httpd sometimes changes the quality values from what would be expected by a strict interpretation of the httpd negotiation algorithm above. This is to get a better result from the algorithm for browsers which do not send full or accurate information. Some of the most popular browsers send `Accept` header information which would otherwise result in the selection of the wrong variant in many cases. If a browser sends full and correct information these fiddles will not be applied.

Media Types and Wildcards

The `Accept:` request header indicates preferences for media types. It can also include 'wildcard' media types, such as "image/*" or "*/*" where the * matches any string. So a request including:

```
Accept:  image/*, */*
```

would indicate that any type starting "image/" is acceptable, as is any other type. Some browsers routinely send wildcards in addition to explicit types they can handle. For example:

```
Accept:  text/html, text/plain, image/gif, image/jpeg, */*
```

The intention of this is to indicate that the explicitly listed types are preferred, but if a different representation is available, that is ok too. Using explicit quality values, what the browser really wants is something like:

```
Accept:  text/html, text/plain, image/gif, image/jpeg, */*; q=0.01
```

The explicit types have no quality factor, so they default to a preference of 1.0 (the highest). The wildcard */* is given a low preference of 0.01, so other types will only be returned if no variant matches an explicitly listed type.

If the `Accept:` header contains *no* q factors at all, httpd sets the q value of "*/*", if present, to 0.01 to emulate the desired behavior. It also sets the q value of wildcards of the format "type/*" to 0.02 (so these are preferred over matches against "*/*". If any media type on the `Accept:` header contains a q factor, these special values are *not* applied, so requests from browsers which send the explicit information to start with work as expected.

Language Negotiation Exceptions

New in httpd 2.0, some exceptions have been added to the negotiation algorithm to allow graceful fallback when language negotiation fails to find a match.

When a client requests a page on your server, but the server cannot find a single page that matches the `Accept-language` sent by the browser, the server will return either a "No Acceptable Variant" or "Multiple Choices" response to the client. To avoid these error messages, it is possible to configure httpd to ignore the `Accept-language` in these cases and provide a document that does not explicitly match the client's request. The FORCELANGUAGEPRIORITY directive can be used to override one or both of these error messages and substitute the servers judgement in the form of the LANGUAGEPRIORITY directive.

The server will also attempt to match language-subsets when no other match can be found. For example, if a client requests documents with the language `en-GB` for British English, the server is not normally allowed by the HTTP/1.1 standard to match that against a document that is marked as simply `en`. (Note that it is almost surely a configuration error to include `en-GB` and not `en` in the `Accept-Language` header, since it is very unlikely that a reader understands British English, but doesn't understand English in general. Unfortunately, many current clients have default configurations that resemble this.) However, if no other language match is possible and the server is about to return a "No Acceptable Variants" error or fallback to the LANGUAGEPRIORITY, the server will ignore the subset specification and match `en-GB` against `en` documents. Implicitly, httpd will add the parent language to the client's acceptable language list with a very low quality value. But note that if the client requests "en-GB; q=0.9, fr; q=0.8", and the server has documents designated "en" and "fr", then the "fr" document will be returned. This is necessary to maintain compliance with the HTTP/1.1 specification and to work effectively with properly configured clients.

In order to support advanced techniques (such as cookies or special URL-paths) to determine the user's preferred language, since httpd 2.0.47 MOD_NEGOTIATION recognizes the environment variable (p. 82) `prefer-language`. If it exists and contains an appropriate language tag, MOD_NEGOTIATION will try to select a matching variant. If there's no such variant, the normal negotiation process applies.

Example

```
SetEnvIf Cookie "language=(.+)" prefer-language=$1
Header append Vary cookie
```

Extensions to Transparent Content Negotiation

httpd extends the transparent content negotiation protocol (RFC 2295) as follows. A new {`encoding ..`} element is used in variant lists to label variants which are available with a specific content-encoding only. The implementation of the RVSA/1.0 algorithm (RFC 2296) is extended to recognize encoded variants in the list, and to use them as candidate variants whenever their encodings are acceptable according to the `Accept-Encoding` request header. The RVSA/1.0 implementation does not round computed quality factors to 5 decimal places before choosing the best variant.

Note on hyperlinks and naming conventions

If you are using language negotiation you can choose between different naming conventions, because files can have more than one extension, and the order of the extensions is normally irrelevant (see the mod_mime (p. 704) documentation for details).

A typical file has a MIME-type extension (*e.g.*, `html`), maybe an encoding extension (*e.g.*, `gz`), and of course a language extension (*e.g.*, `en`) when we have different language variants of this file.

Examples:

- foo.en.html
- foo.html.en
- foo.en.html.gz

Here some more examples of filenames together with valid and invalid hyperlinks:

Filename	**Valid hyperlink**	**Invalid hyperlink**
foo.html.en	foo foo.html	-
foo.en.html	foo	foo.html
foo.html.en.gz	foo foo.html	foo.gz foo.html.gz
foo.en.html.gz	foo	foo.html foo.html.gz foo.gz
foo.gz.html.en	foo foo.gz foo.gz.html	foo.html
foo.html.gz.en	foo foo.html foo.html.gz	foo.gz

Looking at the table above, you will notice that it is always possible to use the name without any extensions in a hyperlink (*e.g.*, `foo`). The advantage is that you can hide the actual type of a document rsp. file and can change it later, *e.g.*, from `html` to `shtml` or `cgi` without changing any hyperlink references.

If you want to continue to use a MIME-type in your hyperlinks (*e.g.* `foo.html`) the language extension (including an encoding extension if there is one) must be on the right hand side of the MIME-type extension (*e.g.*, `foo.html.en`).

Note on Caching

When a cache stores a representation, it associates it with the request URL. The next time that URL is requested, the cache can use the stored representation. But, if the resource is negotiable at the server, this might result in only the first requested variant being cached and subsequent cache hits might return the wrong response. To prevent this, httpd normally marks all responses that are returned after content negotiation as non-cacheable by HTTP/1.0 clients. httpd also supports the HTTP/1.1 protocol features to allow caching of negotiated responses.

For requests which come from a HTTP/1.0 compliant client (either a browser or a cache), the directive CACHENEGOTIATEDDOCS can be used to allow caching of responses which were subject to negotiation. This directive can be given in the server config or virtual host, and takes no arguments. It has no effect on requests from HTTP/1.1 clients.

For HTTP/1.1 clients, httpd sends a `Vary` HTTP response header to indicate the negotiation dimensions for the response. Caches can use this information to determine whether a subsequent request can be served from the local copy. To encourage a cache to use the local copy regardless of the negotiation dimensions, set the `force-no-vary` environment variable (p. 82) .

2.12 Custom Error Responses

Although the Apache HTTP Server provides generic error responses in the event of 4xx or 5xx HTTP status codes, these responses are rather stark, uninformative, and can be intimidating to site users. You may wish to provide custom error responses which are either friendlier, or in some language other than English, or perhaps which are styled more in line with your site layout.

Customized error responses can be defined for any HTTP status code designated as an error condition - that is, any 4xx or 5xx status.

Additionally, a set of values are provided, so that the error document can be customized further based on the values of these variables, using Server Side Includes (p. 233) . Or, you can have error conditions handled by a cgi program, or other dynamic handler (PHP, mod_perl, etc) which makes use of these variables.

Configuration

Custom error documents are configured using the ERRORDOCUMENT directive, which may be used in global, virtualhost, or directory context. It may be used in .htaccess files if ALLOWOVERRIDE is set to FileInfo.

```
ErrorDocument 500 "Sorry, our script crashed. Oh dear"
ErrorDocument 500 /cgi-bin/crash-recover
ErrorDocument 500 http://error.example.com/server_error.html
ErrorDocument 404 /errors/not_found.html
ErrorDocument 401 /subscription/how_to_subscribe.html
```

The syntax of the `ErrorDocument` directive is:

```
ErrorDocument <3-digit-code> <action>
```

where the action will be treated as:

1. A local URL to redirect to (if the action begins with a `"/"`).
2. An external URL to redirect to (if the action is a valid URL).
3. Text to be displayed (if none of the above). The text must be wrapped in quotes (`"`) if it consists of more than one word.

When redirecting to a local URL, additional environment variables are set so that the response can be further customized. They are not sent to external URLs.

Available Variables

Redirecting to another URL can be useful, but only if some information can be passed which can then be used to explain or log the error condition more clearly.

To achieve this, when the error redirect is sent, additional environment variables will be set, which will be generated from the headers provided to the original request by prepending 'REDIRECT_' onto the original header name. This provides the error document the context of the original request.

For example, you might receive, in addition to more usual environment variables, the following.

```
REDIRECT_HTTP_ACCEPT=*/*, image/gif, image/jpeg, image/png
REDIRECT_HTTP_USER_AGENT=Mozilla/5.0 Fedora/3.5.8-1.fc12 Firefox/3.5.8
REDIRECT_PATH=.:/bin:/usr/local/bin:/sbin
REDIRECT_QUERY_STRING=
REDIRECT_REMOTE_ADDR=121.345.78.123
REDIRECT_REMOTE_HOST=client.example.com
REDIRECT_SERVER_NAME=www.example.edu
REDIRECT_SERVER_PORT=80
REDIRECT_SERVER_SOFTWARE=Apache/2.2.15
REDIRECT_URL=/cgi-bin/buggy.pl
```

`REDIRECT_` environment variables are created from the environment variables which existed prior to the redirect. They are renamed with a `REDIRECT_` prefix, *i.e.*, `HTTP_USER_AGENT` becomes `REDIRECT_HTTP_USER_AGENT`.

`REDIRECT_URL`, `REDIRECT_STATUS`, and `REDIRECT_QUERY_STRING` are guaranteed to be set, and the other headers will be set only if they existed prior to the error condition.

None of these will be set if the ERRORDOCUMENT target is an *external* redirect (anything starting with a scheme name like `http:`, even if it refers to the same host as the server).

Customizing Error Responses

If you point your `ErrorDocument` to some variety of dynamic handler such as a server-side include document, CGI script, or some variety of other handler, you may wish to use the available custom environment variables to customize this response.

If the ErrorDocument specifies a local redirect to a CGI script, the script should include a `"Status:"` header field in its output in order to ensure the propagation all the way back to the client of the error condition that caused it to be invoked. For instance, a Perl ErrorDocument script might include the following:

```
...
print  "Content-type: text/html\n";
printf "Status: %s Condition Intercepted\n", $ENV{"REDIRECT_STATUS"};
...
```

If the script is dedicated to handling a particular error condition, such as `404NotFound`, it can use the specific code and error text instead.

Note that if the response contains `Location:` header (in order to issue a client-side redirect), the script *must* emit an appropriate `Status:` header (such as `302Found`). Otherwise the `Location:` header may have no effect.

Multi Language Custom Error Documents

Provided with your installation of the Apache HTTP Server is a directory of custom error documents translated into 16 different languages. There's also a configuration file in the `conf/extra` configuration directory that can be included to enable this feature.

In your server configuration file, you'll see a line such as:

```
# Multi-language error messages
#Include conf/extra/httpd-multilang-errordoc.conf
```

Uncommenting this `Include` line will enable this feature, and provide language-negotiated error messages, based on the language preference set in the client browser.

Additionally, these documents contain various of the `REDIRECT_` variables, so that additional information can be provided to the end-user about what happened, and what they can do now.

These documents can be customized to whatever degree you wish to provide more useful information to users about your site, and what they can expect to find there.

MOD_INCLUDE and MOD_NEGOTIATION must be enabled to use this feature.

2.13 Binding to Addresses and Ports

Configuring Apache HTTP Server to listen on specific addresses and ports.

See also

- Virtual Hosts (p. 114)
- DNS Issues (p. 111)

Overview

Related Modules	Related Directives
CORE	<VIRTUALHOST>
MPM_COMMON	LISTEN

When httpd starts, it binds to some port and address on the local machine and waits for incoming requests. By default, it listens to all addresses on the machine. However, it may need to be told to listen on specific ports, or only on selected addresses, or a combination of both. This is often combined with the Virtual Host (p. 114) feature, which determines how `httpd` responds to different IP addresses, hostnames and ports.

The LISTEN directive tells the server to accept incoming requests only on the specified port(s) or address-and-port combinations. If only a port number is specified in the LISTEN directive, the server listens to the given port on all interfaces. If an IP address is given as well as a port, the server will listen on the given port and interface. Multiple LISTEN directives may be used to specify a number of addresses and ports to listen on. The server will respond to requests from any of the listed addresses and ports.

For example, to make the server accept connections on both port 80 and port 8000, on all interfaces, use:

```
Listen 80
Listen 8000
```

To make the server accept connections on port 80 for one interface, and port 8000 on another, use

```
Listen 192.0.2.1:80
Listen 192.0.2.5:8000
```

IPv6 addresses must be enclosed in square brackets, as in the following example:

```
Listen [2001:db8::a00:20ff:fea7:ccea]:80
```

! Overlapping LISTEN directives will result in a fatal error which will prevent the server from starting up.

```
(48)Address already in use: make_sock: could not bind
to address [::]:80
```

See the discussion in the wiki[a] for further troubleshooting tips.

[a]http://wiki.apache.org/httpd/CouldNotBindToAddress

Special IPv6 Considerations

A growing number of platforms implement IPv6, and APR supports IPv6 on most of these platforms, allowing httpd to allocate IPv6 sockets, and to handle requests sent over IPv6.

One complicating factor for httpd administrators is whether or not an IPv6 socket can handle both IPv4 connections and IPv6 connections. Handling IPv4 connections with an IPv6 socket uses IPv4-mapped IPv6 addresses, which are allowed by default on most platforms, but are disallowed by default on FreeBSD, NetBSD, and OpenBSD, in order to match the system-wide policy on those platforms. On systems where it is disallowed by default, a special `configure` parameter can change this behavior for httpd.

On the other hand, on some platforms, such as Linux and Tru64, the **only** way to handle both IPv6 and IPv4 is to use mapped addresses. If you want `httpd` to handle IPv4 and IPv6 connections with a minimum of sockets, which requires using IPv4-mapped IPv6 addresses, specify the `--enable-v4-mapped configure` option.

`--enable-v4-mapped` is the default on all platforms except FreeBSD, NetBSD, and OpenBSD, so this is probably how your httpd was built.

If you want httpd to handle IPv4 connections only, regardless of what your platform and APR will support, specify an IPv4 address on all LISTEN directives, as in the following examples:

```
Listen 0.0.0.0:80
Listen 192.0.2.1:80
```

If your platform supports it and you want httpd to handle IPv4 and IPv6 connections on separate sockets (i.e., to disable IPv4-mapped addresses), specify the `--disable-v4-mapped configure` option. `--disable-v4-mapped` is the default on FreeBSD, NetBSD, and OpenBSD.

Specifying the protocol with Listen

The optional second *protocol* argument of LISTEN is not required for most configurations. If not specified, `https` is the default for port 443 and `http` the default for all other ports. The protocol is used to determine which module should handle a request, and to apply protocol specific optimizations with the ACCEPTFILTER directive.

You only need to set the protocol if you are running on non-standard ports. For example, running an `https` site on port 8443:

```
Listen 192.170.2.1:8443 https
```

How This Works With Virtual Hosts

The LISTEN directive does not implement Virtual Hosts - it only tells the main server what addresses and ports to listen on. If no <VIRTUALHOST> directives are used, the server will behave in the same way for all accepted requests. However, <VIRTUALHOST> can be used to specify a different behavior for one or more of the addresses or ports. To implement a VirtualHost, the server must first be told to listen to the address and port to be used. Then a <VIRTUALHOST> section should be created for the specified address and port to set the behavior of this virtual host. Note that if the <VIRTUALHOST> is set for an address and port that the server is not listening to, it cannot be accessed.

2.14 Multi-Processing Modules (MPMs)

This document describes what a Multi-Processing Module is and how they are used by the Apache HTTP Server.

Introduction

The Apache HTTP Server is designed to be a powerful and flexible web server that can work on a very wide variety of platforms in a range of different environments. Different platforms and different environments often require different features, or may have different ways of implementing the same feature most efficiently. Apache httpd has always accommodated a wide variety of environments through its modular design. This design allows the webmaster to choose which features will be included in the server by selecting which modules to load either at compile-time or at run-time.

Apache HTTP Server 2.0 extends this modular design to the most basic functions of a web server. The server ships with a selection of Multi-Processing Modules (MPMs) which are responsible for binding to network ports on the machine, accepting requests, and dispatching children to handle the requests.

Extending the modular design to this level of the server allows two important benefits:

- Apache httpd can more cleanly and efficiently support a wide variety of operating systems. In particular, the Windows version of the server is now much more efficient, since MPM_WINNT can use native networking features in place of the POSIX layer used in Apache httpd 1.3. This benefit also extends to other operating systems that implement specialized MPMs.
- The server can be better customized for the needs of the particular site. For example, sites that need a great deal of scalability can choose to use a threaded MPM like WORKER or EVENT, while sites requiring stability or compatibility with older software can use a PREFORK.

At the user level, MPMs appear much like other Apache httpd modules. The main difference is that one and only one MPM must be loaded into the server at any time. The list of available MPMs appears on the module index page (p. 1025) .

MPM Defaults

The following table lists the default MPMs for various operating systems. This will be the MPM selected if you do not make another choice at compile-time.

Netware	MPM_NETWARE
OS/2	MPMT_OS2
Unix	PREFORK, WORKER, or EVENT, depending on platform capabilities
Windows	MPM_WINNT

⟹ Here, 'Unix' is used to mean Unix-like operating systems, such as Linux, BSD, Solaris, Mac OS X, etc.

In the case of Unix, the decision as to which MPM is installed is based on two questions:

1. Does the system support threads?

2. Does the system support thread-safe polling (Specifically, the kqueue and epoll functions)?

If the answer to both questions is 'yes', the default MPM is EVENT.

If The answer to #1 is 'yes', but the answer to #2 is 'no', the default will be WORKER.

If the answer to both questions is 'no', then the default MPM will be PREFORK.

In practical terms, this means that the default will almost always be EVENT, as all modern operating systems support these two features.

Building an MPM as a static module

MPMs can be built as static modules on all platforms. A single MPM is chosen at build time and linked into the server. The server must be rebuilt in order to change the MPM.

To override the default MPM choice, use the `--with-mpm=`*NAME* option of the `configure` script. *NAME* is the name of the desired MPM.

Once the server has been compiled, it is possible to determine which MPM was chosen by using `./httpd -l`. This command will list every module that is compiled into the server, including the MPM.

Building an MPM as a DSO module

On Unix and similar platforms, MPMs can be built as DSO modules and dynamically loaded into the server in the same manner as other DSO modules. Building MPMs as DSO modules allows the MPM to be changed by updating the LOADMODULE directive for the MPM instead of by rebuilding the server.

```
LoadModule mpm_prefork_module modules/mod_mpm_prefork.so
```

Attempting to LOADMODULE more than one MPM will result in a startup failure with the following error.

```
AH00534: httpd: Configuration error: More than one MPM loaded.
```

This feature is enabled using the `--enable-mpms-shared` option of the `configure` script. With argument *`all`*, all possible MPMs for the platform will be installed. Alternately, a list of MPMs can be specified as the argument.

The default MPM, either selected automatically or specified with the `--with-mpm` option of the `configure` script, will be loaded in the generated server configuration file. Edit the LOADMODULE directive to select a different MPM.

2.15 Environment Variables in Apache

There are two kinds of environment variables that affect the Apache HTTP Server.

First, there are the environment variables controlled by the underlying operating system. These are set before the server starts. They can be used in expansions in configuration files, and can optionally be passed to CGI scripts and SSI using the PassEnv directive.

Second, the Apache HTTP Server provides a mechanism for storing information in named variables that are also called *environment variables*. This information can be used to control various operations such as logging or access control. The variables are also used as a mechanism to communicate with external programs such as CGI scripts. This document discusses different ways to manipulate and use these variables.

Although these variables are referred to as *environment variables*, they are not the same as the environment variables controlled by the underlying operating system. Instead, these variables are stored and manipulated in an internal Apache structure. They only become actual operating system environment variables when they are provided to CGI scripts and Server Side Include scripts. If you wish to manipulate the operating system environment under which the server itself runs, you must use the standard environment manipulation mechanisms provided by your operating system shell.

Setting Environment Variables

Related Modules	Related Directives
MOD_CACHE	BROWSERMATCH
MOD_ENV	BROWSERMATCHNOCASE
MOD_REWRITE	PASSENV
MOD_SETENVIF	REWRITERULE
MOD_UNIQUE_ID	SETENV
	SETENVIF
	SETENVIFNOCASE
	UNSETENV

Basic Environment Manipulation

The most basic way to set an environment variable in Apache is using the unconditional SETENV directive. Variables may also be passed from the environment of the shell which started the server using the PASSENV directive.

Conditional Per-Request Settings

For additional flexibility, the directives provided by MOD_SETENVIF allow environment variables to be set on a per-request basis, conditional on characteristics of particular requests. For example, a variable could be set only when a specific browser (User-Agent) is making a request, or only when a specific Referer [sic] header is found. Even more flexibility is available through the MOD_REWRITE's REWRITERULE which uses the `[E=...]` option to set environment variables.

Unique Identifiers

Finally, MOD_UNIQUE_ID sets the environment variable `UNIQUE_ID` for each request to a value which is guaranteed to be unique across "all" requests under very specific conditions.

Standard CGI Variables

In addition to all environment variables set within the Apache configuration and passed from the shell, CGI scripts and SSI pages are provided with a set of environment variables containing meta-information about the request as required by the CGI specification[19].

Some Caveats

- It is not possible to override or change the standard CGI variables using the environment manipulation directives.
- When `suexec` is used to launch CGI scripts, the environment will be cleaned down to a set of *safe* variables before CGI scripts are launched. The list of *safe* variables is defined at compile-time in `suexec.c`.
- For portability reasons, the names of environment variables may contain only letters, numbers, and the underscore character. In addition, the first character may not be a number. Characters which do not match this restriction will be replaced by an underscore when passed to CGI scripts and SSI pages.
- A special case are HTTP headers which are passed to CGI scripts and the like via environment variables (see below). They are converted to uppercase and only dashes are replaced with underscores; if the header contains any other (invalid) character, the whole header is silently dropped. See below for a workaround.
- The SETENV directive runs late during request processing meaning that directives such as SETENVIF and REWRITECOND will not see the variables set with it.
- When the server looks up a path via an internal subrequest such as looking for a DIRECTORYINDEX or generating a directory listing with MOD_AUTOINDEX, per-request environment variables are *not* inherited in the subrequest. Additionally, SETENVIF directives are not separately evaluated in the subrequest due to the API phases MOD_SETENVIF takes action in.

Using Environment Variables

Related Modules	Related Directives
MOD_AUTHZ_HOST	REQUIRE
MOD_CGI	CUSTOMLOG
MOD_EXT_FILTER	DENY
MOD_HEADERS	EXTFILTERDEFINE
MOD_INCLUDE	HEADER
MOD_LOG_CONFIG	LOGFORMAT
MOD_REWRITE	REWRITECOND
	REWRITERULE

CGI Scripts

One of the primary uses of environment variables is to communicate information to CGI scripts. As discussed above, the environment passed to CGI scripts includes standard meta-information about the request in addition to any variables set within the Apache configuration. For more details, see the CGI tutorial (p. 226) .

SSI Pages

Server-parsed (SSI) documents processed by MOD_INCLUDE's `INCLUDES` filter can print environment variables using the `echo` element, and can use environment variables in flow control elements to makes parts of a page conditional on

[19] http://www.ietf.org/rfc/rfc3875

characteristics of a request. Apache also provides SSI pages with the standard CGI environment variables as discussed above. For more details, see the SSI tutorial (p. 233) .

Access Control

Access to the server can be controlled based on the value of environment variables using the `allow from env=` and `deny from env=` directives. In combination with SETENVIF, this allows for flexible control of access to the server based on characteristics of the client. For example, you can use these directives to deny access to a particular browser (User-Agent).

Conditional Logging

Environment variables can be logged in the access log using the LOGFORMAT option `%e`. In addition, the decision on whether or not to log requests can be made based on the status of environment variables using the conditional form of the CUSTOMLOG directive. In combination with SETENVIF this allows for flexible control of which requests are logged. For example, you can choose not to log requests for filenames ending in `gif`, or you can choose to only log requests from clients which are outside your subnet.

Conditional Response Headers

The HEADER directive can use the presence or absence of an environment variable to determine whether or not a certain HTTP header will be placed in the response to the client. This allows, for example, a certain response header to be sent only if a corresponding header is received in the request from the client.

External Filter Activation

External filters configured by MOD_EXT_FILTER using the EXTFILTERDEFINE directive can by activated conditional on an environment variable using the `disableenv=` and `enableenv=` options.

URL Rewriting

The `%{ENV:variable}` form of *TestString* in the REWRITECOND allows MOD_REWRITE's rewrite engine to make decisions conditional on environment variables. Note that the variables accessible in MOD_REWRITE without the `ENV:` prefix are not actually environment variables. Rather, they are variables special to MOD_REWRITE which cannot be accessed from other modules.

Special Purpose Environment Variables

Interoperability problems have led to the introduction of mechanisms to modify the way Apache behaves when talking to particular clients. To make these mechanisms as flexible as possible, they are invoked by defining environment variables, typically with BROWSERMATCH, though SETENV and PASSENV could also be used, for example.

downgrade-1.0

This forces the request to be treated as a HTTP/1.0 request even if it was in a later dialect.

force-gzip

If you have the `DEFLATE` filter activated, this environment variable will ignore the accept-encoding setting of your browser and will send compressed output unconditionally.

force-no-vary

This causes any `Vary` fields to be removed from the response header before it is sent back to the client. Some clients don't interpret this field correctly; setting this variable can work around this problem. Setting this variable also implies **force-response-1.0**.

force-response-1.0

This forces an HTTP/1.0 response to clients making an HTTP/1.0 request. It was originally implemented as a result of a problem with AOL's proxies. Some HTTP/1.0 clients may not behave correctly when given an HTTP/1.1 response, and this can be used to interoperate with them.

gzip-only-text/html

When set to a value of `"1"`, this variable disables the `DEFLATE` output filter provided by MOD_DEFLATE for content-types other than `text/html`. If you'd rather use statically compressed files, MOD_NEGOTIATION evaluates the variable as well (not only for gzip, but for all encodings that differ from `"identity"`).

no-gzip

When set, the `DEFLATE` filter of MOD_DEFLATE will be turned off and MOD_NEGOTIATION will refuse to deliver encoded resources.

no-cache

Available in versions 2.2.12 and later

When set, MOD_CACHE will not save an otherwise cacheable response. This environment variable does not influence whether a response already in the cache will be served for the current request.

nokeepalive

This disables KEEPALIVE when set.

prefer-language

This influences MOD_NEGOTIATION's behaviour. If it contains a language tag (such as `en`, `ja` or `x-klingon`), MOD_NEGOTIATION tries to deliver a variant with that language. If there's no such variant, the normal negotiation (p. 68) process applies.

redirect-carefully

This forces the server to be more careful when sending a redirect to the client. This is typically used when a client has a known problem handling redirects. This was originally implemented as a result of a problem with Microsoft's WebFolders software which has a problem handling redirects on directory resources via DAV methods.

suppress-error-charset

Available in versions after 2.0.54

When Apache issues a redirect in response to a client request, the response includes some actual text to be displayed in case the client can't (or doesn't) automatically follow the redirection. Apache ordinarily labels this text according to the character set which it uses, which is ISO-8859-1.

However, if the redirection is to a page that uses a different character set, some broken browser versions will try to use the character set from the redirection text rather than the actual page. This can result in Greek, for instance, being incorrectly rendered.

Setting this environment variable causes Apache to omit the character set for the redirection text, and these broken browsers will then correctly use that of the destination page.

Security note

Sending error pages without a specified character set may allow a cross-site-scripting attack for existing browsers (MSIE) which do not follow the HTTP/1.1 specification and attempt to "guess" the character set from the content. Such browsers can be easily fooled into using the UTF-7 character set, and UTF-7 content from input data (such as the request-URI) will not be escaped by the usual escaping mechanisms designed to prevent cross-site-scripting attacks.

force-proxy-request-1.0, proxy-nokeepalive, proxy-sendchunked, proxy-sendcl, proxy-chain-auth, proxy-interim-response, proxy-initial-not-pooled

These directives alter the protocol behavior of MOD_PROXY. See the MOD_PROXY and MOD_PROXY_HTTP documentation for more details.

Examples

Passing broken headers to CGI scripts

Starting with version 2.4, Apache is more strict about how HTTP headers are converted to environment variables in MOD_CGI and other modules: Previously any invalid characters in header names were simply translated to underscores. This allowed for some potential cross-site-scripting attacks via header injection (see Unusual Web Bugs[20], slide 19/20).

If you have to support a client which sends broken headers and which can't be fixed, a simple workaround involving MOD_SETENVIF and MOD_HEADERS allows you to still accept these headers:

```
#
# The following works around a client sending a broken Accept_Encoding
# header.
#
```

[20] http://events.ccc.de/congress/2007/Fahrplan/events/2212.en.html

```
SetEnvIfNoCase ^Accept.Encoding$ ^(.*)$ fix_accept_encoding=$1
RequestHeader set Accept-Encoding %{fix_accept_encoding}e env=fix_accept_encoding
```

Changing protocol behavior with misbehaving clients

Earlier versions recommended that the following lines be included in httpd.conf to deal with known client problems. Since the affected clients are no longer seen in the wild, this configuration is likely no-longer necessary.

```
#
# The following directives modify normal HTTP response behavior.
# The first directive disables keepalive for Netscape 2.x and browsers that
# spoof it. There are known problems with these browser implementations.
# The second directive is for Microsoft Internet Explorer 4.0b2
# which has a broken HTTP/1.1 implementation and does not properly
# support keepalive when it is used on 301 or 302 (redirect) responses.
#
BrowserMatch "Mozilla/2" nokeepalive
BrowserMatch "MSIE 4\.0b2;" nokeepalive downgrade-1.0 force-response-1.0

#
# The following directive disables HTTP/1.1 responses to browsers which
# are in violation of the HTTP/1.0 spec by not being able to understand a
# basic 1.1 response.
#
BrowserMatch "RealPlayer 4\.0" force-response-1.0
BrowserMatch "Java/1\.0" force-response-1.0
BrowserMatch "JDK/1\.0" force-response-1.0
```

Do not log requests for images in the access log

This example keeps requests for images from appearing in the access log. It can be easily modified to prevent logging of particular directories, or to prevent logging of requests coming from particular hosts.

```
SetEnvIf Request_URI \.gif image-request
SetEnvIf Request_URI \.jpg image-request
SetEnvIf Request_URI \.png image-request
CustomLog logs/access_log common env=!image-request
```

Prevent "Image Theft"

This example shows how to keep people not on your server from using images on your server as inline-images on their pages. This is not a recommended configuration, but it can work in limited circumstances. We assume that all your images are in a directory called /web/images.

```
SetEnvIf Referer "^http://www\.example\.com/" local_referal
# Allow browsers that do not send Referer info
SetEnvIf Referer "^$" local_referal
<Directory "/web/images">
    Require env local_referal
</Directory>
```

For more information about this technique, see the "Keeping Your Images from Adorning Other Sites[21] " tutorial on ServerWatch.

[21] http://www.serverwatch.com/tutorials/article.php/1132731

2.16 Expressions in Apache HTTP Server

Historically, there are several syntax variants for expressions used to express a condition in the different modules of the Apache HTTP Server. There is some ongoing effort to only use a single variant, called *ap_expr*, for all configuration directives. This document describes the *ap_expr* expression parser.

The *ap_expr* expression is intended to replace most other expression variants in HTTPD. For example, the deprecated SSLREQUIRE expressions can be replaced by Require expr (p. 488) .

See also

- <IF>
- <ELSEIF>
- <ELSE>
- <ERRORDOCUMENT>
- AUTHBASICFAKE
- AUTHFORMLOGINREQUIREDLOCATION
- AUTHFORMLOGINSUCCESSLOCATION
- AUTHFORMLOGOUTLOCATION
- REWRITECOND
- SETENVIFEXPR
- HEADER
- REQUESTHEADER
- FILTERPROVIDER
- Require expr (p. 488)
- Require ldap-user (p. 470)
- Require ldap-group (p. 470)
- Require ldap-dn (p. 470)
- Require ldap-attribute (p. 470)
- Require ldap-filter (p. 470)
- Require dbd-group (p. 496)
- Require dbm-group (p. 500)
- Require group (p. 503)
- Require host (p. 505)
- SSLREQUIRE
- LOGMESSAGE
- MOD_INCLUDE

Grammar in Backus-Naur Form notation

Backus-Naur Form[22] (BNF) is a notation technique for context-free grammars, often used to describe the syntax of languages used in computing. In most cases, expressions are used to express boolean values. For these, the starting point in the BNF is `expr`. However, a few directives like LOGMESSAGE accept expressions that evaluate to a string value. For those, the starting point in the BNF is `string`.

[22]http://en.wikipedia.org/wiki/Backus%E2%80%93Naur_Form

```
expr        ::= "true" | "false"
              | "!" expr
              | expr "&&" expr
              | expr "||" expr
              | "(" expr ")"
              | comp

comp        ::= stringcomp
              | integercomp
              | unaryop word
              | word binaryop word
              | word "in" "{" wordlist "}"
              | word "in" listfunction
              | word "=~" regex
              | word "!~" regex


stringcomp  ::= word "==" word
              | word "!=" word
              | word "<"  word
              | word "<=" word
              | word ">"  word
              | word ">=" word

integercomp ::= word "-eq" word | word "eq" word
              | word "-ne" word | word "ne" word
              | word "-lt" word | word "lt" word
              | word "-le" word | word "le" word
              | word "-gt" word | word "gt" word
              | word "-ge" word | word "ge" word

wordlist    ::= word
              | wordlist "," word

word        ::= word "." word
              | digit
              | "'" string "'"
              | """ string """
              | variable
              | rebackref
              | function

string      ::= stringpart
              | string stringpart

stringpart  ::= cstring
              | variable
              | rebackref

cstring     ::= ...
digit       ::= [0-9]+

variable    ::= "%{" varname "}"
```

```
             | "%{" funcname ":" funcargs "}"

rebackref    ::= "$" [0-9]

function     ::= funcname "(" word ")"

listfunction ::= listfuncname "(" word ")"
```

Variables

The expression parser provides a number of variables of the form %{HTTP_HOST}. Note that the value of a variable may depend on the phase of the request processing in which it is evaluated. For example, an expression used in an <IF > directive is evaluated before authentication is done. Therefore, %{REMOTE_USER} will not be set in this case.

The following variables provide the values of the named HTTP request headers. The values of other headers can be obtained with the `req` function. Using these variables may cause the header name to be added to the Vary header of the HTTP response, except where otherwise noted for the directive accepting the expression. The `req_novary` function may be used to circumvent this behavior.

Name
HTTP_ACCEPT
HTTP_COOKIE
HTTP_FORWARDED
HTTP_HOST
HTTP_PROXY_CONNECTION
HTTP_REFERER
HTTP_USER_AGENT

Other request related variables

Name	Description
REQUEST_METHOD	The HTTP method of the incoming request (e.g. GET)
REQUEST_SCHEME	The scheme part of the request's URI
REQUEST_URI	The path part of the request's URI
DOCUMENT_URI	Same as REQUEST_URI
REQUEST_FILENAME	The full local filesystem path to the file or script matching the request, if this has already been determined by the server at the time REQUEST_FILENAME is referenced. Otherwise, such as when used in virtual host context, the same value as REQUEST_URI
SCRIPT_FILENAME	Same as REQUEST_FILENAME
LAST_MODIFIED	The date and time of last modification of the file in the format 20101231235959, if this has already been determined by the server at the time LAST_MODIFIED is referenced.
SCRIPT_USER	The user name of the owner of the script.
SCRIPT_GROUP	The group name of the group of the script.
PATH_INFO	The trailing path name information, see ACCEPTPATHINFO
QUERY_STRING	The query string of the current request
IS_SUBREQ	"true" if the current request is a subrequest, "false" otherwise
THE_REQUEST	The complete request line (e.g., "GET /index.html HTTP/1.1")
REMOTE_ADDR	The IP address of the remote host
REMOTE_HOST	The host name of the remote host
REMOTE_USER	The name of the authenticated user, if any (not available during <IF >)
REMOTE_IDENT	The user name set by MOD_IDENT
SERVER_NAME	The SERVERNAME of the current vhost

SERVER_PORT	The server port of the current vhost, see ServerName
SERVER_ADMIN	The ServerAdmin of the current vhost
SERVER_PROTOCOL	The protocol used by the request
DOCUMENT_ROOT	The DocumentRoot of the current vhost
AUTH_TYPE	The configured AuthType (e.g. "basic")
CONTENT_TYPE	The content type of the response (not available during <If >)
HANDLER	The name of the handler (p. 98) creating the response
HTTPS	"on" if the request uses https, "off" otherwise
IPV6	"on" if the connection uses IPv6, "off" otherwise
REQUEST_STATUS	The HTTP error status of the request (not available during <If >)
REQUEST_LOG_ID	The error log id of the request (see ErrorLogFormat)
CONN_LOG_ID	The error log id of the connection (see ErrorLogFormat)
CONN_REMOTE_ADDR	The peer IP address of the connection (see the mod_remoteip module)
CONTEXT_PREFIX	
CONTEXT_DOCUMENT_ROOT	

Misc variables

Name	**Description**
TIME_YEAR	The current year (e.g. 2010)
TIME_MON	The current month (1, ..., 12)
TIME_DAY	The current day of the month
TIME_HOUR	The hour part of the current time (0, ..., 23)
TIME_MIN	The minute part of the current time
TIME_SEC	The second part of the current time
TIME_WDAY	The day of the week (starting with 0 for Sunday)
TIME	The date and time in the format 20101231235959
SERVER_SOFTWARE	The server version string
API_VERSION	The date of the API version (module magic number)

Some modules register additional variables, see e.g. mod_ssl.

Binary operators

With the exception of some built-in comparison operators, binary operators have the form "-[a-zA-Z][a-zA-Z0-9_]+", i.e. a minus and at least two characters. The name is not case sensitive. Modules may register additional binary operators.

Comparison operators

Name	Alternative	Description
==	=	String equality
!=		String inequality
<		String less than
<=		String less than or equal
>		String greater than
>=		String greater than or equal
-eq	eq	Integer equality
-ne	ne	Integer inequality
-lt	lt	Integer less than
-le	le	Integer less than or equal
-gt	gt	Integer greater than
-ge	ge	Integer greater than or equal

Other binary operators

Name	Description
-ipmatch	IP address matches address/netmask
-strmatch	left string matches pattern given by right string (containing wildcards *, ?, [])
-strcmatch	same as -strmatch, but case insensitive
-fnmatch	same as -strmatch, but slashes are not matched by wildcards

Unary operators

Unary operators take one argument and have the form "-[a-zA-Z]", i.e. a minus and one character. The name *is* case sensitive. Modules may register additional unary operators.

Name	Description	Restricted
-d	The argument is treated as a filename. True if the file exists and is a directory	yes
-e	The argument is treated as a filename. True if the file (or dir or special) exists	yes
-f	The argument is treated as a filename. True if the file exists and is regular file	yes
-s	The argument is treated as a filename. True if the file exists and is not empty	yes
-L	The argument is treated as a filename. True if the file exists and is symlink	yes
-h	The argument is treated as a filename. True if the file exists and is symlink (same as -L)	yes
-F	True if string is a valid file, accessible via all the server's currently-configured access controls for that path. This uses an internal subrequest to do the check, so use it with care - it can impact your server's performance!	
-U	True if string is a valid URL, accessible via all the server's currently-configured access controls for that path. This uses an internal subrequest to do the check, so use it with care - it can impact your server's performance!	
-A	Alias for -U	
-n	True if string is not empty	
-z	True if string is empty	
-T	False if string is empty, "0", "off", "false", or "no" (case insensitive). True otherwise.	
-R	Same as "%{REMOTE_ADDR} -ipmatch ...", but more efficient	

The operators marked as "restricted" are not available in some modules like MOD_INCLUDE.

Functions

Normal string-valued functions take one string as argument and return a string. Functions names are not case sensitive. Modules may register additional functions.

Name	Description	Restricted
`req`, `http`	Get HTTP request header; header names may be added to the Vary header, see below	
`req_novary`	Same as `req`, but header names will not be added to the Vary header	
`resp`	Get HTTP response header	
`reqenv`	Lookup request environment variable (as a shortcut, `v` can be used too to access variables).	
`osenv`	Lookup operating system environment variable	
`note`	Lookup request note	
`env`	Return first match of `note`, `reqenv`, `osenv`	
`tolower`	Convert string to lower case	
`toupper`	Convert string to upper case	
`escape`	Escape special characters in %hex encoding	
`unescape`	Unescape %hex encoded string, leaving encoded slashes alone; return empty string if %00 is found	
`base64`	Encode the string using base64 encoding	
`unbase64`	Decode base64 encoded string, return truncated string if 0x00 is found	
`md5`	Hash the string using MD5, then encode the hash with hexadecimal encoding	
`sha1`	Hash the string using SHA1, then encode the hash with hexadecimal encoding	
`file`	Read contents from a file (including line endings, when present)	yes
`filesize`	Return size of a file (or 0 if file does not exist or is not regular file)	yes

The functions marked as "restricted" are not available in some modules like MOD_INCLUDE.

When the functions `req` or `http` are used, the header name will automatically be added to the Vary header of the HTTP response, except where otherwise noted for the directive accepting the expression. The `req_novary` function can be used to prevent names from being added to the Vary header.

In addition to string-valued functions, there are also list-valued functions which take one string as argument and return a wordlist, i.e. a list of strings. The wordlist can be used with the special `-in` operator. Functions names are not case sensitive. Modules may register additional functions.

There are no built-in list-valued functions. MOD_SSL provides `PeerExtList`. See the description of SSLREQUIRE for details (but `PeerExtList` is also usable outside of SSLREQUIRE).

Example expressions

The following examples show how expressions might be used to evaluate requests:

```
# Compare the host name to example.com and redirect to www.example.com if it matches
<If "%{HTTP_HOST} == 'example.com'">
    Redirect permanent "/" "http://www.example.com/"
</If>

# Force text/plain if requesting a file with the query string contains 'forcetext'
<If "%{QUERY_STRING} =~ /forcetext/">
    ForceType text/plain
</If>
```

```
# Only allow access to this content during business hours
<Directory "/foo/bar/business">
    Require expr %{TIME_HOUR} -gt 9 && %{TIME_HOUR} -lt 17
</Directory>

# Check a HTTP header for a list of values
<If "%{HTTP:X-example-header} in { 'foo', 'bar', 'baz' }">
    Header set matched true
</If>

# Check an environment variable for a regular expression, negated.
<If "! reqenv('REDIRECT_FOO') =~ /bar/">
    Header set matched true
</If>

# Check result of URI mapping by running in Directory context with -f
<Directory "/var/www">
    AddEncoding x-gzip gz
<If "-f '%{REQUEST_FILENAME}.unzipme' && ! %{HTTP:Accept-Encoding} =~ /gzip/">
      SetOutputFilter INFLATE
</If>
</Directory>

# Function examples in boolean context
<If "md5('foo') == 'acbd18db4cc2f85cedef654fccc4a4d8'">
  Header set checksum-matched true
</If>
<If "md5('foo') == replace('md5:XXXd18db4cc2f85cedef654fccc4a4d8', 'md5:XXX', 'acb')>
  Header set checksum-matched-2 true
</If>

# Function example in string context
Header set foo-checksum "expr=%{md5:foo}"
```

Other

Name	Alternative	Description
`-in`	`in`	string contained in wordlist
`/regexp/`	`m#regexp#`	Regular expression (the second form allows different delimiters than /)
`/regexp/i`	`m#regexp#i`	Case insensitive regular expression
`$0 ... $9`		Regular expression backreferences

Regular expression backreferences

The strings `$0` ... `$9` allow to reference the capture groups from a previously executed, successfully matching regular expressions. They can normally only be used in the same expression as the matching regex, but some modules allow special uses.

Comparison with SSLRequire

The *ap_expr* syntax is mostly a superset of the syntax of the deprecated SSLREQUIRE directive. The differences are described in SSLREQUIRE's documentation.

Version History

The `req_novary` function is available for versions 2.4.4 and later.

2.17 Apache's Handler Use

This document describes the use of Apache's Handlers.

What is a Handler

Related Modules	Related Directives
MOD_ACTIONS	ACTION
MOD_ASIS	ADDHANDLER
MOD_CGI	REMOVEHANDLER
MOD_IMAGEMAP	SETHANDLER
MOD_INFO	
MOD_MIME	
MOD_NEGOTIATION	
MOD_STATUS	

A "handler" is an internal Apache representation of the action to be performed when a file is called. Generally, files have implicit handlers, based on the file type. Normally, all files are simply served by the server, but certain file types are "handled" separately.

Handlers may also be configured explicitly, based on either filename extensions or on location, without relation to file type. This is advantageous both because it is a more elegant solution, and because it also allows for both a type **and** a handler to be associated with a file. (See also Files with Multiple Extensions (p. 704) .)

Handlers can either be built into the server or included in a module, or they can be added with the ACTION directive. The built-in handlers in the standard distribution are as follows:

- **default-handler**: Send the file using the `default_handler()`, which is the handler used by default to handle static content. (core)
- **send-as-is**: Send file with HTTP headers as is. (MOD_ASIS)
- **cgi-script**: Treat the file as a CGI script. (MOD_CGI)
- **imap-file**: Parse as an imagemap rule file. (MOD_IMAGEMAP)
- **server-info**: Get the server's configuration information. (MOD_INFO)
- **server-status**: Get the server's status report. (MOD_STATUS)
- **type-map**: Parse as a type map file for content negotiation. (MOD_NEGOTIATION)

Examples

Modifying static content using a CGI script

The following directives will cause requests for files with the `html` extension to trigger the launch of the `footer.pl` CGI script.

```
Action add-footer /cgi-bin/footer.pl
AddHandler add-footer .html
```

Then the CGI script is responsible for sending the originally requested document (pointed to by the `PATH_TRANSLATED` environment variable) and making whatever modifications or additions are desired.

Files with HTTP headers

The following directives will enable the `send-as-is` handler, which is used for files which contain their own HTTP headers. All files in the `/web/htdocs/asis/` directory will be processed by the `send-as-is` handler, regardless of their filename extensions.

```
<Directory "/web/htdocs/asis">
    SetHandler send-as-is
</Directory>
```

Programmer's Note

In order to implement the handler features, an addition has been made to the Apache API (p. 943) that you may wish to make use of. Specifically, a new record has been added to the `request_rec` structure:

```
char *handler
```

If you wish to have your module engage a handler, you need only to set `r->handler` to the name of the handler at any time prior to the `invoke_handler` stage of the request. Handlers are implemented as they were before, albeit using the handler name instead of a content type. While it is not necessary, the naming convention for handlers is to use a dash-separated word, with no slashes, so as to not invade the media type name-space.

2.18 Filters

This document describes the use of filters in Apache.

Filtering in Apache 2

Related Modules	Related Directives
MOD_FILTER	FILTERCHAIN
MOD_DEFLATE	FILTERDECLARE
MOD_EXT_FILTER	FILTERPROTOCOL
MOD_INCLUDE	FILTERPROVIDER
MOD_CHARSET_LITE	ADDINPUTFILTER
MOD_REFLECTOR	ADDOUTPUTFILTER
MOD_BUFFER	REMOVEINPUTFILTER
MOD_DATA	REMOVEOUTPUTFILTER
MOD_RATELIMIT	REFLECTORHEADER
MOD_REQTIMEOUT	EXTFILTERDEFINE
MOD_REQUEST	EXTFILTEROPTIONS
MOD_SED	SETINPUTFILTER
MOD_SUBSTITUTE	SETOUTPUTFILTER
MOD_XML2ENC	
MOD_PROXY_HTML	

The Filter Chain is available in Apache 2.0 and higher, and enables applications to process incoming and outgoing data in a highly flexible and configurable manner, regardless of where the data comes from. We can pre-process incoming data, and post-process outgoing data, at will. This is basically independent of the traditional request processing phases.

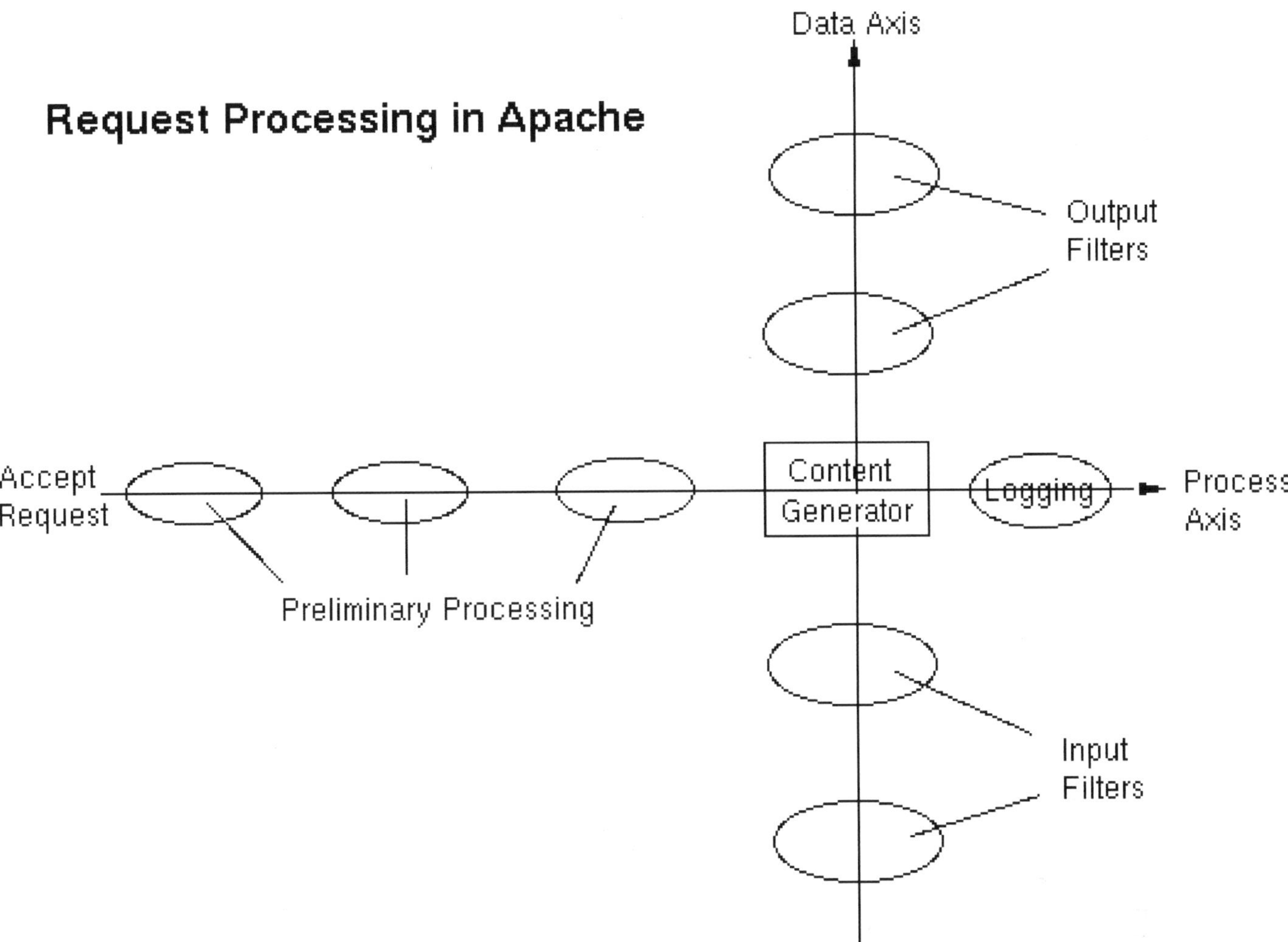

Some examples of filtering in the standard Apache distribution are:

- MOD_INCLUDE, implements server-side includes.
- MOD_SSL, implements SSL encryption (https).
- MOD_DEFLATE, implements compression/decompression on the fly.
- MOD_CHARSET_LITE, transcodes between different character sets.
- MOD_EXT_FILTER, runs an external program as a filter.

Apache also uses a number of filters internally to perform functions like chunking and byte-range handling.

A wider range of applications are implemented by third-party filter modules available from modules.apache.org[23] and elsewhere. A few of these are:

- HTML and XML processing and rewriting
- XSLT transforms and XIncludes
- XML Namespace support

[23] http://modules.apache.org/

- File Upload handling and decoding of HTML Forms
- Image processing
- Protection of vulnerable applications such as PHP scripts
- Text search-and-replace editing

Smart Filtering

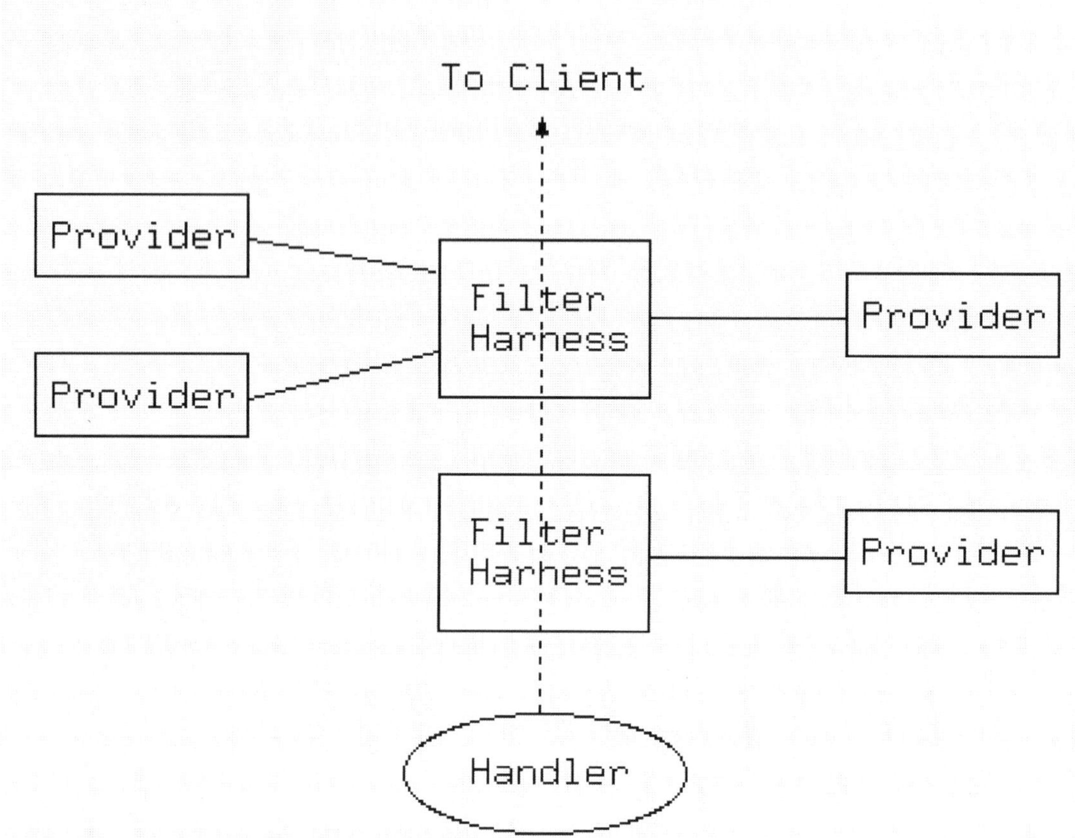

MOD_FILTER, included in Apache 2.1 and later, enables the filter chain to be configured dynamically at run time. So for example you can set up a proxy to rewrite HTML with an HTML filter and JPEG images with a completely separate filter, despite the proxy having no prior information about what the origin server will send. This works by using a filter harness, that dispatches to different providers according to the actual contents at runtime. Any filter may be either inserted directly in the chain and run unconditionally, or used as a provider and inserted dynamically. For example,

- an HTML processing filter will only run if the content is text/html or application/xhtml+xml
- A compression filter will only run if the input is a compressible type and not already compressed
- A charset conversion filter will be inserted if a text document is not already in the desired charset

Exposing Filters as an HTTP Service

Filters can be used to process content originating from the client in addition to processing content originating on the server using the MOD_REFLECTOR module.

MOD_REFLECTOR accepts POST requests from clients, and reflects the content request body received within the POST request back in the response, passing through the output filter stack on the way back to the client.

This technique can be used as an alternative to a web service running within an application server stack, where an output filter provides the transformation required on the request body. For example, the MOD_DEFLATE module might be used to provide a general compression service, or an image transformation filter might be turned into an image transformation service.

Using Filters

There are two ways to use filtering: Simple and Dynamic. In general, you should use one or the other; mixing them can have unexpected consequences (although simple Input filtering can be mixed freely with either simple or dynamic Output filtering).

The Simple Way is the only way to configure input filters, and is sufficient for output filters where you need a static filter chain. Relevant directives are SETINPUTFILTER, SETOUTPUTFILTER, ADDINPUTFILTER, ADDOUTPUTFILTER, REMOVEINPUTFILTER, and REMOVEOUTPUTFILTER.

The Dynamic Way enables both static and flexible, dynamic configuration of output filters, as discussed in the MOD_FILTER page. Relevant directives are FILTERCHAIN, FILTERDECLARE, and FILTERPROVIDER.

One further directive ADDOUTPUTFILTERBYTYPE is still supported, but deprecated. Use dynamic configuration instead.

2.19 Shared Object Cache in Apache HTTP Server

The Shared Object Cache provides a means to share simple data across all a server's workers, regardless of thread and process models (p. 80) . It is used where the advantages of sharing data across processes outweigh the performance overhead of inter-process communication.

Shared Object Cache Providers

The shared object cache as such is an abstraction. Four different modules implement it. To use the cache, one or more of these modules must be present, and configured.

The only configuration required is to select which cache provider to use. This is the responsibility of modules using the cache, and they enable selection using directives such as CACHESOCACHE, AUTHNCACHESOCACHE, SSLSESSIONCACHE, and SSLSTAPLINGCACHE.

Currently available providers are:

"dbm" (MOD_SOCACHE_DBM) This makes use of a DBM hash file. The choice of underlying DBM used may be configurable if the installed APR version supports multiple DBM implementations.

"dc" (MOD_SOCACHE_DC) This makes use of the distcache[24] distributed session caching libraries.

"memcache" (MOD_SOCACHE_MEMCACHE) This makes use of the memcached[25] high-performance, distributed memory object caching system.

"shmcb" (MOD_SOCACHE_SHMCB) This makes use of a high-performance cyclic buffer inside a shared memory segment.

The API provides the following functions:

const char *create(ap_socache_instance_t **instance, const char *arg, apr_pool_t *tmp, apr_pool_t *p); Create a session cache based on the given configuration string. The instance pointer returned in the instance paramater will be passed as the first argument to subsequent invocations.

apr_status_t init(ap_socache_instance_t *instance, const char *cname, const struct ap_socache_hints *hints, server_rec *s, a Initialize the cache. The cname must be of maximum length 16 characters, and uniquely identifies the consumer of the cache within the server; using the module name is recommended, e.g. "mod_ssl-sess". This string may be used within a filesystem path so use of only alphanumeric [a-z0-9_-] characters is recommended. If hints is non-NULL, it gives a set of hints for the provider. Return APR error code.

void destroy(ap_socache_instance_t *instance, server_rec *s) Destroy a given cache instance object.

apr_status_t store(ap_socache_instance_t *instance, server_rec *s, const unsigned char *id, unsigned int idlen, apr_time_t e Store an object in a cache instance.

apr_status_t retrieve(ap_socache_instance_t *instance, server_rec *s, const unsigned char *id, unsigned int idlen, unsigned Retrieve a cached object.

apr_status_t remove(ap_socache_instance_t *instance, server_rec *s, const unsigned char *id, unsigned int idlen, apr_pool_ Remove an object from the cache.

void status(ap_socache_instance_t *instance, request_rec *r, int flags) Dump the status of a cache instance for mod_status.

apr_status_t iterate(ap_socache_instance_t *instance, server_rec *s, void *userctx, ap_socache_iterator_t *iterator, apr_pool Dump all cached objects through an iterator callback.

[24] http://www.distcache.org/

[25] http://memcached.org/

2.20 suEXEC Support

The **suEXEC** feature provides users of the Apache HTTP Server the ability to run **CGI** and **SSI** programs under user IDs different from the user ID of the calling web server. Normally, when a CGI or SSI program executes, it runs as the same user who is running the web server.

Used properly, this feature can reduce considerably the security risks involved with allowing users to develop and run private CGI or SSI programs. However, if suEXEC is improperly configured, it can cause any number of problems and possibly create new holes in your computer's security. If you aren't familiar with managing *setuid root* programs and the security issues they present, we highly recommend that you not consider using suEXEC.

Before we begin

Before jumping head-first into this document, you should be aware that certain assumptions are made about you and the environment in which you will be using suexec.

First, it is assumed that you are using a UNIX derivative operating system that is capable of **setuid** and **setgid** operations. All command examples are given in this regard. Other platforms, if they are capable of supporting suEXEC, may differ in their configuration.

Second, it is assumed you are familiar with some basic concepts of your computer's security and its administration. This involves an understanding of **setuid/setgid** operations and the various effects they may have on your system and its level of security.

Third, it is assumed that you are using an **unmodified** version of suEXEC code. All code for suEXEC has been carefully scrutinized and tested by the developers as well as numerous beta testers. Every precaution has been taken to ensure a simple yet solidly safe base of code. Altering this code can cause unexpected problems and new security risks. It is **highly** recommended you not alter the suEXEC code unless you are well versed in the particulars of security programming and are willing to share your work with the Apache HTTP Server development team for consideration.

Fourth, and last, it has been the decision of the Apache HTTP Server development team to **NOT** make suEXEC part of the default installation of Apache httpd. To this end, suEXEC configuration requires of the administrator careful attention to details. After due consideration has been given to the various settings for suEXEC, the administrator may install suEXEC through normal installation methods. The values for these settings need to be carefully determined and specified by the administrator to properly maintain system security during the use of suEXEC functionality. It is through this detailed process that we hope to limit suEXEC installation only to those who are careful and determined enough to use it.

Still with us? Yes? Good. Let's move on!

suEXEC Security Model

Before we begin configuring and installing suEXEC, we will first discuss the security model you are about to implement. By doing so, you may better understand what exactly is going on inside suEXEC and what precautions are taken to ensure your system's security.

suEXEC is based on a setuid "wrapper" program that is called by the main Apache HTTP Server. This wrapper is called when an HTTP request is made for a CGI or SSI program that the administrator has designated to run as a userid other than that of the main server. When such a request is made, Apache httpd provides the suEXEC wrapper with the program's name and the user and group IDs under which the program is to execute.

The wrapper then employs the following process to determine success or failure – if any one of these conditions fail, the program logs the failure and exits with an error, otherwise it will continue:

1. **Is the user executing this wrapper a valid user of this system?**

   This is to ensure that the user executing the wrapper is truly a user of the system.

2. **Was the wrapper called with the proper number of arguments?**

   The wrapper will only execute if it is given the proper number of arguments. The proper argument format is known to the Apache HTTP Server. If the wrapper is not receiving the proper number of arguments, it is either being hacked, or there is something wrong with the suEXEC portion of your Apache httpd binary.

3. **Is this valid user allowed to run the wrapper?**

   Is this user the user allowed to run this wrapper? Only one user (the Apache user) is allowed to execute this program.

4. **Does the target CGI or SSI program have an unsafe hierarchical reference?**

   Does the target CGI or SSI program's path contain a leading '/' or have a '..' backreference? These are not allowed; the target CGI/SSI program must reside within suEXEC's document root (see `--with-suexec-docroot=`*`DIR`* below).

5. **Is the target user name valid?**

   Does the target user exist?

6. **Is the target group name valid?**

   Does the target group exist?

7. **Is the target user *NOT* superuser?**

   suEXEC does not allow *`root`* to execute CGI/SSI programs.

8. **Is the target userid *ABOVE* the minimum ID number?**

   The minimum user ID number is specified during configuration. This allows you to set the lowest possible userid that will be allowed to execute CGI/SSI programs. This is useful to block out "system" accounts.

9. **Is the target group *NOT* the superuser group?**

   Presently, suEXEC does not allow the *`root`* group to execute CGI/SSI programs.

10. **Is the target groupid *ABOVE* the minimum ID number?**

    The minimum group ID number is specified during configuration. This allows you to set the lowest possible groupid that will be allowed to execute CGI/SSI programs. This is useful to block out "system" groups.

11. **Can the wrapper successfully become the target user and group?**

    Here is where the program becomes the target user and group via setuid and setgid calls. The group access list is also initialized with all of the groups of which the user is a member.

12. **Can we change directory to the one in which the target CGI/SSI program resides?**

    If it doesn't exist, it can't very well contain files. If we can't change directory to it, it might as well not exist.

13. **Is the directory within the httpd webspace?**

    If the request is for a regular portion of the server, is the requested directory within suEXEC's document root? If the request is for a USERDIR, is the requested directory within the directory configured as suEXEC's userdir (see suEXEC's configuration options)?

14. **Is the directory *NOT* writable by anyone else?**

    We don't want to open up the directory to others; only the owner user may be able to alter this directories contents.

15. **Does the target CGI/SSI program exist?**

    If it doesn't exists, it can't very well be executed.

16. **Is the target CGI/SSI program *NOT* writable by anyone else?**

    We don't want to give anyone other than the owner the ability to change the CGI/SSI program.

17. **Is the target CGI/SSI program *NOT* setuid or setgid?**

    We do not want to execute programs that will then change our UID/GID again.

18. **Is the target user/group the same as the program's user/group?**

    Is the user the owner of the file?

19. **Can we successfully clean the process environment to ensure safe operations?**

    suEXEC cleans the process' environment by establishing a safe execution PATH (defined during configuration), as well as only passing through those variables whose names are listed in the safe environment list (also created during configuration).

20. **Can we successfully become the target CGI/SSI program and execute?**

    Here is where suEXEC ends and the target CGI/SSI program begins.

This is the standard operation of the suEXEC wrapper's security model. It is somewhat stringent and can impose new limitations and guidelines for CGI/SSI design, but it was developed carefully step-by-step with security in mind.

For more information as to how this security model can limit your possibilities in regards to server configuration, as well as what security risks can be avoided with a proper suEXEC setup, see the "Beware the Jabberwock" section of this document.

Configuring & Installing suEXEC

Here's where we begin the fun.

suEXEC configuration options

`--enable-suexec` This option enables the suEXEC feature which is never installed or activated by default. At least one `--with-suexec-xxxxx` option has to be provided together with the `--enable-suexec` option to let APACI accept your request for using the suEXEC feature.

`--with-suexec-bin=`*`PATH`* The path to the `suexec` binary must be hard-coded in the server for security reasons. Use this option to override the default path. *e.g.* `--with-suexec-bin=/usr/sbin/suexec`

`--with-suexec-caller=`*`UID`* The username (p. 917) under which httpd normally runs. This is the only user allowed to execute the suEXEC wrapper.

`--with-suexec-userdir=`*`DIR`* Define to be the subdirectory under users' home directories where suEXEC access should be allowed. All executables under this directory will be executable by suEXEC as the user so they should be "safe" programs. If you are using a "simple" USERDIR directive (ie. one without a "*" in it) this should be set to the same value. suEXEC will not work properly in cases where the USERDIR directive points to a location that is not the same as the user's home directory as referenced in the `passwd` file. Default value is "`public_html`".
If you have virtual hosts with a different USERDIR for each, you will need to define them to all reside in one parent directory; then name that parent directory here. **If this is not defined properly, "~userdir" cgi requests will not work!**

`--with-suexec-docroot=`*`DIR`* Define as the DocumentRoot set for httpd. This will be the only hierarchy (aside from USERDIRs) that can be used for suEXEC behavior. The default directory is the `--datadir` value with the suffix "`/htdocs`", *e.g.* if you configure with "`--datadir=/home/apache`" the directory "`/home/apache/htdocs`" is used as document root for the suEXEC wrapper.

--with-suexec-uidmin=*UID* Define this as the lowest UID allowed to be a target user for suEXEC. For most systems, 500 or 100 is common. Default value is 100.

--with-suexec-gidmin=*GID* Define this as the lowest GID allowed to be a target group for suEXEC. For most systems, 100 is common and therefore used as default value.

--with-suexec-logfile=*FILE* This defines the filename to which all suEXEC transactions and errors are logged (useful for auditing and debugging purposes). By default the logfile is named `"suexec_log"` and located in your standard logfile directory (`--logfiledir`).

--with-suexec-safepath=*PATH* Define a safe PATH environment to pass to CGI executables. Default value is `"/usr/local/bin:/usr/bin:/bin"`.

Compiling and installing the suEXEC wrapper

If you have enabled the suEXEC feature with the `--enable-suexec` option the `suexec` binary (together with httpd itself) is automatically built if you execute the `make` command.

After all components have been built you can execute the command `make install` to install them. The binary image `suexec` is installed in the directory defined by the `--sbindir` option. The default location is "/usr/local/apache2/bin/suexec".

Please note that you need ***root privileges*** for the installation step. In order for the wrapper to set the user ID, it must be installed as owner *`root`* and must have the setuserid execution bit set for file modes.

Setting paranoid permissions

Although the suEXEC wrapper will check to ensure that its caller is the correct user as specified with the `--with-suexec-caller configure` option, there is always the possibility that a system or library call suEXEC uses before this check may be exploitable on your system. To counter this, and because it is best-practise in general, you should use filesystem permissions to ensure that only the group httpd runs as may execute suEXEC.

If for example, your web server is configured to run as:

```
User www
Group webgroup
```

and `suexec` is installed at "/usr/local/apache2/bin/suexec", you should run:

```
chgrp webgroup /usr/local/apache2/bin/suexec
chmod 4750 /usr/local/apache2/bin/suexec
```

This will ensure that only the group httpd runs as can even execute the suEXEC wrapper.

Enabling & Disabling suEXEC

Upon startup of httpd, it looks for the file `suexec` in the directory defined by the `--sbindir` option (default is "/usr/local/apache/sbin/suexec"). If httpd finds a properly configured suEXEC wrapper, it will print the following message to the error log:

```
[notice] suEXEC mechanism enabled (wrapper: /path/to/suexec)
```

If you don't see this message at server startup, the server is most likely not finding the wrapper program where it expects it, or the executable is not installed *setuid root*.

If you want to enable the suEXEC mechanism for the first time and an Apache HTTP Server is already running you must kill and restart httpd. Restarting it with a simple HUP or USR1 signal will not be enough.

If you want to disable suEXEC you should kill and restart httpd after you have removed the `suexec` file.

Using suEXEC

Requests for CGI programs will call the suEXEC wrapper only if they are for a virtual host containing a SUEXECUSERGROUP directive or if they are processed by MOD_USERDIR.

Virtual Hosts:
One way to use the suEXEC wrapper is through the SUEXECUSERGROUP directive in VIRTUALHOST definitions. By setting this directive to values different from the main server user ID, all requests for CGI resources will be executed as the *User* and *Group* defined for that <VIRTUALHOST>. If this directive is not specified for a <VIRTUALHOST> then the main server userid is assumed.

User directories:
Requests that are processed by MOD_USERDIR will call the suEXEC wrapper to execute CGI programs under the userid of the requested user directory. The only requirement needed for this feature to work is for CGI execution to be enabled for the user and that the script must meet the scrutiny of the security checks above. See also the `--with-suexec-userdir` compile time option.

Debugging suEXEC

The suEXEC wrapper will write log information to the file defined with the `--with-suexec-logfile` option as indicated above. If you feel you have configured and installed the wrapper properly, have a look at this log and the error_log for the server to see where you may have gone astray.

Beware the Jabberwock: Warnings & Examples

NOTE! This section may not be complete. For the latest revision of this section of the documentation, see the Online Documentation[26] version.

There are a few points of interest regarding the wrapper that can cause limitations on server setup. Please review these before submitting any "bugs" regarding suEXEC.

- **suEXEC Points Of Interest**
- Hierarchy limitations

  For security and efficiency reasons, all suEXEC requests must remain within either a top-level document root for virtual host requests, or one top-level personal document root for userdir requests. For example, if you have four VirtualHosts configured, you would need to structure all of your VHosts' document roots off of one main httpd document hierarchy to take advantage of suEXEC for VirtualHosts. (Example forthcoming.)
- suEXEC's PATH environment variable

  This can be a dangerous thing to change. Make certain every path you include in this define is a **trusted** directory. You don't want to open people up to having someone from across the world running a trojan horse on them.

[26] http://httpd.apache.org/docs/2.4/suexec.html

- Altering the suEXEC code

  Again, this can cause **Big Trouble** if you try this without knowing what you are doing. Stay away from it if at all possible.

2.21 Issues Regarding DNS and Apache HTTP Server

This page could be summarized with the statement: don't configure Apache HTTP Server in such a way that it relies on DNS resolution for parsing of the configuration files. If httpd requires DNS resolution to parse the configuration files then your server may be subject to reliability problems (ie. it might not start up), or denial and theft of service attacks (including virtual hosts able to steal hits from other virtual hosts).

A Simple Example

```
# This is a misconfiguration example, do not use on your server
<VirtualHost www.example.dom>
  ServerAdmin webgirl@example.dom
  DocumentRoot "/www/example"
</VirtualHost>
```

In order for the server to function properly, it absolutely needs to have two pieces of information about each virtual host: the SERVERNAME and at least one IP address that the server will bind and respond to. The above example does not include the IP address, so httpd must use DNS to find the address of `www.example.dom`. If for some reason DNS is not available at the time your server is parsing its config file, then this virtual host **will not be configured**. It won't be able to respond to any hits to this virtual host.

Suppose that `www.example.dom` has address 192.0.2.1. Then consider this configuration snippet:

```
# This is a misconfiguration example, do not use on your server
<VirtualHost 192.0.2.1>
  ServerAdmin webgirl@example.dom
  DocumentRoot "/www/example"
</VirtualHost>
```

This time httpd needs to use reverse DNS to find the `ServerName` for this virtualhost. If that reverse lookup fails then it will partially disable the virtualhost. If the virtual host is name-based then it will effectively be totally disabled, but if it is IP-based then it will mostly work. However, if httpd should ever have to generate a full URL for the server which includes the server name (such as when a Redirect is issued), then it will fail to generate a valid URL.

Here is a snippet that avoids both of these problems:

```
<VirtualHost 192.0.2.1>
  ServerName www.example.dom
  ServerAdmin webgirl@example.dom
  DocumentRoot "/www/example"
</VirtualHost>
```

Denial of Service

Consider this configuration snippet:

```
<VirtualHost www.example1.dom>
  ServerAdmin webgirl@example1.dom
  DocumentRoot "/www/example1"
</VirtualHost>
<VirtualHost www.example2.dom>
  ServerAdmin webguy@example2.dom
```

```
  DocumentRoot "/www/example2"
</VirtualHost>
```

Suppose that you've assigned 192.0.2.1 to www.example1.dom and 192.0.2.2 to www.example2.dom. Furthermore, suppose that example1.dom has control of their own DNS. With this config you have put example1.dom into a position where they can steal all traffic destined to example2.dom. To do so, all they have to do is set www.example1.dom to 192.0.2.2. Since they control their own DNS you can't stop them from pointing the www.example1.dom record wherever they wish.

Requests coming in to 192.0.2.2 (including all those where users typed in URLs of the form http://www.example2.dom/whatever) will all be served by the example1.dom virtual host. To better understand why this happens requires a more in-depth discussion of how httpd matches up incoming requests with the virtual host that will serve it. A rough document describing this is available (p. 131) .

The "main server" Address

Name-based virtual host support (p. 115) requires httpd to know the IP address(es) of the host that httpd is running on. To get this address it uses either the global SERVERNAME (if present) or calls the C function gethostname (which should return the same as typing "hostname" at the command prompt). Then it performs a DNS lookup on this address. At present there is no way to avoid this lookup.

If you fear that this lookup might fail because your DNS server is down then you can insert the hostname in /etc/hosts (where you probably already have it so that the machine can boot properly). Then ensure that your machine is configured to use /etc/hosts in the event that DNS fails. Depending on what OS you are using this might be accomplished by editing /etc/resolv.conf, or maybe /etc/nsswitch.conf.

If your server doesn't have to perform DNS for any other reason then you might be able to get away with running httpd with the HOSTRESORDER environment variable set to "local". This all depends on what OS and resolver libraries you are using. It also affects CGIs unless you use MOD_ENV to control the environment. It's best to consult the man pages or FAQs for your OS.

Tips to Avoid These Problems

- use IP addresses in VIRTUALHOST
- use IP addresses in LISTEN
- ensure all virtual hosts have an explicit SERVERNAME
- create a <VirtualHost _default_:*> server that has no pages to serve

Chapter 3

Apache Virtual Host documentation

3.1 Apache Virtual Host documentation

The term *Virtual Host* refers to the practice of running more than one web site (such as `company1.example.com` and `company2.example.com`) on a single machine. Virtual hosts can be "IP-based (p. 118) ", meaning that you have a different IP address for every web site, or "name-based (p. 115) ", meaning that you have multiple names running on each IP address. The fact that they are running on the same physical server is not apparent to the end user.

Apache was one of the first servers to support IP-based virtual hosts right out of the box. Versions 1.1 and later of Apache support both IP-based and name-based virtual hosts (vhosts). The latter variant of virtual hosts is sometimes also called *host-based* or *non-IP virtual hosts*.

Below is a list of documentation pages which explain all details of virtual host support in Apache HTTP Server:

See also

- MOD_VHOST_ALIAS
- Name-based virtual hosts (p. 115)
- IP-based virtual hosts (p. 118)
- Virtual host examples (p. 124)
- File descriptor limits (p. 134)
- Mass virtual hosting (p. 120)
- Details of host matching (p. 131)

Virtual Host Support

- Name-based Virtual Hosts (p. 115) (More than one web site per IP address)
- IP-based Virtual Hosts (p. 118) (An IP address for each web site)
- Virtual Host examples for common setups (p. 124)
- File Descriptor Limits (p. 134) (or, *Too many log files*)
- Dynamically Configured Mass Virtual Hosting (p. 120)
- In-Depth Discussion of Virtual Host Matching (p. 131)

Configuration directives

- <VIRTUALHOST>
- SERVERNAME
- SERVERALIAS
- SERVERPATH

If you are trying to debug your virtual host configuration, you may find the Apache `-S` command line switch useful. That is, type the following command:

```
/usr/local/apache2/bin/httpd -S
```

This command will dump out a description of how Apache parsed the configuration file. Careful examination of the IP addresses and server names may help uncover configuration mistakes. (See the docs for the `httpd` program for other command line options)

3.2 Name-based Virtual Host Support

This document describes when and how to use name-based virtual hosts.

See also

- IP-based Virtual Host Support (p. 118)
- An In-Depth Discussion of Virtual Host Matching (p. 131)
- Dynamically configured mass virtual hosting (p. 120)
- Virtual Host examples for common setups (p. 124)

Name-based vs. IP-based Virtual Hosts

IP-based virtual hosts (p. 118) use the IP address of the connection to determine the correct virtual host to serve. Therefore you need to have a separate IP address for each host.

With name-based virtual hosting, the server relies on the client to report the hostname as part of the HTTP headers. Using this technique, many different hosts can share the same IP address.

Name-based virtual hosting is usually simpler, since you need only configure your DNS server to map each hostname to the correct IP address and then configure the Apache HTTP Server to recognize the different hostnames. Name-based virtual hosting also eases the demand for scarce IP addresses. Therefore you should use name-based virtual hosting unless you are using equipment that explicitly demands IP-based hosting. Historical reasons for IP-based virtual hosting based on client support are no longer applicable to a general-purpose web server.

Name-based virtual hosting builds off of the IP-based virtual host selection algorithm, meaning that searches for the proper server name occur only between virtual hosts that have the best IP-based address.

How the server selects the proper name-based virtual host

It is important to recognize that the first step in name-based virtual host resolution is IP-based resolution. Name-based virtual host resolution only chooses the most appropriate name-based virtual host after narrowing down the candidates to the best IP-based match. Using a wildcard (*) for the IP address in all of the VirtualHost directives makes this IP-based mapping irrelevant.

When a request arrives, the server will find the best (most specific) matching <VirtualHost> argument based on the IP address and port used by the request. If there is more than one virtual host containing this best-match address and port combination, Apache will further compare the ServerName and ServerAlias directives to the server name present in the request.

If you omit the ServerName directive from any name-based virtual host, the server will default to a fully qualified domain name (FQDN) derived from the system hostname. This implicitly set server name can lead to counter-intuitive virtual host matching and is discouraged.

The default name-based vhost for an IP and port combination

If no matching ServerName or ServerAlias is found in the set of virtual hosts containing the most specific matching IP address and port combination, then **the first listed virtual host** that matches that will be used.

Using Name-based Virtual Hosts

Related Modules	Related Directives
CORE	DOCUMENTROOT SERVERALIAS SERVERNAME <VIRTUALHOST>

The first step is to create a <VIRTUALHOST> block for each different host that you would like to serve. Inside each <VIRTUALHOST> block, you will need at minimum a SERVERNAME directive to designate which host is served and a DOCUMENTROOT directive to show where in the filesystem the content for that host lives.

**Main host goes away**

Any request that doesn't match an existing <VIRTUALHOST> is handled by the global server configuration, regardless of the hostname or ServerName.

When you add a name-based virtual host to an existing server, and the virtual host arguments match preexisting IP and port combinations, requests will now be handled by an explicit virtual host. In this case, it's usually wise to create a default virtual host with a SERVERNAME matching that of the base server. New domains on the same interface and port, but requiring separate configurations, can then be added as subsequent (non-default) virtual hosts.

**ServerName inheritance**

It is best to always explicitly list a SERVERNAME in every name-based virtual host.

If a VIRTUALHOST doesn't specify a SERVERNAME, a server name will be inherited from the base server configuration. If no server name was specified globally, one is detected at startup through reverse DNS resolution of the first listening address. In either case, this inherited server name will influence name-based virtual host resolution, so it is best to always explicitly list a SERVERNAME in every name-based virtual host.

For example, suppose that you are serving the domain `www.example.com` and you wish to add the virtual host `other.example.com`, which points at the same IP address. Then you simply add the following to `httpd.conf`:

```
<VirtualHost *:80>
    # This first-listed virtual host is also the default for *:80
    ServerName www.example.com
    ServerAlias example.com
    DocumentRoot "/www/domain"
</VirtualHost>

<VirtualHost *:80>
    ServerName other.example.com
    DocumentRoot "/www/otherdomain"
</VirtualHost>
```

You can alternatively specify an explicit IP address in place of the * in <VIRTUALHOST> directives. For example, you might want to do this in order to run some name-based virtual hosts on one IP address, and either IP-based, or another set of name-based virtual hosts on another address.

Many servers want to be accessible by more than one name. This is possible with the SERVERALIAS directive, placed inside the <VIRTUALHOST> section. For example in the first <VIRTUALHOST> block above, the SERVERALIAS directive indicates that the listed names are other names which people can use to see that same web site:

```
ServerAlias example.com *.example.com
```

then requests for all hosts in the `example.com` domain will be served by the `www.example.com` virtual host. The wildcard characters `*` and `?` can be used to match names. Of course, you can't just make up names and place them in SERVERNAME or `ServerAlias`. You must first have your DNS server properly configured to map those names to an IP address associated with your server.

Name-based virtual hosts for the best-matching set of <VIRTUALHOST>s are processed in the order they appear in the configuration. The first matching SERVERNAME or SERVERALIAS is used, with no different precedence for wildcards (nor for ServerName vs. ServerAlias).

The complete list of names in the VIRTUALHOST directive are treated just like a (non wildcard) SERVERALIAS.

Finally, you can fine-tune the configuration of the virtual hosts by placing other directives inside the <VIRTUALHOST> containers. Most directives can be placed in these containers and will then change the configuration only of the relevant virtual host. To find out if a particular directive is allowed, check the Context (p. 351) of the directive. Configuration directives set in the *main server context* (outside any <VIRTUALHOST> container) will be used only if they are not overridden by the virtual host settings.

3.3 Apache IP-based Virtual Host Support

See also

- Name-based Virtual Hosts Support (p. 115)

What is IP-based virtual hosting

IP-based virtual hosting is a method to apply different directives based on the IP address and port a request is received on. Most commonly, this is used to serve different websites on different ports or interfaces.

In many cases, name-based virtual hosts (p. 115) are more convenient, because they allow many virtual hosts to share a single address/port. See Name-based vs. IP-based Virtual Hosts (p. 115) to help you decide.

System requirements

As the term *IP-based* indicates, the server **must have a different IP address/port combination for each IP-based virtual host**. This can be achieved by the machine having several physical network connections, or by use of virtual interfaces which are supported by most modern operating systems (see system documentation for details, these are frequently called "ip aliases", and the "ifconfig" command is most commonly used to set them up), and/or using multiple port numbers.

In the terminology of Apache HTTP Server, using a single IP address but multiple TCP ports, is also IP-based virtual hosting.

How to set up Apache

There are two ways of configuring apache to support multiple hosts. Either by running a separate `httpd` daemon for each hostname, or by running a single daemon which supports all the virtual hosts.

Use multiple daemons when:

- There are security partitioning issues, such as company1 does not want anyone at company2 to be able to read their data except via the web. In this case you would need two daemons, each running with different USER, GROUP, LISTEN, and SERVERROOT settings.
- You can afford the memory and file descriptor requirements of listening to every IP alias on the machine. It's only possible to LISTEN to the "wildcard" address, or to specific addresses. So if you have a need to listen to a specific address for whatever reason, then you will need to listen to all specific addresses. (Although one `httpd` could listen to N-1 of the addresses, and another could listen to the remaining address.)

Use a single daemon when:

- Sharing of the httpd configuration between virtual hosts is acceptable.
- The machine services a large number of requests, and so the performance loss in running separate daemons may be significant.

Setting up multiple daemons

Create a separate `httpd` installation for each virtual host. For each installation, use the LISTEN directive in the configuration file to select which IP address (or virtual host) that daemon services. e.g.

```
Listen 192.0.2.100:80
```

It is recommended that you use an IP address instead of a hostname (see DNS caveats (p. 111)).

Setting up a single daemon with virtual hosts

For this case, a single `httpd` will service requests for the main server and all the virtual hosts. The VIRTUALHOST directive in the configuration file is used to set the values of SERVERADMIN, SERVERNAME, DOCUMENTROOT, ERRORLOG and TRANSFERLOG or CUSTOMLOG configuration directives to different values for each virtual host. e.g.

```
<VirtualHost 172.20.30.40:80>
    ServerAdmin webmaster@www1.example.com
    DocumentRoot "/www/vhosts/www1"
    ServerName www1.example.com
    ErrorLog "/www/logs/www1/error_log"
    CustomLog "/www/logs/www1/access_log" combined
</VirtualHost>

<VirtualHost 172.20.30.50:80>
    ServerAdmin webmaster@www2.example.org
    DocumentRoot "/www/vhosts/www2"
    ServerName www2.example.org
    ErrorLog "/www/logs/www2/error_log"
    CustomLog "/www/logs/www2/access_log" combined
</VirtualHost>
```

It is recommended that you use an IP address instead of a hostname in the <VirtualHost> directive (see DNS caveats (p. 111)).

Specific IP addresses or ports have precedence over their wildcard equivalents, and any virtual host that matches has precedence over the servers base configuration.

Almost **any** configuration directive can be put in the VirtualHost directive, with the exception of directives that control process creation and a few other directives. To find out if a directive can be used in the VirtualHost directive, check the Context (p. 351) using the directive index (p. 1030) .

SUEXECUSERGROUP may be used inside a VirtualHost directive if the suEXEC wrapper (p. 105) is used.

SECURITY: When specifying where to write log files, be aware of some security risks which are present if anyone other than the user that starts Apache has write access to the directory where they are written. See the security tips (p. 338) document for details.

3.4 Dynamically Configured Mass Virtual Hosting

This document describes how to efficiently serve an arbitrary number of virtual hosts with the Apache HTTP Server. A separate document (p. 152) discusses using MOD_REWRITE to create dynamic mass virtual hosts.

Motivation

The techniques described here are of interest if your `httpd.conf` contains many `<VirtualHost>` sections that are substantially the same, for example:

```
<VirtualHost 111.22.33.44>
    ServerName                customer-1.example.com
    DocumentRoot         "/www/hosts/customer-1.example.com/docs"
    ScriptAlias  "/cgi-bin/"  "/www/hosts/customer-1.example.com/cgi-bin"
</VirtualHost>

<VirtualHost 111.22.33.44>
    ServerName                customer-2.example.com
    DocumentRoot         "/www/hosts/customer-2.example.com/docs"
    ScriptAlias  "/cgi-bin/"  "/www/hosts/customer-2.example.com/cgi-bin"
</VirtualHost>

<VirtualHost 111.22.33.44>
    ServerName                customer-N.example.com
    DocumentRoot         "/www/hosts/customer-N.example.com/docs"
    ScriptAlias  "/cgi-bin/"  "/www/hosts/customer-N.example.com/cgi-bin"
</VirtualHost>
```

We wish to replace these multiple `<VirtualHost>` blocks with a mechanism that works them out dynamically. This has a number of advantages:

1. Your configuration file is smaller, so Apache starts more quickly and uses less memory. Perhaps more importantly, the smaller configuration is easier to maintain, and leaves less room for errors.

2. Adding virtual hosts is simply a matter of creating the appropriate directories in the filesystem and entries in the DNS - you don't need to reconfigure or restart Apache.

The main disadvantage is that you cannot have a different log file for each virtual host; however, if you have many virtual hosts, doing this can be a bad idea anyway, because of the number of file descriptors needed (p. 134) . It is better to log to a pipe or a fifo (p. 53) , and arrange for the process at the other end to split up the log files into one per virtual host. One example of such a process can be found in the split-logfile (p. 323) utility.

Overview

A virtual host is defined by two pieces of information: its IP address, and the contents of the `Host:` header in the HTTP request. The dynamic mass virtual hosting technique used here is based on automatically inserting this information into the pathname of the file that is used to satisfy the request. This can be most easily done by using MOD_VHOST_ALIAS with Apache httpd. Alternatively, mod_rewrite can be used (p. 152) .

Both of these modules are disabled by default; you must enable one of them when configuring and building Apache httpd if you want to use this technique.

A couple of things need to be determined from the request in order to make the dynamic virtual host look like a normal one. The most important is the server name, which is used by the server to generate self-referential URLs etc. It is configured with the `ServerName` directive, and it is available to CGIs via the `SERVER_NAME` environment variable. The actual value used at run time is controlled by the USECANONICALNAME setting. With `UseCanonicalName Off`, the server name is taken from the contents of the `Host:` header in the request. With `UseCanonicalName DNS`, it is taken from a reverse DNS lookup of the virtual host's IP address. The former setting is used for name-based dynamic virtual hosting, and the latter is used for IP-based hosting. If httpd cannot work out the server name because there is no `Host:` header, or the DNS lookup fails, then the value configured with `ServerName` is used instead.

The other thing to determine is the document root (configured with `DocumentRoot` and available to CGI scripts via the `DOCUMENT_ROOT` environment variable). In a normal configuration, this is used by the core module when mapping URIs to filenames, but when the server is configured to do dynamic virtual hosting, that job must be taken over by another module (either MOD_VHOST_ALIAS or MOD_REWRITE), which has a different way of doing the mapping. Neither of these modules is responsible for setting the `DOCUMENT_ROOT` environment variable so if any CGIs or SSI documents make use of it, they will get a misleading value.

Dynamic Virtual Hosts with mod_vhost_alias

This extract from `httpd.conf` implements the virtual host arrangement outlined in the Motivation section above using MOD_VHOST_ALIAS.

```
# get the server name from the Host: header
UseCanonicalName Off

# this log format can be split per-virtual-host based on the first field
# using the split-logfile utility.
LogFormat "%V %h %l %u %t \"%r\" %s %b" vcommon
CustomLog "logs/access_log" vcommon

# include the server name in the filenames used to satisfy requests
VirtualDocumentRoot "/www/hosts/%0/docs"
VirtualScriptAlias  "/www/hosts/%0/cgi-bin"
```

This configuration can be changed into an IP-based virtual hosting solution by just turning `UseCanonicalName Off` into `UseCanonicalName DNS`. The server name that is inserted into the filename is then derived from the IP address of the virtual host. The variable `%0` references the requested servername, as indicated in the `Host:` header.

See the MOD_VHOST_ALIAS documentation for more usage examples.

Simplified Dynamic Virtual Hosts

This is an adjustment of the above system, tailored for an ISP's web hosting server. Using `%2`, we can select substrings of the server name to use in the filename so that, for example, the documents for `www.user.example.com` are found in `/home/user/www`. It uses a single `cgi-bin` directory instead of one per virtual host.

```
UseCanonicalName Off

LogFormat "%V %h %l %u %t \"%r\" %s %b" vcommon
CustomLog logs/access_log vcommon

# include part of the server name in the filenames
VirtualDocumentRoot "/home/%2/www"
```

```
# single cgi-bin directory
ScriptAlias  "/cgi-bin/"  "/www/std-cgi/"
```

There are examples of more complicated `VirtualDocumentRoot` settings in the MOD_VHOST_ALIAS documentation.

Using Multiple Virtual Hosting Systems on the Same Server

With more complicated setups, you can use httpd's normal <VirtualHost> directives to control the scope of the various virtual hosting configurations. For example, you could have one IP address for general customers' homepages, and another for commercial customers, with the following setup. This can be combined with conventional <VirtualHost> configuration sections, as shown below.

```
UseCanonicalName Off

LogFormat "%V %h %l %u %t \"%r\" %s %b" vcommon

<Directory "/www/commercial">
    Options FollowSymLinks
    AllowOverride All
</Directory>

<Directory "/www/homepages">
    Options FollowSymLinks
    AllowOverride None
</Directory>

<VirtualHost 111.22.33.44>
    ServerName www.commercial.example.com

    CustomLog "logs/access_log.commercial" vcommon

    VirtualDocumentRoot "/www/commercial/%0/docs"
    VirtualScriptAlias  "/www/commercial/%0/cgi-bin"
</VirtualHost>

<VirtualHost 111.22.33.45>
    ServerName www.homepages.example.com

    CustomLog "logs/access_log.homepages" vcommon

    VirtualDocumentRoot "/www/homepages/%0/docs"
    ScriptAlias         "/cgi-bin/" "/www/std-cgi/"
</VirtualHost>
```

⟹ **Note**

If the first VirtualHost block does *not* include a SERVERNAME directive, the reverse DNS of the relevant IP will be used instead. If this is not the server name you wish to use, a bogus entry (eg. `ServerName none.example.com`) can be added to get around this behaviour.

More Efficient IP-Based Virtual Hosting

The configuration changes suggested to turn the first example into an IP-based virtual hosting setup result in a rather inefficient setup. A new DNS lookup is required for every request. To avoid this overhead, the filesystem can be arranged to correspond to the IP addresses, instead of to the host names, thereby negating the need for a DNS lookup. Logging will also have to be adjusted to fit this system.

```
# get the server name from the reverse DNS of the IP address
UseCanonicalName DNS

# include the IP address in the logs so they may be split
LogFormat "%A %h %l %u %t \"%r\" %s %b" vcommon
CustomLog "logs/access_log" vcommon

# include the IP address in the filenames
VirtualDocumentRootIP "/www/hosts/%0/docs"
VirtualScriptAliasIP  "/www/hosts/%0/cgi-bin"
```

Mass virtual hosts with mod_rewrite

Mass virtual hosting may also be accomplished using MOD_REWRITE, either using simple REWRITERULE directives, or using more complicated techniques such as storing the vhost definitions externally and accessing them via REWRITEMAP. These techniques are discussed in the rewrite documentation (p. 152) .

3.5 VirtualHost Examples

This document attempts to answer the commonly-asked questions about setting up virtual hosts (p. 114) . These scenarios are those involving multiple web sites running on a single server, via name-based (p. 115) or IP-based (p. 118) virtual hosts.

Running several name-based web sites on a single IP address.

Your server has a single IP address, and multiple aliases (CNAMES) point to this machine in DNS. You want to run a web server for `www.example.com` and `www.example.org` on this machine.

**Note**

Creating virtual host configurations on your Apache server does not magically cause DNS entries to be created for those host names. You *must* have the names in DNS, resolving to your IP address, or nobody else will be able to see your web site. You can put entries in your `hosts` file for local testing, but that will work only from the machine with those `hosts` entries.

```
# Ensure that Apache listens on port 80
Listen 80
<VirtualHost *:80>
    DocumentRoot "/www/example1"
    ServerName www.example.com

    # Other directives here
</VirtualHost>

<VirtualHost *:80>
    DocumentRoot "/www/example2"
    ServerName www.example.org

    # Other directives here
</VirtualHost>
```

The asterisks match all addresses, so the main server serves no requests. Due to the fact that the virtual host with `ServerName www.example.com` is first in the configuration file, it has the highest priority and can be seen as the *default* or *primary* server. That means that if a request is received that does not match one of the specified `ServerName` directives, it will be served by this first `VirtualHost`.

**Note**

You can, if you wish, replace `*` with the actual IP address of the system, when you don't care to discriminate based on the IP address or port.
However, it is additionally useful to use `*` on systems where the IP address is not predictable - for example if you have a dynamic IP address with your ISP, and you are using some variety of dynamic DNS solution. Since `*` matches any IP address, this configuration would work without changes whenever your IP address changes.

The above configuration is what you will want to use in almost all name-based virtual hosting situations. The only thing that this configuration will not work for, in fact, is when you are serving different content based on differing IP addresses or ports.

Name-based hosts on more than one IP address.

**Note**

Any of the techniques discussed here can be extended to any number of IP addresses.

The server has two IP addresses. On one (172.20.30.40), we will serve the "main" server, server.example.com and on the other (172.20.30.50), we will serve two or more virtual hosts.

```
Listen 80

# This is the "main" server running on 172.20.30.40
ServerName server.example.com
DocumentRoot "/www/mainserver"

<VirtualHost 172.20.30.50>
    DocumentRoot "/www/example1"
    ServerName www.example.com

    # Other directives here ...
</VirtualHost>

<VirtualHost 172.20.30.50>
    DocumentRoot "/www/example2"
    ServerName www.example.org

    # Other directives here ...
</VirtualHost>
```

Any request to an address other than 172.20.30.50 will be served from the main server. A request to 172.20.30.50 with an unknown hostname, or no Host: header, will be served from www.example.com.

Serving the same content on different IP addresses (such as an internal and external address).

The server machine has two IP addresses (192.168.1.1 and 172.20.30.40). The machine is sitting between an internal (intranet) network and an external (internet) network. Outside of the network, the name server.example.com resolves to the external address (172.20.30.40), but inside the network, that same name resolves to the internal address (192.168.1.1).

The server can be made to respond to internal and external requests with the same content, with just one VirtualHost section.

```
<VirtualHost 192.168.1.1 172.20.30.40>
    DocumentRoot "/www/server1"
    ServerName server.example.com
    ServerAlias server
</VirtualHost>
```

Now requests from both networks will be served from the same VirtualHost.

**Note:**

On the internal network, one can just use the name server rather than the fully qualified host name server.example.com.

Note also that, in the above example, you can replace the list of IP addresses with *, which will cause the server to respond the same on all addresses.

Running different sites on different ports.

You have multiple domains going to the same IP and also want to serve multiple ports. The example below illustrates that the name-matching takes place after the best matching IP address and port combination is determined.

```
Listen 80
Listen 8080

<VirtualHost 172.20.30.40:80>
    ServerName www.example.com
    DocumentRoot "/www/domain-80"
</VirtualHost>

<VirtualHost 172.20.30.40:8080>
    ServerName www.example.com
    DocumentRoot "/www/domain-8080"
</VirtualHost>

<VirtualHost 172.20.30.40:80>
    ServerName www.example.org
    DocumentRoot "/www/otherdomain-80"
</VirtualHost>

<VirtualHost 172.20.30.40:8080>
    ServerName www.example.org
    DocumentRoot "/www/otherdomain-8080"
</VirtualHost>
```

IP-based virtual hosting

The server has two IP addresses (172.20.30.40 and 172.20.30.50) which resolve to the names www.example.com and www.example.org respectively.

```
Listen 80

<VirtualHost 172.20.30.40>
    DocumentRoot "/www/example1"
    ServerName www.example.com
</VirtualHost>

<VirtualHost 172.20.30.50>
    DocumentRoot "/www/example2"
    ServerName www.example.org
</VirtualHost>
```

Requests for any address not specified in one of the <VirtualHost> directives (such as localhost, for example) will go to the main server, if there is one.

Mixed port-based and ip-based virtual hosts

The server machine has two IP addresses (172.20.30.40 and 172.20.30.50) which resolve to the names www.example.com and www.example.org respectively. In each case, we want to run hosts on ports 80 and

8080.

```
Listen 172.20.30.40:80
Listen 172.20.30.40:8080
Listen 172.20.30.50:80
Listen 172.20.30.50:8080

<VirtualHost 172.20.30.40:80>
    DocumentRoot "/www/example1-80"
    ServerName www.example.com
</VirtualHost>

<VirtualHost 172.20.30.40:8080>
    DocumentRoot "/www/example1-8080"
    ServerName www.example.com
</VirtualHost>

<VirtualHost 172.20.30.50:80>
    DocumentRoot "/www/example2-80"
    ServerName www.example.org
</VirtualHost>

<VirtualHost 172.20.30.50:8080>
    DocumentRoot "/www/example2-8080"
    ServerName www.example.org
</VirtualHost>
```

Mixed name-based and IP-based vhosts

Any address mentioned in the argument to a virtualhost that never appears in another virtual host is a strictly IP-based virtual host.

```
Listen 80
<VirtualHost 172.20.30.40>
    DocumentRoot "/www/example1"
    ServerName www.example.com
</VirtualHost>

<VirtualHost 172.20.30.40>
    DocumentRoot "/www/example2"
    ServerName www.example.org
</VirtualHost>

<VirtualHost 172.20.30.40>
    DocumentRoot "/www/example3"
    ServerName www.example.net
</VirtualHost>

# IP-based
<VirtualHost 172.20.30.50>
    DocumentRoot "/www/example4"
    ServerName www.example.edu
```

```
</VirtualHost>

<VirtualHost 172.20.30.60>
    DocumentRoot "/www/example5"
    ServerName www.example.gov
</VirtualHost>
```

Using `Virtual_host` and mod_proxy together

The following example allows a front-end machine to proxy a virtual host through to a server running on another machine. In the example, a virtual host of the same name is configured on a machine at `192.168.111.2`. The PROXYPRESERVEHOST ON directive is used so that the desired hostname is passed through, in case we are proxying multiple hostnames to a single machine.

```
<VirtualHost *:*>
    ProxyPreserveHost On
    ProxyPass "/" "http://192.168.111.2/"
    ProxyPassReverse "/" "http://192.168.111.2/"
    ServerName hostname.example.com
</VirtualHost>
```

Using `_default_` vhosts

`_default_` vhosts for all ports

Catching *every* request to any unspecified IP address and port, *i.e.*, an address/port combination that is not used for any other virtual host.

```
<VirtualHost _default_:*>
    DocumentRoot "/www/default"
</VirtualHost>
```

Using such a default vhost with a wildcard port effectively prevents any request going to the main server.

A default vhost never serves a request that was sent to an address/port that is used for name-based vhosts. If the request contained an unknown or no `Host:` header it is always served from the primary name-based vhost (the vhost for that address/port appearing first in the configuration file).

You can use ALIASMATCH or REWRITERULE to rewrite any request to a single information page (or script).

`_default_` vhosts for different ports

Same as setup 1, but the server listens on several ports and we want to use a second `_default_` vhost for port 80.

```
<VirtualHost _default_:80>
    DocumentRoot "/www/default80"
    # ...
</VirtualHost>

<VirtualHost _default_:*>
    DocumentRoot "/www/default"
    # ...
</VirtualHost>
```

The default vhost for port 80 (which *must* appear before any default vhost with a wildcard port) catches all requests that were sent to an unspecified IP address. The main server is never used to serve a request.

default vhosts for one port

We want to have a default vhost for port 80, but no other default vhosts.

```
<VirtualHost _default_:80>
DocumentRoot "/www/default"
...
</VirtualHost>
```

A request to an unspecified address on port 80 is served from the default vhost. Any other request to an unspecified address and port is served from the main server.

Any use of * in a virtual host declaration will have higher precedence than `_default_`.

Migrating a name-based vhost to an IP-based vhost

The name-based vhost with the hostname `www.example.org` (from our name-based example, setup 2) should get its own IP address. To avoid problems with name servers or proxies who cached the old IP address for the name-based vhost we want to provide both variants during a migration phase.

The solution is easy, because we can simply add the new IP address (`172.20.30.50`) to the `VirtualHost` directive.

```
Listen 80
ServerName www.example.com
DocumentRoot "/www/example1"

<VirtualHost 172.20.30.40 172.20.30.50>
    DocumentRoot "/www/example2"
    ServerName www.example.org
    # ...
</VirtualHost>

<VirtualHost 172.20.30.40>
    DocumentRoot "/www/example3"
    ServerName www.example.net
    ServerAlias *.example.net
    # ...
</VirtualHost>
```

The vhost can now be accessed through the new address (as an IP-based vhost) and through the old address (as a name-based vhost).

Using the ServerPath directive

We have a server with two name-based vhosts. In order to match the correct virtual host a client must send the correct `Host:` header. Old HTTP/1.0 clients do not send such a header and Apache has no clue what vhost the client tried to reach (and serves the request from the primary vhost). To provide as much backward compatibility as possible we create a primary vhost which returns a single page containing links with an URL prefix to the name-based virtual hosts.

```
<VirtualHost 172.20.30.40>
    # primary vhost
    DocumentRoot "/www/subdomain"
    RewriteEngine On
    RewriteRule "." "/www/subdomain/index.html"
    # ...
</VirtualHost>

<VirtualHost 172.20.30.40>
DocumentRoot "/www/subdomain/sub1"
    ServerName www.sub1.domain.tld
    ServerPath "/sub1/"
    RewriteEngine On
    RewriteRule "^(/sub1/.*)" "/www/subdomain$1"
    # ...
</VirtualHost>

<VirtualHost 172.20.30.40>
    DocumentRoot "/www/subdomain/sub2"
    ServerName www.sub2.domain.tld
    ServerPath "/sub2/"
    RewriteEngine On
    RewriteRule "^(/sub2/.*)" "/www/subdomain$1"
    # ...
</VirtualHost>
```

Due to the SERVERPATH directive a request to the URL `http://www.sub1.domain.tld/sub1/` is *always* served from the sub1-vhost.
A request to the URL `http://www.sub1.domain.tld/` is only served from the sub1-vhost if the client sent a correct `Host:` header. If no `Host:` header is sent the client gets the information page from the primary host.

Please note that there is one oddity: A request to `http://www.sub2.domain.tld/sub1/` is also served from the sub1-vhost if the client sent no `Host:` header.

The REWRITERULE directives are used to make sure that a client which sent a correct `Host:` header can use both URL variants, *i.e.*, with or without URL prefix.

3.6 An In-Depth Discussion of Virtual Host Matching

This document attempts to explain exactly what Apache HTTP Server does when deciding what virtual host to serve a request from.

Most users should read about Name-based vs. IP-based Virtual Hosts (p. 115) to decide which type they want to use, then read more about name-based (p. 115) or IP-based (p. 118) virtualhosts, and then see some examples (p. 124) .

If you want to understand all the details, then you can come back to this page.

See also

- IP-based Virtual Host Support (p. 118)
- Name-based Virtual Hosts Support (p. 115)
- Virtual Host examples for common setups (p. 124)
- Dynamically configured mass virtual hosting (p. 120)

Configuration File

There is a *main server* which consists of all the definitions appearing outside of `<VirtualHost>` sections.

There are virtual servers, called *vhosts*, which are defined by <VIRTUALHOST> sections.

Each `VirtualHost` directive includes one or more addresses and optional ports.

Hostnames can be used in place of IP addresses in a virtual host definition, but they are resolved at startup and if any name resolutions fail, those virtual host definitions are ignored. This is, therefore, not recommended.

The address can be specified as `*`, which will match a request if no other vhost has the explicit address on which the request was received.

The address appearing in the `VirtualHost` directive can have an optional port. If the port is unspecified, it is treated as a wildcard port, which can also be indicated explicitly using `*`. The wildcard port matches any port.

(Port numbers specified in the `VirtualHost` directive do not influence what port numbers Apache will listen on, they only control which `VirtualHost` will be selected to handle a request. Use the LISTEN directive to control the addresses and ports on which the server listens.)

Collectively the entire set of addresses (including multiple results from DNS lookups) are called the vhost's *address set*.

Apache automatically discriminates on the basis of the HTTP `Host` header supplied by the client whenever the most specific match for an IP address and port combination is listed in multiple virtual hosts.

The SERVERNAME directive may appear anywhere within the definition of a server. However, each appearance overrides the previous appearance (within that server). If no `ServerName` is specified, the server attempts to deduce it from the server's IP address.

The first name-based vhost in the configuration file for a given IP:port pair is significant because it is used for all requests received on that address and port for which no other vhost for that IP:port pair has a matching ServerName or ServerAlias. It is also used for all SSL connections if the server does not support Server Name Indication.

The complete list of names in the `VirtualHost` directive are treated just like a (non wildcard) `ServerAlias` (but are not overridden by any `ServerAlias` statement).

For every vhost various default values are set. In particular:

1. If a vhost has no SERVERADMIN, TIMEOUT, KEEPALIVETIMEOUT, KEEPALIVE, MAXKEEPALIVEREQUESTS, RECEIVEBUFFERSIZE, or SENDBUFFERSIZE directive then the respective value is inherited from the main server. (That is, inherited from whatever the final setting of that value is in the main server.)

2. The "lookup defaults" that define the default directory permissions for a vhost are merged with those of the main server. This includes any per-directory configuration information for any module.
3. The per-server configs for each module from the main server are merged into the vhost server.

Essentially, the main server is treated as "defaults" or a "base" on which to build each vhost. But the positioning of these main server definitions in the config file is largely irrelevant – the entire config of the main server has been parsed when this final merging occurs. So even if a main server definition appears after a vhost definition it might affect the vhost definition.

If the main server has no `ServerName` at this point, then the hostname of the machine that `httpd` is running on is used instead. We will call the *main server address set* those IP addresses returned by a DNS lookup on the `ServerName` of the main server.

For any undefined `ServerName` fields, a name-based vhost defaults to the address given first in the `VirtualHost` statement defining the vhost.

Any vhost that includes the magic `_default_` wildcard is given the same `ServerName` as the main server.

Virtual Host Matching

The server determines which vhost to use for a request as follows:

IP address lookup

When the connection is first received on some address and port, the server looks for all the `VirtualHost` definitions that have the same IP address and port.

If there are no exact matches for the address and port, then wildcard (*) matches are considered.

If no matches are found, the request is served by the main server.

If there are `VirtualHost` definitions for the IP address, the next step is to decide if we have to deal with an IP-based or a name-based vhost.

IP-based vhost

If there is exactly one `VirtualHost` directive listing the IP address and port combination that was determined to be the best match, no further actions are performed and the request is served from the matching vhost.

Name-based vhost

If there are multiple `VirtualHost` directives listing the IP address and port combination that was determined to be the best match, the "list" in the remaining steps refers to the list of vhosts that matched, in the order they were in the configuration file.

If the connection is using SSL, the server supports Server Name Indication, and the SSL client handshake includes the TLS extension with the requested hostname, then that hostname is used below just like the `Host:` header would be used on a non-SSL connection. Otherwise, the first name-based vhost whose address matched is used for SSL connections. This is significant because the vhost determines which certificate the server will use for the connection.

If the request contains a `Host:` header field, the list is searched for the first vhost with a matching `ServerName` or `ServerAlias`, and the request is served from that vhost. A `Host:` header field can contain a port number, but Apache always ignores it and matches against the real port to which the client sent the request.

The first vhost in the config file with the specified IP address has the highest priority and catches any request to an unknown server name, or a request without a `Host:` header field (such as a HTTP/1.0 request).

Persistent connections

The *IP lookup* described above is only done *once* for a particular TCP/IP session while the *name lookup* is done on *every* request during a KeepAlive/persistent connection. In other words, a client may request pages from different name-based vhosts during a single persistent connection.

Absolute URI

If the URI from the request is an absolute URI, and its hostname and port match the main server or one of the configured virtual hosts *and* match the address and port to which the client sent the request, then the scheme/hostname/port prefix is stripped off and the remaining relative URI is served by the corresponding main server or virtual host. If it does not match, then the URI remains untouched and the request is taken to be a proxy request.

Observations

- Name-based virtual hosting is a process applied after the server has selected the best matching IP-based virtual host.
- If you don't care what IP address the client has connected to, use a `"*"` as the address of every virtual host, and name-based virtual hosting is applied across all configured virtual hosts.
- `ServerName` and `ServerAlias` checks are never performed for an IP-based vhost.
- Only the ordering of name-based vhosts for a specific address set is significant. The one name-based vhosts that comes first in the configuration file has the highest priority for its corresponding address set.
- Any port in the `Host:` header field is never used during the matching process. Apache always uses the real port to which the client sent the request.
- If two vhosts have an address in common, those common addresses act as name-based virtual hosts implicitly. This is new behavior as of 2.3.11.
- The main server is only used to serve a request if the IP address and port number to which the client connected does not match any vhost (including a `*` vhost). In other words, the main server only catches a request for an unspecified address/port combination (unless there is a `_default_` vhost which matches that port).
- You should never specify DNS names in `VirtualHost` directives because it will force your server to rely on DNS to boot. Furthermore it poses a security threat if you do not control the DNS for all the domains listed. There's more information (p. 111) available on this and the next two topics.
- `ServerName` should always be set for each vhost. Otherwise A DNS lookup is required for each vhost.

Tips

In addition to the tips on the DNS Issues (p. 111) page, here are some further tips:

- Place all main server definitions before any `VirtualHost` definitions. (This is to aid the readability of the configuration – the post-config merging process makes it non-obvious that definitions mixed in around virtual hosts might affect all virtual hosts.)

3.7 File Descriptor Limits

When using a large number of Virtual Hosts, Apache may run out of available file descriptors (sometimes called *file handles*) if each Virtual Host specifies different log files. The total number of file descriptors used by Apache is one for each distinct error log file, one for every other log file directive, plus 10-20 for internal use. Unix operating systems limit the number of file descriptors that may be used by a process; the limit is typically 64, and may usually be increased up to a large hard-limit.

Although Apache attempts to increase the limit as required, this may not work if:

1. Your system does not provide the `setrlimit()` system call.
2. The `setrlimit(RLIMIT_NOFILE)` call does not function on your system (such as Solaris 2.3)
3. The number of file descriptors required exceeds the hard limit.
4. Your system imposes other limits on file descriptors, such as a limit on stdio streams only using file descriptors below 256. (Solaris 2)

In the event of problems you can:

- Reduce the number of log files; don't specify log files in the <VIRTUALHOST> sections, but only log to the main log files. (See Splitting up your log files, below, for more information on doing this.)
- If you system falls into 1 or 2 (above), then increase the file descriptor limit before starting Apache, using a script like

```
#!/bin/sh
ulimit -S -n 100
exec httpd
```

Splitting up your log files

If you want to log multiple virtual hosts to the same log file, you may want to split up the log files afterwards in order to run statistical analysis of the various virtual hosts. This can be accomplished in the following manner.

First, you will need to add the virtual host information to the log entries. This can be done using the LOGFORMAT directive, and the `%v` variable. Add this to the beginning of your log format string:

```
LogFormat "%v %h %l %u %t \"%r\" %>s %b" vhost
CustomLog logs/multiple_vhost_log vhost
```

This will create a log file in the common log format, but with the canonical virtual host (whatever appears in the SERVERNAME directive) prepended to each line. (See MOD_LOG_CONFIG for more about customizing your log files.)

When you wish to split your log file into its component parts (one file per virtual host) you can use the program `split-logfile` (p. 323) to accomplish this. You'll find this program in the `support` directory of the Apache distribution.

Run this program with the command:

```
split-logfile < /logs/multiple_vhost_log
```

This program, when run with the name of your vhost log file, will generate one file for each virtual host that appears in your log file. Each file will be called `hostname.log`.

Chapter 4

URL Rewriting Guide

4.1 Apache mod_rewrite

MOD_REWRITE provides a way to modify incoming URL requests, dynamically, based on regular expression (p. 137) rules. This allows you to map arbitrary URLs onto your internal URL structure in any way you like.

It supports an unlimited number of rules and an unlimited number of attached rule conditions for each rule to provide a really flexible and powerful URL manipulation mechanism. The URL manipulations can depend on various tests: server variables, environment variables, HTTP headers, time stamps, external database lookups, and various other external programs or handlers, can be used to achieve granular URL matching.

Rewrite rules can operate on the full URLs, including the path-info and query string portions, and may be used in per-server context (`httpd.conf`), per-virtualhost context (<VIRTUALHOST> blocks), or per-directory context (`.htaccess` files and <DIRECTORY> blocks). The rewritten result can lead to further rules, internal sub-processing, external request redirection, or proxy passthrough, depending on what flags (p. 168) you attach to the rules.

Since mod_rewrite is so powerful, it can indeed be rather complex. This document supplements the reference documentation (p. 804) , and attempts to allay some of that complexity, and provide highly annotated examples of common scenarios that you may handle with mod_rewrite. But we also attempt to show you when you should not use mod_rewrite, and use other standard Apache features instead, thus avoiding this unnecessary complexity.

See also

- mod_rewrite reference documentation (p. 804)
- Mapping URLs to the Filesystem (p. 61)
- mod_rewrite wiki[1]
- Glossary (p. 1020)

[1]http://wiki.apache.org/httpd/Rewrite

4.2 Apache mod_rewrite Introduction

This document supplements the MOD_REWRITE reference documentation (p. 804) . It describes the basic concepts necessary for use of MOD_REWRITE. Other documents go into greater detail, but this doc should help the beginner get their feet wet.

See also

- Module documentation (p. 804)
- Redirection and remapping (p. 142)
- Controlling access (p. 149)
- Virtual hosts (p. 152)
- Proxying (p. 155)
- Using RewriteMap (p. 156)
- Advanced techniques (p. 162)
- When not to use mod_rewrite (p. 165)

Introduction

The Apache module MOD_REWRITE is a very powerful and sophisticated module which provides a way to do URL manipulations. With it, you can do nearly all types of URL rewriting that you may need. It is, however, somewhat complex, and may be intimidating to the beginner. There is also a tendency to treat rewrite rules as magic incantation, using them without actually understanding what they do.

This document attempts to give sufficient background so that what follows is understood, rather than just copied blindly.

Remember that many common URL-manipulation tasks don't require the full power and complexity of MOD_REWRITE. For simple tasks, see MOD_ALIAS and the documentation on mapping URLs to the filesystem (p. 61) .

Finally, before proceeding, be sure to configure MOD_REWRITE's log level to one of the trace levels using the LOGLEVEL directive. Although this can give an overwhelming amount of information, it is indispensable in debugging problems with MOD_REWRITE configuration, since it will tell you exactly how each rule is processed.

Regular Expressions

mod_rewrite uses the Perl Compatible Regular Expression[2] vocabulary. In this document, we do not attempt to provide a detailed reference to regular expressions. For that, we recommend the PCRE man pages[3], the Perl regular expression man page[4], and Mastering Regular Expressions, by Jeffrey Friedl[5].

In this document, we attempt to provide enough of a regex vocabulary to get you started, without being overwhelming, in the hope that REWRITERULEs will be scientific formulae, rather than magical incantations.

[2] http://pcre.org/
[3] http://pcre.org/pcre.txt
[4] http://perldoc.perl.org/perlre.html
[5] http://shop.oreilly.com/product/9780596528126.do

Regex vocabulary

The following are the minimal building blocks you will need, in order to write regular expressions and REWRITERULES. They certainly do not represent a complete regular expression vocabulary, but they are a good place to start, and should help you read basic regular expressions, as well as write your own.

Character	Meaning	Example
.	Matches any single character	`c.t` will match `cat`, `cot`, `cut`, etc.
+	Repeats the previous match one or more times	`a+` matches `a`, `aa`, `aaa`, etc
*	Repeats the previous match zero or more times.	`a*` matches all the same things `a+` matches, but will also match an empty string.
?	Makes the match optional.	`colou?r` will match `color` and `colour`.
^	Called an anchor, matches the beginning of the string	`^a` matches a string that begins with `a`
$	The other anchor, this matches the end of the string.	`a$` matches a string that ends with `a`.
( )	Groups several characters into a single unit, and captures a match for use in a backreference.	`(ab)+` matches `ababab` - that is, the + applies to the group. For more on back-references see below.
[ ]	A character class - matches one of the characters	`c[uoa]t` matches `cut`, `cot` or `cat`.
[^]	Negative character class - matches any character not specified	`c[^/]t` matches `cat` or `c=t` but not `c/t`

In MOD_REWRITE the ! character can be used before a regular expression to negate it. This is, a string will be considered to have matched only if it does not match the rest of the expression.

Regex Back-Reference Availability

One important thing here has to be remembered: Whenever you use parentheses in *Pattern* or in one of the *CondPattern*, back-references are internally created which can be used with the strings `$N` and `%N` (see below). These are available for creating the *Substitution* parameter of a REWRITERULE or the *TestString* parameter of a REWRITECOND.

Captures in the REWRITERULE patterns are (counterintuitively) available to all preceding REWRITECOND directives, because the REWRITERULE expression is evaluated before the individual conditions.

Figure 1 shows to which locations the back-references are transferred for expansion as well as illustrating the flow of the RewriteRule, RewriteCond matching. In the next chapters, we will be exploring how to use these back-references, so do not fret if it seems a bit alien to you at first.

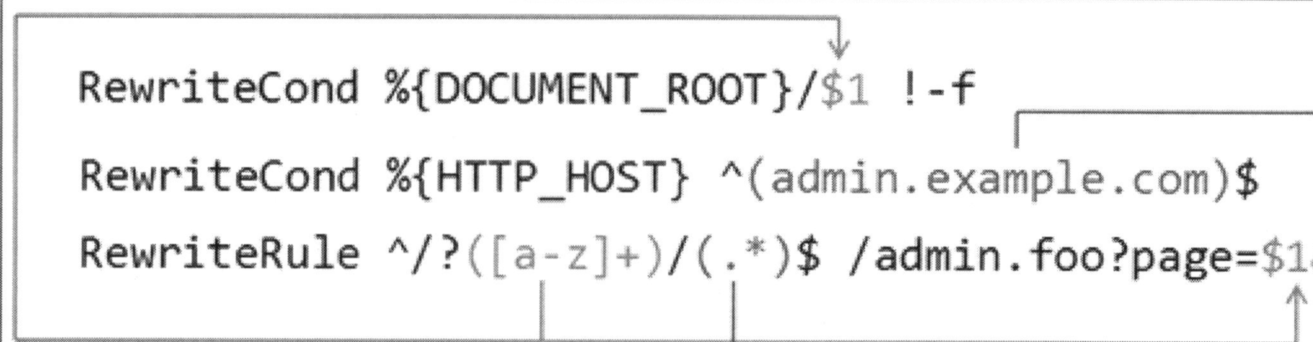

Figure 1: The back-reference flow through a rule.

In this example, a request for `/test/1234` would be transformed into `/admin.foo?page=test&id=1234&host=admin.example.com`.

RewriteRule Basics

A REWRITERULE consists of three arguments separated by spaces. The arguments are

1. *Pattern*: which incoming URLs should be affected by the rule;
2. *Substitution*: where should the matching requests be sent;
3. *[flags]*: options affecting the rewritten request.

The *Pattern* is a regular expression. It is initially (for the first rewrite rule or until a substitution occurs) matched against the URL-path of the incoming request (the part after the hostname but before any question mark indicating the beginning of a query string) or, in per-directory context, against the request's path relative to the directory for which the rule is defined. Once a substitution has occurred, the rules that follow are matched against the substituted value.

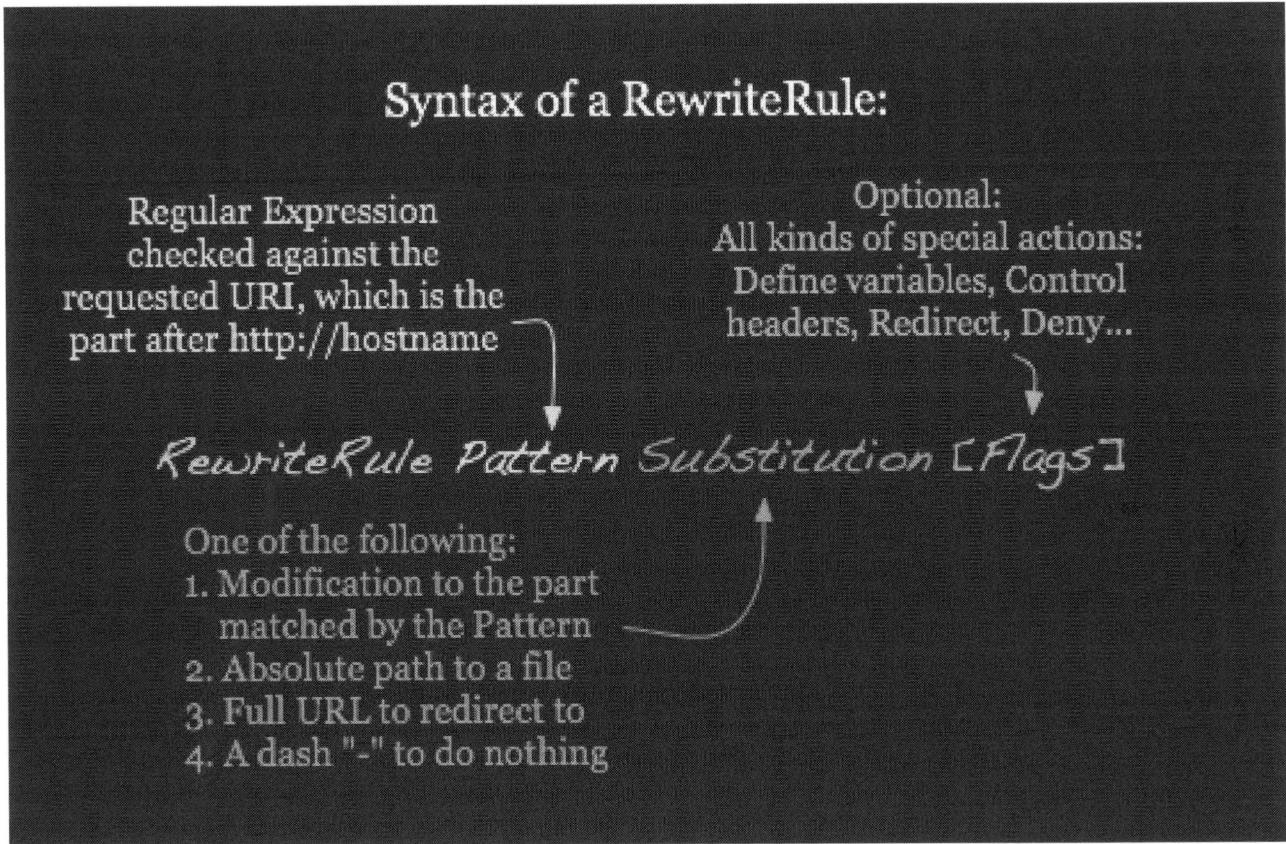

Figure 2: Syntax of the RewriteRule directive.

The *Substitution* can itself be one of three things:

A full filesystem path to a resource `RewriteRule "^/games" "/usr/local/games/web"`

This maps a request to an arbitrary location on your filesystem, much like the ALIAS directive.

A web-path to a resource `RewriteRule "^/foo$" "/bar"`

If DOCUMENTROOT is set to `/usr/local/apache2/htdocs`, then this directive would map requests for `http://example.com/foo` to the path `/usr/local/apache2/htdocs/bar`.

An absolute URL `RewriteRule "^/product/view$" "http://site2.example.com/seeproduct.html" [R]`

This tells the client to make a new request for the specified URL.

The *Substitution* can also contain *back-references* to parts of the incoming URL-path matched by the *Pattern*. Consider the following:

```
RewriteRule "^/product/(.*)/view$" "/var/web/productdb/$1"
```

The variable `$1` will be replaced with whatever text was matched by the expression inside the parenthesis in the *Pattern*. For example, a request for `http://example.com/product/r14df/view` will be mapped to the path `/var/web/productdb/r14df`.

If there is more than one expression in parenthesis, they are available in order in the variables `$1`, `$2`, `$3`, and so on.

Rewrite Flags

The behavior of a REWRITERULE can be modified by the application of one or more flags to the end of the rule. For example, the matching behavior of a rule can be made case-insensitive by the application of the `[NC]` flag:

```
RewriteRule "^puppy.html" "smalldog.html" [NC]
```

For more details on the available flags, their meanings, and examples, see the Rewrite Flags (p. 168) document.

Rewrite Conditions

One or more REWRITECOND directives can be used to restrict the types of requests that will be subject to the following REWRITERULE. The first argument is a variable describing a characteristic of the request, the second argument is a regular expression that must match the variable, and a third optional argument is a list of flags that modify how the match is evaluated.

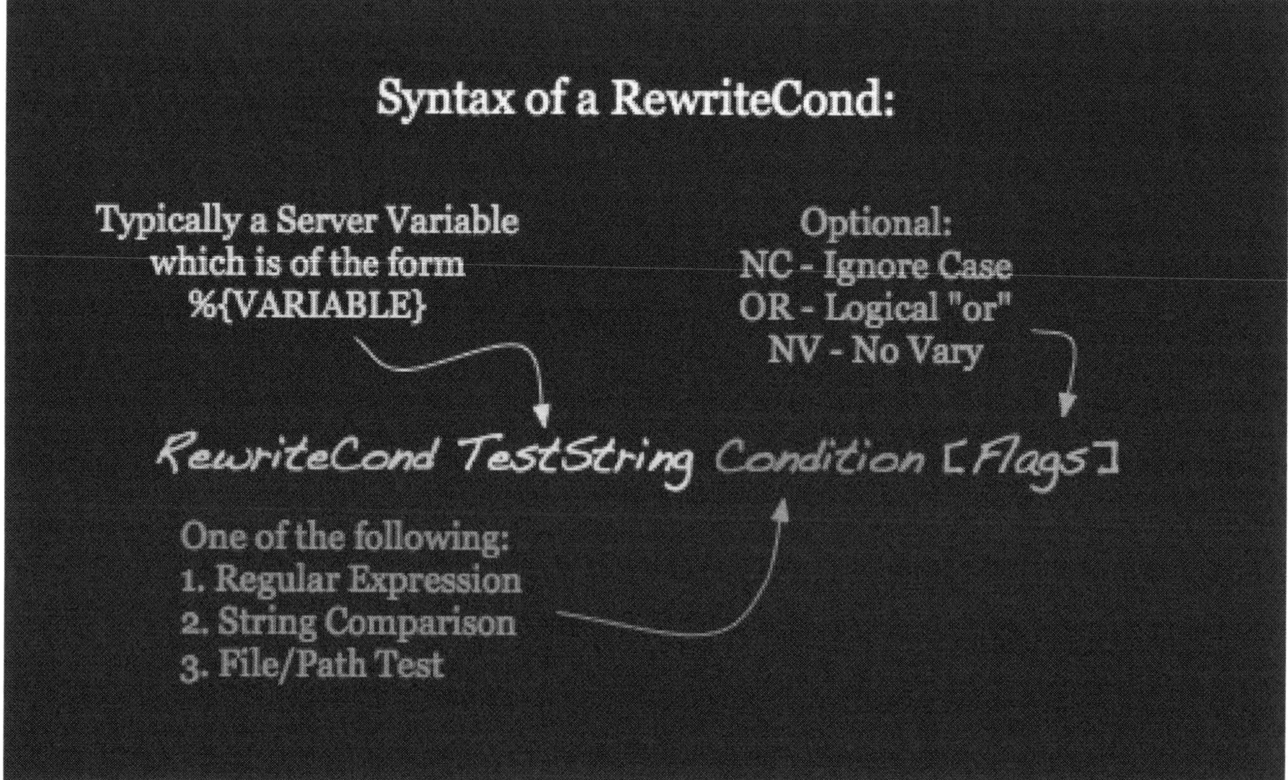

Figure 3: Syntax of the RewriteCond directive

For example, to send all requests from a particular IP range to a different server, you could use:

```
RewriteCond "%{REMOTE_ADDR}" "^10\.2\."
RewriteRule "(.*)" "http://intranet.example.com$1"
```

When more than one REWRITECOND is specified, they must all match for the REWRITERULE to be applied. For example, to deny requests that contain the word "hack" in their query string, unless they also contain a cookie containing the word "go", you could use:

```
RewriteCond "%{QUERY_STRING}" "hack"
RewriteCond "%{HTTP_COOKIE}" "!go"
RewriteRule "." "-" [F]
```

Notice that the exclamation mark specifies a negative match, so the rule is only applied if the cookie does not contain "go".

Matches in the regular expressions contained in the REWRITECONDs can be used as part of the *Substitution* in the REWRITERULE using the variables `%1`, `%2`, etc. For example, this will direct the request to a different directory depending on the hostname used to access the site:

```
RewriteCond "%{HTTP_HOST}" "(.*)"
RewriteRule "^/(.*)" "/sites/%1/$1"
```

If the request was for `http://example.com/foo/bar`, then `%1` would contain `example.com` and `$1` would contain `foo/bar`.

Rewrite maps

The REWRITEMAP directive provides a way to call an external function, so to speak, to do your rewriting for you. This is discussed in greater detail in the RewriteMap supplementary documentation (p. 156).

.htaccess files

Rewriting is typically configured in the main server configuration setting (outside any <DIRECTORY> section) or inside <VIRTUALHOST> containers. This is the easiest way to do rewriting and is recommended. It is possible, however, to do rewriting inside <DIRECTORY> sections or `.htaccess` files (p. 239) at the expense of some additional complexity. This technique is called per-directory rewrites.

The main difference with per-server rewrites is that the path prefix of the directory containing the `.htaccess` file is stripped before matching in the REWRITERULE. In addition, the REWRITEBASE should be used to assure the request is properly mapped.

4.3 Redirecting and Remapping with mod_rewrite

This document supplements the MOD_REWRITE reference documentation (p. 804) . It describes how you can use MOD_REWRITE to redirect and remap request. This includes many examples of common uses of mod_rewrite, including detailed descriptions of how each works.

Note that many of these examples won't work unchanged in your particular server configuration, so it's important that you understand them, rather than merely cutting and pasting the examples into your configuration.

See also

- Module documentation (p. 804)
- mod_rewrite introduction (p. 137)
- Controlling access (p. 149)
- Virtual hosts (p. 152)
- Proxying (p. 155)
- Using RewriteMap (p. 156)
- Advanced techniques (p. 162)
- When not to use mod_rewrite (p. 165)

From Old to New (internal)

Description: Assume we have recently renamed the page `foo.html` to `bar.html` and now want to provide the old URL for backward compatibility. However, we want that users of the old URL even not recognize that the pages was renamed - that is, we don't want the address to change in their browser.

Solution: We rewrite the old URL to the new one internally via the following rule:

```
RewriteEngine  on
RewriteRule    "^/foo\.html$"  "/bar.html" [PT]
```

Rewriting From Old to New (external)

Description: Assume again that we have recently renamed the page `foo.html` to `bar.html` and now want to provide the old URL for backward compatibility. But this time we want that the users of the old URL get hinted to the new one, i.e. their browsers Location field should change, too.

Solution: We force a HTTP redirect to the new URL which leads to a change of the browsers and thus the users view:

```
RewriteEngine  on
RewriteRule    "^/foo\.html$"  "bar.html"  [R]
```

Discussion In this example, as contrasted to the internal example above, we can simply use the Redirect directive. mod_rewrite was used in that earlier example in order to hide the redirect from the client:

```
Redirect "/foo.html" "/bar.html"
```

Resource Moved to Another Server

Description: If a resource has moved to another server, you may wish to have URLs continue to work for a time on the old server while people update their bookmarks.

Solution: You can use MOD_REWRITE to redirect these URLs to the new server, but you might also consider using the Redirect or RedirectMatch directive.

```
#With mod_rewrite
RewriteEngine on
RewriteRule    "^/docs/(.+)"  "http://new.example.com/docs/$1"  [R,L]

#With RedirectMatch
RedirectMatch "^/docs/(.*)" "http://new.example.com/docs/$1"

#With Redirect
Redirect "/docs/" "http://new.example.com/docs/"
```

From Static to Dynamic

Description: How can we transform a static page `foo.html` into a dynamic variant `foo.cgi` in a seamless way, i.e. without notice by the browser/user.

Solution: We just rewrite the URL to the CGI-script and force the handler to be **cgi-script** so that it is executed as a CGI program. This way a request to `/~quux/foo.html` internally leads to the invocation of `/~quux/foo.cgi`.

```
RewriteEngine  on
RewriteBase    "/~quux/"
RewriteRule    "^foo\.html$"  "foo.cgi"  [H=cgi-script]
```

Backward Compatibility for file extension change

Description: How can we make URLs backward compatible (still existing virtually) after migrating `document.YYYY` to `document.XXXX`, e.g. after translating a bunch of `.html` files to `.php`?

Solution: We rewrite the name to its basename and test for existence of the new extension. If it exists, we take that name, else we rewrite the URL to its original state.

```
#   backward compatibility ruleset for
#   rewriting document.html to document.php
#   when and only when document.php exists
<Directory "/var/www/htdocs">
    RewriteEngine on
    RewriteBase "/var/www/htdocs"

    RewriteCond "$1.php" -f
    RewriteCond "$1.html" !-f
    RewriteRule "^(.*).html$" "$1.php"
</Directory>
```

Discussion This example uses an often-overlooked feature of mod_rewrite, by taking advantage of the order of execution of the ruleset. In particular, mod_rewrite evaluates the left-hand-side of the RewriteRule before it evaluates the RewriteCond directives. Consequently, $1 is already defined by the time the RewriteCond directives are evaluated. This allows us to test for the existence of the original (`document.html`) and target (`document.php`) files using the same base filename.

This ruleset is designed to use in a per-directory context (In a <Directory> block or in a .htaccess file), so that the `-f` checks are looking at the correct directory path. You may need to set a REWRITEBASE directive to specify the directory base that you're working in.

Canonical Hostnames

Description: The goal of this rule is to force the use of a particular hostname, in preference to other hostnames which may be used to reach the same site. For example, if you wish to force the use of **www.example.com** instead of **example.com**, you might use a variant of the following recipe.

Solution: The very best way to solve this doesn't involve mod_rewrite at all, but rather uses the REDIRECT directive placed in a virtual host for the non-canonical hostname(s).

```
<VirtualHost *:80>
  ServerName undesired.example.com
  ServerAlias example.com notthis.example.com

  Redirect "/" "http://www.example.com/"
</VirtualHost>

<VirtualHost *:80>
  ServerName www.example.com
</VirtualHost>
```

You can alternatively accomplish this using the <IF> directive:

```
<If "%{HTTP_HOST} != 'www.example.com'">
Redirect "/" "http://www.example.com/"
</If>
```

Or, for example, to redirect a portion of your site to HTTPS, you might do the following:

```
<If "%{SERVER_PROTOCOL} != 'HTTPS'">
Redirect "/admin/" "https://www.example.com/admin/"
</If>
```

If, for whatever reason, you still want to use `mod_rewrite` - if, for example, you need this to work with a larger set of RewriteRules - you might use one of the recipes below.

For sites running on a port other than 80:

```
RewriteCond "%{HTTP_HOST}"   "!^www\.example\.com" [NC]
RewriteCond "%{HTTP_HOST}"   "!^$"
RewriteCond "%{SERVER_PORT}" "!^80$"
RewriteRule "^/?(.*)"        "http://www.example.com:%{SERVER_PORT}/$1" [L,R,NE]
```

And for a site running on port 80

```
RewriteCond "%{HTTP_HOST}"    "!^www\.example\.com" [NC]
RewriteCond "%{HTTP_HOST}"    "!^$"
RewriteRule "^/?(.*)"         "http://www.example.com/$1" [L,R,NE]
```

If you wanted to do this generically for all domain names - that is, if you want to redirect **example.com** to **www.example.com** for all possible values of **example.com**, you could use the following recipe:

```
RewriteCond "%{HTTP_HOST}" "!^www\." [NC]
RewriteCond "%{HTTP_HOST}" "!^$"
RewriteRule "^/?(.*)"      "http://www.%{HTTP_HOST}/$1" [L,R,NE]
```

These rulesets will work either in your main server configuration file, or in a `.htaccess` file placed in the DocumentRoot of the server.

Search for pages in more than one directory

Description: A particular resource might exist in one of several places, and we want to look in those places for the resource when it is requested. Perhaps we've recently rearranged our directory structure, dividing content into several locations.

Solution: The following ruleset searches in two directories to find the resource, and, if not finding it in either place, will attempt to just serve it out of the location requested.

```
RewriteEngine on

#   first try to find it in dir1/...
#   ...and if found stop and be happy:
RewriteCond         "%{DOCUMENT_ROOT}/dir1/%{REQUEST_URI}"  -f
RewriteRule "^(.+)" "%{DOCUMENT_ROOT}/dir1/$1"  [L]

#   second try to find it in dir2/...
#   ...and if found stop and be happy:
RewriteCond         "%{DOCUMENT_ROOT}/dir2/%{REQUEST_URI}"  -f
RewriteRule "^(.+)" "%{DOCUMENT_ROOT}/dir2/$1"  [L]

#   else go on for other Alias or ScriptAlias directives,
#   etc.
RewriteRule   "^"   "-"   [PT]
```

Redirecting to Geographically Distributed Servers

Description: We have numerous mirrors of our website, and want to redirect people to the one that is located in the country where they are located.

Solution: Looking at the hostname of the requesting client, we determine which country they are coming from. If we can't do a lookup on their IP address, we fall back to a default server.

We'll use a RewriteMap directive to build a list of servers that we wish to use.

```
HostnameLookups on
RewriteEngine on
RewriteMap    multiplex         "txt:/path/to/map.mirrors"
RewriteCond   "%{REMOTE_HOST}"  "([a-z]+)$" [NC]
RewriteRule   "^/(.*)$"  "${multiplex:%1|http://www.example.com/}$1"  [R,L]
```

```
## map.mirrors -- Multiplexing Map
de http://www.example.de/
uk http://www.example.uk/
com http://www.example.com/
##EOF##
```

Discussion ! This ruleset relies on HostNameLookups being set `on`, which can be a significant performance hit.

The RewriteCond directive captures the last portion of the hostname of the requesting client - the country code - and the following RewriteRule uses that value to look up the appropriate mirror host in the map file.

Browser Dependent Content

Description: We wish to provide different content based on the browser, or user-agent, which is requesting the content.

Solution: We have to decide, based on the HTTP header "User-Agent", which content to serve. The following config does the following: If the HTTP header "User-Agent" contains "Mozilla/3", the page `foo.html` is rewritten to `foo.NS.html` and the rewriting stops. If the browser is "Lynx" or "Mozilla" of version 1 or 2, the URL becomes `foo.20.html`. All other browsers receive page `foo.32.html`. This is done with the following ruleset:

```
RewriteCond "%{HTTP_USER_AGENT}"  "^Mozilla/3.*"
RewriteRule "^foo\.html$"         "foo.NS.html"          [L]

RewriteCond "%{HTTP_USER_AGENT}"  "^Lynx/" [OR]
RewriteCond "%{HTTP_USER_AGENT}"  "^Mozilla/[12]"
RewriteRule "^foo\.html$"         "foo.20.html"          [L]

RewriteRule "^foo\.html$"         "foo.32.html"          [L]
```

Canonical URLs

Description: On some webservers there is more than one URL for a resource. Usually there are canonical URLs (which are be actually used and distributed) and those which are just shortcuts, internal ones, and so on. Independent of which URL the user supplied with the request, they should finally see the canonical one in their browser address bar.

Solution: We do an external HTTP redirect for all non-canonical URLs to fix them in the location view of the Browser and for all subsequent requests. In the example ruleset below we replace `/puppies` and `/canines` by the canonical `/dogs`.

```
RewriteRule   "^/(puppies|canines)/(.*)"    "/dogs/$2"  [R]
```

Discussion: This should really be accomplished with Redirect or RedirectMatch directives:

```
RedirectMatch "^/(puppies|canines)/(.*)" "/dogs/$2"
```

Moved DocumentRoot

Description: Usually the DOCUMENTROOT of the webserver directly relates to the URL "/". But often this data is not really of top-level priority. For example, you may wish for visitors, on first entering a site, to go to a particular subdirectory /about/. This may be accomplished using the following ruleset:

Solution: We redirect the URL / to /about/:

```
RewriteEngine on
RewriteRule    "^/$"   "/about/"   [R]
```

Note that this can also be handled using the REDIRECTMATCH directive:

```
RedirectMatch "^/$" "http://example.com/about/"
```

Note also that the example rewrites only the root URL. That is, it rewrites a request for http://example.com/, but not a request for http://example.com/page.html. If you have in fact changed your document root - that is, if **all** of your content is in fact in that subdirectory, it is greatly preferable to simply change your DOCUMENTROOT directive, or move all of the content up one directory, rather than rewriting URLs.

Fallback Resource

Description: You want a single resource (say, a certain file, like index.php) to handle all requests that come to a particular directory, except those that should go to an existing resource such as an image, or a css file.

Solution: As of version 2.2.16, you should use the FALLBACKRESOURCE directive for this:

```
<Directory "/var/www/my_blog">
  FallbackResource "index.php"
</Directory>
```

However, in earlier versions of Apache, or if your needs are more complicated than this, you can use a variation of the following rewrite set to accomplish the same thing:

```
<Directory "/var/www/my_blog">
  RewriteBase "/my_blog"

  RewriteCond "/var/www/my_blog/%{REQUEST_FILENAME}" !-f
  RewriteCond "/var/www/my_blog/%{REQUEST_FILENAME}" !-d
  RewriteRule "^" "index.php" [PT]
</Directory>
```

If, on the other hand, you wish to pass the requested URI as a query string argument to index.php, you can replace that RewriteRule with:

```
RewriteRule "(.*)" "index.php?$1" [PT,QSA]
```

Note that these rulesets can be used in a .htaccess file, as well as in a <Directory> block.

Rewrite query string

Description: You want to capture a particular value from a query string and either replace it or incorporate it into another component of the URL.

Solutions: Many of the solutions in this section will all use the same condition, which leaves the matched value in the %2 backreference. %1 is the begining of the query string (up to the key of intererest), and %3 is the remainder. This condition is a bit complex for flexibility and to avoid double '&&' in the substitutions.

- This solution removes the matching key and value:

```
# Remove mykey=???
RewriteCond "%{QUERY_STRING}" "(.*(?:^|&))mykey=([^&]*)&?(.*)&?$"
RewriteRule "(.*)" "$1?%1%3"
```

- This solution uses the captured value in the URL subsitution, discarding the rest of the original query by appending a '?':

```
# Copy from query string to PATH_INFO
RewriteCond "%{QUERY_STRING}" "(.*(?:^|&))mykey=([^&]*)&?(.*)&?$"
RewriteRule "(.*)" "$1/products/%2/?" [PT]
```

- This solution checks the captured value in a subsequent condition:

```
# Capture the value of mykey in the query string
RewriteCond "%{QUERY_STRING}" "(.*(?:^|&))mykey=([^&]*)&?(.*)&?$"
RewriteCond "%2" !=not-so-secret-value
RewriteRule "(.*)" - [F]
```

- This solution shows the reverse of the previous ones, copying path components (perhaps PATH_INFO) from the URL into the query string.

```
# The desired URL might be /products/kitchen-sink, and the script expects
# /path?products=kitchen-sink.
RewriteRule "^/?path/([^/]+)/([^/]+)" "/path?$1=$2" [PT]
```

4.4 Using mod_rewrite to control access

This document supplements the MOD_REWRITE reference documentation (p. 804) . It describes how you can use MOD_REWRITE to control access to various resources, and other related techniques. This includes many examples of common uses of mod_rewrite, including detailed descriptions of how each works.

Note that many of these examples won't work unchanged in your particular server configuration, so it's important that you understand them, rather than merely cutting and pasting the examples into your configuration.

See also

- Module documentation (p. 804)
- mod_rewrite introduction (p. 137)
- Redirection and remapping (p. 142)
- Virtual hosts (p. 152)
- Proxying (p. 155)
- Using RewriteMap (p. 156)
- Advanced techniques (p. 162)
- When not to use mod_rewrite (p. 165)

Forbidding Image "Hotlinking"

Description: The following technique forbids the practice of other sites including your images inline in their pages. This practice is often referred to as "hotlinking", and results in your bandwidth being used to serve content for someone else's site.

Solution: This technique relies on the value of the HTTP_REFERER variable, which is optional. As such, it's possible for some people to circumvent this limitation. However, most users will experience the failed request, which should, over time, result in the image being removed from that other site.

There are several ways that you can handle this situation.

In this first example, we simply deny the request, if it didn't initiate from a page on our site. For the purpose of this example, we assume that our site is www.example.com.

```
RewriteCond "%{HTTP_REFERER}" "!^$"
RewriteCond "%{HTTP_REFERER}" "!www.example.com" [NC]
RewriteRule "\.(gif|jpg|png)$"    "-"    [F,NC]
```

In this second example, instead of failing the request, we display an alternate image instead.

```
RewriteCond "%{HTTP_REFERER}" "!^$"
RewriteCond "%{HTTP_REFERER}" "!www.example.com" [NC]
RewriteRule "\.(gif|jpg|png)$"    "/images/go-away.png"    [R,NC]
```

In the third example, we redirect the request to an image on some other site.

```
RewriteCond "%{HTTP_REFERER}" "!^$"
RewriteCond "%{HTTP_REFERER}" "!www.example.com" [NC]
RewriteRule "\.(gif|jpg|png)$" "http://other.example.com/image.gif"    [R,NC]
```

Of these techniques, the last two tend to be the most effective in getting people to stop hotlinking your images, because they will simply not see the image that they expected to see.

Discussion: If all you wish to do is deny access to the resource, rather than redirecting that request elsewhere, this can be accomplished without the use of mod_rewrite:

```
SetEnvIf Referer "example\.com" localreferer
<FilesMatch "\.(jpg|png|gif)$">
    Require env localreferer
</FilesMatch>
```

Blocking of Robots

Description: In this recipe, we discuss how to block persistent requests from a particular robot, or user agent.

The standard for robot exclusion defines a file, `/robots.txt` that specifies those portions of your website where you wish to exclude robots. However, some robots do not honor these files.

Note that there are methods of accomplishing this which do not use mod_rewrite. Note also that any technique that relies on the clients `USER_AGENT` string can be circumvented very easily, since that string can be changed.

Solution: We use a ruleset that specifies the directory to be protected, and the client `USER_AGENT` that identifies the malicious or persistent robot.

In this example, we are blocking a robot called `NameOfBadRobot` from a location `/secret/files`. You may also specify an IP address range, if you are trying to block that user agent only from the particular source.

```
RewriteCond "%{HTTP_USER_AGENT}"   "^NameOfBadRobot"
RewriteCond "%{REMOTE_ADDR}"       "=123\.45\.67\.[8-9]"
RewriteRule "^/secret/files/"   "-"   [F]
```

Discussion: Rather than using mod_rewrite for this, you can accomplish the same end using alternate means, as illustrated here:

```
SetEnvIfNoCase User-Agent "^NameOfBadRobot" goaway
<Location "/secret/files">
    <RequireAll>
        Require all granted
        Require not env goaway
    </RequireAll>
</Location>
```

As noted above, this technique is trivial to circumvent, by simply modifying the `USER_AGENT` request header. If you are experiencing a sustained attack, you should consider blocking it at a higher level, such as at your firewall.

Denying Hosts in a Blacklist

Description: We wish to maintain a blacklist of hosts, rather like `hosts.deny`, and have those hosts blocked from accessing our server.

Solution:

```
RewriteEngine on
RewriteMap    hosts-deny  "txt:/path/to/hosts.deny"
RewriteCond   "${hosts-deny:%{REMOTE_ADDR}|NOT-FOUND}" "!=NOT-FOUND" [OR]
RewriteCond   "${hosts-deny:%{REMOTE_HOST}|NOT-FOUND}" "!=NOT-FOUND"
RewriteRule   "^"  "-"  [F]
```

```
##
## hosts.deny
##
## ATTENTION! This is a map, not a list, even when we treat it as
such.
## mod_rewrite parses it for key/value pairs, so at least a
## dummy value "-" must be present for each entry.
##
193.102.180.41 -
bsdti1.sdm.de -
192.76.162.40 -
```

Discussion: The second RewriteCond assumes that you have HostNameLookups turned on, so that client IP addresses will be resolved. If that's not the case, you should drop the second RewriteCond, and drop the `[OR]` flag from the first RewriteCond.

Referer-based Deflector

Description: Redirect requests based on the Referer from which the request came, with different targets per Referer.

Solution: The following ruleset uses a map file to associate each Referer with a redirection target.

```
RewriteMap  deflector "txt:/path/to/deflector.map"

RewriteCond "%{HTTP_REFERER}" !=""
RewriteCond "${deflector:%{HTTP_REFERER}}" "=-"
RewriteRule "^" "%{HTTP_REFERER}" [R,L]

RewriteCond "%{HTTP_REFERER}" !=""
RewriteCond "${deflector:%{HTTP_REFERER}|NOT-FOUND}" "!=NOT-FOUND"
RewriteRule "^" "${deflector:%{HTTP_REFERER}}" [R,L]
```

The map file lists redirection targets for each referer, or, if we just wish to redirect back to where they came from, a `"-"` is placed in the map:

```
##
##  deflector.map
##

http://badguys.example.com/bad/index.html     -
http://badguys.example.com/bad/index2.html    -
http://badguys.example.com/bad/index3.html    http://somewhere.example.com/
```

4.5 Dynamic mass virtual hosts with mod_rewrite

This document supplements the MOD_REWRITE reference documentation (p. 804) . It describes how you can use MOD_REWRITE to create dynamically configured virtual hosts.

mod_rewrite is not the best way to configure virtual hosts. You should first consider the alternatives (p. 120) before resorting to mod_rewrite. See also the "how to avoid mod_rewrite (p. 165) document.

See also

- Module documentation (p. 804)
- mod_rewrite introduction (p. 137)
- Redirection and remapping (p. 142)
- Controlling access (p. 149)
- Proxying (p. 155)
- RewriteMap (p. 156)
- Advanced techniques (p. 162)
- When not to use mod_rewrite (p. 165)

Virtual Hosts For Arbitrary Hostnames

Description: We want to automatically create a virtual host for every hostname which resolves in our domain, without having to create new VirtualHost sections.

In this recipe, we assume that we'll be using the hostname `www.SITE.example.com` for each user, and serve their content out of `/home/SITE/www`.

Solution:
```
RewriteEngine on

RewriteMap     lowercase int:tolower

RewriteCond    "${lowercase:%{HTTP_HOST}}"    "^www\.([^.]+)\.example\.com$"
RewriteRule    "^(.*)" "/home/%1/www$1"
```

Discussion  You will need to take care of the DNS resolution - Apache does not handle name resolution. You'll need either to create CNAME records for each hostname, or a DNS wildcard record. Creating DNS records is beyond the scope of this document.

The internal `tolower` RewriteMap directive is used to ensure that the hostnames being used are all lowercase, so that there is no ambiguity in the directory structure which must be created.

Parentheses used in a REWRITECOND are captured into the backreferences `%1`, `%2`, etc, while parentheses used in REWRITERULE are captured into the backreferences `$1`, `$2`, etc.

As with many techniques discussed in this document, mod_rewrite really isn't the best way to accomplish this task. You should, instead, consider using MOD_VHOST_ALIAS instead, as it will much more gracefully handle anything beyond serving static files, such as any dynamic content, and Alias resolution.

Dynamic Virtual Hosts Using MOD_REWRITE

This extract from `httpd.conf` does the same thing as the first example. The first half is very similar to the corresponding part above, except for some changes, required for backward compatibility and to make the `mod_rewrite` part work properly; the second half configures `mod_rewrite` to do the actual work.

Because `mod_rewrite` runs before other URI translation modules (e.g., `mod_alias`), `mod_rewrite` must be told to explicitly ignore any URLs that would have been handled by those modules. And, because these rules would otherwise bypass any `ScriptAlias` directives, we must have `mod_rewrite` explicitly enact those mappings.

```
# get the server name from the Host: header
UseCanonicalName Off

# splittable logs
LogFormat "%{Host}i %h %l %u %t \"%r\" %s %b" vcommon
CustomLog "logs/access_log" vcommon

<Directory "/www/hosts">
    # ExecCGI is needed here because we can't force
    # CGI execution in the way that ScriptAlias does
    Options FollowSymLinks ExecCGI
</Directory>

RewriteEngine On

# a ServerName derived from a Host: header may be any case at all
RewriteMap  lowercase  int:tolower

## deal with normal documents first:
# allow Alias "/icons/" to work - repeat for other aliases
RewriteCond  "%{REQUEST_URI}"  "!^/icons/"
# allow CGIs to work
RewriteCond  "%{REQUEST_URI}"  "!^/cgi-bin/"
# do the magic
RewriteRule  "^/(.*)$"  "/www/hosts/${lowercase:%{SERVER_NAME}}/docs/$1"

## and now deal with CGIs - we have to force a handler
RewriteCond  "%{REQUEST_URI}"  "^/cgi-bin/"
RewriteRule  "^/(.*)$"  "/www/hosts/${lowercase:%{SERVER_NAME}}/cgi-bin/$1"  [H=cgi-script
```

Using a Separate Virtual Host Configuration File

This arrangement uses more advanced MOD_REWRITE features to work out the translation from virtual host to document root, from a separate configuration file. This provides more flexibility, but requires more complicated configuration.

The `vhost.map` file should look something like this:

```
customer-1.example.com /www/customers/1
customer-2.example.com /www/customers/2
# ...
customer-N.example.com /www/customers/N
```

The `httpd.conf` should contain the following:

```
RewriteEngine on

RewriteMap   lowercase  int:tolower

# define the map file
RewriteMap   vhost      "txt:/www/conf/vhost.map"

# deal with aliases as above
RewriteCond  "%{REQUEST_URI}"                "!^/icons/"
RewriteCond  "%{REQUEST_URI}"                "!^/cgi-bin/"
RewriteCond  "${lowercase:%{SERVER_NAME}}"   "^(.+)$"
# this does the file-based remap
RewriteCond  "${vhost:%1}"                   "^(/.*)$"
RewriteRule  "^/(.*)$"                       "%1/docs/$1"

RewriteCond  "%{REQUEST_URI}"                "^/cgi-bin/"
RewriteCond  "${lowercase:%{SERVER_NAME}}"   "^(.+)$"
RewriteCond  "${vhost:%1}"                   "^(/.*)$"
RewriteRule  "^/(.*)$"                       "%1/cgi-bin/$1" [H=cgi-script]
```

4.6 Using mod_rewrite for Proxying

This document supplements the MOD_REWRITE reference documentation (p. 804) . It describes how to use the RewriteRule's [P] flag to proxy content to another server. A number of recipes are provided that describe common scenarios.

See also

- Module documentation (p. 804)
- mod_rewrite introduction (p. 137)
- Redirection and remapping (p. 142)
- Controlling access (p. 149)
- Virtual hosts (p. 152)
- Using RewriteMap (p. 156)
- Advanced techniques (p. 162)
- When not to use mod_rewrite (p. 165)

Proxying Content with mod_rewrite

Description: mod_rewrite provides the [P] flag, which allows URLs to be passed, via mod_proxy, to another server. Two examples are given here. In one example, a URL is passed directly to another server, and served as though it were a local URL. In the other example, we proxy missing content to a back-end server.

Solution: To simply map a URL to another server, we use the [P] flag, as follows:

```
RewriteEngine  on
RewriteBase    "/products/"
RewriteRule    "^widget/(.*)$"  "http://product.example.com/widget/$1"  [P]
ProxyPassReverse "/products/widget/" "http://product.example.com/widget/"
```

In the second example, we proxy the request only if we can't find the resource locally. This can be very useful when you're migrating from one server to another, and you're not sure if all the content has been migrated yet.

```
RewriteCond "%{REQUEST_FILENAME}"       !-f
RewriteCond "%{REQUEST_FILENAME}"       !-d
RewriteRule "^/(.*)" "http://old.example.com/$1" [P]
ProxyPassReverse "/" "http://old.example.com/"
```

Discussion: In each case, we add a PROXYPASSREVERSE directive to ensure that any redirects issued by the backend are correctly passed on to the client.

Consider using either PROXYPASS or PROXYPASSMATCH whenever possible in preference to mod_rewrite.

4.7 Using RewriteMap

This document supplements the MOD_REWRITE reference documentation (p. 804) . It describes the use of the REWRITEMAP directive, and provides examples of each of the various `RewriteMap` types.

Note that many of these examples won't work unchanged in your particular server configuration, so it's important that you understand them, rather than merely cutting and pasting the examples into your configuration.

See also

- Module documentation (p. 804)
- mod_rewrite introduction (p. 137)
- Redirection and remapping (p. 142)
- Controlling access (p. 149)
- Virtual hosts (p. 152)
- Proxying (p. 155)
- Advanced techniques (p. 162)
- When not to use mod_rewrite (p. 165)

Introduction

The REWRITEMAP directive defines an external function which can be called in the context of REWRITERULE or REWRITECOND directives to perform rewriting that is too complicated, or too specialized to be performed just by regular expressions. The source of this lookup can be any of the types listed in the sections below, and enumerated in the REWRITEMAP reference documentation.

The syntax of the `RewriteMap` directive is as follows:

```
RewriteMap MapName MapType:MapSource
```

The *MapName* is an arbitray name that you assign to the map, and which you will use in directives later on. Arguments are passed to the map via the following syntax:

`$`{ *MapName* : *LookupKey* }
`$`{ *MapName* : *LookupKey* | *DefaultValue* }

When such a construct occurs, the map *MapName* is consulted and the key *LookupKey* is looked-up. If the key is found, the map-function construct is substituted by *SubstValue*. If the key is not found then it is substituted by *DefaultValue* or by the empty string if no *DefaultValue* was specified.

For example, you might define a REWRITEMAP as:

```
RewriteMap examplemap "txt:/path/to/file/map.txt"
```

You would then be able to use this map in a REWRITERULE as follows:

```
RewriteRule "^/ex/(.*)" "${examplemap:$1}"
```

A default value can be specified in the event that nothing is found in the map:

```
RewriteRule "^/ex/(.*)" "${examplemap:$1|/not_found.html}"
```

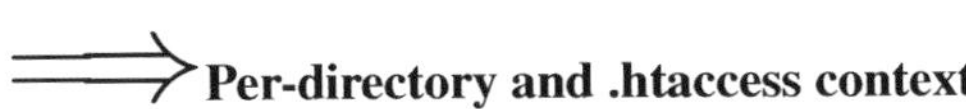

Per-directory and .htaccess context

> The `RewriteMap` directive may not be used in <Directory> sections or `.htaccess` files. You must declare the map in server or virtualhost context. You may use the map, once created, in your `RewriteRule` and `RewriteCond` directives in those scopes. You just can't **declare** it in those scopes.

The sections that follow describe the various *MapTypes* that may be used, and give examples of each.

txt: Plain text maps

When a MapType of `txt` is used, the MapSource is a filesystem path to a plain-text mapping file, containing space-separated key/value pair per line. Optionally, a line may be contain a comment, starting with a '#' character.

For example, the following might be valid entries in a map file.

\# Comment line
MatchingKey SubstValue
MatchingKey SubstValue # comment

When the RewriteMap is invoked the argument is looked for in the first argument of a line, and, if found, the substitution value is returned.

For example, we might use a mapfile to translate product names to product IDs for easier-to-remember URLs, using the following recipe:

Product to ID configuration

```
RewriteMap product2id "txt:/etc/apache2/productmap.txt"
RewriteRule "^/product/(.*)" "/prods.php?id=${product2id:$1|NOTFOUND}" [PT]
```

We assume here that the `prods.php` script knows what to do when it received an argument of `id=NOTFOUND` when a product is not found in the lookup map.

The file `/etc/apache2/productmap.txt` then contains the following:

Product to ID map

```
##
## productmap.txt - Product to ID map file
##
television 993
stereo 198
fishingrod 043
basketball 418
telephone 328
```

Thus, when `http://example.com/product/television` is requested, the `RewriteRule` is applied, and the request is internally mapped to `/prods.php?id=993`.

⟹ **Note: .htaccess files**

> The example given is crafted to be used in server or virtualhost scope. If you're planning to use this in a `.htaccess` file, you'll need to remove the leading slash from the rewrite pattern in order for it to match anything:

```
RewriteRule "^product/(.*)" "/prods.php?id=${product2id:$1|NOTFOUND}" [PT]
```

**Cached lookups**

The looked-up keys are cached by httpd until the `mtime` (modified time) of the mapfile changes, or the httpd server is restarted. This ensures better performance on maps that are called by many requests.

rnd: Randomized Plain Text

When a MapType of `rnd` is used, the MapSource is a filesystem path to a plain-text mapping file, each line of which contains a key, and one or more values separated by `|`. One of these values will be chosen at random if the key is matched.

For example, you might use the following map file and directives to provide a random load balancing between several back-end servers, via a reverse-proxy. Images are sent to one of the servers in the 'static' pool, while everything else is sent to one of the 'dynamic' pool.

Rewrite map file

```
##
## map.txt -- rewriting map
##
static www1|www2|www3|www4
dynamic www5|www6
```

Configuration directives

```
RewriteMap servers "rnd:/path/to/file/map.txt"

RewriteRule "^/(.*\.(png|gif|jpg))" "http://${servers:static}/$1" [NC,P,L]
RewriteRule "^/(.*)" "http://${servers:dynamic}/$1" [P,L]
```

So, when an image is requested and the first of these rules is matched, `RewriteMap` looks up the string `static` in the map file, which returns one of the specified hostnames at random, which is then used in the `RewriteRule` target.

If you wanted to have one of the servers more likely to be chosen (for example, if one of the server has more memory than the others, and so can handle more requests) simply list it more times in the map file.

```
static www1|www1|www2|www3|www4
```

dbm: DBM Hash File

When a MapType of `dbm` is used, the MapSource is a filesystem path to a DBM database file containing key/value pairs to be used in the mapping. This works exactly the same way as the `txt` map, but is much faster, because a DBM is indexed, whereas a text file is not. This allows more rapid access to the desired key.

You may optionally specify a particular dbm type:

```
RewriteMap examplemap "dbm=sdbm:/etc/apache/mapfile.dbm"
```

The type can be sdbm, gdbm, ndbm or db. However, it is recommended that you just use the httxt2dbm (p. 315) utility that is provided with Apache HTTP Server, as it will use the correct DBM library, matching the one that was used when httpd itself was built.

To create a dbm file, first create a text map file as described in the txt section. Then run `httxt2dbm`:

```
$ httxt2dbm -i mapfile.txt -o mapfile.map
```

You can then reference the resulting file in your `RewriteMap` directive:

```
RewriteMap mapname "dbm:/etc/apache/mapfile.map"
```

⟹ Note that with some dbm types, more than one file is generated, with a common base name. For example, you may have two files named `mapfile.map.dir` and `mapfiile.map.pag`. This is normal, and you need only use the base name `mapfile.map` in your `RewriteMap` directive.

**Cached lookups**

The looked-up keys are cached by httpd until the `mtime` (modified time) of the mapfile changes, or the httpd server is restarted. This ensures better performance on maps that are called by many requests.

int: Internal Function

When a MapType of `int` is used, the MapSource is one of the available internal RewriteMap functions. Module authors can provide additional internal functions by registering them with the `ap_register_rewrite_mapfunc` API. The functions that are provided by default are:

- **toupper**:
  Converts the key to all upper case.
- **tolower**:
  Converts the key to all lower case.
- **escape**:
  Translates special characters in the key to hex-encodings.
- **unescape**:
  Translates hex-encodings in the key back to special characters.

To use one of these functions, create a `RewriteMap` referencing the int function, and then use that in your `RewriteRule`:

Redirect a URI to an all-lowercase version of itself

```
RewriteMap lc int:tolower
RewriteRule "(.*?[A-Z]+.*)" "${lc:$1}" [R]
```

⟹ Please note that the example offered here is for illustration purposes only, and is not a recommendation. If you want to make URLs case-insensitive, consider using MOD_SPELING instead.

prg: External Rewriting Program

When a MapType of `prg` is used, the MapSource is a filesystem path to an executable program which will providing the mapping behavior. This can be a compiled binary file, or a program in an interpreted language such as Perl or Python.

This program is started once, when the Apache HTTP Server is started, and then communicates with the rewriting engine via `STDIN` and `STDOUT`. That is, for each map function lookup, it expects one argument via `STDIN`, and should return one new-line terminated response string on `STDOUT`. If there is no corresponding lookup value, the map program should return the four-character string `"NULL"` to indicate this.

External rewriting programs are not started if they're defined in a context that does not have REWRITEENGINE set to `on`.

This feature utilizes the `rewrite-map` mutex, which is required for reliable communication with the program. The mutex mechanism and lock file can be configured with the MUTEX directive.

A simple example is shown here which will replace all dashes with underscores in a request URI.

Rewrite configuration

```
RewriteMap d2u "prg:/www/bin/dash2under.pl"
RewriteRule "-" "${d2u:%{REQUEST_URI}}"
```

dash2under.pl

```
#!/usr/bin/perl
$| = 1; # Turn off I/O buffering
while (<STDIN>) {
    s/-/_/g; # Replace dashes with underscores
    print $_;
}
```

⟹ **Caution!**

- Keep your rewrite map program as simple as possible. If the program hangs, it will cause httpd to wait indefinitely for a response from the map, which will, in turn, cause httpd to stop responding to requests.
- Be sure to turn off buffering in your program. In Perl this is done by the second line in the example script: `$| = 1;` This will of course vary in other languages. Buffered I/O will cause httpd to wait for the output, and so it will hang.
- Remember that there is only one copy of the program, started at server startup. All requests will need to go through this one bottleneck. This can cause significant slowdowns if many requests must go through this process, or if the script itself is very slow.

dbd or fastdbd: SQL Query

When a MapType of `dbd` or `fastdbd` is used, the MapSource is a SQL SELECT statement that takes a single argument and returns a single value.

MOD_DBD will need to be configured to point at the right database for this statement to be executed.

There are two forms of this MapType. Using a MapType of `dbd` causes the query to be executed with each map request, while using `fastdbd` caches the database lookups internally. So, while `fastdbd` is more efficient, and therefore faster, it won't pick up on changes to the database until the server is restarted.

If a query returns more than one row, a random row from the result set is used.

Example

```
RewriteMap myquery "fastdbd:SELECT destination FROM rewrite WHERE source = %s"
```

Summary

The RewriteMap directive can occur more than once. For each mapping-function use one RewriteMap directive to declare its rewriting mapfile.

While you cannot **declare** a map in per-directory context (`.htaccess` files or <Directory> blocks) it is possible to **use** this map in per-directory context.

4.8 Advanced Techniques with mod_rewrite

This document supplements the MOD_REWRITE reference documentation (p. 804) . It provides a few advanced techniques using mod_rewrite.

Note that many of these examples won't work unchanged in your particular server configuration, so it's important that you understand them, rather than merely cutting and pasting the examples into your configuration.

See also

- Module documentation (p. 804)
- mod_rewrite introduction (p. 137)
- Redirection and remapping (p. 142)
- Controlling access (p. 149)
- Virtual hosts (p. 152)
- Proxying (p. 155)
- Using RewriteMap (p. 156)
- When not to use mod_rewrite (p. 165)

URL-based sharding across multiple backends

Description: A common technique for distributing the burden of server load or storage space is called "sharding". When using this method, a front-end server will use the url to consistently "shard" users or objects to separate backend servers.

Solution: A mapping is maintained, from users to target servers, in external map files. They look like:

```
user1 physical_host_of_user1
user2 physical_host_of_user2
:  :
```

We put this into a `map.users-to-hosts` file. The aim is to map;

```
/u/user1/anypath
```

to

```
http://physical_host_of_user1/u/user/anypath
```

thus every URL path need not be valid on every backend physical host. The following ruleset does this for us with the help of the map files assuming that server0 is a default server which will be used if a user has no entry in the map:

```
RewriteEngine on
RewriteMap      users-to-hosts   "txt:/path/to/map.users-to-hosts"
RewriteRule   "^/u/([^/]+)/?(.*)"   "http://${users-to-hosts:$1|server0}/u/$1/$2"
```

See the REWRITEMAP documentation for more discussion of the syntax of this directive.

On-the-fly Content-Regeneration

Description: We wish to dynamically generate content, but store it statically once it is generated. This rule will check for the existence of the static file, and if it's not there, generate it. The static files can be removed periodically, if desired (say, via cron) and will be regenerated on demand.

Solution: This is done via the following ruleset:

```
# This example is valid in per-directory context only
RewriteCond "%{REQUEST_URI}"   "!-U"
RewriteRule "^(.+)\.html$"          "/regenerate_page.cgi"   [PT,L]
```

The `-U` operator determines whether the test string (in this case, `REQUEST_URI`) is a valid URL. It does this via a subrequest. In the event that this subrequest fails - that is, the requested resource doesn't exist - this rule invokes the CGI program `/regenerate_page.cgi`, which generates the requested resource and saves it into the document directory, so that the next time it is requested, a static copy can be served.

In this way, documents that are infrequently updated can be served in static form. if documents need to be refreshed, they can be deleted from the document directory, and they will then be regenerated the next time they are requested.

Load Balancing

Description: We wish to randomly distribute load across several servers using mod_rewrite.

Solution: We'll use REWRITEMAP and a list of servers to accomplish this.

```
RewriteEngine on
RewriteMap lb "rnd:/path/to/serverlist.txt"
RewriteRule "^/(.*)" "http://${lb:servers}/$1" [P,L]
```

`serverlist.txt` will contain a list of the servers:

```
## serverlist.txt
servers one.example.com|two.example.com|three.example.com
```

If you want one particular server to get more of the load than the others, add it more times to the list.

Discussion Apache comes with a load-balancing module - MOD_PROXY_BALANCER - which is far more flexible and featureful than anything you can cobble together using mod_rewrite.

Structured Userdirs

Description: Some sites with thousands of users use a structured homedir layout, *i.e.* each homedir is in a subdirectory which begins (for instance) with the first character of the username. So, `/~larry/anypath` is `/home/`**`l`**`/larry/public_html/anypath` while `/~waldo/anypath` is `/home/`**`w`**`/waldo/public_html/anypath`.

Solution: We use the following ruleset to expand the tilde URLs into the above layout.

```
RewriteEngine on
RewriteRule   "^/~(([a-z])[a-z0-9]+)(.*)"  "/home/$2/$1/public_html$3"
```

Redirecting Anchors

Description: By default, redirecting to an HTML anchor doesn't work, because mod_rewrite escapes the # character, turning it into `%23`. This, in turn, breaks the redirection.

Solution: Use the `[NE]` flag on the `RewriteRule`. NE stands for No Escape.

Discussion: This technique will of course also work with other special characters that mod_rewrite, by default, URL-encodes.

Time-Dependent Rewriting

Description: We wish to use mod_rewrite to serve different content based on the time of day.

Solution: There are a lot of variables named `TIME_xxx` for rewrite conditions. In conjunction with the special lexicographic comparison patterns `<STRING`, `>STRING` and `=STRING` we can do time-dependent redirects:

```
RewriteEngine on
RewriteCond   "%{TIME_HOUR}%{TIME_MIN}" ">0700"
RewriteCond   "%{TIME_HOUR}%{TIME_MIN}" "<1900"
RewriteRule   "^foo\.html$"             "foo.day.html" [L]
RewriteRule   "^foo\.html$"             "foo.night.html"
```

This provides the content of `foo.day.html` under the URL `foo.html` from `07:01-18:59` and at the remaining time the contents of `foo.night.html`.

> ! MOD_CACHE, intermediate proxies and browsers may each cache responses and cause the either page to be shown outside of the time-window configured. MOD_EXPIRES may be used to control this effect. You are, of course, much better off simply serving the content dynamically, and customizing it based on the time of day.

Set Environment Variables Based On URL Parts

Description: At time, we want to maintain some kind of status when we perform a rewrite. For example, you want to make a note that you've done that rewrite, so that you can check later to see if a request can via that rewrite. One way to do this is by setting an environment variable.

Solution: Use the [E] flag to set an environment variable.

```
RewriteEngine on
RewriteRule   "^/horse/(.*)"   "/pony/$1" [E=rewritten:1]
```

Later in your ruleset you might check for this environment variable using a RewriteCond:

```
RewriteCond "%{ENV:rewritten}" "=1"
```

Note that environment variables do not survive an external redirect. You might consider using the [CO] flag to set a cookie.

4.9 When not to use mod_rewrite

This document supplements the MOD_REWRITE reference documentation (p. 804) . It describes perhaps one of the most important concepts about mod_rewrite - namely, when to avoid using it.

mod_rewrite should be considered a last resort, when other alternatives are found wanting. Using it when there are simpler alternatives leads to configurations which are confusing, fragile, and hard to maintain. Understanding what other alternatives are available is a very important step towards mod_rewrite mastery.

Note that many of these examples won't work unchanged in your particular server configuration, so it's important that you understand them, rather than merely cutting and pasting the examples into your configuration.

The most common situation in which MOD_REWRITE is the right tool is when the very best solution requires access to the server configuration files, and you don't have that access. Some configuration directives are only available in the server configuration file. So if you are in a hosting situation where you only have .htaccess files to work with, you may need to resort to MOD_REWRITE.

See also

- Module documentation (p. 804)
- mod_rewrite introduction (p. 137)
- Redirection and remapping (p. 142)
- Controlling access (p. 149)
- Virtual hosts (p. 152)
- Proxying (p. 155)
- Using RewriteMap (p. 156)
- Advanced techniques (p. 162)

Simple Redirection

MOD_ALIAS provides the REDIRECT and REDIRECTMATCH directives, which provide a means to redirect one URL to another. This kind of simple redirection of one URL, or a class of URLs, to somewhere else, should be accomplished using these directives rather than REWRITERULE. `RedirectMatch` allows you to include a regular expression in your redirection criteria, providing many of the benefits of using `RewriteRule`.

A common use for `RewriteRule` is to redirect an entire class of URLs. For example, all URLs in the `/one` directory must be redirected to `http://one.example.com/`, or perhaps all `http` requests must be redirected to `https`.

These situations are better handled by the `Redirect` directive. Remember that `Redirect` preserves path information. That is to say, a redirect for a URL `/one` will also redirect all URLs under that, such as `/one/two.html` and `/one/three/four.html`.

To redirect URLs under `/one` to `http://one.example.com`, do the following:

```
Redirect /one/ http://one.example.com/
```

To redirect one hostname to another, for example `example.com` to `www.example.com`, see the Canonical Hostnames (p. 142) recipe.

To redirect `http` URLs to `https`, do the following:

```
<VirtualHost *:80>
    ServerName www.example.com
    Redirect "/" "https://www.example.com/"
```

```
</VirtualHost >

<VirtualHost *:443>
    ServerName www.example.com
    # ... SSL configuration goes here
</VirtualHost >
```

The use of RewriteRule to perform this task may be appropriate if there are other RewriteRule directives in the same scope. This is because, when there are Redirect and RewriteRule directives in the same scope, the RewriteRule directives will run first, regardless of the order of appearance in the configuration file.

In the case of the *http-to-https* redirection, the use of RewriteRule would be appropriate if you don't have access to the main server configuration file, and are obliged to perform this task in a .htaccess file instead.

URL Aliasing

The ALIAS directive provides mapping from a URI to a directory - usually a directory outside of your DOCUMENTROOT. Although it is possible to perform this mapping with mod_rewrite, Alias is the preferred method, for reasons of simplicity and performance.

Using Alias

```
Alias "/cats" "/var/www/virtualhosts/felines/htdocs"
```

The use of mod_rewrite to perform this mapping may be appropriate when you do not have access to the server configuration files. Alias may only be used in server or virtualhost context, and not in a .htaccess file.

Symbolic links would be another way to accomplish the same thing, if you have Options FollowSymLinks enabled on your server.

Virtual Hosting

Although it is possible to handle virtual hosts with mod_rewrite (p. 152) , it is seldom the right way. Creating individual <VirtualHost> blocks is almost always the right way to go. In the event that you have an enormous number of virtual hosts, consider using MOD_VHOST_ALIAS to create these hosts automatically.

Modules such as MOD_MACRO are also useful for creating a large number of virtual hosts dynamically.

Using MOD_REWRITE for vitualhost creation may be appropriate if you are using a hosting service that does not provide you access to the server configuration files, and you are therefore restricted to configuration using .htaccess files.

See the virtual hosts with mod_rewrite (p. 152) document for more details on how you might accomplish this if it still seems like the right approach.

Simple Proxying

RewriteRule provides the [P] (p. 168) flag to pass rewritten URIs through MOD_PROXY.

```
RewriteRule "^/?images(.*)" "http://imageserver.local/images$1" [P]
```

However, in many cases, when there is no actual pattern matching needed, as in the example shown above, the PROXYPASS directive is a better choice. The example here could be rendered as:

```
ProxyPass "/images/" "http://imageserver.local/images/"
```

Note that whether you use REWRITERULE or PROXYPASS, you'll still need to use the PROXYPASSREVERSE directive to catch redirects issued from the back-end server:

```
ProxyPassReverse "/images/" "http://imageserver.local/images/"
```

You may need to use `RewriteRule` instead when there are other `RewriteRules` in effect in the same scope, as a `RewriteRule` will usually take effect before a `ProxyPass`, and so may preempt what you're trying to accomplish.

Environment Variable Testing

MOD_REWRITE is frequently used to take a particular action based on the presence or absence of a particular environment variable or request header. This can be done more efficiently using the <IF>.

Consider, for example, the common scenario where REWRITERULE is used to enforce a canonical hostname, such as `www.example.com` instead of `example.com`. This can be done using the <IF> directive, as shown here:

```
<If "req('Host') != 'www.example.com'">
    Redirect "/" "http://www.example.com/"
</If>
```

This technique can be used to take actions based on any request header, response header, or environment variable, replacing MOD_REWRITE in many common scenarios.

See especially the expression evaluation documentation (p. 89) for a overview of what types of expressions you can use in <If> sections, and in certain other directives.

4.10 RewriteRule Flags

This document discusses the flags which are available to the REWRITERULE directive, providing detailed explanations and examples.

See also

- Module documentation (p. 804)
- mod_rewrite introduction (p. 137)
- Redirection and remapping (p. 142)
- Controlling access (p. 149)
- Virtual hosts (p. 152)
- Proxying (p. 155)
- Using RewriteMap (p. 156)
- Advanced techniques (p. 162)
- When not to use mod_rewrite (p. 165)

Introduction

A REWRITERULE can have its behavior modified by one or more flags. Flags are included in square brackets at the end of the rule, and multiple flags are separated by commas.

```
RewriteRule pattern target [Flag1,Flag2,Flag3]
```

Each flag (with a few exceptions) has a short form, such as `CO`, as well as a longer form, such as `cookie`. While it is most common to use the short form, it is recommended that you familiarize yourself with the long form, so that you remember what each flag is supposed to do. Some flags take one or more arguments. Flags are not case sensitive.

Flags that alter metadata associated with the request (T=, H=, E=) have no affect in per-directory and htaccess context, when a substitution (other than '-') is performed during the same round of rewrite processing.

Presented here are each of the available flags, along with an example of how you might use them.

B (escape backreferences)

The [B] flag instructs REWRITERULE to escape non-alphanumeric characters before applying the transformation.

`mod_rewrite` has to unescape URLs before mapping them, so backreferences are unescaped at the time they are applied. Using the B flag, non-alphanumeric characters in backreferences will be escaped. For example, consider the rule:

```
RewriteRule "^search/(.*)$" "/search.php?term=$1"
```

Given a search term of 'x & y/z', a browser will encode it as 'x%20%26%20y%2Fz', making the request 'search/x%20%26%20y%2Fz'. Without the B flag, this rewrite rule will map to 'search.php?term=x & y/z', which isn't a valid URL, and so would be encoded as `search.php?term=x%20&y%2Fz=`, which is not what was intended.

With the B flag set on this same rule, the parameters are re-encoded before being passed on to the output URL, resulting in a correct mapping to `/search.php?term=x%20%26%20y%2Fz`.

Note that you may also need to set ALLOWENCODEDSLASHES to `On` to get this particular example to work, as httpd does not allow encoded slashes in URLs, and returns a 404 if it sees one.

This escaping is particularly necessary in a proxy situation, when the backend may break if presented with an unescaped URL.

C—chain

The [C] or [chain] flag indicates that the REWRITERULE is chained to the next rule. That is, if the rule matches, then it is processed as usual and control moves on to the next rule. However, if it does not match, then the next rule, and any other rules that are chained together, are skipped.

CO—cookie

The [CO], or [cookie] flag, allows you to set a cookie when a particular REWRITERULE matches. The argument consists of three required fields and four optional fields.

The full syntax for the flag, including all attributes, is as follows:

```
[CO=NAME:VALUE:DOMAIN:lifetime:path:secure:httponly]
```

If a literal ':' character is needed in any of the cookie fields, an alternate syntax is available. To opt-in to the alternate syntax, the cookie "Name" should be preceded with a ';' character, and field separators should be specified as ';'.

```
[CO=;NAME;VALUE:MOREVALUE;DOMAIN;lifetime;path;secure;httponly]
```

You must declare a name, a value, and a domain for the cookie to be set.

Domain The domain for which you want the cookie to be valid. This may be a hostname, such as `www.example.com`, or it may be a domain, such as `.example.com`. It must be at least two parts separated by a dot. That is, it may not be merely `.com` or `.net`. Cookies of that kind are forbidden by the cookie security model.

You may optionally also set the following values:

Lifetime The time for which the cookie will persist, in minutes. A value of 0 indicates that the cookie will persist only for the current browser session. This is the default value if none is specified.

Path The path, on the current website, for which the cookie is valid, such as `/customers/` or `/files/download/`. By default, this is set to / - that is, the entire website.

Secure If set to `secure`, `true`, or `1`, the cookie will only be permitted to be translated via secure (https) connections.

httponly If set to `HttpOnly`, `true`, or `1`, the cookie will have the `HttpOnly` flag set, which means that the cookie is inaccessible to JavaScript code on browsers that support this feature.

Consider this example:

```
RewriteEngine On
RewriteRule "^/index\.html" "-" [CO=frontdoor:yes:.example.com:1440:/]
```

In the example give, the rule doesn't rewrite the request. The "-" rewrite target tells mod_rewrite to pass the request through unchanged. Instead, it sets a cookie called 'frontdoor' to a value of 'yes'. The cookie is valid for any host in the `.example.com` domain. It is set to expire in 1440 minutes (24 hours) and is returned for all URIs.

DPI—discardpath

The DPI flag causes the PATH_INFO portion of the rewritten URI to be discarded.

This flag is available in version 2.2.12 and later.

In per-directory context, the URI each REWRITERULE compares against is the concatenation of the current values of the URI and PATH_INFO.

The current URI can be the initial URI as requested by the client, the result of a previous round of mod_rewrite processing, or the result of a prior rule in the current round of mod_rewrite processing.

In contrast, the PATH_INFO that is appended to the URI before each rule reflects only the value of PATH_INFO before this round of mod_rewrite processing. As a consequence, if large portions of the URI are matched and copied into a substitution in multiple REWRITERULE directives, without regard for which parts of the URI came from the current PATH_INFO, the final URI may have multiple copies of PATH_INFO appended to it.

Use this flag on any substitution where the PATH_INFO that resulted from the previous mapping of this request to the filesystem is not of interest. This flag permanently forgets the PATH_INFO established before this round of mod_rewrite processing began. PATH_INFO will not be recalculated until the current round of mod_rewrite processing completes. Subsequent rules during this round of processing will see only the direct result of substitutions, without any PATH_INFO appended.

E—env

With the [E], or [env] flag, you can set the value of an environment variable. Note that some environment variables may be set after the rule is run, thus unsetting what you have set. See the Environment Variables document (p. 82) for more details on how Environment variables work.

The full syntax for this flag is:

```
[E=VAR:VAL] [E=!VAR]
```

`VAL` may contain backreferences (`$N` or `%N`) which are expanded.

Using the short form

```
[E=VAR]
```

you can set the environment variable named `VAR` to an empty value.

The form

```
[E=!VAR]
```

allows to unset a previously set environment variable named `VAR`.

Environment variables can then be used in a variety of contexts, including CGI programs, other RewriteRule directives, or CustomLog directives.

The following example sets an environment variable called 'image' to a value of '1' if the requested URI is an image file. Then, that environment variable is used to exclude those requests from the access log.

```
RewriteRule "\.(png|gif|jpg)$" "-" [E=image:1]
CustomLog "logs/access_log" combined env=!image
```

Note that this same effect can be obtained using SETENVIF. This technique is offered as an example, not as a recommendation.

END

Using the [END] flag terminates not only the current round of rewrite processing (like [L]) but also prevents any subsequent rewrite processing from occurring in per-directory (htaccess) context.

This does not apply to new requests resulting from external redirects.

F—forbidden

Using the [F] flag causes the server to return a 403 Forbidden status code to the client. While the same behavior can be accomplished using the DENY directive, this allows more flexibility in assigning a Forbidden status.

The following rule will forbid `.exe` files from being downloaded from your server.

```
RewriteRule "\.exe" "-" [F]
```

This example uses the `"-"` syntax for the rewrite target, which means that the requested URI is not modified. There's no reason to rewrite to another URI, if you're going to forbid the request.

When using [F], an [L] is implied - that is, the response is returned immediately, and no further rules are evaluated.

G—gone

The [G] flag forces the server to return a 410 Gone status with the response. This indicates that a resource used to be available, but is no longer available.

As with the [F] flag, you will typically use the `"-"` syntax for the rewrite target when using the [G] flag:

```
RewriteRule "oldproduct" "-" [G,NC]
```

When using [G], an [L] is implied - that is, the response is returned immediately, and no further rules are evaluated.

H—handler

Forces the resulting request to be handled with the specified handler. For example, one might use this to force all files without a file extension to be parsed by the php handler:

```
RewriteRule "!\." "-" [H=application/x-httpd-php]
```

The regular expression above - `!\.` - will match any request that does not contain the literal `.` character.

This can be also used to force the handler based on some conditions. For example, the following snippet used in per-server context allows `.php` files to be *displayed* by `mod_php` if they are requested with the `.phps` extension:

```
RewriteRule "^(/source/.+\.php)s$" "$1" [H=application/x-httpd-php-source]
```

The regular expression above - `^(/source/.+\.php)s$` - will match any request that starts with `/source/` followed by 1 or n characters followed by `.phps` literally. The backreference $1 referrers to the captured match within parenthesis of the regular expression.

L—last

The [L] flag causes MOD_REWRITE to stop processing the rule set. In most contexts, this means that if the rule matches, no further rules will be processed. This corresponds to the `last` command in Perl, or the `break` command in C. Use this flag to indicate that the current rule should be applied immediately without considering further rules.

If you are using REWRITERULE in either `.htaccess` files or in <DIRECTORY> sections, it is important to have some understanding of how the rules are processed. The simplified form of this is that once the rules have been processed, the rewritten request is handed back to the URL parsing engine to do what it may with it. It is possible that as the rewritten request is handled, the `.htaccess` file or <DIRECTORY> section may be encountered again, and thus the ruleset may be run again from the start. Most commonly this will happen if one of the rules causes a redirect - either internal or external - causing the request process to start over.

It is therefore important, if you are using REWRITERULE directives in one of these contexts, that you take explicit steps to avoid rules looping, and not count solely on the [L] flag to terminate execution of a series of rules, as shown below.

An alternative flag, [END], can be used to terminate not only the current round of rewrite processing but prevent any subsequent rewrite processing from occurring in per-directory (htaccess) context. This does not apply to new requests resulting from external redirects.

The example given here will rewrite any request to `index.php`, giving the original request as a query string argument to `index.php`, however, the REWRITECOND ensures that if the request is already for `index.php`, the REWRITERULE will be skipped.

```
RewriteBase "/"
RewriteCond "%{REQUEST_URI}" "!=/index.php"
RewriteRule "^(.*)" "/index.php?req=$1" [L,PT]
```

N—next

The [N] flag causes the ruleset to start over again from the top, using the result of the ruleset so far as a starting point. Use with extreme caution, as it may result in loop.

The [Next] flag could be used, for example, if you wished to replace a certain string or letter repeatedly in a request. The example shown here will replace A with B everywhere in a request, and will continue doing so until there are no more As to be replaced.

```
RewriteRule "(.*)A(.*)" "$1B$2" [N]
```

You can think of this as a `while` loop: While this pattern still matches (i.e., while the URI still contains an `A`), perform this substitution (i.e., replace the `A` with a `B`).

In 2.4.8 and later, this module returns an error after 32,000 iterations to protect against unintended looping. An alternative maximum number of iterations can be specified by adding to the N flag.

```
# Be willing to replace 1 character in each pass of the loop
RewriteRule "(.+)[><;]$" "$1" [N=64000]
# ... or, give up if after 10 loops
RewriteRule "(.+)[><;]$" "$1" [N=10]
```

NC—nocase

Use of the [NC] flag causes the REWRITERULE to be matched in a case-insensitive manner. That is, it doesn't care whether letters appear as upper-case or lower-case in the matched URI.

In the example below, any request for an image file will be proxied to your dedicated image server. The match is case-insensitive, so that `.jpg` and `.JPG` files are both acceptable, for example.

```
RewriteRule "(.*\.(jpg|gif|png))$" "http://images.example.com$1" [P,NC]
```

NE—noescape

By default, special characters, such as `&` and `?`, for example, will be converted to their hexcode equivalent. Using the [NE] flag prevents that from happening.

```
RewriteRule "^/anchor/(.+)" "/bigpage.html#$1" [NE,R]
```

The above example will redirect `/anchor/xyz` to `/bigpage.html#xyz`. Omitting the [NE] will result in the # being converted to its hexcode equivalent, `%23`, which will then result in a 404 Not Found error condition.

NS—nosubreq

Use of the [NS] flag prevents the rule from being used on subrequests. For example, a page which is included using an SSI (Server Side Include) is a subrequest, and you may want to avoid rewrites happening on those subrequests. Also, when MOD_DIR tries to find out information about possible directory default files (such as `index.html` files), this is an internal subrequest, and you often want to avoid rewrites on such subrequests. On subrequests, it is not always useful, and can even cause errors, if the complete set of rules are applied. Use this flag to exclude problematic rules.

To decide whether or not to use this rule: if you prefix URLs with CGI-scripts, to force them to be processed by the CGI-script, it's likely that you will run into problems (or significant overhead) on sub-requests. In these cases, use this flag.

Images, javascript files, or css files, loaded as part of an HTML page, are not subrequests - the browser requests them as separate HTTP requests.

P—proxy

Use of the [P] flag causes the request to be handled by MOD_PROXY, and handled via a proxy request. For example, if you wanted all image requests to be handled by a back-end image server, you might do something like the following:

```
RewriteRule "/(.*)\.(jpg|gif|png)$" "http://images.example.com/$1.$2" [P]
```

Use of the [P] flag implies [L] - that is, the request is immediately pushed through the proxy, and any following rules will not be considered.

You must make sure that the substitution string is a valid URI (typically starting with `http://`*hostname*) which can be handled by the MOD_PROXY. If not, you will get an error from the proxy module. Use this flag to achieve a more powerful implementation of the PROXYPASS directive, to map remote content into the namespace of the local server.

Security Warning

Take care when constructing the target URL of the rule, considering the security impact from allowing the client influence over the set of URLs to which your server will act as a proxy. Ensure that the scheme and hostname part of the URL is either fixed, or does not allow the client undue influence.

! Performance warning

Using this flag triggers the use of MOD_PROXY, without handling of persistent connections. This means the performance of your proxy will be better if you set it up with PROXYPASS or PROXYPASSMATCH
This is because this flag triggers the use of the default worker, which does not handle connection pooling.
Avoid using this flag and prefer those directives, whenever you can.

Note: MOD_PROXY must be enabled in order to use this flag.

PT—passthrough

The target (or substitution string) in a RewriteRule is assumed to be a file path, by default. The use of the [PT] flag causes it to be treated as a URI instead. That is to say, the use of the [PT] flag causes the result of the REWRITERULE to be passed back through URL mapping, so that location-based mappings, such as ALIAS, REDIRECT, or SCRIPTALIAS, for example, might have a chance to take effect.

If, for example, you have an ALIAS for /icons, and have a REWRITERULE pointing there, you should use the [PT] flag to ensure that the ALIAS is evaluated.

```
Alias "/icons" "/usr/local/apache/icons"
RewriteRule "/pics/(.+)\.jpg$" "/icons/$1.gif" [PT]
```

Omission of the [PT] flag in this case will cause the Alias to be ignored, resulting in a 'File not found' error being returned.

The `PT` flag implies the `L` flag: rewriting will be stopped in order to pass the request to the next phase of processing.

Note that the `PT` flag is implied in per-directory contexts such as <DIRECTORY> sections or in `.htaccess` files. The only way to circumvent that is to rewrite to `-`.

QSA—qsappend

When the replacement URI contains a query string, the default behavior of REWRITERULE is to discard the existing query string, and replace it with the newly generated one. Using the [QSA] flag causes the query strings to be combined.

Consider the following rule:

```
RewriteRule "/pages/(.+)" "/page.php?page=$1" [QSA]
```

With the [QSA] flag, a request for `/pages/123?one=two` will be mapped to `/page.php?page=123&one=two`. Without the [QSA] flag, that same request will be mapped to `/page.php?page=123` - that is, the existing query string will be discarded.

QSD—qsdiscard

When the requested URI contains a query string, and the target URI does not, the default behavior of REWRITERULE is to copy that query string to the target URI. Using the [QSD] flag causes the query string to be discarded.

This flag is available in version 2.4.0 and later.

Using [QSD] and [QSA] together will result in [QSD] taking precedence.

If the target URI has a query string, the default behavior will be observed - that is, the original query string will be discarded and replaced with the query string in the `RewriteRule` target URI.

R—redirect

Use of the [R] flag causes a HTTP redirect to be issued to the browser. If a fully-qualified URL is specified (that is, including `http://servername/`) then a redirect will be issued to that location. Otherwise, the current protocol, servername, and port number will be used to generate the URL sent with the redirect.

Any valid HTTP response status code may be specified, using the syntax [R=305], with a 302 status code being used by default if none is specified. The status code specified need not necessarily be a redirect (3xx) status code. However, if a status code is outside the redirect range (300-399) then the substitution string is dropped entirely, and rewriting is stopped as if the `L` were used.

In addition to response status codes, you may also specify redirect status using their symbolic names: `temp` (default), `permanent`, or `seeother`.

You will almost always want to use [R] in conjunction with [L] (that is, use [R,L]) because on its own, the [R] flag prepends `http://thishost[:thisport]` to the URI, but then passes this on to the next rule in the ruleset, which can often result in 'Invalid URI in request' warnings.

S—skip

The [S] flag is used to skip rules that you don't want to run. The syntax of the skip flag is [S=*N*], where *N* signifies the number of rules to skip (provided the REWRITERULE matches). This can be thought of as a `goto` statement in your rewrite ruleset. In the following example, we only want to run the REWRITERULE if the requested URI doesn't correspond with an actual file.

```
# Is the request for a non-existent file?
RewriteCond "%{REQUEST_FILENAME}" "!-f"
RewriteCond "%{REQUEST_FILENAME}" "!-d"
# If so, skip these two RewriteRules
RewriteRule ".?" "-" [S=2]

RewriteRule "(.*\.gif)" "images.php?$1"
RewriteRule "(.*\.html)" "docs.php?$1"
```

This technique is useful because a REWRITECOND only applies to the REWRITERULE immediately following it. Thus, if you want to make a `RewriteCond` apply to several `RewriteRules`, one possible technique is to negate those conditions and add a `RewriteRule` with a [Skip] flag. You can use this to make pseudo if-then-else constructs: The last rule of the then-clause becomes `skip=N`, where N is the number of rules in the else-clause:

```
# Does the file exist?
RewriteCond "%{REQUEST_FILENAME}" "!-f"
RewriteCond "%{REQUEST_FILENAME}" "!-d"
# Create an if-then-else construct by skipping 3 lines if we meant to go to the "else" sta
RewriteRule ".?" "-" [S=3]

# IF the file exists, then:
    RewriteRule "(.*\.gif)" "images.php?$1"
    RewriteRule "(.*\.html)" "docs.php?$1"
```

```
    # Skip past the "else" stanza.
    RewriteRule ".?" "-" [S=1]
# ELSE...
    RewriteRule "(.*)" "404.php?file=$1"
# END
```

It is probably easier to accomplish this kind of configuration using the <IF>, <ELSEIF>, and <ELSE> directives instead.

T—type

Sets the MIME type with which the resulting response will be sent. This has the same effect as the ADDTYPE directive.

For example, you might use the following technique to serve Perl source code as plain text, if requested in a particular way:

```
# Serve .pl files as plain text
RewriteRule "\.pl$" "-" [T=text/plain]
```

Or, perhaps, if you have a camera that produces jpeg images without file extensions, you could force those images to be served with the correct MIME type by virtue of their file names:

```
# Files with 'IMG' in the name are jpg images.
RewriteRule "IMG" "-" [T=image/jpg]
```

Please note that this is a trivial example, and could be better done using <FILESMATCH> instead. Always consider the alternate solutions to a problem before resorting to rewrite, which will invariably be a less efficient solution than the alternatives.

If used in per-directory context, use only - (dash) as the substitution *for the entire round of mod_rewrite processing*, otherwise the MIME-type set with this flag is lost due to an internal re-processing (including subsequent rounds of mod_rewrite processing). The `L` flag can be useful in this context to end the *current* round of mod_rewrite processing.

4.11 Apache mod_rewrite Technical Details

This document discusses some of the technical details of mod_rewrite and URL matching.

See also

- Module documentation (p. 804)
- mod_rewrite introduction (p. 137)
- Redirection and remapping (p. 142)
- Controlling access (p. 149)
- Virtual hosts (p. 152)
- Proxying (p. 155)
- Using RewriteMap (p. 156)
- Advanced techniques (p. 162)
- When not to use mod_rewrite (p. 165)

API Phases

The Apache HTTP Server handles requests in several phases. At each of these phases, one or more modules may be called upon to handle that portion of the request lifecycle. Phases include things like URL-to-filename translation, authentication, authorization, content, and logging. (This is not an exhaustive list.)

mod_rewrite acts in two of these phases (or "hooks", as they are often called) to influence how URLs may be rewritten.

First, it uses the URL-to-filename translation hook, which occurs after the HTTP request has been read, but before any authorization starts. Secondly, it uses the Fixup hook, which is after the authorization phases, and after per-directory configuration files (`.htaccess` files) have been read, but before the content handler is called.

So, after a request comes in and a corresponding server or virtual host has been determined, the rewriting engine starts processing any `mod_rewrite` directives appearing in the per-server configuration. (i.e., in the main server configuration file and <VIRTUALHOST> sections.) This happens in the URL-to-filename phase.

A few steps later, once the final data directories have been found, the per-directory configuration directives (`.htaccess` files and <DIRECTORY> blocks) are applied. This happens in the Fixup phase.

In each of these cases, mod_rewrite rewrites the `REQUEST_URI` either to a new URL, or to a filename.

In per-directory context (i.e., within `.htaccess` files and `Directory` blocks), these rules are being applied after a URL has already been translated to a filename. Because of this, the URL-path that mod_rewrite initially compares REWRITERULE directives against is the full filesystem path to the translated filename with the current directories path (including a trailing slash) removed from the front.

To illustrate: If rules are in /var/www/foo/.htaccess and a request for /foo/bar/baz is being processed, an expression like ^bar/baz$ would match.

If a substitution is made in per-directory context, a new internal subrequest is issued with the new URL, which restarts processing of the request phases. If the substitution is a relative path, the REWRITEBASE directive determines the URL-path prefix prepended to the substitution. In per-directory context, care must be taken to create rules which will eventually (in some future "round" of per-directory rewrite processing) not perform a substitution to avoid looping. (See RewriteLooping[6] for further discussion of this problem.)

Because of this further manipulation of the URL in per-directory context, you'll need to take care to craft your rewrite rules differently in that context. In particular, remember that the leading directory path will be stripped off of the URL that your rewrite rules will see. Consider the examples below for further clarification.

---

[6] http://wiki.apache.org/httpd/RewriteLooping

Location of rule	Rule
VirtualHost section	RewriteRule "^/images/(.+)\.jpg" "/images/$1.gif"
.htaccess file in document root	RewriteRule "^images/(.+)\.jpg" "images/$1.gif"
.htaccess file in images directory	RewriteRule "^(.+)\.jpg" "$1.gif"

For even more insight into how mod_rewrite manipulates URLs in different contexts, you should consult the log entries (p. 804) made during rewriting.

Ruleset Processing

Now when mod_rewrite is triggered in these two API phases, it reads the configured rulesets from its configuration structure (which itself was either created on startup for per-server context or during the directory walk of the Apache kernel for per-directory context). Then the URL rewriting engine is started with the contained ruleset (one or more rules together with their conditions). The operation of the URL rewriting engine itself is exactly the same for both configuration contexts. Only the final result processing is different.

The order of rules in the ruleset is important because the rewriting engine processes them in a special (and not very obvious) order. The rule is this: The rewriting engine loops through the ruleset rule by rule (REWRITERULE directives) and when a particular rule matches it optionally loops through existing corresponding conditions (`RewriteCond` directives). For historical reasons the conditions are given first, and so the control flow is a little bit long-winded. See Figure 1 for more details.

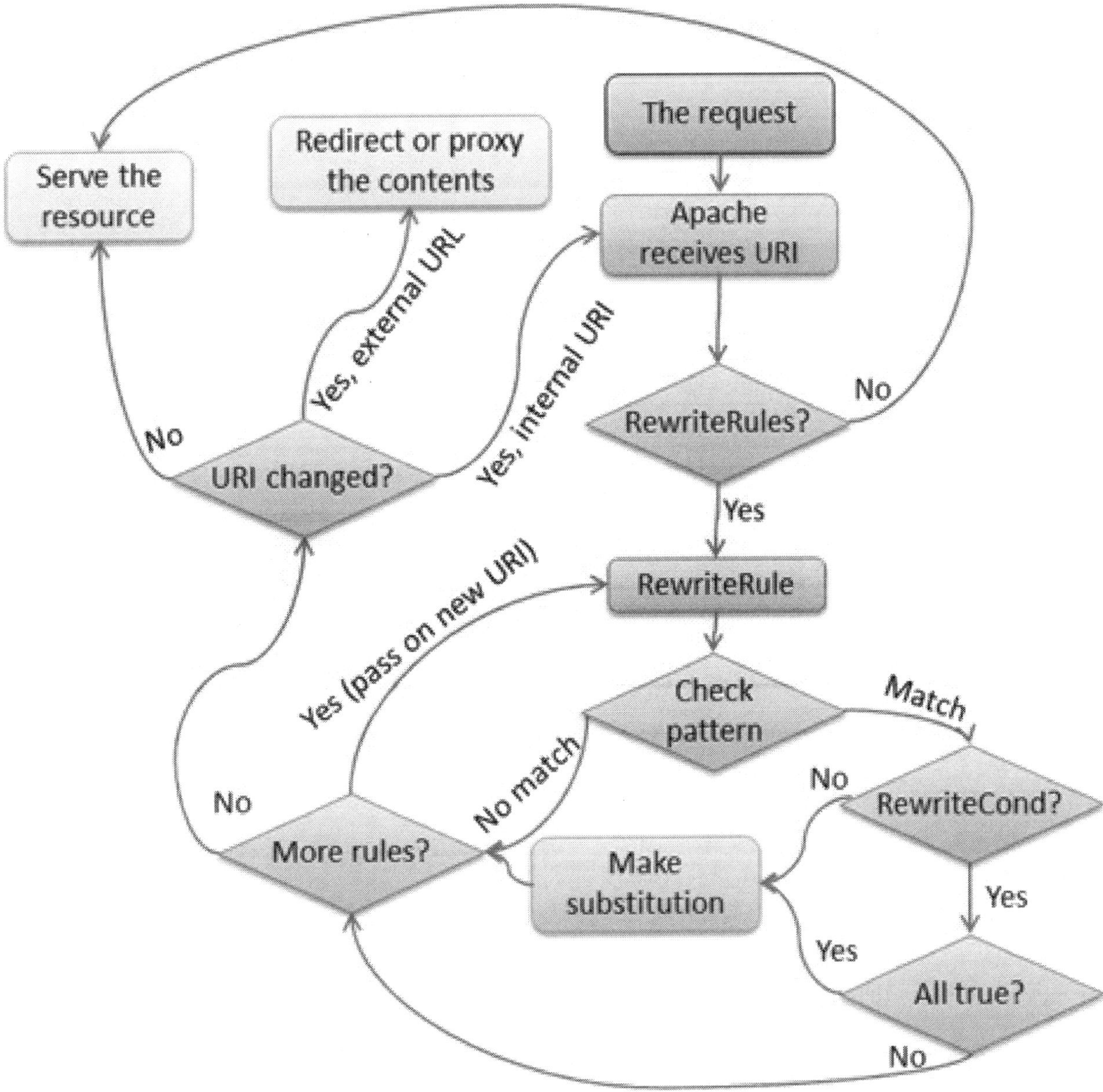

*Figure 1:*The control flow through the rewriting ruleset

First the URL is matched against the *Pattern* of each rule. If it fails, mod_rewrite immediately stops processing this rule, and continues with the next rule. If the *Pattern* matches, mod_rewrite looks for corresponding rule conditions (RewriteCond directives, appearing immediately above the RewriteRule in the configuration). If none are present, it substitutes the URL with a new value, which is constructed from the string *Substitution*, and goes on with its rule-looping. But if conditions exist, it starts an inner loop for processing them in the order that they are listed. For conditions, the logic is different: we don't match a pattern against the current URL. Instead we first create a string *TestString* by expanding variables, back-references, map lookups, *etc.* and then we try to match *CondPattern* against it. If the pattern doesn't match, the complete set of conditions and the corresponding rule fails. If the pattern matches, then the next condition is processed until no more conditions are available. If all conditions match, processing is continued with the substitution of the URL with *Substitution*.

Chapter 5

Apache SSL/TLS Encryption

5.1 Apache SSL/TLS Encryption

The Apache HTTP Server module MOD_SSL provides an interface to the OpenSSL[1] library, which provides Strong Encryption using the Secure Sockets Layer and Transport Layer Security protocols.

Documentation

- mod_ssl Configuration How-To (p. 196)
- Introduction To SSL (p. 183)
- Compatibility (p. 192)
- Frequently Asked Questions (p. 202)
- Glossary (p. 1020)

mod_ssl

Extensive documentation on the directives and environment variables provided by this module is provided in the mod_ssl reference documentation (p. 853) .

[1] http://www.openssl.org/

5.2 SSL/TLS Strong Encryption: An Introduction

As an introduction this chapter is aimed at readers who are familiar with the Web, HTTP, and Apache, but are not security experts. It is not intended to be a definitive guide to the SSL protocol, nor does it discuss specific techniques for managing certificates in an organization, or the important legal issues of patents and import and export restrictions. Rather, it is intended to provide a common background to MOD_SSL users by pulling together various concepts, definitions, and examples as a starting point for further exploration.

Cryptographic Techniques

Understanding SSL requires an understanding of cryptographic algorithms, message digest functions (aka. one-way or hash functions), and digital signatures. These techniques are the subject of entire books (see for instance [AC96]) and provide the basis for privacy, integrity, and authentication.

Cryptographic Algorithms

Suppose Alice wants to send a message to her bank to transfer some money. Alice would like the message to be private, since it will include information such as her account number and transfer amount. One solution is to use a cryptographic algorithm, a technique that would transform her message into an encrypted form, unreadable until it is decrypted. Once in this form, the message can only be decrypted by using a secret key. Without the key the message is useless: good cryptographic algorithms make it so difficult for intruders to decode the original text that it isn't worth their effort.

There are two categories of cryptographic algorithms: conventional and public key.

Conventional cryptography also known as symmetric cryptography, requires the sender and receiver to share a key: a secret piece of information that may be used to encrypt or decrypt a message. As long as this key is kept secret, nobody other than the sender or recipient can read the message. If Alice and the bank know a secret key, then they can send each other private messages. The task of sharing a key between sender and recipient before communicating, while also keeping it secret from others, can be problematic.

Public key cryptography also known as asymmetric cryptography, solves the key exchange problem by defining an algorithm which uses two keys, each of which may be used to encrypt a message. If one key is used to encrypt a message then the other must be used to decrypt it. This makes it possible to receive secure messages by simply publishing one key (the public key) and keeping the other secret (the private key).

Anyone can encrypt a message using the public key, but only the owner of the private key will be able to read it. In this way, Alice can send private messages to the owner of a key-pair (the bank), by encrypting them using their public key. Only the bank will be able to decrypt them.

Message Digests

Although Alice may encrypt her message to make it private, there is still a concern that someone might modify her original message or substitute it with a different one, in order to transfer the money to themselves, for instance. One way of guaranteeing the integrity of Alice's message is for her to create a concise summary of her message and send this to the bank as well. Upon receipt of the message, the bank creates its own summary and compares it with the one Alice sent. If the summaries are the same then the message has been received intact.

A summary such as this is called a *message digest*, *one-way function* or *hash function*. Message digests are used to create a short, fixed-length representation of a longer, variable-length message. Digest algorithms are designed to produce a unique digest for each message. Message digests are designed to make it impractically difficult to determine the message from the digest and (in theory) impossible to find two different messages which create the same digest – thus eliminating the possibility of substituting one message for another while maintaining the same digest.

Another challenge that Alice faces is finding a way to send the digest to the bank securely; if the digest is not sent securely, its integrity may be compromised and with it the possibility for the bank to determine the integrity of the original message. Only if the digest is sent securely can the integrity of the associated message be determined.

One way to send the digest securely is to include it in a digital signature.

Digital Signatures

When Alice sends a message to the bank, the bank needs to ensure that the message is really from her, so an intruder cannot request a transaction involving her account. A *digital signature*, created by Alice and included with the message, serves this purpose.

Digital signatures are created by encrypting a digest of the message and other information (such as a sequence number) with the sender's private key. Though anyone can *decrypt* the signature using the public key, only the sender knows the private key. This means that only the sender can have signed the message. Including the digest in the signature means the signature is only good for that message; it also ensures the integrity of the message since no one can change the digest and still sign it.

To guard against interception and reuse of the signature by an intruder at a later date, the signature contains a unique sequence number. This protects the bank from a fraudulent claim from Alice that she did not send the message – only she could have signed it (non-repudiation).

Certificates

Although Alice could have sent a private message to the bank, signed it and ensured the integrity of the message, she still needs to be sure that she is really communicating with the bank. This means that she needs to be sure that the public key she is using is part of the bank's key-pair, and not an intruder's. Similarly, the bank needs to verify that the message signature really was signed by the private key that belongs to Alice.

If each party has a certificate which validates the other's identity, confirms the public key and is signed by a trusted agency, then both can be assured that they are communicating with whom they think they are. Such a trusted agency is called a *Certificate Authority* and certificates are used for authentication.

Certificate Contents

A certificate associates a public key with the real identity of an individual, server, or other entity, known as the subject. As shown in Table 1, information about the subject includes identifying information (the distinguished name) and the public key. It also includes the identification and signature of the Certificate Authority that issued the certificate and the period of time during which the certificate is valid. It may have additional information (or extensions) as well as administrative information for the Certificate Authority's use, such as a serial number.

Table 1: Certificate Information

Subject	Distinguished Name, Public Key
Issuer	Distinguished Name, Signature
Period of Validity	Not Before Date, Not After Date
Administrative Information	Version, Serial Number
Extended Information	Basic Constraints, Netscape Flags, etc.

A distinguished name is used to provide an identity in a specific context – for instance, an individual might have a personal certificate as well as one for their identity as an employee. Distinguished names are defined by the X.509 standard [X509], which defines the fields, field names and abbreviations used to refer to the fields (see Table 2).

Table 2: Distinguished Name Information

DN Field	Abbrev.	Description	Example
Common Name	CN	Name being certified	CN=Joe Average
Organization or Company	O	Name is associated with this organization	O=Snake Oil, Ltd.
Organizational Unit	OU	Name is associated with this organization unit, such as a department	OU=Research Institute
City/Locality	L	Name is located in this City	L=Snake City
State/Province	ST	Name is located in this State/Province	ST=Desert
Country	C	Name is located in this Country (ISO code)	C=XZ

A Certificate Authority may define a policy specifying which distinguished field names are optional and which are required. It may also place requirements upon the field contents, as may users of certificates. For example, a Netscape browser requires that the Common Name for a certificate representing a server matches a wildcard pattern for the domain name of that server, such as `*.snakeoil.com`.

The binary format of a certificate is defined using the ASN.1 notation [ASN1] [PKCS]. This notation defines how to specify the contents and encoding rules define how this information is translated into binary form. The binary encoding of the certificate is defined using Distinguished Encoding Rules (DER), which are based on the more general Basic Encoding Rules (BER). For those transmissions which cannot handle binary, the binary form may be translated into an ASCII form by using Base64 encoding [MIME]. When placed between begin and end delimiter lines (as below), this encoded version is called a PEM ("Privacy Enhanced Mail") encoded certificate.

Example of a PEM-encoded certificate (snakeoil.crt)


```
-----BEGIN CERTIFICATE-----
MIIC7jCCAlegAwIBAgIBATANBgkqhkiG9w0BAQQFADCBqTELMAkGA1UEBhMCWFkx
FTATBgNVBAgTDFNuYWtlIERlc2VydDETMBEGA1UEBxMKU25ha2UgVG93bjEXMBUG
A1UEChMOU25ha2UgT2lsLCBMdGQxHjAcBgNVBAsTFUNlcnRpZmljYXRlIEF1dGhv
cml0eTEVMBMGA1UEAxMMU25ha2UgT2lsIENBMR4wHAYJKoZIhvcNAQkBFg9jYUBz
bmFrZW9pbC5kb20wHhcNOTgxMDIxMDg1ODM2WhcNOTkxMDIxMDg1ODM2WjCBpzEL
MAkGA1UEBhMCWFkxFTATBgNVBAgTDFNuYWtlIERlc2VydDETMBEGA1UEBxMKU25h
a2UgVG93bjEXMBUGA1UEChMOU25ha2UgT2lsLCBMdGQxFzAVBgNVBAsTDldlYnNl
cnZlciBUZWFtMRkwFwYDVQQDExB3d3cuc25ha2VvaWwuZG9tMR8wHQYJKoZIhvcN
AQkBFhB3d3dAc25ha2VvaWwuZG9tMIGfMA0GCSqGSIb3DQEBAQUAA4GNADCBiQKB
gQDH9Ge/s2zcH+da+rPTx/DPRp3xGjHZ4GG6pCmvADIEtBtKBFAcZ64n+Dy7Np8b
vKR+yy5DGQiijsH1D/j8H1GE+q4TZ8OFk7BNBFazHxFbYI4OKMiCxdKzdif1yfaa
lWoANFlAzlSdbxeGVHoT0K+gT5w3UxwZKv2DLbCTzLZyPwIDAQABoyYwJDAPBgNV
HRMECDAGAQH/AgEAMBEGCWCGSAGG+EIBAQQEAwIAQDANBgkqhkiG9w0BAQQFAAOB
gQAZUIHAL4D09oE6Lv2k56Gp38OBDuILvwLg1v1KL8mQR+KFjghCrtpqaztZqcDt
2q2QoyulCgSzHbEGmi0EsdkPfg6mp0penssIFePYNI+/8u9HT4LuKMJX15hxBam7
dUHzICxBVC1lnHyYGjDuAMhe396lYAn8bCld1/L4NMGBCQ==
-----END CERTIFICATE-----
```


Certificate Authorities

By verifying the information in a certificate request before granting the certificate, the Certificate Authority assures itself of the identity of the private key owner of a key-pair. For instance, if Alice requests a personal certificate, the Certificate Authority must first make sure that Alice really is the person the certificate request claims she is.

Certificate Chains

A Certificate Authority may also issue a certificate for another Certificate Authority. When examining a certificate, Alice may need to examine the certificate of the issuer, for each parent Certificate Authority, until reaching one which she has confidence in. She may decide to trust only certificates with a limited chain of issuers, to reduce her risk of a "bad" certificate in the chain.

Creating a Root-Level CA

As noted earlier, each certificate requires an issuer to assert the validity of the identity of the certificate subject, up to the top-level Certificate Authority (CA). This presents a problem: who can vouch for the certificate of the top-level authority, which has no issuer? In this unique case, the certificate is "self-signed", so the issuer of the certificate is the same as the subject. Browsers are preconfigured to trust well-known certificate authorities, but it is important to exercise extra care in trusting a self-signed certificate. The wide publication of a public key by the root authority reduces the risk in trusting this key – it would be obvious if someone else publicized a key claiming to be the authority.

A number of companies, such as Thawte[2] and VeriSign[3] have established themselves as Certificate Authorities. These companies provide the following services:

- Verifying certificate requests
- Processing certificate requests
- Issuing and managing certificates

It is also possible to create your own Certificate Authority. Although risky in the Internet environment, it may be useful within an Intranet where the organization can easily verify the identities of individuals and servers.

Certificate Management

Establishing a Certificate Authority is a responsibility which requires a solid administrative, technical and management framework. Certificate Authorities not only issue certificates, they also manage them – that is, they determine for how long certificates remain valid, they renew them and keep lists of certificates that were issued in the past but are no longer valid (Certificate Revocation Lists, or CRLs).

For example, if Alice is entitled to a certificate as an employee of a company but has now left that company, her certificate may need to be revoked. Because certificates are only issued after the subject's identity has been verified and can then be passed around to all those with whom the subject may communicate, it is impossible to tell from the certificate alone that it has been revoked. Therefore when examining certificates for validity it is necessary to contact the issuing Certificate Authority to check CRLs – this is usually not an automated part of the process.

**Note**

If you use a Certificate Authority that browsers are not configured to trust by default, it is necessary to load the Certificate Authority certificate into the browser, enabling the browser to validate server certificates signed by that Certificate Authority. Doing so may be dangerous, since once loaded, the browser will accept all certificates signed by that Certificate Authority.

Secure Sockets Layer (SSL)

The Secure Sockets Layer protocol is a protocol layer which may be placed between a reliable connection-oriented network layer protocol (e.g. TCP/IP) and the application protocol layer (e.g. HTTP). SSL provides for secure communication between client and server by allowing mutual authentication, the use of digital signatures for integrity and encryption for privacy.

[2] http://www.thawte.com/

[3] http://www.verisign.com/

The protocol is designed to support a range of choices for specific algorithms used for cryptography, digests and signatures. This allows algorithm selection for specific servers to be made based on legal, export or other concerns and also enables the protocol to take advantage of new algorithms. Choices are negotiated between client and server when establishing a protocol session.

Table 4: Versions of the SSL protocol

Version	Source	Description
SSL v2.0	Vendor Standard (from Netscape Corp.)	First SSL protocol for which implementations exist
SSL v3.0	Expired Internet Draft (from Netscape Corp.) [SSL3]	Revisions to prevent specific security attacks, add non-RSA ciphers and support for certificate chains
TLS v1.0	Proposed Internet Standard (from IETF) [TLS1]	Revision of SSL 3.0 to update the MAC layer to HMAC, add block padding for block ciphers, message order standardization and more alert messages.
TLS v1.1	Proposed Internet Standard (from IETF) [TLS11]	Update of TLS 1.0 to add protection against Cipher block chaining (CBC) attacks.
TLS v1.2	Proposed Internet Standard (from IETF) [TLS12]	Update of TLS 1.2 deprecating MD5 as hash, and adding incompatibility to SSL so it will never negotiate the use of SSLv2.

There are a number of versions of the SSL protocol, as shown in Table 4. As noted there, one of the benefits in SSL 3.0 is that it adds support of certificate chain loading. This feature allows a server to pass a server certificate along with issuer certificates to the browser. Chain loading also permits the browser to validate the server certificate, even if Certificate Authority certificates are not installed for the intermediate issuers, since they are included in the certificate chain. SSL 3.0 is the basis for the Transport Layer Security [TLS] protocol standard, currently in development by the Internet Engineering Task Force (IETF).

Establishing a Session

The SSL session is established by following a handshake sequence between client and server, as shown in Figure 1. This sequence may vary, depending on whether the server is configured to provide a server certificate or request a client certificate. Although cases exist where additional handshake steps are required for management of cipher information, this article summarizes one common scenario. See the SSL specification for the full range of possibilities.

**Note**

Once an SSL session has been established, it may be reused. This avoids the performance penalty of repeating the many steps needed to start a session. To do this, the server assigns each SSL session a unique session identifier which is cached in the server and which the client can use in future connections to reduce the handshake time (until the session identifier expires from the cache of the server).

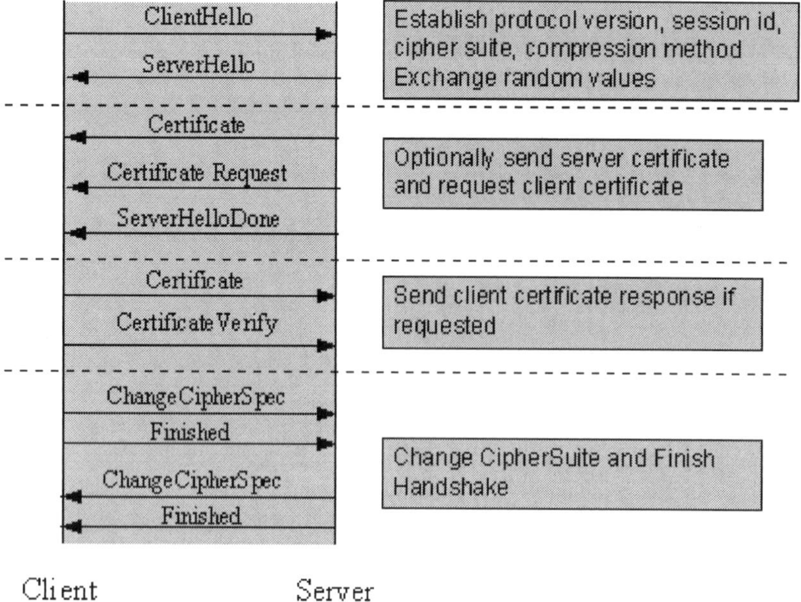

Figure 1: Simplified SSL Handshake Sequence

The elements of the handshake sequence, as used by the client and server, are listed below:

1. Negotiate the Cipher Suite to be used during data transfer
2. Establish and share a session key between client and server
3. Optionally authenticate the server to the client
4. Optionally authenticate the client to the server

The first step, Cipher Suite Negotiation, allows the client and server to choose a Cipher Suite supported by both of them. The SSL3.0 protocol specification defines 31 Cipher Suites. A Cipher Suite is defined by the following components:

- Key Exchange Method
- Cipher for Data Transfer
- Message Digest for creating the Message Authentication Code (MAC)

These three elements are described in the sections that follow.

Key Exchange Method

The key exchange method defines how the shared secret symmetric cryptography key used for application data transfer will be agreed upon by client and server. SSL 2.0 uses RSA key exchange only, while SSL 3.0 supports a choice of key exchange algorithms including RSA key exchange (when certificates are used), and Diffie-Hellman key exchange (for exchanging keys without certificates, or without prior communication between client and server).

One variable in the choice of key exchange methods is digital signatures – whether or not to use them, and if so, what kind of signatures to use. Signing with a private key provides protection against a man-in-the-middle-attack during the information exchange used to generating the shared key [AC96, p516].

Cipher for Data Transfer

SSL uses conventional symmetric cryptography, as described earlier, for encrypting messages in a session. There are nine choices of how to encrypt, including the option not to encrypt:

- No encryption
- Stream Ciphers
  - RC4 with 40-bit keys
  - RC4 with 128-bit keys
- CBC Block Ciphers
  - RC2 with 40 bit key
  - DES with 40 bit key
  - DES with 56 bit key
  - Triple-DES with 168 bit key
  - Idea (128 bit key)
  - Fortezza (96 bit key)

"CBC" refers to Cipher Block Chaining, which means that a portion of the previously encrypted cipher text is used in the encryption of the current block. "DES" refers to the Data Encryption Standard [AC96, ch12], which has a number of variants (including DES40 and 3DES_EDE). "Idea" is currently one of the best and cryptographically strongest algorithms available, and "RC2" is a proprietary algorithm from RSA DSI [AC96, ch13].

Digest Function

The choice of digest function determines how a digest is created from a record unit. SSL supports the following:

- No digest (Null choice)
- MD5, a 128-bit hash
- Secure Hash Algorithm (SHA-1), a 160-bit hash

The message digest is used to create a Message Authentication Code (MAC) which is encrypted with the message to verify integrity and to protect against replay attacks.

Handshake Sequence Protocol

The handshake sequence uses three protocols:

- The *SSL Handshake Protocol* for performing the client and server SSL session establishment.
- The *SSL Change Cipher Spec Protocol* for actually establishing agreement on the Cipher Suite for the session.
- The *SSL Alert Protocol* for conveying SSL error messages between client and server.

These protocols, as well as application protocol data, are encapsulated in the *SSL Record Protocol*, as shown in Figure 2. An encapsulated protocol is transferred as data by the lower layer protocol, which does not examine the data. The encapsulated protocol has no knowledge of the underlying protocol.

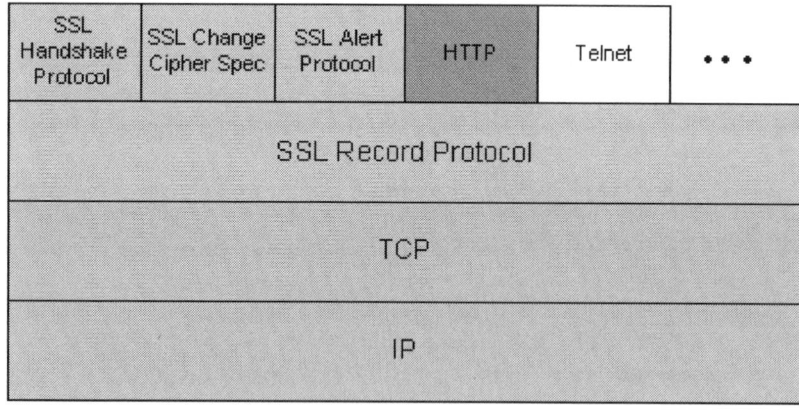

Figure 2: SSL Protocol Stack

The encapsulation of SSL control protocols by the record protocol means that if an active session is renegotiated the control protocols will be transmitted securely. If there was no previous session, the Null cipher suite is used, which means there will be no encryption and messages will have no integrity digests, until the session has been established.

Data Transfer

The SSL Record Protocol, shown in Figure 3, is used to transfer application and SSL Control data between the client and server, where necessary fragmenting this data into smaller units, or combining multiple higher level protocol data messages into single units. It may compress, attach digest signatures, and encrypt these units before transmitting them using the underlying reliable transport protocol (Note: currently, no major SSL implementations include support for compression).

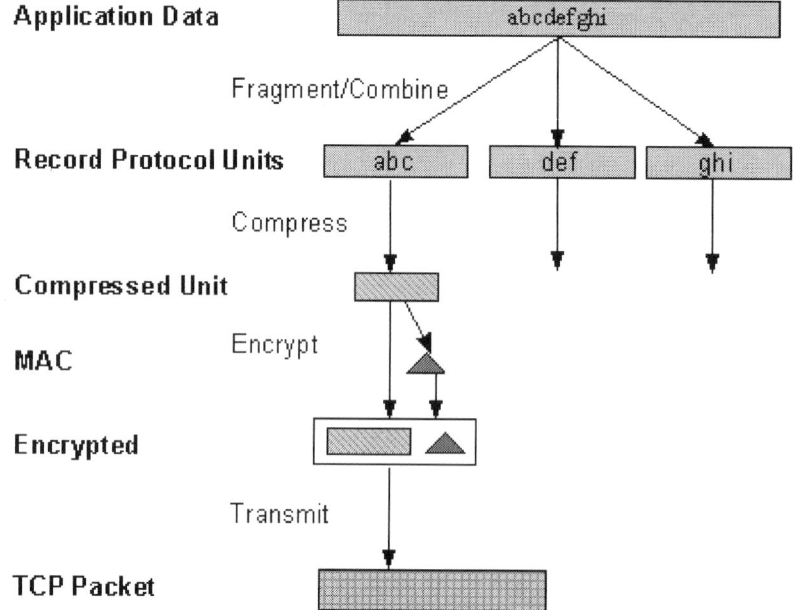

Figure 3: SSL Record Protocol

Securing HTTP Communication

One common use of SSL is to secure Web HTTP communication between a browser and a webserver. This does not preclude the use of non-secured HTTP - the secure version (called HTTPS) is the same as plain HTTP over SSL, but uses the URL scheme `https` rather than `http`, and a different server port (by default, port 443). This functionality is a large part of what MOD_SSL provides for the Apache webserver.

References

[AC96] Bruce Schneier, *Applied Cryptography*, 2nd Edition, Wiley, 1996. See http://www.counterpane.com/ for various other materials by Bruce Schneier.

[ASN1] ITU-T Recommendation X.208, *Specification of Abstract Syntax Notation One (ASN.1)*, last updated 2008. See http://www.itu.int/ITU-T/asn1/.

[X509] ITU-T Recommendation X.509, *The Directory - Authentication Framework*. For references, see http://en.wikipedia.org/wiki/X.509.

[PKCS] *Public Key Cryptography Standards (PKCS)*, RSA Laboratories Technical Notes, See http://www.rsasecurity.com/rsalabs/pkcs/.

[MIME] N. Freed, N. Borenstein, *Multipurpose Internet Mail Extensions (MIME) Part One: Format of Internet Message Bodies*, RFC2045. See for instance http://tools.ietf.org/html/rfc2045.

[SSL3] Alan O. Freier, Philip Karlton, Paul C. Kocher, *The SSL Protocol Version 3.0*, 1996. See http://www.netscape.com/eng/ssl3/draft302.txt.

[TLS1] Tim Dierks, Christopher Allen, *The TLS Protocol Version 1.0*, 1999. See http://ietf.org/rfc/rfc2246.txt.

[TLS11] *The TLS Protocol Version 1.1*, 2006. See http://tools.ietf.org/html/rfc4346.

[TLS12] *The TLS Protocol Version 1.2*, 2008. See http://tools.ietf.org/html/rfc5246.

5.3 SSL/TLS Strong Encryption: Compatibility

This page covers backwards compatibility between mod_ssl and other SSL solutions. mod_ssl is not the only SSL solution for Apache; four additional products are (or were) also available: Ben Laurie's freely available Apache-SSL[4] (from where mod_ssl were originally derived in 1998), Red Hat's commercial Secure Web Server (which was based on mod_ssl), Covalent's commercial Raven SSL Module (also based on mod_ssl) and finally C2Net's (now Red Hat's) commercial product Stronghold[5] (based on a different evolution branch, named Sioux up to Stronghold 2.x, and based on mod_ssl since Stronghold 3.x).

mod_ssl mostly provides a superset of the functionality of all the other solutions, so it's simple to migrate from one of the older modules to mod_ssl. The configuration directives and environment variable names used by the older SSL solutions vary from those used in mod_ssl; mapping tables are included here to give the equivalents used by mod_ssl.

Configuration Directives

The mapping between configuration directives used by Apache-SSL 1.x and mod_ssl 2.0.x is given in Table 1. The mapping from Sioux 1.x and Stronghold 2.x is only partial because of special functionality in these interfaces which mod_ssl doesn't provide.

Table 1: Configuration Directive Mapping

Old Directive	mod_ssl Directive	Comment
Apache-SSL 1.x & mod_ssl 2.0.x compatibility:		
`SSLEnable`	`SSLEngine on`	compactified
`SSLDisable`	`SSLEngine off`	compactified
`SSLLogFile` *file*		Use per-module LOGLEVEL setting instead.
`SSLRequiredCiphers` *spec*	`SSLCipherSuite` *spec*	renamed
`SSLRequireCipher` *c1* ...	`SSLRequire %{SSL_CIPHER} in {"c1", ...}`	generalized
`SSLBanCipher` *c1* ...	`SSLRequire not (%{SSL_CIPHER} in {"c1", ...})`	generalized
`SSLFakeBasicAuth`	`SSLOptions +FakeBasicAuth`	merged
`SSLCacheServerPath` *dir*	-	functionality removed
`SSLCacheServerPort` *integer*	-	functionality removed
Apache-SSL 1.x compatibility:		
`SSLExportClientCertificates`	`SSLOptions +ExportCertData`	merged
`SSLCacheServerRunDir` *dir*	-	functionality not supported
Sioux 1.x compatibility:		
`SSL_CertFile` *file*	`SSLCertificateFile` *file*	renamed
`SSL_KeyFile` *file*	`SSLCertificateKeyFile` *file*	renamed
`SSL_CipherSuite` *arg*	`SSLCipherSuite` *arg*	renamed
`SSL_X509VerifyDir` *arg*	`SSLCACertificatePath` *arg*	renamed
`SSL_Log` *file*	–	Use per-module LOGLEVEL setting instead.
`SSL_Connect` *flag*	`SSLEngine` *flag*	renamed
`SSL_ClientAuth` *arg*	`SSLVerifyClient` *arg*	renamed
`SSL_X509VerifyDepth` *arg*	`SSLVerifyDepth` *arg*	renamed

[4] http://www.apache-ssl.org/
[5] http://www.redhat.com/explore/stronghold/

SSL_FetchKeyPhraseFrom *arg*	-	not directly mappable; use SSLPassPhraseDialog
SSL_SessionDir *dir*	-	not directly mappable; use SSLSession-Cache
SSL_Require *expr*	-	not directly mappable; use SSLRequire
SSL_CertFileType *arg*	-	functionality not supported
SSL_KeyFileType *arg*	-	functionality not supported
SSL_X509VerifyPolicy *arg*	-	functionality not supported
SSL_LogX509Attributes *arg*	-	functionality not supported
Stronghold 2.x compatibility:		
StrongholdAccelerator *engine*	SSLCryptoDevice *engine*	renamed
StrongholdKey *dir*	-	functionality not needed
StrongholdLicenseFile *dir*	-	functionality not needed
SSLFlag *flag*	SSLEngine *flag*	renamed
SSLSessionLockFile *file*	SSLMutex *file*	renamed
SSLCipherList *spec*	SSLCipherSuite *spec*	renamed
RequireSSL	SSLRequireSSL	renamed
SSLErrorFile *file*	-	functionality not supported
SSLRoot *dir*	-	functionality not supported
SSL_CertificateLogDir *dir*	-	functionality not supported
AuthCertDir *dir*	-	functionality not supported
SSL_Group *name*	-	functionality not supported
SSLProxyMachineCertPath *dir*	SSLProxyMachineCertificatePath *dir*	renamed
SSLProxyMachineCertFile *file*	SSLProxyMachineCertificateFile *file*	renamed
SSLProxyCipherList *spec*	SSLProxyCipherSpec *spec*	renamed

Environment Variables

The mapping between environment variable names used by the older SSL solutions and the names used by mod_ssl is given in Table 2.

Table 2: Environment Variable Derivation

Old Variable	mod_ssl Variable	Comment
SSL_PROTOCOL_VERSION	SSL_PROTOCOL	renamed
SSLEAY_VERSION	SSL_VERSION_LIBRARY	renamed
HTTPS_SECRETKEYSIZE	SSL_CIPHER_USEKEYSIZE	renamed
HTTPS_KEYSIZE	SSL_CIPHER_ALGKEYSIZE	renamed
HTTPS_CIPHER	SSL_CIPHER	renamed
HTTPS_EXPORT	SSL_CIPHER_EXPORT	renamed
SSL_SERVER_KEY_SIZE	SSL_CIPHER_ALGKEYSIZE	renamed
SSL_SERVER_CERTIFICATE	SSL_SERVER_CERT	renamed
SSL_SERVER_CERT_START	SSL_SERVER_V_START	renamed
SSL_SERVER_CERT_END	SSL_SERVER_V_END	renamed
SSL_SERVER_CERT_SERIAL	SSL_SERVER_M_SERIAL	renamed
SSL_SERVER_SIGNATURE_ALGORITHM	SSL_SERVER_A_SIG	renamed
SSL_SERVER_DN	SSL_SERVER_S_DN	renamed
SSL_SERVER_CN	SSL_SERVER_S_DN_CN	renamed
SSL_SERVER_EMAIL	SSL_SERVER_S_DN_Email	renamed
SSL_SERVER_O	SSL_SERVER_S_DN_O	renamed
SSL_SERVER_OU	SSL_SERVER_S_DN_OU	renamed

SSL_SERVER_C	SSL_SERVER_S_DN_C	renamed
SSL_SERVER_SP	SSL_SERVER_S_DN_SP	renamed
SSL_SERVER_L	SSL_SERVER_S_DN_L	renamed
SSL_SERVER_IDN	SSL_SERVER_I_DN	renamed
SSL_SERVER_ICN	SSL_SERVER_I_DN_CN	renamed
SSL_SERVER_IEMAIL	SSL_SERVER_I_DN_Email	renamed
SSL_SERVER_IO	SSL_SERVER_I_DN_O	renamed
SSL_SERVER_IOU	SSL_SERVER_I_DN_OU	renamed
SSL_SERVER_IC	SSL_SERVER_I_DN_C	renamed
SSL_SERVER_ISP	SSL_SERVER_I_DN_SP	renamed
SSL_SERVER_IL	SSL_SERVER_I_DN_L	renamed
SSL_CLIENT_CERTIFICATE	SSL_CLIENT_CERT	renamed
SSL_CLIENT_CERT_START	SSL_CLIENT_V_START	renamed
SSL_CLIENT_CERT_END	SSL_CLIENT_V_END	renamed
SSL_CLIENT_CERT_SERIAL	SSL_CLIENT_M_SERIAL	renamed
SSL_CLIENT_SIGNATURE_ALGORITHM	SSL_CLIENT_A_SIG	renamed
SSL_CLIENT_DN	SSL_CLIENT_S_DN	renamed
SSL_CLIENT_CN	SSL_CLIENT_S_DN_CN	renamed
SSL_CLIENT_EMAIL	SSL_CLIENT_S_DN_Email	renamed
SSL_CLIENT_O	SSL_CLIENT_S_DN_O	renamed
SSL_CLIENT_OU	SSL_CLIENT_S_DN_OU	renamed
SSL_CLIENT_C	SSL_CLIENT_S_DN_C	renamed
SSL_CLIENT_SP	SSL_CLIENT_S_DN_SP	renamed
SSL_CLIENT_L	SSL_CLIENT_S_DN_L	renamed
SSL_CLIENT_IDN	SSL_CLIENT_I_DN	renamed
SSL_CLIENT_ICN	SSL_CLIENT_I_DN_CN	renamed
SSL_CLIENT_IEMAIL	SSL_CLIENT_I_DN_Email	renamed
SSL_CLIENT_IO	SSL_CLIENT_I_DN_O	renamed
SSL_CLIENT_IOU	SSL_CLIENT_I_DN_OU	renamed
SSL_CLIENT_IC	SSL_CLIENT_I_DN_C	renamed
SSL_CLIENT_ISP	SSL_CLIENT_I_DN_SP	renamed
SSL_CLIENT_IL	SSL_CLIENT_I_DN_L	renamed
SSL_EXPORT	SSL_CIPHER_EXPORT	renamed
SSL_KEYSIZE	SSL_CIPHER_ALGKEYSIZE	renamed
SSL_SECKEYSIZE	SSL_CIPHER_USEKEYSIZE	renamed
SSL_SSLEAY_VERSION	SSL_VERSION_LIBRARY	renamed
SSL_STRONG_CRYPTO	-	Not supported by mod_ssl
SSL_SERVER_KEY_EXP	-	Not supported by mod_ssl
SSL_SERVER_KEY_ALGORITHM	-	Not supported by mod_ssl
SSL_SERVER_KEY_SIZE	-	Not supported by mod_ssl
SSL_SERVER_SESSIONDIR	-	Not supported by mod_ssl
SSL_SERVER_CERTIFICATELOGDIR	-	Not supported by mod_ssl
SSL_SERVER_CERTFILE	-	Not supported by mod_ssl
SSL_SERVER_KEYFILE	-	Not supported by mod_ssl
SSL_SERVER_KEYFILETYPE	-	Not supported by mod_ssl
SSL_CLIENT_KEY_EXP	-	Not supported by mod_ssl
SSL_CLIENT_KEY_ALGORITHM	-	Not supported by mod_ssl
SSL_CLIENT_KEY_SIZE	-	Not supported by mod_ssl

Custom Log Functions

When mod_ssl is enabled, additional functions exist for the Custom Log Format (p. 661) of MOD_LOG_CONFIG as documented in the Reference Chapter. Beside the "%{*varname*}x" eXtension format function which can be used to expand any variables provided by any module, an additional Cryptography "%{*name*}c" cryptography format function exists for backward compatibility. The currently implemented function calls are listed in Table 3.

Table 3: Custom Log Cryptography Function

Function Call	Description
`%...{version}c`	SSL protocol version
`%...{cipher}c`	SSL cipher
`%...{subjectdn}c`	Client Certificate Subject Distinguished Name
`%...{issuerdn}c`	Client Certificate Issuer Distinguished Name
`%...{errcode}c`	Certificate Verification Error (numerical)
`%...{errstr}c`	Certificate Verification Error (string)

5.4 SSL/TLS Strong Encryption: How-To

This document is intended to get you started, and get a few things working. You are strongly encouraged to read the rest of the SSL documentation, and arrive at a deeper understanding of the material, before progressing to the advanced techniques.

Basic Configuration Example

Your SSL configuration will need to contain, at minimum, the following directives.

```
LoadModule ssl_module modules/mod_ssl.so

Listen 443
<VirtualHost *:443>
    ServerName www.example.com
    SSLEngine on
    SSLCertificateFile "/path/to/www.example.com.cert"
    SSLCertificateKeyFile "/path/to/www.example.com.key"
</VirtualHost>
```

Cipher Suites and Enforcing Strong Security

- How can I create an SSL server which accepts strong encryption only?
- How can I create an SSL server which accepts all types of ciphers in general, but requires a strong cipher for access to a particular URL?

How can I create an SSL server which accepts strong encryption only?

The following enables only the strongest ciphers:

```
SSLCipherSuite HIGH:!aNULL:!MD5
```

While with the following configuration you specify a preference for specific speed-optimized ciphers (which will be selected by mod_ssl, provided that they are supported by the client):

```
SSLCipherSuite RC4-SHA:AES128-SHA:HIGH:!aNULL:!MD5
SSLHonorCipherOrder on
```

How can I create an SSL server which accepts all types of ciphers in general, but requires a strong ciphers for access to a particular URL?

Obviously, a server-wide SSLCIPHERSUITE which restricts ciphers to the strong variants, isn't the answer here. However, MOD_SSL can be reconfigured within `Location` blocks, to give a per-directory solution, and can automatically force a renegotiation of the SSL parameters to meet the new configuration. This can be done as follows:

```
# be liberal in general
SSLCipherSuite ALL:!aNULL:RC4+RSA:+HIGH:+MEDIUM:+LOW:+EXP:+eNULL

<Location "/strong/area">
```

```
# but https://hostname/strong/area/ and below
# requires strong ciphers
SSLCipherSuite HIGH:!aNULL:!MD5
</Location>
```

OCSP Stapling

The Online Certificate Status Protocol (OCSP) is a mechanism for determining whether or not a server certificate has been revoked, and OCSP Stapling is a special form of this in which the server, such as httpd and mod_ssl, maintains current OCSP responses for its certificates and sends them to clients which communicate with the server. Most certificates contain the address of an OCSP responder maintained by the issuing Certificate Authority, and mod_ssl can communicate with that responder to obtain a signed response that can be sent to clients communicating with the server.

Because the client can obtain the certificate revocation status from the server, without requiring an extra connection from the client to the Certificate Authority, OCSP Stapling is the preferred way for the revocation status to be obtained. Other benefits of eliminating the communication between clients and the Certificate Authority are that the client browsing history is not exposed to the Certificate Authority and obtaining status is more reliable by not depending on potentially heavily loaded Certificate Authority servers.

Because the response obtained by the server can be reused for all clients using the same certificate during the time that the response is valid, the overhead for the server is minimal.

Once general SSL support has been configured properly, enabling OCSP Stapling generally requires only very minor modifications to the httpd configuration - the addition of these two directives:

```
SSLUseStapling On
SSLStaplingCache "shmcb:logs/ssl_stapling(32768)"
```

These directives are placed at global scope (i.e., not within a virtual host definition) wherever other global SSL configuration directives are placed, such as in `conf/extra/httpd-ssl.conf` for normal open source builds of httpd, `/etc/apache2/mods-enabled/ssl.conf` for the Ubuntu or Debian-bundled httpd, etc.

The path on the SSLSTAPLINGCACHE directive (e.g., `logs/`) should match the one on the SSLSESSIONCACHE directive. This path is relative to SERVERROOT.

This particular SSLSTAPLINGCACHE directive requires MOD_SOCACHE_SHMCB (from the `shmcb` prefix on the directive's argument). This module is usually enabled already for SSLSESSIONCACHE or on behalf of some module other than MOD_SSL. If you enabled an SSL session cache using a mechanism other than MOD_SOCACHE_SHMCB, use that alternative mechanism for SSLSTAPLINGCACHE as well. For example:

```
SSLSessionCache "dbm:logs/ssl_scache"
SSLStaplingCache "dbm:logs/ssl_stapling"
```

You can use the openssl command-line program to verify that an OCSP response is sent by your server:

```
$ openssl s_client -connect www.example.com:443 -status -servername www.example.com
...
OCSP response:
======================================
OCSP Response Data:
    OCSP Response Status: successful (0x0)
    Response Type: Basic OCSP Response
...
    Cert Status: Good
...
```

The following sections highlight the most common situations which require further modification to the configuration. Refer also to the MOD_SSL reference manual.

If more than a few SSL certificates are used for the server

OCSP responses are stored in the SSL stapling cache. While the responses are typically a few hundred to a few thousand bytes in size, mod_ssl supports OCSP responses up to around 10K bytes in size. With more than a few certificates, the stapling cache size (32768 bytes in the example above) may need to be increased. Error message AH01929 will be logged in case of an error storing a response.

If the certificate does not point to an OCSP responder, or if a different address must be used

Refer to the SSLSTAPLINGFORCEURL directive.

You can confirm that a server certificate points to an OCSP responder using the openssl command-line program, as follows:

```
$ openssl x509 -in ./www.example.com.crt -text | grep 'OCSP.*http'
OCSP - URI:http://ocsp.example.com
```

If the OCSP URI is provided and the web server can communicate to it directly without using a proxy, no configuration is required. Note that firewall rules that control outbound connections from the web server may need to be adjusted.

If no OCSP URI is provided, contact your Certificate Authority to determine if one is available; if so, configure it with SSLSTAPLINGFORCEURL in the virtual host that uses the certificate.

If multiple SSL-enabled virtual hosts are configured and OCSP Stapling should be disabled for some

Add `SSLUseStapling Off` to the virtual hosts for which OCSP Stapling should be disabled.

If the OCSP responder is slow or unreliable

Several directives are available to handle timeouts and errors. Refer to the documentation for the SSLSTAPLINGFAKETRYLATER, SSLSTAPLINGRESPONDERTIMEOUT, and SSLSTAPLINGRETURNRESPONDERERRORS directives.

If mod_ssl logs error AH02217

```
AH02217: ssl_stapling_init_cert: Can't retrieve issuer certificate!
```

In order to support OCSP Stapling when a particular server certificate is used, the certificate chain for that certificate must be configured. If it was not configured as part of enabling SSL, the AH02217 error will be issued when stapling is enabled, and an OCSP response will not be provided for clients using the certificate.

Refer to the SSLCERTIFICATECHAINFILE and SSLCERTIFICATEFILE for instructions for configuring the certificate chain.

Client Authentication and Access Control

- How can I force clients to authenticate using certificates?
- How can I force clients to authenticate using certificates for a particular URL, but still allow arbitrary clients to access the rest of the server?
- How can I allow only clients who have certificates to access a particular URL, but allow all clients to access the rest of the server?
- How can I require HTTPS with strong ciphers, and either basic authentication or client certificates, for access to part of the Intranet website, for clients coming from the Internet?

How can I force clients to authenticate using certificates?

When you know all of your users (eg, as is often the case on a corporate Intranet), you can require plain certificate authentication. All you need to do is to create client certificates signed by your own CA certificate (`ca.crt`) and then verify the clients against this certificate.

```
# require a client certificate which has to be directly
# signed by our CA certificate in ca.crt
SSLVerifyClient require
SSLVerifyDepth 1
SSLCACertificateFile "conf/ssl.crt/ca.crt"
```

How can I force clients to authenticate using certificates for a particular URL, but still allow arbitrary clients to access the rest of the server?

To force clients to authenticate using certificates for a particular URL, you can use the per-directory reconfiguration features of MOD_SSL:

```
SSLVerifyClient none
SSLCACertificateFile "conf/ssl.crt/ca.crt"

<Location "/secure/area">
SSLVerifyClient require
SSLVerifyDepth 1
</Location>
```

How can I allow only clients who have certificates to access a particular URL, but allow all clients to access the rest of the server?

The key to doing this is checking that part of the client certificate matches what you expect. Usually this means checking all or part of the Distinguished Name (DN), to see if it contains some known string. There are two ways to do this, using either MOD_AUTH_BASIC or SSLREQUIRE.

The MOD_AUTH_BASIC method is generally required when the certificates are completely arbitrary, or when their DNs have no common fields (usually the organisation, etc.). In this case, you should establish a password database containing *all* clients allowed, as follows:

```
SSLVerifyClient      none
SSLCACertificateFile "conf/ssl.crt/ca.crt"
SSLCACertificatePath "conf/ssl.crt"
```

```
<Directory "/usr/local/apache2/htdocs/secure/area">
    SSLVerifyClient       require
    SSLVerifyDepth        5
    SSLOptions            +FakeBasicAuth
    SSLRequireSSL
    AuthName              "Snake Oil Authentication"
    AuthType              Basic
    AuthBasicProvider     file
    AuthUserFile          "/usr/local/apache2/conf/httpd.passwd"
    Require               valid-user
</Directory>
```

The password used in this example is the DES encrypted string "password". See the SSLOPTIONS docs for more information.

httpd.passwd

```
/C=DE/L=Munich/O=Snake Oil, Ltd./OU=Staff/CN=Foo:xxj31ZMTZzkVA
/C=US/L=S.F./O=Snake Oil, Ltd./OU=CA/CN=Bar:xxj31ZMTZzkVA
/C=US/L=L.A./O=Snake Oil, Ltd./OU=Dev/CN=Quux:xxj31ZMTZzkVA
```

When your clients are all part of a common hierarchy, which is encoded into the DN, you can match them more easily using SSLREQUIRE, as follows:

```
SSLVerifyClient      none
SSLCACertificateFile "conf/ssl.crt/ca.crt"
SSLCACertificatePath "conf/ssl.crt"

<Directory "/usr/local/apache2/htdocs/secure/area">
  SSLVerifyClient       require
  SSLVerifyDepth        5
  SSLOptions            +FakeBasicAuth
  SSLRequireSSL
  SSLRequire        %{SSL_CLIENT_S_DN_O}  eq "Snake Oil, Ltd." \
                and %{SSL_CLIENT_S_DN_OU} in {"Staff", "CA", "Dev"}
</Directory>
```

How can I require HTTPS with strong ciphers, and either basic authentication or client certificates, for access to part of the Intranet website, for clients coming from the Internet? I still want to allow plain HTTP access for clients on the Intranet.

These examples presume that clients on the Intranet have IPs in the range 192.168.1.0/24, and that the part of the Intranet website you want to allow internet access to is `/usr/local/apache2/htdocs/subarea`. This configuration should remain outside of your HTTPS virtual host, so that it applies to both HTTPS and HTTP.

```
SSLCACertificateFile "conf/ssl.crt/company-ca.crt"

<Directory "/usr/local/apache2/htdocs">
    #   Outside the subarea only Intranet access is granted
    Require               ip 192.168.1.0/24
</Directory>

<Directory "/usr/local/apache2/htdocs/subarea">
```

```
    #   Inside the subarea any Intranet access is allowed
    #   but from the Internet only HTTPS + Strong-Cipher + Password
    #   or the alternative HTTPS + Strong-Cipher + Client-Certificate

    #   If HTTPS is used, make sure a strong cipher is used.
    #   Additionally allow client certs as alternative to basic auth.
    SSLVerifyClient      optional
    SSLVerifyDepth       1
    SSLOptions           +FakeBasicAuth +StrictRequire
    SSLRequire           %{SSL_CIPHER_USEKEYSIZE} >= 128

    #   Force clients from the Internet to use HTTPS
    RewriteEngine        on
    RewriteCond          "%{REMOTE_ADDR}" "!^192\.168\.1\.[0-9]+$"
    RewriteCond          "%{HTTPS}" "!=on"
    RewriteRule          "." "-" [F]

    #   Allow Network Access and/or Basic Auth
    Satisfy              any

    #   Network Access Control
    Require              ip 192.168.1.0/24

    #   HTTP Basic Authentication
    AuthType             basic
    AuthName             "Protected Intranet Area"
    AuthBasicProvider    file
    AuthUserFile         "conf/protected.passwd"
    Require              valid-user
</Directory>
```

Logging

MOD_SSL can log extremely verbose debugging information to the error log, when its LOGLEVEL is set to the higher trace levels. On the other hand, on a very busy server, level `info` may already be too much. Remember that you can configure the LOGLEVEL per module to suite your needs.

5.5 SSL/TLS Strong Encryption: FAQ

The wise man doesn't give the right answers, he poses the right questions.
– *Claude Levi-Strauss*

Installation

- Why do I get permission errors related to SSLMutex when I start Apache?
- Why does mod_ssl stop with the error "Failed to generate temporary 512 bit RSA private key" when I start Apache?

Why do I get permission errors related to SSLMutex when I start Apache?

Errors such as "`mod_ssl: Child could not open SSLMutex lockfile /opt/apache/logs/ssl_mutex.18332 (System error follows) [...] System: Permission denied (errno: 13)`" are usually caused by overly restrictive permissions on the *parent* directories. Make sure that all parent directories (here `/opt`, `/opt/apache` and `/opt/apache/logs`) have the x-bit set for, at minimum, the UID under which Apache's children are running (see the USER directive).

Why does mod_ssl stop with the error "Failed to generate temporary 512 bit RSA private key" when I start Apache?

Cryptographic software needs a source of unpredictable data to work correctly. Many open source operating systems provide a "randomness device" that serves this purpose (usually named `/dev/random`). On other systems, applications have to seed the OpenSSL Pseudo Random Number Generator (PRNG) manually with appropriate data before generating keys or performing public key encryption. As of version 0.9.5, the OpenSSL functions that need randomness report an error if the PRNG has not been seeded with at least 128 bits of randomness.

To prevent this error, MOD_SSL has to provide enough entropy to the PRNG to allow it to work correctly. This can be done via the SSLRANDOMSEED directive.

Configuration

- Is it possible to provide HTTP and HTTPS from the same server?
- Which port does HTTPS use?
- How do I speak HTTPS manually for testing purposes?
- Why does the connection hang when I connect to my SSL-aware Apache server?
- Why do I get "Connection Refused" errors, when trying to access my newly installed Apache+mod_ssl server via HTTPS?
- Why are the `SSL_XXX` variables not available to my CGI & SSI scripts?
- How can I switch between HTTP and HTTPS in relative hyperlinks?

Is it possible to provide HTTP and HTTPS from the same server?

Yes. HTTP and HTTPS use different server ports (HTTP binds to port 80, HTTPS to port 443), so there is no direct conflict between them. You can either run two separate server instances bound to these ports, or use Apache's elegant virtual hosting facility to create two virtual servers, both served by the same instance of Apache - one responding over HTTP to requests on port 80, and the other responding over HTTPS to requests on port 443.

Which port does HTTPS use?

You can run HTTPS on any port, but the standards specify port 443, which is where any HTTPS compliant browser will look by default. You can force your browser to look on a different port by specifying it in the URL. For example, if your server is set up to serve pages over HTTPS on port 8080, you can access them at `https://example.com:8080/`

How do I speak HTTPS manually for testing purposes?

While you usually just use

```
$ telnet localhost 80
GET / HTTP/1.0
```

for simple testing of Apache via HTTP, it's not so easy for HTTPS because of the SSL protocol between TCP and HTTP. With the help of OpenSSL's `s_client` command, however, you can do a similar check via HTTPS:

```
$ openssl s_client -connect localhost:443 -state -debug
GET / HTTP/1.0
```

Before the actual HTTP response you will receive detailed information about the SSL handshake. For a more general command line client which directly understands both HTTP and HTTPS, can perform GET and POST operations, can use a proxy, supports byte ranges, etc. you should have a look at the nifty cURL[6] tool. Using this, you can check that Apache is responding correctly to requests via HTTP and HTTPS as follows:

```
$ curl http://localhost/
$ curl https://localhost/
```

Why does the connection hang when I connect to my SSL-aware Apache server?

This can happen when you try to connect to a HTTPS server (or virtual server) via HTTP (eg, using `http://example.com/` instead of `https://example.com`). It can also happen when trying to connect via HTTPS to a HTTP server (eg, using `https://example.com/` on a server which doesn't support HTTPS, or which supports it on a non-standard port). Make sure that you're connecting to a (virtual) server that supports SSL.

Why do I get "Connection Refused" messages, when trying to access my newly installed Apache+mod_ssl server via HTTPS?

This error can be caused by an incorrect configuration. Please make sure that your LISTEN directives match your <VIRTUALHOST> directives. If all else fails, please start afresh, using the default configuration provided by MOD_SSL.

Why are the `SSL_XXX` variables not available to my CGI & SSI scripts?

Please make sure you have "`SSLOptions +StdEnvVars`" enabled for the context of your CGI/SSI requests.

[6] http://curl.haxx.se/

How can I switch between HTTP and HTTPS in relative hyperlinks?

Usually, to switch between HTTP and HTTPS, you have to use fully-qualified hyperlinks (because you have to change the URL scheme). Using MOD_REWRITE however, you can manipulate relative hyperlinks, to achieve the same effect.

```
RewriteEngine on
RewriteRule    "^/(.*)_SSL$"    "https://%{SERVER_NAME}/$1" [R,L]
RewriteRule    "^/(.*)_NOSSL$" "http://%{SERVER_NAME}/$1"  [R,L]
```

This rewrite ruleset lets you use hyperlinks of the form `<a href="document.html_SSL">`, to switch to HTTPS in a relative link. (Replace SSL with NOSSL to switch to HTTP.)

Certificates

- What are RSA Private Keys, CSRs and Certificates?
- Is there a difference on startup between a non-SSL-aware Apache and an SSL-aware Apache?
- How do I create a self-signed SSL Certificate for testing purposes?
- How do I create a real SSL Certificate?
- How do I create and use my own Certificate Authority (CA)?
- How can I change the pass-phrase on my private key file?
- How can I get rid of the pass-phrase dialog at Apache startup time?
- How do I verify that a private key matches its Certificate?
- How can I convert a certificate from PEM to DER format?
- Why do browsers complain that they cannot verify my server certificate?

What are RSA Private Keys, CSRs and Certificates?

An RSA private key file is a digital file that you can use to decrypt messages sent to you. It has a public component which you distribute (via your Certificate file) which allows people to encrypt those messages to you.

A Certificate Signing Request (CSR) is a digital file which contains your public key and your name. You send the CSR to a Certifying Authority (CA), who will convert it into a real Certificate, by signing it.

A Certificate contains your RSA public key, your name, the name of the CA, and is digitally signed by the CA. Browsers that know the CA can verify the signature on that Certificate, thereby obtaining your RSA public key. That enables them to send messages which only you can decrypt.

See the Introduction (p. 183) chapter for a general description of the SSL protocol.

Is there a difference on startup between a non-SSL-aware Apache and an SSL-aware Apache?

Yes. In general, starting Apache with MOD_SSL built-in is just like starting Apache without it. However, if you have a passphrase on your SSL private key file, a startup dialog will pop up which asks you to enter the pass phrase.

Having to manually enter the passphrase when starting the server can be problematic - for example, when starting the server from the system boot scripts. In this case, you can follow the steps below to remove the passphrase from your private key. Bear in mind that doing so brings additional security risks - proceed with caution!

How do I create a self-signed SSL Certificate for testing purposes?

1. Make sure OpenSSL is installed and in your `PATH`.

2. Run the following command, to create `server.key` and `server.crt` files:
   `$ openssl req -new -x509 -nodes -out server.crt -keyout server.key`
   These can be used as follows in your `httpd.conf` file:

   ```
   SSLCertificateFile    "/path/to/this/server.crt"
   SSLCertificateKeyFile "/path/to/this/server.key"
   ```

3. It is important that you are aware that this `server.key` does *not* have any passphrase. To add a passphrase to the key, you should run the following command, and enter & verify the passphrase as requested.
   `$ openssl rsa -des3 -in server.key -out server.key.new`
   `$ mv server.key.new server.key`
   Please backup the `server.key` file, and the passphrase you entered, in a secure location.

How do I create a real SSL Certificate?

Here is a step-by-step description:

1. Make sure OpenSSL is installed and in your `PATH`.

2. Create a RSA private key for your Apache server (will be Triple-DES encrypted and PEM formatted):
   `$ openssl genrsa -des3 -out server.key 2048`
   Please backup this `server.key` file and the pass-phrase you entered in a secure location. You can see the details of this RSA private key by using the command:

   `$ openssl rsa -noout -text -in server.key`
   If necessary, you can also create a decrypted PEM version (not recommended) of this RSA private key with:
   `$ openssl rsa -in server.key -out server.key.unsecure`

3. Create a Certificate Signing Request (CSR) with the server RSA private key (output will be PEM formatted):
   `$ openssl req -new -key server.key -out server.csr`
   Make sure you enter the FQDN ("Fully Qualified Domain Name") of the server when OpenSSL prompts you for the "CommonName", i.e. when you generate a CSR for a website which will be later accessed via `https://www.foo.dom/`, enter "www.foo.dom" here. You can see the details of this CSR by using

   `$ openssl req -noout -text -in server.csr`

4. You now have to send this Certificate Signing Request (CSR) to a Certifying Authority (CA) to be signed. Once the CSR has been signed, you will have a real Certificate, which can be used by Apache. You can have a CSR signed by a commercial CA, or you can create your own CA to sign it.
   Commercial CAs usually ask you to post the CSR into a web form, pay for the signing, and then send a signed Certificate, which you can store in a server.crt file.

For details on how to create your own CA, and use this to sign a CSR, see below.

Once your CSR has been signed, you can see the details of the Certificate as follows:
$ openssl x509 -noout -text -in server.crt

5. You should now have two files: `server.key` and `server.crt`. These can be used as follows in your `httpd.conf` file:

```
SSLCertificateFile    "/path/to/this/server.crt"
SSLCertificateKeyFile "/path/to/this/server.key"
```

The `server.csr` file is no longer needed.

How do I create and use my own Certificate Authority (CA)?

The short answer is to use the `CA.sh` or `CA.pl` script provided by OpenSSL. Unless you have a good reason not to, you should use these for preference. If you cannot, you can create a self-signed certificate as follows:

1. Create a RSA private key for your server (will be Triple-DES encrypted and PEM formatted):
$ openssl genrsa -des3 -out server.key 2048
Please backup this `server.key` file and the pass-phrase you entered in a secure location. You can see the details of this RSA private key by using the command:
$ openssl rsa -noout -text -in server.key
If necessary, you can also create a decrypted PEM version (not recommended) of this RSA private key with:
$ openssl rsa -in server.key -out server.key.unsecure

2. Create a self-signed certificate (X509 structure) with the RSA key you just created (output will be PEM formatted):
$ openssl req -new -x509 -nodes -sha1 -days 365 -key server.key -out server.crt -extensions usr_cert
This signs the server CSR and results in a `server.crt` file.
You can see the details of this Certificate using:
$ openssl x509 -noout -text -in server.crt

How can I change the pass-phrase on my private key file?

You simply have to read it with the old pass-phrase and write it again, specifying the new pass-phrase. You can accomplish this with the following commands:

```
$ openssl rsa -des3 -in server.key -out server.key.new
$ mv server.key.new server.key
```

The first time you're asked for a PEM pass-phrase, you should enter the old pass-phrase. After that, you'll be asked again to enter a pass-phrase - this time, use the new pass-phrase. If you are asked to verify the pass-phrase, you'll need to enter the new pass-phrase a second time.

How can I get rid of the pass-phrase dialog at Apache startup time?

The reason this dialog pops up at startup and every re-start is that the RSA private key inside your server.key file is stored in encrypted format for security reasons. The pass-phrase is needed to decrypt this file, so it can be read and parsed. Removing the pass-phrase removes a layer of security from your server - proceed with caution!

1. Remove the encryption from the RSA private key (while keeping a backup copy of the original file):
   ```
   $ cp server.key server.key.org
   $ openssl rsa -in server.key.org -out server.key
   ```

2. Make sure the server.key file is only readable by root:
   ```
   $ chmod 400 server.key
   ```

Now `server.key` contains an unencrypted copy of the key. If you point your server at this file, it will not prompt you for a pass-phrase. HOWEVER, if anyone gets this key they will be able to impersonate you on the net. PLEASE make sure that the permissions on this file are such that only root or the web server user can read it (preferably get your web server to start as root but run as another user, and have the key readable only by root).

As an alternative approach you can use the "`SSLPassPhraseDialog exec:/path/to/program`" facility. Bear in mind that this is neither more nor less secure, of course.

How do I verify that a private key matches its Certificate?

A private key contains a series of numbers. Two of these numbers form the "public key", the others are part of the "private key". The "public key" bits are included when you generate a CSR, and subsequently form part of the associated Certificate.

To check that the public key in your Certificate matches the public portion of your private key, you simply need to compare these numbers. To view the Certificate and the key run the commands:

```
$ openssl x509 -noout -text -in server.crt
$ openssl rsa -noout -text -in server.key
```

The 'modulus' and the 'public exponent' portions in the key and the Certificate must match. As the public exponent is usually 65537 and it's difficult to visually check that the long modulus numbers are the same, you can use the following approach:

```
$ openssl x509 -noout -modulus -in server.crt | openssl md5
$ openssl rsa -noout -modulus -in server.key | openssl md5
```

This leaves you with two rather shorter numbers to compare. It is, in theory, possible that these numbers may be the same, without the modulus numbers being the same, but the chances of this are overwhelmingly remote.

Should you wish to check to which key or certificate a particular CSR belongs you can perform the same calculation on the CSR as follows:

```
$ openssl req -noout -modulus -in server.csr | openssl md5
```

How can I convert a certificate from PEM to DER format?

The default certificate format for OpenSSL is PEM, which is simply Base64 encoded DER, with header and footer lines. For some applications (e.g. Microsoft Internet Explorer) you need the certificate in plain DER format. You can convert a PEM file `cert.pem` into the corresponding DER file `cert.der` using the following command: **`$ openssl x509 -in cert.pem -out cert.der -outform DER`**

Why do browsers complain that they cannot verify my server certificate?

One reason this might happen is because your server certificate is signed by an intermediate CA. Various CAs, such as Verisign or Thawte, have started signing certificates not with their root certificate but with intermediate certificates.

Intermediate CA certificates lie between the root CA certificate (which is installed in the browsers) and the server certificate (which you installed on the server). In order for the browser to be able to traverse and verify the trust chain from the server certificate to the root certificate it needs need to be given the intermediate certificates. The CAs should be able to provide you such intermediate certificate packages that can be installed on the server.

You need to include those intermediate certificates with the SSLCertificateChainFile directive.

The SSL Protocol

- Why do I get lots of random SSL protocol errors under heavy server load?
- Why does my webserver have a higher load, now that it serves SSL encrypted traffic?
- Why do HTTPS connections to my server sometimes take up to 30 seconds to establish a connection?
- What SSL Ciphers are supported by mod_ssl?
- Why do I get "no shared cipher" errors, when trying to use Anonymous Diffie-Hellman (ADH) ciphers?
- Why do I get a 'no shared ciphers' error when connecting to my newly installed server?
- Why can't I use SSL with name-based/non-IP-based virtual hosts?
- Is it possible to use Name-Based Virtual Hosting to identify different SSL virtual hosts?
- How do I get SSL compression working?
- When I use Basic Authentication over HTTPS the lock icon in Netscape browsers stays unlocked when the dialog pops up. Does this mean the username/password is being sent unencrypted?
- Why do I get I/O errors when connecting via HTTPS to an Apache+mod_ssl server with Microsoft Internet Explorer (MSIE)?
- How do I enable TLS-SRP?
- Why do I get handshake failures with Java-based clients when using a certificate with more than 1024 bits?

Why do I get lots of random SSL protocol errors under heavy server load?

There can be a number of reasons for this, but the main one is problems with the SSL session Cache specified by the SSLSessionCache directive. The DBM session cache is the most likely source of the problem, so using the SHM session cache (or no cache at all) may help.

Why does my webserver have a higher load, now that it serves SSL encrypted traffic?

SSL uses strong cryptographic encryption, which necessitates a lot of number crunching. When you request a webpage via HTTPS, everything (even the images) is encrypted before it is transferred. So increased HTTPS traffic leads to load increases.

Why do HTTPS connections to my server sometimes take up to 30 seconds to establish a connection?

This is usually caused by a `/dev/random` device for SSLRandomSeed which blocks the read(2) call until enough entropy is available to service the request. More information is available in the reference manual for the SSLRandomSeed directive.

What SSL Ciphers are supported by mod_ssl?

Usually, any SSL ciphers supported by the version of OpenSSL in use, are also supported by MOD_SSL. Which ciphers are available can depend on the way you built OpenSSL. Typically, at least the following ciphers are supported:

1. RC4 with SHA1
2. AES with SHA1
3. Triple-DES with SHA1

To determine the actual list of ciphers available, you should run the following:

```
$ openssl ciphers -v
```

Why do I get "no shared cipher" errors, when trying to use Anonymous Diffie-Hellman (ADH) ciphers?

By default, OpenSSL does *not* allow ADH ciphers, for security reasons. Please be sure you are aware of the potential side-effects if you choose to enable these ciphers.

In order to use Anonymous Diffie-Hellman (ADH) ciphers, you must build OpenSSL with "`-DSSL_ALLOW_ADH`", and then add "`ADH`" into your SSLCipherSuite.

Why do I get a 'no shared ciphers' error when connecting to my newly installed server?

Either you have made a mistake with your SSLCipherSuite directive (compare it with the pre-configured example in `extra/httpd-ssl.conf`) or you chose to use DSA/DH algorithms instead of RSA when you generated your private key and ignored or overlooked the warnings. If you have chosen DSA/DH, then your server cannot communicate using RSA-based SSL ciphers (at least until you configure an additional RSA-based certificate/key pair). Modern browsers like NS or IE can only communicate over SSL using RSA ciphers. The result is the `"no shared ciphers"` error. To fix this, regenerate your server certificate/key pair, using the RSA algorithm.

Why can't I use SSL with name-based/non-IP-based virtual hosts?

The reason is very technical, and a somewhat `"chicken and egg"` problem. The SSL protocol layer stays below the HTTP protocol layer and encapsulates HTTP. When an SSL connection (HTTPS) is established Apache/mod_ssl has to negotiate the SSL protocol parameters with the client. For this, mod_ssl has to consult the configuration of the virtual server (for instance it has to look for the cipher suite, the server certificate, etc.). But in order to go to the correct virtual server Apache has to know the `Host` HTTP header field. To do this, the HTTP request header has to be read. This cannot be done before the SSL handshake is finished, but the information is needed in order to complete the SSL handshake phase. See the next question for how to circumvent this issue.

Note that if you have a wildcard SSL certificate, or a certificate that has multiple hostnames on it using subjectAltName fields, you can use SSL on name-based virtual hosts without further workarounds.

Is it possible to use Name-Based Virtual Hosting to identify different SSL virtual hosts?

Name-Based Virtual Hosting is a very popular method of identifying different virtual hosts. It allows you to use the same IP address and the same port number for many different sites. When people move on to SSL, it seems natural to assume that the same method can be used to have lots of different SSL virtual hosts on the same server.

It is possible, but only if using a 2.2.12 or later web server, built with 0.9.8j or later OpenSSL. This is because it requires a feature that only the most recent revisions of the SSL specification added, called Server Name Indication (SNI).

Note that if you have a wildcard SSL certificate, or a certificate that has multiple hostnames on it using subjectAltName fields, you can use SSL on name-based virtual hosts without further workarounds.

The reason is that the SSL protocol is a separate layer which encapsulates the HTTP protocol. So the SSL session is a separate transaction, that takes place before the HTTP session has begun. The server receives an SSL request on IP address X and port Y (usually 443). Since the SSL request did not contain any Host: field, the server had no way to decide which SSL virtual host to use. Usually, it just used the first one it found which matched the port and IP address specified.

If you are using a version of the web server and OpenSSL that support SNI, though, and the client's browser also supports SNI, then the hostname is included in the original SSL request, and the web server can select the correct SSL virtual host.

You can, of course, use Name-Based Virtual Hosting to identify many non-SSL virtual hosts (all on port 80, for example) and then have a single SSL virtual host (on port 443). But if you do this, you must make sure to put the non-SSL port number on the NameVirtualHost directive, e.g.

```
NameVirtualHost 192.168.1.1:80
```

Other workaround solutions include:

Using separate IP addresses for different SSL hosts. Using different port numbers for different SSL hosts.

How do I get SSL compression working?

Although SSL compression negotiation was defined in the specification of SSLv2 and TLS, it took until May 2004 for RFC 3749 to define DEFLATE as a negotiable standard compression method.

OpenSSL 0.9.8 started to support this by default when compiled with the `zlib` option. If both the client and the server support compression, it will be used. However, most clients still try to initially connect with an SSLv2 Hello. As SSLv2 did not include an array of preferred compression algorithms in its handshake, compression cannot be negotiated with these clients. If the client disables support for SSLv2, either an SSLv3 or TLS Hello may be sent, depending on which SSL library is used, and compression may be set up. You can verify whether clients make use of SSL compression by logging the `%{SSL_COMPRESS_METHOD}x` variable.

When I use Basic Authentication over HTTPS the lock icon in Netscape browsers stays unlocked when the dialog pops up. Does this mean the username/password is being sent unencrypted?

No, the username/password is transmitted encrypted. The icon in Netscape browsers is not actually synchronized with the SSL/TLS layer. It only toggles to the locked state when the first part of the actual webpage data is transferred, which may confuse people. The Basic Authentication facility is part of the HTTP layer, which is above the SSL/TLS layer in HTTPS. Before any HTTP data communication takes place in HTTPS, the SSL/TLS layer has already completed its handshake phase, and switched to encrypted communication. So don't be confused by this icon.

Why do I get I/O errors when connecting via HTTPS to an Apache+mod_ssl server with older versions of Microsoft Internet Explorer (MSIE)?

The first reason is that the SSL implementation in some MSIE versions has some subtle bugs related to the HTTP keep-alive facility and the SSL close notify alerts on socket connection close. Additionally the interaction between SSL and HTTP/1.1 features are problematic in some MSIE versions. You can work around these problems by forcing

Apache not to use HTTP/1.1, keep-alive connections or send the SSL close notify messages to MSIE clients. This can be done by using the following directive in your SSL-aware virtual host section:

```
SetEnvIf User-Agent "MSIE [2-5]" \
         nokeepalive ssl-unclean-shutdown \
         downgrade-1.0 force-response-1.0
```

Further, some MSIE versions have problems with particular ciphers. Unfortunately, it is not possible to implement a MSIE-specific workaround for this, because the ciphers are needed as early as the SSL handshake phase. So a MSIE-specific SETENVIF won't solve these problems. Instead, you will have to make more drastic adjustments to the global parameters. Before you decide to do this, make sure your clients really have problems. If not, do not make these changes - they will affect *all* your clients, MSIE or otherwise.

How do I enable TLS-SRP?

TLS-SRP (Secure Remote Password key exchange for TLS, specified in RFC 5054) can supplement or replace certificates in authenticating an SSL connection. To use TLS-SRP, set the SSLSRPVERIFIERFILE directive to point to an OpenSSL SRP verifier file. To create the verifier file, use the `openssl` tool:

```
openssl srp -srpvfile passwd.srpv -add username
```

After creating this file, specify it in the SSL server configuration:

```
SSLSRPVerifierFile /path/to/passwd.srpv
```

To force clients to use non-certificate TLS-SRP cipher suites, use the following directive:

```
SSLCipherSuite "!DSS:!aRSA:SRP"
```

Why do I get handshake failures with Java-based clients when using a certificate with more than 1024 bits?

Beginning with version 2.4.7, MOD_SSL will use DH parameters which include primes with lengths of more than 1024 bits. Java 7 and earlier limit their support for DH prime sizes to a maximum of 1024 bits, however.

If your Java-based client aborts with exceptions such as `java.lang.RuntimeException: Could not generate DH keypair` and `java.security.InvalidAlgorithmParameterException: Prime size must be multiple of 64, and can only range from 512 to 1024 (inclusive)`, and httpd logs `tlsv1 alert internal error (SSL alert number 80)` (at LOGLEVEL `info` or higher), you can either rearrange mod_ssl's cipher list with SSLCIPHERSUITE (possibly in conjunction with SSLHONORCIPHERORDER), or you can use custom DH parameters with a 1024-bit prime, which will always have precedence over any of the built-in DH parameters.

To generate custom DH parameters, use the `openssl dhparam 1024` command. Alternatively, you can use the following standard 1024-bit DH parameters from RFC 2409[7], section 6.2:

```
-----BEGIN DH PARAMETERS-----
MIGHAoGBAP//////////yQ/aoiFowjTExmKLgNwc0SkCTgiKZ8x0Agu+pjsTmyJR
Sgh5jjQE3e+VGbPNOkMbMCsKbfJfFDdP4TVtbVHCReSFtXZiXn7G9ExC6aY37WsL
/1y29Aa37e44a/taiZ+lrp8kEXxLH+ZJKGZR7OZTgf//////////AgEC
-----END DH PARAMETERS-----
```

[7] http://www.ietf.org/rfc/rfc2409.txt

Add the custom parameters including the "BEGIN DH PARAMETERS" and "END DH PARAMETERS" lines to the end of the first certificate file you have configured using the SSLCertificateFile directive.

mod_ssl Support

- What information resources are available in case of mod_ssl problems?
- What support contacts are available in case of mod_ssl problems?
- What information should I provide when writing a bug report?
- I had a core dump, can you help me?
- How do I get a backtrace, to help find the reason for my core dump?

What information resources are available in case of mod_ssl problems?

The following information resources are available. In case of problems you should search here first.

Answers in the User Manual's F.A.Q. List (this) http://httpd.apache.org/docs/2.4/ssl/ssl_faq.html[8]
First check the F.A.Q. (this text). If your problem is a common one, it may have been answered several times before, and been included in this doc.

What support contacts are available in case of mod_ssl problems?

The following lists all support possibilities for mod_ssl, in order of preference. Please go through these possibilities *in this order* - don't just pick the one you like the look of.

1. *Send a Problem Report to the Apache httpd Users Support Mailing List*

   users@httpd.apache.org[9]
   This is the second way of submitting your problem report. Again, you must subscribe to the list first, but you can then easily discuss your problem with the whole Apache httpd user community.

2. *Write a Problem Report in the Bug Database*

   http://httpd.apache.org/bug_report.html[10]
   This is the last way of submitting your problem report. You should only do this if you've already posted to the mailing lists, and had no success. Please follow the instructions on the above page *carefully*.

What information should I provide when writing a bug report?

You should always provide at least the following information:

Apache httpd and OpenSSL version information The Apache version can be determined by running `httpd -v`. The OpenSSL version can be determined by running `openssl version`. Alternatively, if you have Lynx installed, you can run the command `lynx -mime_header http://localhost/ | grep Server` to gather this information in a single step.

[8] http://httpd.apache.org/docs/2.4/ssl/ssl_faq.html
[9] mailto:users@httpd.apache.org
[10] http://httpd.apache.org/bug_report.html

The details on how you built and installed Apache httpd and OpenSSL For this you can provide a logfile of your terminal session which shows the configuration and install steps. If this is not possible, you should at least provide the `configure` command line you used.

In case of core dumps please include a Backtrace If your Apache httpd dumps its core, please attach a stack-frame "backtrace" (see below for information on how to get this). This information is required in order to find a reason for your core dump.

A detailed description of your problem Don't laugh, we really mean it! Many problem reports don't include a description of what the actual problem is. Without this, it's very difficult for anyone to help you. So, it's in your own interest (you want the problem be solved, don't you?) to include as much detail as possible, please. Of course, you should still include all the essentials above too.

I had a core dump, can you help me?

In general no, at least not unless you provide more details about the code location where Apache dumped core. What is usually always required in order to help you is a backtrace (see next question). Without this information it is mostly impossible to find the problem and help you in fixing it.

How do I get a backtrace, to help find the reason for my core dump?

Following are the steps you will need to complete, to get a backtrace:

1. Make sure you have debugging symbols available, at least in Apache. On platforms where you use GCC/GDB, you will have to build Apache+mod_ssl with "`OPTIM="-g -ggdb3"`" to get this. On other platforms at least "`OPTIM="-g"`" is needed.

2. Start the server and try to reproduce the core-dump. For this you may want to use a directive like "`CoreDumpDirectory /tmp`" to make sure that the core-dump file can be written. This should result in a `/tmp/core` or `/tmp/httpd.core` file. If you don't get one of these, try running your server under a non-root UID. Many modern kernels do not allow a process to dump core after it has done a `setuid()` (unless it does an `exec()`) for security reasons (there can be privileged information left over in memory). If necessary, you can run `/path/to/httpd -X` manually to force Apache to not fork.

3. Analyze the core-dump. For this, run `gdb /path/to/httpd /tmp/httpd.core` or a similar command. In GDB, all you have to do then is to enter `bt`, and voila, you get the backtrace. For other debuggers consult your local debugger manual.

Chapter 6

Guides, Tutorials, and HowTos

6.1 How-To / Tutorials

How-To / Tutorials

Authentication and Authorization Authentication is any process by which you verify that someone is who they claim they are. Authorization is any process by which someone is allowed to be where they want to go, or to have information that they want to have.

See: Authentication, Authorization (p. 217)

Access Control Access control refers to the process of restricting, or granting access to a resource based on arbitrary criteria. There are a variety of different ways that this can be accomplished.

See: Access Control (p. 224)

Dynamic Content with CGI The CGI (Common Gateway Interface) defines a way for a web server to interact with external content-generating programs, which are often referred to as CGI programs or CGI scripts. It is a simple way to put dynamic content on your web site. This document will be an introduction to setting up CGI on your Apache web server, and getting started writing CGI programs.

See: CGI: Dynamic Content (p. 226)

`.htaccess` files `.htaccess` files provide a way to make configuration changes on a per-directory basis. A file, containing one or more configuration directives, is placed in a particular document directory, and the directives apply to that directory, and all subdirectories thereof.

See: `.htaccess` files (p. 239)

Introduction to Server Side Includes SSI (Server Side Includes) are directives that are placed in HTML pages, and evaluated on the server while the pages are being served. They let you add dynamically generated content to an existing HTML page, without having to serve the entire page via a CGI program, or other dynamic technology.

See: Server Side Includes (SSI) (p. 233)

Per-user web directories On systems with multiple users, each user can be permitted to have a web site in their home directory using the USERDIR directive. Visitors to a URL `http://example.com/~username/` will get content out of the home directory of the user `"username"`, out of the subdirectory specified by the USERDIR directive.

See: User web directories (`public_html`) (p. 245)

6.2 Authentication and Authorization

Authentication is any process by which you verify that someone is who they claim they are. Authorization is any process by which someone is allowed to be where they want to go, or to have information that they want to have.

For general access control, see the Access Control How-To (p. 224) .

Related Modules and Directives

There are three types of modules involved in the authentication and authorization process. You will usually need to choose at least one module from each group.

- Authentication type (see the AUTHTYPE directive)
  - MOD_AUTH_BASIC
  - MOD_AUTH_DIGEST
- Authentication provider (see the AUTHBASICPROVIDER and AUTHDIGESTPROVIDER directives)
  - MOD_AUTHN_ANON
  - MOD_AUTHN_DBD
  - MOD_AUTHN_DBM
  - MOD_AUTHN_FILE
  - MOD_AUTHNZ_LDAP
  - MOD_AUTHN_SOCACHE
- Authorization (see the REQUIRE directive)
  - MOD_AUTHNZ_LDAP
  - MOD_AUTHZ_DBD
  - MOD_AUTHZ_DBM
  - MOD_AUTHZ_GROUPFILE
  - MOD_AUTHZ_HOST
  - MOD_AUTHZ_OWNER
  - MOD_AUTHZ_USER

In addition to these modules, there are also MOD_AUTHN_CORE and MOD_AUTHZ_CORE. These modules implement core directives that are core to all auth modules.

The module MOD_AUTHNZ_LDAP is both an authentication and authorization provider. The module MOD_AUTHZ_HOST provides authorization and access control based on hostname, IP address or characteristics of the request, but is not part of the authentication provider system. For backwards compatibility with the mod_access, there is a new module MOD_ACCESS_COMPAT.

You probably also want to take a look at the Access Control (p. 224) howto, which discusses the various ways to control access to your server.

Introduction

If you have information on your web site that is sensitive or intended for only a small group of people, the techniques in this article will help you make sure that the people that see those pages are the people that you wanted to see them.

This article covers the "standard" way of protecting parts of your web site that most of you are going to use.

**Note:**

If your data really needs to be secure, consider using MOD_SSL in addition to any authentication.

The Prerequisites

The directives discussed in this article will need to go either in your main server configuration file (typically in a <DIRECTORY> section), or in per-directory configuration files (`.htaccess` files).

If you plan to use `.htaccess` files, you will need to have a server configuration that permits putting authentication directives in these files. This is done with the ALLOWOVERRIDE directive, which specifies which directives, if any, may be put in per-directory configuration files.

Since we're talking here about authentication, you will need an ALLOWOVERRIDE directive like the following:

```
AllowOverride AuthConfig
```

Or, if you are just going to put the directives directly in your main server configuration file, you will of course need to have write permission to that file.

And you'll need to know a little bit about the directory structure of your server, in order to know where some files are kept. This should not be terribly difficult, and I'll try to make this clear when we come to that point.

You will also need to make sure that the modules MOD_AUTHN_CORE and MOD_AUTHZ_CORE have either been built into the httpd binary or loaded by the httpd.conf configuration file. Both of these modules provide core directives and functionality that are critical to the configuration and use of authentication and authorization in the web server.

Getting it working

Here's the basics of password protecting a directory on your server.

First, you need to create a password file. Exactly how you do this will vary depending on what authentication provider you have chosen. More on that later. To start with, we'll use a text password file.

This file should be placed somewhere not accessible from the web. This is so that folks cannot download the password file. For example, if your documents are served out of `/usr/local/apache/htdocs`, you might want to put the password file(s) in `/usr/local/apache/passwd`.

To create the file, use the `htpasswd` utility that came with Apache. This will be located in the `bin` directory of wherever you installed Apache. If you have installed Apache from a third-party package, it may be in your execution path.

To create the file, type:

```
htpasswd -c /usr/local/apache/passwd/passwords rbowen
```

`htpasswd` will ask you for the password, and then ask you to type it again to confirm it:

```
# htpasswd -c /usr/local/apache/passwd/passwords rbowen
New password:  mypassword
Re-type new password:  mypassword
Adding password for user rbowen
```

If `htpasswd` is not in your path, of course you'll have to type the full path to the file to get it to run. With a default installation, it's located at `/usr/local/apache2/bin/htpasswd`

Next, you'll need to configure the server to request a password and tell the server which users are allowed access. You can do this either by editing the `httpd.conf` file or using an `.htaccess` file. For example, if you wish to protect the directory `/usr/local/apache/htdocs/secret`, you can use the following directives, either placed in the file `/usr/local/apache/htdocs/secret/.htaccess`, or placed in `httpd.conf` inside a <Directory "/usr/local/apache/htdocs/secret"> section.

```
AuthType Basic
AuthName "Restricted Files"
# (Following line optional)
AuthBasicProvider file
AuthUserFile "/usr/local/apache/passwd/passwords"
Require user rbowen
```

Let's examine each of those directives individually. The AUTHTYPE directive selects that method that is used to authenticate the user. The most common method is `Basic`, and this is the method implemented by MOD_AUTH_BASIC. It is important to be aware, however, that Basic authentication sends the password from the client to the server unencrypted. This method should therefore not be used for highly sensitive data, unless accompanied by MOD_SSL. Apache supports one other authentication method: `AuthType Digest`. This method is implemented by MOD_AUTH_DIGEST and was intended to be more secure. This is no longer the case and the connection should be encrypted with MOD_SSL instead.

The AUTHNAME directive sets the *Realm* to be used in the authentication. The realm serves two major functions. First, the client often presents this information to the user as part of the password dialog box. Second, it is used by the client to determine what password to send for a given authenticated area.

So, for example, once a client has authenticated in the `"Restricted Files"` area, it will automatically retry the same password for any area on the same server that is marked with the `"Restricted Files"` Realm. Therefore, you can prevent a user from being prompted more than once for a password by letting multiple restricted areas share the same realm. Of course, for security reasons, the client will always need to ask again for the password whenever the hostname of the server changes.

The AUTHBASICPROVIDER is, in this case, optional, since `file` is the default value for this directive. You'll need to use this directive if you are choosing a different source for authentication, such as MOD_AUTHN_DBM or MOD_AUTHN_DBD.

The AUTHUSERFILE directive sets the path to the password file that we just created with `htpasswd`. If you have a large number of users, it can be quite slow to search through a plain text file to authenticate the user on each request. Apache also has the ability to store user information in fast database files. The MOD_AUTHN_DBM module provides the AUTHDBMUSERFILE directive. These files can be created and manipulated with the `dbmmanage` and `htdbm` programs. Many other types of authentication options are available from third party modules in the Apache Modules Database[1].

Finally, the REQUIRE directive provides the authorization part of the process by setting the user that is allowed to access this region of the server. In the next section, we discuss various ways to use the REQUIRE directive.

Letting more than one person in

The directives above only let one person (specifically someone with a username of `rbowen`) into the directory. In most cases, you'll want to let more than one person in. This is where the AUTHGROUPFILE comes in.

[1] http://modules.apache.org/

If you want to let more than one person in, you'll need to create a group file that associates group names with a list of users in that group. The format of this file is pretty simple, and you can create it with your favorite editor. The contents of the file will look like this:

```
GroupName:  rbowen dpitts sungo rshersey
```

That's just a list of the members of the group in a long line separated by spaces.

To add a user to your already existing password file, type:

```
htpasswd /usr/local/apache/passwd/passwords dpitts
```

You'll get the same response as before, but it will be appended to the existing file, rather than creating a new file. (It's the `-c` that makes it create a new password file).

Now, you need to modify your `.htaccess` file or <DIRECTORY> block to look like the following:

```
AuthType Basic
AuthName "By Invitation Only"
# Optional line:
AuthBasicProvider file
AuthUserFile "/usr/local/apache/passwd/passwords"
AuthGroupFile "/usr/local/apache/passwd/groups"
Require group GroupName
```

Now, anyone that is listed in the group `GroupName`, and has an entry in the `password` file, will be let in, if they type the correct password.

There's another way to let multiple users in that is less specific. Rather than creating a group file, you can just use the following directive:

```
Require valid-user
```

Using that rather than the `Require user rbowen` line will allow anyone in that is listed in the password file, and who correctly enters their password.

Possible problems

Because of the way that Basic authentication is specified, your username and password must be verified every time you request a document from the server. This is even if you're reloading the same page, and for every image on the page (if they come from a protected directory). As you can imagine, this slows things down a little. The amount that it slows things down is proportional to the size of the password file, because it has to open up that file, and go down the list of users until it gets to your name. And it has to do this every time a page is loaded.

A consequence of this is that there's a practical limit to how many users you can put in one password file. This limit will vary depending on the performance of your particular server machine, but you can expect to see slowdowns once you get above a few hundred entries, and may wish to consider a different authentication method at that time.

Alternate password storage

Because storing passwords in plain text files has the above problems, you may wish to store your passwords somewhere else, such as in a database.

MOD_AUTHN_DBM and MOD_AUTHN_DBD are two modules which make this possible. Rather than selecting AUTHBASICPROVIDER `file`, instead you can choose `dbm` or `dbd` as your storage format.

To select a dbm file rather than a text file, for example:

```
<Directory "/www/docs/private">
    AuthName "Private"
    AuthType Basic
    AuthBasicProvider dbm
    AuthDBMUserFile "/www/passwords/passwd.dbm"
    Require valid-user
</Directory>
```

Other options are available. Consult the MOD_AUTHN_DBM documentation for more details.

Using multiple providers

With the introduction of the new provider based authentication and authorization architecture, you are no longer locked into a single authentication or authorization method. In fact any number of the providers can be mixed and matched to provide you with exactly the scheme that meets your needs. In the following example, both the file and LDAP based authentication providers are being used.

```
<Directory "/www/docs/private">
    AuthName "Private"
    AuthType Basic
    AuthBasicProvider file ldap
    AuthUserFile "/usr/local/apache/passwd/passwords"
    AuthLDAPURL ldap://ldaphost/o=yourorg
    Require valid-user
</Directory>
```

In this example the file provider will attempt to authenticate the user first. If it is unable to authenticate the user, the LDAP provider will be called. This allows the scope of authentication to be broadened if your organization implements more than one type of authentication store. Other authentication and authorization scenarios may include mixing one type of authentication with a different type of authorization. For example, authenticating against a password file yet authorizing against an LDAP directory.

Just as multiple authentication providers can be implemented, multiple authorization methods can also be used. In this example both file group authorization as well as LDAP group authorization is being used.

```
<Directory "/www/docs/private">
    AuthName "Private"
    AuthType Basic
    AuthBasicProvider file
    AuthUserFile "/usr/local/apache/passwd/passwords"
    AuthLDAPURL ldap://ldaphost/o=yourorg
    AuthGroupFile "/usr/local/apache/passwd/groups"
    Require group GroupName
    Require ldap-group cn=mygroup,o=yourorg
</Directory>
```

To take authorization a little further, authorization container directives such as <REQUIREALL> and <REQUIRE-ANY> allow logic to be applied so that the order in which authorization is handled can be completely controlled through the configuration. See Authorization Containers (p. 488) for an example of how they may be applied.

Beyond just authorization

The way that authorization can be applied is now much more flexible than just a single check against a single data store. Ordering, logic and choosing how authorization will be done is now possible.

Applying logic and ordering

Controlling how and in what order authorization will be applied has been a bit of a mystery in the past. In Apache 2.2 a provider-based authentication mechanism was introduced to decouple the actual authentication process from authorization and supporting functionality. One of the side benefits was that authentication providers could be configured and called in a specific order which didn't depend on the load order of the auth module itself. This same provider based mechanism has been brought forward into authorization as well. What this means is that the REQUIRE directive not only specifies which authorization methods should be used, it also specifies the order in which they are called. Multiple authorization methods are called in the same order in which the REQUIRE directives appear in the configuration.

With the introduction of authorization container directives such as <REQUIREALL> and <REQUIREANY>, the configuration also has control over when the authorization methods are called and what criteria determines when access is granted. See Authorization Containers (p. 488) for an example of how they may be used to express complex authorization logic.

By default all REQUIRE directives are handled as though contained within a <REQUIREANY> container directive. In other words, if any of the specified authorization methods succeed, then authorization is granted.

Using authorization providers for access control

Authentication by username and password is only part of the story. Frequently you want to let people in based on something other than who they are. Something such as where they are coming from.

The authorization providers `all`, `env`, `host` and `ip` let you allow or deny access based on other host based criteria such as host name or ip address of the machine requesting a document.

The usage of these providers is specified through the REQUIRE directive. This directive registers the authorization providers that will be called during the authorization stage of the request processing. For example:

```
Require ip address
```

where *address* is an IP address (or a partial IP address) or:

```
Require host domain_name
```

where *domain_name* is a fully qualified domain name (or a partial domain name); you may provide multiple addresses or domain names, if desired.

For example, if you have someone spamming your message board, and you want to keep them out, you could do the following:

```
<RequireAll>
    Require all granted
    Require not ip 10.252.46.165
</RequireAll>
```

Visitors coming from that address will not be able to see the content covered by this directive. If, instead, you have a machine name, rather than an IP address, you can use that.

```
<RequireAll>
    Require all granted
    Require not host host.example.com
</RequireAll>
```

And, if you'd like to block access from an entire domain, you can specify just part of an address or domain name:

```
<RequireAll>
    Require all granted
    Require not ip 192.168.205
    Require not host phishers.example.com moreidiots.example
    Require not host ke
</RequireAll>
```

Using <REQUIREALL> with multiple <REQUIRE> directives, each negated with `not`, will only allow access, if all of negated conditions are true. In other words, access will be blocked, if any of the negated conditions fails.

Access Control backwards compatibility

One of the side effects of adopting a provider based mechanism for authentication is that the previous access control directives ORDER, ALLOW, DENY and SATISFY are no longer needed. However to provide backwards compatibility for older configurations, these directives have been moved to the MOD_ACCESS_COMPAT module.

Authentication Caching

There may be times when authentication puts an unacceptable load on a provider or on your network. This is most likely to affect users of MOD_AUTHN_DBD (or third-party/custom providers). To deal with this, HTTPD 2.3/2.4 introduces a new caching provider MOD_AUTHN_SOCACHE to cache credentials and reduce the load on the origin provider(s).

This may offer a substantial performance boost to some users.

More information

You should also read the documentation for MOD_AUTH_BASIC and MOD_AUTHZ_HOST which contain some more information about how this all works. The directive <AUTHNPROVIDERALIAS> can also help in simplifying certain authentication configurations.

The various ciphers supported by Apache for authentication data are explained in Password Encryptions (p. 345) .

And you may want to look at the Access Control (p. 224) howto, which discusses a number of related topics.

6.3 Access Control

Access control refers to any means of controlling access to any resource. This is separate from authentication and authorization (p. 217) .

Related Modules and Directives

Access control can be done by several different modules. The most important of these are MOD_AUTHZ_CORE and MOD_AUTHZ_HOST. Also discussed in this document is access control using MOD_REWRITE.

Access control by host

If you wish to restrict access to portions of your site based on the host address of your visitors, this is most easily done using MOD_AUTHZ_HOST.

The REQUIRE provides a variety of different ways to allow or deny access to resources. In conjunction with the REQUIREALL, REQUIREANY, and REQUIRENONE directives, these requirements may be combined in arbitrarily complex ways, to enforce whatever your access policy happens to be.

The ALLOW, DENY, and ORDER directives, provided by MOD_ACCESS_COMPAT, are deprecated and will go away in a future version. You should avoid using them, and avoid outdated tutorials recommending their use.

The usage of these directives is:

```
Require host address
Require ip ip.address
```

In the first form, *address* is a fully qualified domain name (or a partial domain name); you may provide multiple addresses or domain names, if desired.

In the second form, *ip.address* is an IP address, a partial IP address, a network/netmask pair, or a network/nnn CIDR specification. Either IPv4 or IPv6 addresses may be used.

See the mod_authz_host documentation (p. 505) for further examples of this syntax.

You can insert `not` to negate a particular requirement. Note, that since a `not` is a negation of a value, it cannot be used by itself to allow or deny a request, as *not true* does not constitute *false*. Thus, to deny a visit using a negation, the block must have one element that evaluates as true or false. For example, if you have someone spamming your message board, and you want to keep them out, you could do the following:

```
<RequireAll>
    Require all granted
    Require not ip 10.252.46.165
</RequireAll>
```

Visitors coming from that address (`10.252.46.165`) will not be able to see the content covered by this directive. If, instead, you have a machine name, rather than an IP address, you can use that.

```
Require not host host.example.com
```

And, if you'd like to block access from an entire domain, you can specify just part of an address or domain name:

```
Require not ip 192.168.205
Require not host phishers.example.com moreidiots.example
Require not host gov
```

Use of the REQUIREALL, REQUIREANY, and REQUIRENONE directives may be used to enforce more complex sets of requirements.

Access control by arbitrary variables

Using the <IF>, you can allow or deny access based on arbitrary environment variables or request header values. For example, to deny access based on user-agent (the browser type) you might do the following:

```
<If "%{HTTP_USER_AGENT} == 'BadBot'">
    Require all denied
</If>
```

Using the REQUIRE `expr` syntax, this could also be written as:

```
Require expr %{HTTP_USER_AGENT} != 'BadBot'
```

**Warning:**
Access control by `User-Agent` is an unreliable technique, since the `User-Agent` header can be set to anything at all, at the whim of the end user.

See the expressions document (p. 89) for a further discussion of what expression syntaxes and variables are available to you.

Access control with mod_rewrite

The `[F]` REWRITERULE flag causes a 403 Forbidden response to be sent. Using this, you can deny access to a resource based on arbitrary criteria.

For example, if you wish to block access to a resource between 8pm and 6am, you can do this using MOD_REWRITE.

```
RewriteEngine On
RewriteCond "%{TIME_HOUR}" ">=20" [OR]
RewriteCond "%{TIME_HOUR}" "<07"
RewriteRule "^/fridge" "-" [F]
```

This will return a 403 Forbidden response for any request after 8pm or before 7am. This technique can be used for any criteria that you wish to check. You can also redirect, or otherwise rewrite these requests, if that approach is preferred.

The <IF> directive, added in 2.4, replaces many things that MOD_REWRITE has traditionally been used to do, and you should probably look there first before resorting to mod_rewrite.

More information

The expression engine (p. 89) gives you a great deal of power to do a variety of things based on arbitrary server variables, and you should consult that document for more detail.

Also, you should read the MOD_AUTHZ_CORE documentation for examples of combining multiple access requirements and specifying how they interact.

See also the Authentication and Authorization (p. 217) howto.

6.4 Apache Tutorial: Dynamic Content with CGI

Introduction

Related Modules	Related Directives
MOD_ALIAS	ADDHANDLER
MOD_CGI	OPTIONS
	SCRIPTALIAS

The CGI (Common Gateway Interface) defines a way for a web server to interact with external content-generating programs, which are often referred to as CGI programs or CGI scripts. It is the simplest, and most common, way to put dynamic content on your web site. This document will be an introduction to setting up CGI on your Apache web server, and getting started writing CGI programs.

Configuring Apache to permit CGI

In order to get your CGI programs to work properly, you'll need to have Apache configured to permit CGI execution. There are several ways to do this.

> **!** Note: If Apache has been built with shared module support you need to ensure that the module is loaded; in your `httpd.conf` you need to make sure the LOADMODULE directive has not been commented out. A correctly configured directive may look like this:
>
> ```
> LoadModule cgi_module modules/mod_cgi.so
> ```

ScriptAlias

The SCRIPTALIAS

directive tells Apache that a particular directory is set aside for CGI programs. Apache will assume that every file in this directory is a CGI program, and will attempt to execute it, when that particular resource is requested by a client.

The SCRIPTALIAS directive looks like:

```
ScriptAlias "/cgi-bin/" "/usr/local/apache2/cgi-bin/"
```

The example shown is from your default `httpd.conf` configuration file, if you installed Apache in the default location. The SCRIPTALIAS directive is much like the ALIAS directive, which defines a URL prefix that is to mapped to a particular directory. ALIAS and SCRIPTALIAS are usually used for directories that are outside of the DOCUMENTROOT directory. The difference between ALIAS and SCRIPTALIAS is that SCRIPTALIAS has the added meaning that everything under that URL prefix will be considered a CGI program. So, the example above tells Apache that any request for a resource beginning with `/cgi-bin/` should be served from the directory `/usr/local/apache2/cgi-bin/`, and should be treated as a CGI program.

For example, if the URL `http://www.example.com/cgi-bin/test.pl` is requested, Apache will attempt to execute the file `/usr/local/apache2/cgi-bin/test.pl` and return the output. Of course, the file will have to exist, and be executable, and return output in a particular way, or Apache will return an error message.

CGI outside of ScriptAlias directories

CGI programs are often restricted to SCRIPTALIAS'ed directories for security reasons. In this way, administrators can tightly control who is allowed to use CGI programs. However, if the proper security precautions are taken, there is no reason why CGI programs cannot be run from arbitrary directories. For example, you may wish to let users have web content in their home directories with the USERDIR directive. If they want to have their own CGI programs, but don't have access to the main cgi-bin directory, they will need to be able to run CGI programs elsewhere.

There are two steps to allowing CGI execution in an arbitrary directory. First, the cgi-script handler must be activated using the ADDHANDLER or SETHANDLER directive. Second, ExecCGI must be specified in the OPTIONS directive.

Explicitly using Options to permit CGI execution

You could explicitly use the OPTIONS directive, inside your main server configuration file, to specify that CGI execution was permitted in a particular directory:

```
<Directory "/usr/local/apache2/htdocs/somedir">
    Options +ExecCGI
</Directory>
```

The above directive tells Apache to permit the execution of CGI files. You will also need to tell the server what files are CGI files. The following ADDHANDLER directive tells the server to treat all files with the cgi or pl extension as CGI programs:

```
AddHandler cgi-script .cgi .pl
```

.htaccess files

The .htaccess tutorial (p. 239) shows how to activate CGI programs if you do not have access to httpd.conf.

User Directories

To allow CGI program execution for any file ending in .cgi in users' directories, you can use the following configuration.

```
<Directory "/home/*/public_html">
    Options +ExecCGI
    AddHandler cgi-script .cgi
</Directory>
```

If you wish designate a cgi-bin subdirectory of a user's directory where everything will be treated as a CGI program, you can use the following.

```
<Directory "/home/*/public_html/cgi-bin">
    Options ExecCGI
    SetHandler cgi-script
</Directory>
```

Writing a CGI program

There are two main differences between "regular" programming, and CGI programming.

First, all output from your CGI program must be preceded by a MIME-type header. This is HTTP header that tells the client what sort of content it is receiving. Most of the time, this will look like:

```
Content-type:  text/html
```

Secondly, your output needs to be in HTML, or some other format that a browser will be able to display. Most of the time, this will be HTML, but occasionally you might write a CGI program that outputs a gif image, or other non-HTML content.

Apart from those two things, writing a CGI program will look a lot like any other program that you might write.

Your first CGI program

The following is an example CGI program that prints one line to your browser. Type in the following, save it to a file called `first.pl`, and put it in your `cgi-bin` directory.

```
#!/usr/bin/perl
print "Content-type: text/html\n\n";
print "Hello, World.";
```

Even if you are not familiar with Perl, you should be able to see what is happening here. The first line tells Apache (or whatever shell you happen to be running under) that this program can be executed by feeding the file to the interpreter found at the location `/usr/bin/perl`. The second line prints the content-type declaration we talked about, followed by two carriage-return newline pairs. This puts a blank line after the header, to indicate the end of the HTTP headers, and the beginning of the body. The third line prints the string "Hello, World.". And that's the end of it.

If you open your favorite browser and tell it to get the address

```
http://www.example.com/cgi-bin/first.pl
```

or wherever you put your file, you will see the one line `Hello, World.` appear in your browser window. It's not very exciting, but once you get that working, you'll have a good chance of getting just about anything working.

But it's still not working!

There are four basic things that you may see in your browser when you try to access your CGI program from the web:

The output of your CGI program Great! That means everything worked fine. If the output is correct, but the browser is not processing it correctly, make sure you have the correct `Content-Type` set in your CGI program.

The source code of your CGI program or a "POST Method Not Allowed" message That means that you have not properly configured Apache to process your CGI program. Reread the section on configuring Apache and try to find what you missed.

A message starting with "Forbidden" That means that there is a permissions problem. Check the Apache error log and the section below on file permissions.

A message saying "Internal Server Error" If you check the Apache error log, you will probably find that it says "Premature end of script headers", possibly along with an error message generated by your CGI program. In this case, you will want to check each of the below sections to see what might be preventing your CGI program from emitting the proper HTTP headers.

File permissions

Remember that the server does not run as you. That is, when the server starts up, it is running with the permissions of an unprivileged user - usually `nobody`, or `www` - and so it will need extra permissions to execute files that are owned by you. Usually, the way to give a file sufficient permissions to be executed by `nobody` is to give everyone execute permission on the file:

```
chmod a+x first.pl
```

Also, if your program reads from, or writes to, any other files, those files will need to have the correct permissions to permit this.

Path information and environment

When you run a program from your command line, you have certain information that is passed to the shell without you thinking about it. For example, you have a `PATH`, which tells the shell where it can look for files that you reference.

When a program runs through the web server as a CGI program, it may not have the same `PATH`. Any programs that you invoke in your CGI program (like `sendmail`, for example) will need to be specified by a full path, so that the shell can find them when it attempts to execute your CGI program.

A common manifestation of this is the path to the script interpreter (often `perl`) indicated in the first line of your CGI program, which will look something like:

```
#!/usr/bin/perl
```

Make sure that this is in fact the path to the interpreter.

! When editing CGI scripts on Windows, end-of-line characters may be appended to the interpreter path. Ensure that files are then transferred to the server in ASCII mode. Failure to do so may result in "Command not found" warnings from the OS, due to the unrecognized end-of-line character being interpreted as a part of the interpreter filename.

Missing environment variables

If your CGI program depends on non-standard environment variables, you will need to assure that those variables are passed by Apache.

When you miss HTTP headers from the environment, make sure they are formatted according to RFC 2616[2], section 4.2: Header names must start with a letter, followed only by letters, numbers or hyphen. Any header violating this rule will be dropped silently.

Program errors

Most of the time when a CGI program fails, it's because of a problem with the program itself. This is particularly true once you get the hang of this CGI stuff, and no longer make the above two mistakes. The first thing to do is to make sure that your program runs from the command line before testing it via the web server. For example, try:

```
cd /usr/local/apache2/cgi-bin
./first.pl
```

[2] http://tools.ietf.org/html/rfc2616

(Do not call the `perl` interpreter. The shell and Apache should find the interpreter using the path information on the first line of the script.)

The first thing you see written by your program should be a set of HTTP headers, including the `Content-Type`, followed by a blank line. If you see anything else, Apache will return the `Premature end of script headers` error if you try to run it through the server. See Writing a CGI program above for more details.

Error logs

The error logs are your friend. Anything that goes wrong generates message in the error log. You should always look there first. If the place where you are hosting your web site does not permit you access to the error log, you should probably host your site somewhere else. Learn to read the error logs, and you'll find that almost all of your problems are quickly identified, and quickly solved.

Suexec

The suexec (p. 105) support program allows CGI programs to be run under different user permissions, depending on which virtual host or user home directory they are located in. Suexec has very strict permission checking, and any failure in that checking will result in your CGI programs failing with `Premature end of script headers`.

To check if you are using suexec, run `apachectl -V` and check for the location of `SUEXEC_BIN`. If Apache finds an `suexec` binary there on startup, suexec will be activated.

Unless you fully understand suexec, you should not be using it. To disable suexec, simply remove (or rename) the `suexec` binary pointed to by `SUEXEC_BIN` and then restart the server. If, after reading about suexec (p. 105) , you still wish to use it, then run `suexec -V` to find the location of the suexec log file, and use that log file to find what policy you are violating.

What's going on behind the scenes?

As you become more advanced in CGI programming, it will become useful to understand more about what's happening behind the scenes. Specifically, how the browser and server communicate with one another. Because although it's all very well to write a program that prints "Hello, World.", it's not particularly useful.

Environment variables

Environment variables are values that float around you as you use your computer. They are useful things like your path (where the computer searches for the actual file implementing a command when you type it), your username, your terminal type, and so on. For a full list of your normal, every day environment variables, type `env` at a command prompt.

During the CGI transaction, the server and the browser also set environment variables, so that they can communicate with one another. These are things like the browser type (Netscape, IE, Lynx), the server type (Apache, IIS, WebSite), the name of the CGI program that is being run, and so on.

These variables are available to the CGI programmer, and are half of the story of the client-server communication. The complete list of required variables is at Common Gateway Interface RFC[3].

This simple Perl CGI program will display all of the environment variables that are being passed around. Two similar programs are included in the `cgi-bin`

[3]http://www.ietf.org/rfc/rfc3875

directory of the Apache distribution. Note that some variables are required, while others are optional, so you may see some variables listed that were not in the official list. In addition, Apache provides many different ways for you to add your own environment variables (p. 82) to the basic ones provided by default.

```
#!/usr/bin/perl
use strict;
use warnings;

print "Content-type: text/html\n\n";
foreach my $key (keys %ENV) {
    print "$key --> $ENV{$key}<br>";
}
```

STDIN and STDOUT

Other communication between the server and the client happens over standard input (`STDIN`) and standard output (`STDOUT`). In normal everyday context, `STDIN` means the keyboard, or a file that a program is given to act on, and `STDOUT` usually means the console or screen.

When you `POST` a web form to a CGI program, the data in that form is bundled up into a special format and gets delivered to your CGI program over `STDIN`. The program then can process that data as though it was coming in from the keyboard, or from a file

The "special format" is very simple. A field name and its value are joined together with an equals (=) sign, and pairs of values are joined together with an ampersand (&). Inconvenient characters like spaces, ampersands, and equals signs, are converted into their hex equivalent so that they don't gum up the works. The whole data string might look something like:

```
name=Rich%20Bowen&city=Lexington&state=KY&sidekick=Squirrel%20Monkey
```

You'll sometimes also see this type of string appended to a URL. When that is done, the server puts that string into the environment variable called `QUERY_STRING`. That's called a `GET` request. Your HTML form specifies whether a `GET` or a `POST` is used to deliver the data, by setting the `METHOD` attribute in the `FORM` tag.

Your program is then responsible for splitting that string up into useful information. Fortunately, there are libraries and modules available to help you process this data, as well as handle other of the aspects of your CGI program.

CGI modules/libraries

When you write CGI programs, you should consider using a code library, or module, to do most of the grunt work for you. This leads to fewer errors, and faster development.

If you're writing CGI programs in Perl, modules are available on CPAN[4]. The most popular module for this purpose is `CGI.pm`. You might also consider `CGI::Lite`, which implements a minimal set of functionality, which is all you need in most programs.

If you're writing CGI programs in C, there are a variety of options. One of these is the `CGIC` library, from http://www.boutell.com/cgic/.

[4] http://www.cpan.org/

For more information

The current CGI specification is available in the Common Gateway Interface RFC[5].

When you post a question about a CGI problem that you're having, whether to a mailing list, or to a newsgroup, make sure you provide enough information about what happened, what you expected to happen, and how what actually happened was different, what server you're running, what language your CGI program was in, and, if possible, the offending code. This will make finding your problem much simpler.

Note that questions about CGI problems should **never** be posted to the Apache bug database unless you are sure you have found a problem in the Apache source code.

[5]http://www.ietf.org/rfc/rfc3875

6.5 Apache httpd Tutorial: Introduction to Server Side Includes

Server-side includes provide a means to add dynamic content to existing HTML documents.

Introduction

Related Modules	Related Directives
MOD_INCLUDE	OPTIONS
MOD_CGI	XBITHACK
MOD_EXPIRES	ADDTYPE
	SETOUTPUTFILTER
	BROWSERMATCHNOCASE

This article deals with Server Side Includes, usually called simply SSI. In this article, I'll talk about configuring your server to permit SSI, and introduce some basic SSI techniques for adding dynamic content to your existing HTML pages.

In the latter part of the article, we'll talk about some of the somewhat more advanced things that can be done with SSI, such as conditional statements in your SSI directives.

What are SSI?

SSI (Server Side Includes) are directives that are placed in HTML pages, and evaluated on the server while the pages are being served. They let you add dynamically generated content to an existing HTML page, without having to serve the entire page via a CGI program, or other dynamic technology.

For example, you might place a directive into an existing HTML page, such as:

```
<!--#echo var="DATE_LOCAL" -->
```

And, when the page is served, this fragment will be evaluated and replaced with its value:

```
Tuesday, 15-Jan-2013 19:28:54 EST
```

The decision of when to use SSI, and when to have your page entirely generated by some program, is usually a matter of how much of the page is static, and how much needs to be recalculated every time the page is served. SSI is a great way to add small pieces of information, such as the current time - shown above. But if a majority of your page is being generated at the time that it is served, you need to look for some other solution.

Configuring your server to permit SSI

To permit SSI on your server, you must have the following directive either in your `httpd.conf` file, or in a `.htaccess` file:

```
Options +Includes
```

This tells Apache that you want to permit files to be parsed for SSI directives. Note that most configurations contain multiple OPTIONS directives that can override each other. You will probably need to apply the `Options` to the specific directory where you want SSI enabled in order to assure that it gets evaluated last.

Not just any file is parsed for SSI directives. You have to tell Apache which files should be parsed. There are two ways to do this. You can tell Apache to parse any file with a particular file extension, such as .shtml, with the following directives:

```
AddType text/html .shtml
AddOutputFilter INCLUDES .shtml
```

One disadvantage to this approach is that if you wanted to add SSI directives to an existing page, you would have to change the name of that page, and all links to that page, in order to give it a .shtml extension, so that those directives would be executed.

The other method is to use the XBITHACK directive:

```
XBitHack on
```

XBITHACK tells Apache to parse files for SSI directives if they have the execute bit set. So, to add SSI directives to an existing page, rather than having to change the file name, you would just need to make the file executable using chmod.

```
chmod +x pagename.html
```

A brief comment about what not to do. You'll occasionally see people recommending that you just tell Apache to parse all .html files for SSI, so that you don't have to mess with .shtml file names. These folks have perhaps not heard about XBITHACK. The thing to keep in mind is that, by doing this, you're requiring that Apache read through every single file that it sends out to clients, even if they don't contain any SSI directives. This can slow things down quite a bit, and is not a good idea.

Of course, on Windows, there is no such thing as an execute bit to set, so that limits your options a little.

In its default configuration, Apache does not send the last modified date or content length HTTP headers on SSI pages, because these values are difficult to calculate for dynamic content. This can prevent your document from being cached, and result in slower perceived client performance. There are two ways to solve this:

1. Use the XBitHack Full configuration. This tells Apache to determine the last modified date by looking only at the date of the originally requested file, ignoring the modification date of any included files.

2. Use the directives provided by MOD_EXPIRES to set an explicit expiration time on your files, thereby letting browsers and proxies know that it is acceptable to cache them.

Basic SSI directives

SSI directives have the following syntax:

```
<!--#function attribute=value attribute=value ... -->
```

It is formatted like an HTML comment, so if you don't have SSI correctly enabled, the browser will ignore it, but it will still be visible in the HTML source. If you have SSI correctly configured, the directive will be replaced with its results.

The function can be one of a number of things, and we'll talk some more about most of these in the next installment of this series. For now, here are some examples of what you can do with SSI

Today's date

```
<!--#echo var="DATE_LOCAL" -->
```

The `echo` function just spits out the value of a variable. There are a number of standard variables, which include the whole set of environment variables that are available to CGI programs. Also, you can define your own variables with the `set` function.

If you don't like the format in which the date gets printed, you can use the `config` function, with a `timefmt` attribute, to modify that formatting.

```
<!--#config timefmt="%A %B %d, %Y" -->
Today is <!--#echo var="DATE_LOCAL" -->
```

Modification date of the file

```
This document last modified <!--#flastmod file="index.html" -->
```

This function is also subject to `timefmt` format configurations.

Including the results of a CGI program

This is one of the more common uses of SSI - to output the results of a CGI program, such as everybody's favorite, a "hit counter."

```
<!--#include virtual="/cgi-bin/counter.pl" -->
```

Additional examples

Following are some specific examples of things you can do in your HTML documents with SSI.

When was this document modified?

Earlier, we mentioned that you could use SSI to inform the user when the document was most recently modified. However, the actual method for doing that was left somewhat in question. The following code, placed in your HTML document, will put such a time stamp on your page. Of course, you will have to have SSI correctly enabled, as discussed above.

```
<!--#config timefmt="%A %B %d, %Y" -->
This file last modified <!--#flastmod file="ssi.shtml" -->
```

Of course, you will need to replace the `ssi.shtml` with the actual name of the file that you're referring to. This can be inconvenient if you're just looking for a generic piece of code that you can paste into any file, so you probably want to use the `LAST_MODIFIED` variable instead:

```
<!--#config timefmt="%D" -->
This file last modified <!--#echo var="LAST_MODIFIED" -->
```

For more details on the `timefmt` format, go to your favorite search site and look for `strftime`. The syntax is the same.

Including a standard footer

If you are managing any site that is more than a few pages, you may find that making changes to all those pages can be a real pain, particularly if you are trying to maintain some kind of standard look across all those pages.

Using an include file for a header and/or a footer can reduce the burden of these updates. You just have to make one footer file, and then include it into each page with the `include` SSI command. The `include` function can determine what file to include with either the `file` attribute, or the `virtual` attribute. The `file` attribute is a file path, *relative to the current directory*. That means that it cannot be an absolute file path (starting with /), nor can it contain ../ as part of that path. The `virtual` attribute is probably more useful, and should specify a URL relative to the document being served. It can start with a /, but must be on the same server as the file being served.

```
<!--#include virtual="/footer.html" -->
```

I'll frequently combine the last two things, putting a `LAST_MODIFIED` directive inside a footer file to be included. SSI directives can be contained in the included file, and includes can be nested - that is, the included file can include another file, and so on.

What else can I config?

In addition to being able to `config` the time format, you can also `config` two other things.

Usually, when something goes wrong with your SSI directive, you get the message

```
[an error occurred while processing this directive]
```

If you want to change that message to something else, you can do so with the `errmsg` attribute to the `config` function:

```
<!--#config errmsg="[It appears that you don't know how to use SSI]"
-->
```

Hopefully, end users will never see this message, because you will have resolved all the problems with your SSI directives before your site goes live. (Right?)

And you can `config` the format in which file sizes are returned with the `sizefmt` attribute. You can specify `bytes` for a full count in bytes, or `abbrev` for an abbreviated number in Kb or Mb, as appropriate.

Executing commands

I expect that I'll have an article some time in the coming months about using SSI with small CGI programs. For now, here's something else that you can do with the `exec` function. You can actually have SSI execute a command using the shell (`/bin/sh`, to be precise - or the DOS shell, if you're on Win32). The following, for example, will give you a directory listing.

```
<pre>
<!--#exec cmd="ls" -->
</pre>
```

or, on Windows

```
<pre>
<!--#exec cmd="dir" -->
</pre>
```

You might notice some strange formatting with this directive on Windows, because the output from `dir` contains the string "`<dir>`" in it, which confuses browsers.

Note that this feature is exceedingly dangerous, as it will execute whatever code happens to be embedded in the `exec` tag. If you have any situation where users can edit content on your web pages, such as with a "guestbook", for example, make sure that you have this feature disabled. You can allow SSI, but not the `exec` feature, with the `IncludesNOEXEC` argument to the `Options` directive.

Advanced SSI techniques

In addition to spitting out content, Apache SSI gives you the option of setting variables, and using those variables in comparisons and conditionals.

Setting variables

Using the `set` directive, you can set variables for later use. We'll need this later in the discussion, so we'll talk about it here. The syntax of this is as follows:

```
<!--#set var="name" value="Rich" -->
```

In addition to merely setting values literally like that, you can use any other variable, including environment variables (p. 82) or the variables discussed above (like `LAST_MODIFIED`, for example) to give values to your variables. You will specify that something is a variable, rather than a literal string, by using the dollar sign ($) before the name of the variable.

```
<!--#set var="modified" value="$LAST_MODIFIED" -->
```

To put a literal dollar sign into the value of your variable, you need to escape the dollar sign with a backslash.

```
<!--#set var="cost" value="\$100" -->
```

Finally, if you want to put a variable in the midst of a longer string, and there's a chance that the name of the variable will run up against some other characters, and thus be confused with those characters, you can place the name of the variable in braces, to remove this confusion. (It's hard to come up with a really good example of this, but hopefully you'll get the point.)

```
<!--#set var="date" value="${DATE_LOCAL}_${DATE_GMT}" -->
```

Conditional expressions

Now that we have variables, and are able to set and compare their values, we can use them to express conditionals. This lets SSI be a tiny programming language of sorts. MOD_INCLUDE provides an `if`, `elif`, `else`, `endif` structure for building conditional statements. This allows you to effectively generate multiple logical pages out of one actual page.

The structure of this conditional construct is:

```
<!--#if expr="test_condition" -->
<!--#elif expr="test_condition" -->
<!--#else -->
<!--#endif -->
```

A *test_condition* can be any sort of logical comparison - either comparing values to one another, or testing the "truth" of a particular value. (A given string is true if it is nonempty.) For a full list of the comparison operators available to you, see the MOD_INCLUDE documentation.

For example, if you wish to customize the text on your web page based on the time of day, you could use the following recipe, placed in the HTML page:

```
Good <!--#if expr="%{TIME_HOUR} <12" -->
morning!
<!--#else -->
afternoon!
<!--#endif -->
```

Any other variable (either ones that you define, or normal environment variables) can be used in conditional statements. See Expressions in Apache HTTP Server (p. 89) for more information on the expression evaluation engine.

With Apache's ability to set environment variables with the `SetEnvIf` directives, and other related directives, this functionality can let you do a wide variety of dynamic content on the server side without resorting a full web application.

Conclusion

SSI is certainly not a replacement for CGI, or other technologies used for generating dynamic web pages. But it is a great way to add small amounts of dynamic content to pages, without doing a lot of extra work.

6.6 Apache HTTP Server Tutorial: .htaccess files

`.htaccess` files provide a way to make configuration changes on a per-directory basis.

.htaccess files

Related Modules	Related Directives
CORE	ACCESSFILENAME
MOD_AUTHN_FILE	ALLOWOVERRIDE
MOD_AUTHZ_GROUPFILE	OPTIONS
MOD_CGI	ADDHANDLER
MOD_INCLUDE	SETHANDLER
MOD_MIME	AUTHTYPE
	AUTHNAME
	AUTHUSERFILE
	AUTHGROUPFILE
	REQUIRE

⟹ You should avoid using `.htaccess` files completely if you have access to httpd main server config file. Using `.htaccess` files slows down your Apache http server. Any directive that you can include in a `.htaccess` file is better set in a DIRECTORY block, as it will have the same effect with better performance.

What they are/How to use them

`.htaccess` files (or "distributed configuration files") provide a way to make configuration changes on a per-directory basis. A file, containing one or more configuration directives, is placed in a particular document directory, and the directives apply to that directory, and all subdirectories thereof.

Note:

If you want to call your `.htaccess` file something else, you can change the name of the file using the ACCESSFILENAME directive. For example, if you would rather call the file `.config` then you can put the following in your server configuration file:

```
AccessFileName ".config"
```

In general, `.htaccess` files use the same syntax as the main configuration files (p. 30) . What you can put in these files is determined by the ALLOWOVERRIDE directive. This directive specifies, in categories, what directives will be honored if they are found in a `.htaccess` file. If a directive is permitted in a `.htaccess` file, the documentation for that directive will contain an Override section, specifying what value must be in ALLOWOVERRIDE in order for that directive to be permitted.

For example, if you look at the documentation for the ADDDEFAULTCHARSET directive, you will find that it is permitted in `.htaccess` files. (See the Context line in the directive summary.) The Override (p. 351) line reads `FileInfo`. Thus, you must have at least `AllowOverride FileInfo` in order for this directive to be honored in `.htaccess` files.

Example:

Context: (p. 351)	server config, virtual host, directory, .htaccess
Override: (p. 351)	FileInfo

If you are unsure whether a particular directive is permitted in a `.htaccess` file, look at the documentation for that directive, and check the Context line for ".htaccess".

When (not) to use .htaccess files

In general, you should only use `.htaccess` files when you don't have access to the main server configuration file. There is, for example, a common misconception that user authentication should always be done in `.htaccess` files, and, in more recent years, another misconception that MOD_REWRITE directives must go in `.htaccess` files. This is simply not the case. You can put user authentication configurations in the main server configuration, and this is, in fact, the preferred way to do things. Likewise, `mod_rewrite` directives work better, in many respects, in the main server configuration.

`.htaccess` files should be used in a case where the content providers need to make configuration changes to the server on a per-directory basis, but do not have root access on the server system. In the event that the server administrator is not willing to make frequent configuration changes, it might be desirable to permit individual users to make these changes in `.htaccess` files for themselves. This is particularly true, for example, in cases where ISPs are hosting multiple user sites on a single machine, and want their users to be able to alter their configuration.

However, in general, use of `.htaccess` files should be avoided when possible. Any configuration that you would consider putting in a `.htaccess` file, can just as effectively be made in a <DIRECTORY> section in your main server configuration file.

There are two main reasons to avoid the use of `.htaccess` files.

The first of these is performance. When ALLOWOVERRIDE is set to allow the use of `.htaccess` files, httpd will look in every directory for `.htaccess` files. Thus, permitting `.htaccess` files causes a performance hit, whether or not you actually even use them! Also, the `.htaccess` file is loaded every time a document is requested.

Further note that httpd must look for `.htaccess` files in all higher-level directories, in order to have a full complement of directives that it must apply. (See section on how directives are applied.) Thus, if a file is requested out of a directory `/www/htdocs/example`, httpd must look for the following files:

```
/.htaccess
/www/.htaccess
/www/htdocs/.htaccess
/www/htdocs/example/.htaccess
```

And so, for each file access out of that directory, there are 4 additional file-system accesses, even if none of those files are present. (Note that this would only be the case if `.htaccess` files were enabled for `/`, which is not usually the case.)

In the case of REWRITERULE directives, in `.htaccess` context these regular expressions must be re-compiled with every request to the directory, whereas in main server configuration context they are compiled once and cached. Additionally, the rules themselves are more complicated, as one must work around the restrictions that come with per-directory context and `mod_rewrite`. Consult the Rewrite Guide (p. 137) for more detail on this subject.

The second consideration is one of security. You are permitting users to modify server configuration, which may result in changes over which you have no control. Carefully consider whether you want to give your users this privilege. Note also that giving users less privileges than they need will lead to additional technical support requests. Make sure you clearly tell your users what level of privileges you have given them. Specifying exactly what you have set ALLOWOVERRIDE to, and pointing them to the relevant documentation, will save yourself a lot of confusion later.

Note that it is completely equivalent to put a `.htaccess` file in a directory `/www/htdocs/example` containing a directive, and to put that same directive in a Directory section `<Directory "/www/htdocs/example">` in your main server configuration:

`.htaccess` file in `/www/htdocs/example`:

Contents of .htaccess file in `/www/htdocs/example`

```
AddType text/example ".exm"
```

Section from your `httpd.conf` file

```
<Directory "/www/htdocs/example">
    AddType text/example ".exm"
</Directory>
```

However, putting this configuration in your server configuration file will result in less of a performance hit, as the configuration is loaded once when httpd starts, rather than every time a file is requested.

The use of `.htaccess` files can be disabled completely by setting the ALLOWOVERRIDE directive to `none`:

```
AllowOverride None
```

How directives are applied

The configuration directives found in a `.htaccess` file are applied to the directory in which the `.htaccess` file is found, and to all subdirectories thereof. However, it is important to also remember that there may have been `.htaccess` files in directories higher up. Directives are applied in the order that they are found. Therefore, a `.htaccess` file in a particular directory may override directives found in `.htaccess` files found higher up in the directory tree. And those, in turn, may have overridden directives found yet higher up, or in the main server configuration file itself.

Example:

In the directory `/www/htdocs/example1` we have a `.htaccess` file containing the following:

```
Options +ExecCGI
```

(Note: you must have "`AllowOverride Options`" in effect to permit the use of the "OPTIONS" directive in `.htaccess` files.)

In the directory `/www/htdocs/example1/example2` we have a `.htaccess` file containing:

```
Options Includes
```

Because of this second `.htaccess` file, in the directory `/www/htdocs/example1/example2`, CGI execution is not permitted, as only `Options Includes` is in effect, which completely overrides any earlier setting that may have been in place.

Merging of .htaccess with the main configuration files

As discussed in the documentation on Configuration Sections (p. 33), `.htaccess` files can override the <DIRECTORY> sections for the corresponding directory, but will be overridden by other types of configuration sections from the main configuration files. This fact can be used to enforce certain configurations, even in the presence of a liberal ALLOWOVERRIDE setting. For example, to prevent script execution while allowing anything else to be set in `.htaccess` you can use:

```
<Directory "/www/htdocs">
    AllowOverride All
</Directory>

<Location "/">
    Options +IncludesNoExec -ExecCGI
</Location>
```

⟹ This example assumes that your DOCUMENTROOT is `/www/htdocs`.

Authentication example

If you jumped directly to this part of the document to find out how to do authentication, it is important to note one thing. There is a common misconception that you are required to use `.htaccess` files in order to implement password authentication. This is not the case. Putting authentication directives in a <DIRECTORY> section, in your main server configuration file, is the preferred way to implement this, and `.htaccess` files should be used only if you don't have access to the main server configuration file. See above for a discussion of when you should and should not use `.htaccess` files.

Having said that, if you still think you need to use a `.htaccess` file, you may find that a configuration such as what follows may work for you.

`.htaccess` file contents:

```
AuthType Basic
AuthName "Password Required"
AuthUserFile "/www/passwords/password.file"
AuthGroupFile "/www/passwords/group.file"
Require group admins
```

Note that `AllowOverride AuthConfig` must be in effect for these directives to have any effect.

Please see the authentication tutorial (p. 217) for a more complete discussion of authentication and authorization.

Server Side Includes example

Another common use of `.htaccess` files is to enable Server Side Includes for a particular directory. This may be done with the following configuration directives, placed in a `.htaccess` file in the desired directory:

```
Options +Includes
AddType text/html shtml
AddHandler server-parsed shtml
```

Note that `AllowOverride Options` and `AllowOverride FileInfo` must both be in effect for these directives to have any effect.

Please see the SSI tutorial (p. 233) for a more complete discussion of server-side includes.

Rewrite Rules in .htaccess files

When using REWRITERULE in `.htaccess` files, be aware that the per-directory context changes things a bit. In particular, rules are taken to be relative to the current directory, rather than being the original requested URI. Consider the following examples:

```
# In httpd.conf
RewriteRule "^/images/(.+)\.jpg" "/images/$1.png"

# In .htaccess in root dir
RewriteRule "^images/(.+)\.jpg" "images/$1.png"

# In .htaccess in images/
RewriteRule "^(.+)\.jpg" "$1.png"
```

In a `.htaccess` in your document directory, the leading slash is removed from the value supplied to REWRITERULE, and in the `images` subdirectory, `/images/` is removed from it. Thus, your regular expression needs to omit that portion as well.

Consult the mod_rewrite documentation (p. 136) for further details on using `mod_rewrite`.

CGI example

Finally, you may wish to use a `.htaccess` file to permit the execution of CGI programs in a particular directory. This may be implemented with the following configuration:

```
Options +ExecCGI
AddHandler cgi-script cgi pl
```

Alternately, if you wish to have all files in the given directory be considered to be CGI programs, this may be done with the following configuration:

```
Options +ExecCGI
SetHandler cgi-script
```

Note that `AllowOverride Options` and `AllowOverride FileInfo` must both be in effect for these directives to have any effect.

Please see the CGI tutorial (p. 226) for a more complete discussion of CGI programming and configuration.

Troubleshooting

When you put configuration directives in a `.htaccess` file, and you don't get the desired effect, there are a number of things that may be going wrong.

Most commonly, the problem is that ALLOWOVERRIDE is not set such that your configuration directives are being honored. Make sure that you don't have a `AllowOverride None` in effect for the file scope in question. A good test for this is to put garbage in your `.htaccess` file and reload the page. If a server error is not generated, then you almost certainly have `AllowOverride None` in effect.

If, on the other hand, you are getting server errors when trying to access documents, check your httpd error log. It will likely tell you that the directive used in your `.htaccess` file is not permitted.

```
[Fri Sep 17 18:43:16 2010] [alert] [client 192.168.200.51]
/var/www/html/.htaccess: DirectoryIndex not allowed here
```

This will indicate either that you've used a directive that is never permitted in `.htaccess` files, or that you simply don't have ALLOWOVERRIDE set to a level sufficient for the directive you've used. Consult the documentation for that particular directive to determine which is the case.

Alternately, it may tell you that you had a syntax error in your usage of the directive itself.

```
[Sat Aug 09 16:22:34 2008] [alert] [client 192.168.200.51]
/var/www/html/.htaccess:  RewriteCond:  bad flag delimiters
```

In this case, the error message should be specific to the particular syntax error that you have committed.

6.7 Per-user web directories

On systems with multiple users, each user can be permitted to have a web site in their home directory using the USERDIR directive. Visitors to a URL `http://example.com/~username/` will get content out of the home directory of the user "`username`", out of the subdirectory specified by the USERDIR directive.

Note that, by default, access to these directories is **not** enabled. You can enable access when using USERDIR by uncommenting the line

```
#Include conf/extra/httpd-userdir.conf
```

in the default config file `conf/httpd.conf`, and adapting the `httpd-userdir.conf` file as necessary, or by including the appropriate directives in a `Directory` block within the main config file.

See also

- Mapping URLs to the Filesystem (p. 61)

Per-user web directories

Related Modules	Related Directives
MOD_USERDIR	USERDIR DIRECTORYMATCH ALLOWOVERRIDE

Setting the file path with UserDir

The USERDIR directive specifies a directory out of which per-user content is loaded. This directive may take several different forms.

If a path is given which does not start with a leading slash, it is assumed to be a directory path relative to the home directory of the specified user. Given this configuration:

```
UserDir public_html
```

the URL `http://example.com/~rbowen/file.html` will be translated to the file path `/home/rbowen/public_html/file.html`

If a path is given starting with a slash, a directory path will be constructed using that path, plus the username specified. Given this configuration:

```
UserDir /var/html
```

the URL `http://example.com/~rbowen/file.html` will be translated to the file path `/var/html/rbowen/file.html`

If a path is provided which contains an asterisk (*), a path is used in which the asterisk is replaced with the username. Given this configuration:

```
UserDir /var/www/*/docs
```

the URL `http://example.com/~rbowen/file.html` will be translated to the file path `/var/www/rbowen/docs/file.html`

Multiple directories or directory paths can also be set.

```
UserDir public_html /var/html
```

For the URL `http://example.com/~rbowen/file.html`, Apache will search for `~rbowen`. If it isn't found, Apache will search for `rbowen` in `/var/html`. If found, the above URL will then be translated to the file path `/var/html/rbowen/file.html`

Redirecting to external URLs

The USERDIR directive can be used to redirect user directory requests to external URLs.

```
UserDir http://example.org/users/*/
```

The above example will redirect a request for `http://example.com/~bob/abc.html` to `http://example.org/users/bob/abc.html`.

Restricting what users are permitted to use this feature

Using the syntax shown in the UserDir documentation, you can restrict what users are permitted to use this functionality:

```
UserDir disabled root jro fish
```

The configuration above will enable the feature for all users except for those listed in the `disabled` statement. You can, likewise, disable the feature for all but a few users by using a configuration like the following:

```
UserDir disabled
UserDir enabled rbowen krietz
```

See USERDIR documentation for additional examples.

Enabling a cgi directory for each user

In order to give each user their own cgi-bin directory, you can use a <DIRECTORY> directive to make a particular subdirectory of a user's home directory cgi-enabled.

```
<Directory "/home/*/public_html/cgi-bin/">
    Options ExecCGI
    SetHandler cgi-script
</Directory>
```

Then, presuming that `UserDir` is set to `public_html`, a cgi program `example.cgi` could be loaded from that directory as:

```
http://example.com/~rbowen/cgi-bin/example.cgi
```

Allowing users to alter configuration

If you want to allows users to modify the server configuration in their web space, they will need to use `.htaccess` files to make these changes. Ensure that you have set ALLOWOVERRIDE to a value sufficient for the directives that you want to permit the users to modify. See the .htaccess tutorial (p. 239) for additional details on how this works.

Chapter 7

Platform-specific Notes

7.1 Platform Specific Notes

Microsoft Windows

Using Apache This document explains how to install, configure and run Apache 2.4 under Microsoft Windows.

See: Using Apache with Microsoft Windows (p. 251)

Compiling Apache There are many important points before you begin compiling Apache. This document explain them.

See: Compiling Apache for Microsoft Windows (p. 259)

Unix Systems

RPM Based Systems (Redhat / CentOS / Fedora) This document explains how to build, install, and run Apache 2.4 on systems supporting the RPM packaging format.

See: Using Apache With RPM Based Systems (p. 265)

Other Platforms

Novell NetWare This document explains how to install, configure and run Apache 2.4 under Novell NetWare 5.1 and above.

See: Using Apache With Novell NetWare (p. 268)

EBCDIC Version 1.3 of the Apache HTTP Server is the first version which includes a port to a (non-ASCII) mainframe machine which uses the EBCDIC character set as its native codeset.

> **Warning:** This document has not been updated to take into account changes made in the 2.4 version of the Apache HTTP Server. Some of the information may still be relevant, but please use it with care.

See: The Apache EBCDIC Port (p. 277)

7.2 Using Apache HTTP Server on Microsoft Windows

This document explains how to install, configure and run Apache 2.4 under Microsoft Windows. If you have questions after reviewing the documentation (and any event and error logs), you should consult the peer-supported users' mailing list[1].

This document assumes that you are installing a binary distribution of Apache. If you want to compile Apache yourself (possibly to help with development or tracking down bugs), see Compiling Apache for Microsoft Windows (p. 259) .

Operating System Requirements

The primary Windows platform for running Apache 2.4 is Windows 2000 or later. Always obtain and install the current service pack to avoid operating system bugs.

⟹ Apache HTTP Server versions later than 2.2 will not run on any operating system earlier than Windows 2000.

Downloading Apache for Windows

The Apache HTTP Server Project itself does not provide binary releases of software, only source code. Individual committers *may* provide binary packages as a convenience, but it is not a release deliverable.

If you cannot compile the Apache HTTP Server yourself, you can obtain a binary package from numerous binary distributions available on the Internet.

Popular options for deploying Apache httpd, and, optionally, PHP and MySQL, on Microsoft Windows, include:

- ApacheHaus[2]
- Apache Lounge[3]
- BitNami WAMP Stack[4]
- WampServer[5]
- XAMPP[6]

Customizing Apache for Windows

Apache is configured by the files in the `conf` subdirectory. These are the same files used to configure the Unix version, but there are a few different directives for Apache on Windows. See the directive index (p. 1030) for all the available directives.

The main differences in Apache for Windows are:

- Because Apache for Windows is multithreaded, it does not use a separate process for each request, as Apache can on Unix. Instead there are usually only two Apache processes running: a parent process, and a child which handles the requests. Within the child process each request is handled by a separate thread.

  The process management directives are also different:

[1] http://httpd.apache.org/userslist.html
[2] http://www.apachehaus.com/cgi-bin/download.plx
[3] http://www.apachelounge.com/download/
[4] http://bitnami.com/stack/wamp
[5] http://www.wampserver.com/
[6] http://www.apachefriends.org/en/xampp.html

MAXCONNECTIONSPERCHILD: Like the Unix directive, this controls how many connections a single child process will serve before exiting. However, unlike on Unix, a replacement process is not instantly available. Use the default `MaxConnectionsPerChild 0`, unless instructed to change the behavior to overcome a memory leak in third party modules or in-process applications.

Warning: The server configuration file is reread when a new child process is started. If you have modified `httpd.conf`, the new child may not start or you may receive unexpected results.

THREADSPERCHILD: This directive is new. It tells the server how many threads it should use. This is the maximum number of connections the server can handle at once, so be sure to set this number high enough for your site if you get a lot of hits. The recommended default is `ThreadsPerChild 150`, but this must be adjusted to reflect the greatest anticipated number of simultaneous connections to accept.

- The directives that accept filenames as arguments must use Windows filenames instead of Unix ones. However, because Apache may interpret backslashes as an "escape character" sequence, you should consistently use forward slashes in path names, not backslashes.
- While filenames are generally case-insensitive on Windows, URLs are still treated internally as case-sensitive before they are mapped to the filesystem. For example, the <LOCATION>, ALIAS, and PROXYPASS directives all use case-sensitive arguments. For this reason, it is particularly important to use the <DIRECTORY> directive when attempting to limit access to content in the filesystem, since this directive applies to any content in a directory, regardless of how it is accessed. If you wish to assure that only lowercase is used in URLs, you can use something like:

```
RewriteEngine On
RewriteMap lowercase int:tolower
RewriteCond "%{REQUEST_URI}" "[A-Z]"
RewriteRule "(.*)" "${lowercase:$1}" [R,L]
```

- When running, Apache needs write access only to the logs directory and any configured cache directory tree. Due to the issue of case insensitive and short 8.3 format names, Apache must validate all path names given. This means that each directory which Apache evaluates, from the drive root up to the directory leaf, must have read, list and traverse directory permissions. If Apache2.4 is installed at C:\Program Files, then the root directory, Program Files and Apache2.4 must all be visible to Apache.
- Apache for Windows contains the ability to load modules at runtime, without recompiling the server. If Apache is compiled normally, it will install a number of optional modules in the `\Apache2.4\modules` directory. To activate these or other modules, the LOADMODULE directive must be used. For example, to activate the status module, use the following (in addition to the status-activating directives in `access.conf`):

```
LoadModule status_module modules/mod_status.so
```

  Information on creating loadable modules (p. 845) is also available.
- Apache can also load ISAPI (Internet Server Application Programming Interface) extensions such as those used by Microsoft IIS and other Windows servers. More information is available (p. 640) . Note that Apache **cannot** load ISAPI Filters, and ISAPI Handlers with some Microsoft feature extensions will not work.
- When running CGI scripts, the method Apache uses to find the interpreter for the script is configurable using the SCRIPTINTERPRETERSOURCE directive.
- Since it is often difficult to manage files with names like `.htaccess` in Windows, you may find it useful to change the name of this per-directory configuration file using the ACCESSFILENAME directive.
- Any errors during Apache startup are logged into the Windows event log when running on Windows NT. This mechanism acts as a backup for those situations where Apache is not yet prepared to use the `error.log` file. You can review the Windows Application Event Log by using the Event Viewer, e.g. Start - Settings - Control Panel - Administrative Tools - Event Viewer.

Running Apache as a Service

Apache comes with a utility called the Apache Service Monitor. With it you can see and manage the state of all installed Apache services on any machine on your network. To be able to manage an Apache service with the monitor, you have to first install the service (either automatically via the installation or manually).

You can install Apache as a Windows NT service as follows from the command prompt at the Apache `bin` subdirectory:

```
httpd.exe -k install
```

If you need to specify the name of the service you want to install, use the following command. You have to do this if you have several different service installations of Apache on your computer. If you specify a name during the install, you have to also specify it during any other -k operation.

```
httpd.exe -k install -n "MyServiceName"
```

If you need to have specifically named configuration files for different services, you must use this:

```
httpd.exe -k install -n "MyServiceName" -f "c:\files\my.conf"
```

If you use the first command without any special parameters except `-k install`, the service will be called `Apache2.4` and the configuration will be assumed to be `conf\httpd.conf`.

Removing an Apache service is easy. Just use:

```
httpd.exe -k uninstall
```

The specific Apache service to be uninstalled can be specified by using:

```
httpd.exe -k uninstall -n "MyServiceName"
```

Normal starting, restarting and shutting down of an Apache service is usually done via the Apache Service Monitor, by using commands like `NET START Apache2.4` and `NET STOP Apache2.4` or via normal Windows service management. Before starting Apache as a service by any means, you should test the service's configuration file by using:

```
httpd.exe -n "MyServiceName" -t
```

You can control an Apache service by its command line switches, too. To start an installed Apache service you'll use this:

```
httpd.exe -k start -n "MyServiceName"
```

To stop an Apache service via the command line switches, use this:

```
httpd.exe -k stop -n "MyServiceName"
```

or

```
httpd.exe -k shutdown -n "MyServiceName"
```

You can also restart a running service and force it to reread its configuration file by using:

```
httpd.exe -k restart -n "MyServiceName"
```

By default, all Apache services are registered to run as the system user (the `LocalSystem` account). The `LocalSystem` account has no privileges to your network via any Windows-secured mechanism, including the file system, named pipes, DCOM, or secure RPC. It has, however, wide privileges locally.

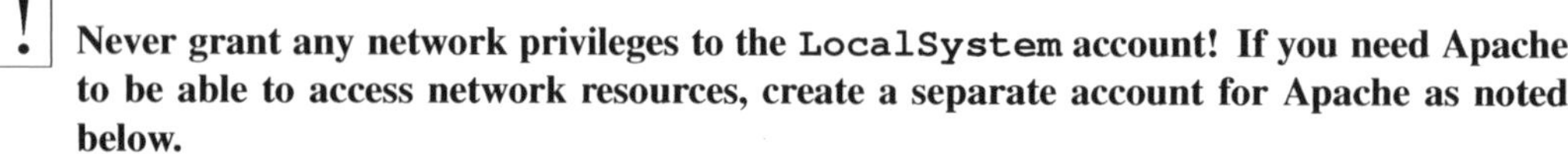
Never grant any network privileges to the `LocalSystem` account! If you need Apache to be able to access network resources, create a separate account for Apache as noted below.

It is recommended that users create a separate account for running Apache service(s). If you have to access network resources via Apache, this is required.

1. Create a normal domain user account, and be sure to memorize its password.
2. Grant the newly-created user a privilege of `Log on as a service` and `Act as part of the operating system`. On Windows NT 4.0 these privileges are granted via User Manager for Domains, but on Windows 2000 and XP you probably want to use Group Policy for propagating these settings. You can also manually set these via the Local Security Policy MMC snap-in.
3. Confirm that the created account is a member of the Users group.
4. Grant the account read and execute (RX) rights to all document and script folders (`htdocs` and `cgi-bin` for example).
5. Grant the account change (RWXD) rights to the Apache `logs` directory.
6. Grant the account read and execute (RX) rights to the `httpd.exe` binary executable.

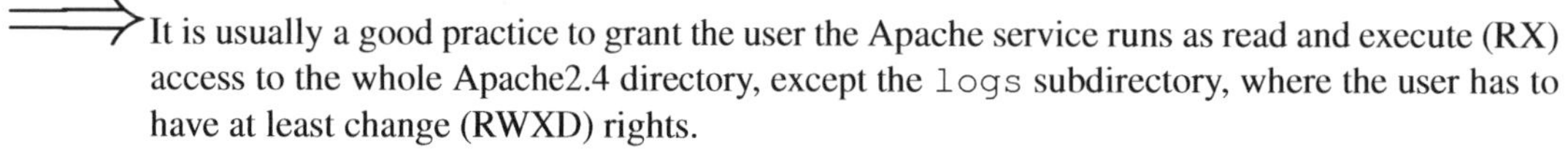
It is usually a good practice to grant the user the Apache service runs as read and execute (RX) access to the whole Apache2.4 directory, except the `logs` subdirectory, where the user has to have at least change (RWXD) rights.

If you allow the account to log in as a user and as a service, then you can log on with that account and test that the account has the privileges to execute the scripts, read the web pages, and that you can start Apache in a console window. If this works, and you have followed the steps above, Apache should execute as a service with no problems.

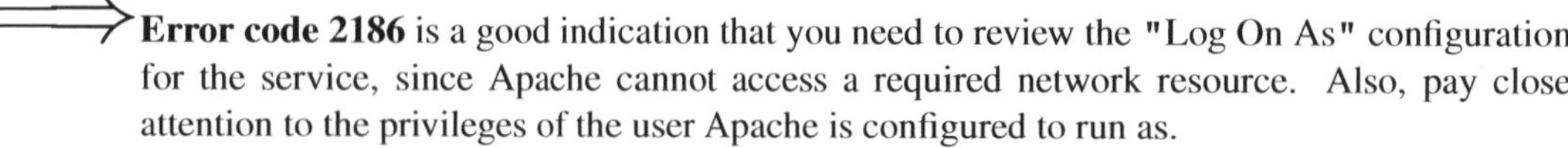
Error code 2186 is a good indication that you need to review the "Log On As" configuration for the service, since Apache cannot access a required network resource. Also, pay close attention to the privileges of the user Apache is configured to run as.

When starting Apache as a service you may encounter an error message from the Windows Service Control Manager. For example, if you try to start Apache by using the Services applet in the Windows Control Panel, you may get the following message:

```
Could not start the Apache2.4 service on \\COMPUTER
Error 1067; The process terminated unexpectedly.
```

You will get this generic error if there is any problem with starting the Apache service. In order to see what is really causing the problem you should follow the instructions for Running Apache for Windows from the Command Prompt.

If you are having problems with the service, it is suggested you follow the instructions below to try starting httpd.exe from a console window, and work out the errors before struggling to start it as a service again.

Running Apache as a Console Application

Running Apache as a service is usually the recommended way to use it, but it is sometimes easier to work from the command line, especially during initial configuration and testing.

To run Apache from the command line as a console application, use the following command:

```
httpd.exe
```

Apache will execute, and will remain running until it is stopped by pressing Control-C.

You can also run Apache via the shortcut Start Apache in Console placed to `Start Menu --> Programs --> Apache HTTP Server 2.4.xx --> Control Apache Server` during the installation. This will open a console window and start Apache inside it. If you don't have Apache installed as a service, the window will remain visible until you stop Apache by pressing Control-C in the console window where Apache is running in. The server will exit in a few seconds. However, if you do have Apache installed as a service, the shortcut starts the service. If the Apache service is running already, the shortcut doesn't do anything.

If Apache is running as a service, you can tell it to stop by opening another console window and entering:

```
httpd.exe -k shutdown
```

Running as a service should be preferred over running in a console window because this lets Apache end any current operations and clean up gracefully.

But if the server is running in a console window, you can only stop it by pressing Control-C in the same window.

You can also tell Apache to restart. This forces it to reread the configuration file. Any operations in progress are allowed to complete without interruption. To restart Apache, either press Control-Break in the console window you used for starting Apache, or enter

```
httpd.exe -k restart
```

if the server is running as a service.

⟹ Note for people familiar with the Unix version of Apache: these commands provide a Windows equivalent to `kill -TERM` *pid* and `kill -USR1` *pid*. The command line option used, `-k`, was chosen as a reminder of the `kill` command used on Unix.

If the Apache console window closes immediately or unexpectedly after startup, open the Command Prompt from the Start Menu –> Programs. Change to the folder to which you installed Apache, type the command `httpd.exe`, and read the error message. Then change to the logs folder, and review the `error.log` file for configuration mistakes. Assuming httpd was installed into `C:\Program Files\Apache Software Foundation\Apache2.4\`, you can do the following:

```
c:
cd "\Program Files\Apache Software Foundation\Apache2.4\bin"
httpd.exe
```

Then wait for Apache to stop, or press Control-C. Then enter the following:

```
cd ..\logs
more < error.log
```

When working with Apache it is important to know how it will find the configuration file. You can specify a configuration file on the command line in two ways:

- `-f` specifies an absolute or relative path to a particular configuration file:

  ```
  httpd.exe -f "c:\my server files\anotherconfig.conf"
  ```

  or

  ```
  httpd.exe -f files\anotherconfig.conf
  ```

- `-n` specifies the installed Apache service whose configuration file is to be used:

  ```
  httpd.exe -n "MyServiceName"
  ```

In both of these cases, the proper SERVERROOT should be set in the configuration file.

If you don't specify a configuration file with `-f` or `-n`, Apache will use the file name compiled into the server, such as `conf\httpd.conf`. This built-in path is relative to the installation directory. You can verify the compiled file name from a value labelled as `SERVER_CONFIG_FILE` when invoking Apache with the `-V` switch, like this:

```
httpd.exe -V
```

Apache will then try to determine its SERVERROOT by trying the following, in this order:

1. A SERVERROOT directive via the `-C` command line switch.
2. The `-d` switch on the command line.
3. Current working directory.
4. A registry entry which was created if you did a binary installation.
5. The server root compiled into the server. This is `/apache` by default, you can verify it by using `httpd.exe -V` and looking for a value labelled as `HTTPD_ROOT`.

If you did not do a binary install, Apache will in some scenarios complain about the missing registry key. This warning can be ignored if the server was otherwise able to find its configuration file.

The value of this key is the SERVERROOT directory which contains the `conf` subdirectory. When Apache starts it reads the `httpd.conf` file from that directory. If this file contains a SERVERROOT directive which contains a different directory from the one obtained from the registry key above, Apache will forget the registry key and use the directory from the configuration file. If you copy the Apache directory or configuration files to a new location it is vital that you update the SERVERROOT directive in the `httpd.conf` file to reflect the new location.

Testing the Installation

After starting Apache (either in a console window or as a service) it will be listening on port 80 (unless you changed the LISTEN directive in the configuration files or installed Apache only for the current user). To connect to the server and access the default page, launch a browser and enter this URL:

```
http://localhost/
```

Apache should respond with a welcome page and you should see "It Works!". If nothing happens or you get an error, look in the `error.log` file in the `logs` subdirectory. If your host is not connected to the net, or if you have serious problems with your DNS (Domain Name Service) configuration, you may have to use this URL:

```
http://127.0.0.1/
```

If you happen to be running Apache on an alternate port, you need to explicitly put that in the URL:

```
http://127.0.0.1:8080/
```

Once your basic installation is working, you should configure it properly by editing the files in the `conf` subdirectory. Again, if you change the configuration of the Windows NT service for Apache, first attempt to start it from the command line to make sure that the service starts with no errors.

Because Apache **cannot** share the same port with another TCP/IP application, you may need to stop, uninstall or reconfigure certain other services before running Apache. These conflicting services include other WWW servers, some firewall implementations, and even some client applications (such as Skype) which will use port 80 to attempt to bypass firewall issues.

Configuring Access to Network Resources

Access to files over the network can be specified using two mechanisms provided by Windows:

Mapped drive letters e.g., `Alias "/images/" "Z:/"`

UNC paths e.g., `Alias "/images/" "//imagehost/www/images/"`

Mapped drive letters allow the administrator to maintain the mapping to a specific machine and path outside of the Apache httpd configuration. However, these mappings are associated only with interactive sessions and are not directly available to Apache httpd when it is started as a service. **Use only UNC paths for network resources in httpd.conf** so that the resources can be accessed consistently regardless of how Apache httpd is started. (Arcane and error prone procedures may work around the restriction on mapped drive letters, but this is not recommended.)

Example DocumentRoot with UNC path

```
DocumentRoot "//dochost/www/html/"
```

Example DocumentRoot with IP address in UNC path

```
DocumentRoot "//192.168.1.50/docs/"
```

Example Alias and corresponding Directory with UNC path

```
Alias "/images/" "//imagehost/www/images/"

<Directory "//imagehost/www/images/">
#...
<Directory>
```

When running Apache httpd as a service, you must create a separate account in order to access network resources, as described above.

Windows Tuning

- If more than a few dozen piped loggers are used on an operating system instance, scaling up the "desktop heap" is often necessary. For more detailed information, refer to the piped logging (p. 53) documentation.

7.3 Compiling Apache for Microsoft Windows

There are many important points to consider before you begin compiling Apache HTTP Server (httpd). See Using Apache HTTP Server on Microsoft Windows (p. 251) before you begin.

httpd can be built on Windows using a cmake-based build system or with Visual Studio project files maintained by httpd developers. The cmake-based build system directly supports more versions of Visual Studio but currently has considerable functional limitations.

Building httpd with the included Visual Studio project files

Requirements

Compiling Apache requires the following environment to be properly installed:

- Disk Space

  Make sure you have at least 200 MB of free disk space available. After installation Apache requires approximately 80 MB of disk space, plus space for log and cache files, which can grow rapidly. The actual disk space requirements will vary considerably based on your chosen configuration and any third-party modules or libraries, especially when OpenSSL is also built. Because many files are text and very easily compressed, NTFS filesystem compression cuts these requirements in half.

- Appropriate Patches

  The httpd binary is built with the help of several patches to third party packages, which ensure the released code is buildable and debuggable. These patches are available and distributed from http://www.apache.org/dist/httpd/binaries/win32/patches_applied/ and are recommended to be applied to obtain identical results as the "official" ASF distributed binaries.

- Microsoft Visual C++ 6.0 (Visual Studio 97) or later.

  Apache can be built using the command line tools, or from within the Visual Studio IDE Workbench. The command line build requires the environment to reflect the `PATH`, `INCLUDE`, `LIB` and other variables that can be configured with the `vcvars32.bat` script.

  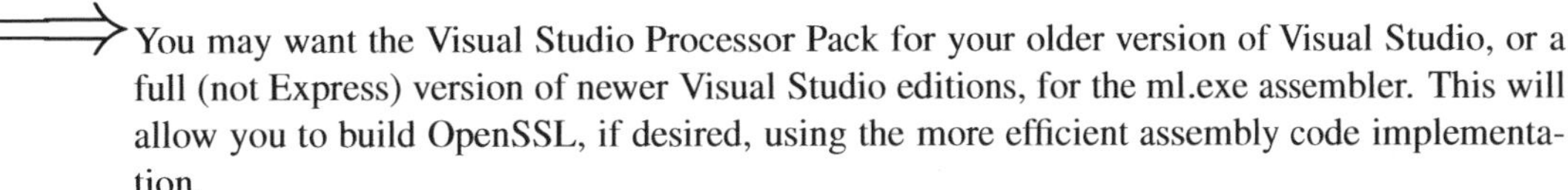

  ⟹ You may want the Visual Studio Processor Pack for your older version of Visual Studio, or a full (not Express) version of newer Visual Studio editions, for the ml.exe assembler. This will allow you to build OpenSSL, if desired, using the more efficient assembly code implementation.

  ⟹ Only the Microsoft compiler tool chain is actively supported by the active httpd contributors. Although the project regularly accepts patches to ensure MinGW and other alternative builds work and improve upon them, they are not actively maintained and are often broken in the course of normal development.

- Updated Microsoft Windows Platform SDK, February 2003 or later.

  An appropriate Windows Platform SDK is included by default in the full (not express/lite) versions of Visual C++ 7.1 (Visual Studio 2002) and later, these users can ignore these steps unless explicitly choosing a newer or different version of the Platform SDK.

  To use Visual C++ 6.0 or 7.0 (Studio 2000 .NET), the Platform SDK environment must be prepared using the `setenv.bat` script (installed by the Platform SDK) before starting the command line build or launching the msdev/devenv GUI environment. Installing the Platform SDK for Visual Studio Express versions (2003 and later) should adjust the default environment appropriately.

```
"c:\Program Files\Microsoft Visual Studio\VC98\Bin\VCVARS32"
"c:\Program Files\Platform SDK\setenv.bat"
```

- Perl and awk

  Several steps recommended here require a perl interpreter during the build preparation process, but it is otherwise not required.

  To install Apache within the build system, several files are modified using the `awk.exe` utility. awk was chosen since it is a very small download (compared with Perl or WSH/VB) and accomplishes the task of modifying configuration files upon installation. Brian Kernighan's http://www.cs.princeton.edu/~bwk/btl.mirror/ site has a compiled native Win32 binary, http://www.cs.princeton.edu/~bwk/btl.mirror/awk95.exe which you must save with the name `awk.exe` (rather than `awk95.exe`).

  ⟹ If awk.exe is not found, Makefile.win's install target will not perform substitutions in the installed .conf files. You must manually modify the installed .conf files to allow the server to start. Search and replace all "@token@" tags as appropriate.

  ⟹ The Visual Studio IDE will only find `awk.exe` from the PATH, or executable path specified in the menu option Tools -> Options -> (Projects ->) Directories. Ensure awk.exe is in your system path.

  ⟹ Also note that if you are using Cygwin tools (http://www.cygwin.com/) the awk utility is named `gawk.exe` and that the file `awk.exe` is really a symlink to the `gawk.exe` file. The Windows command shell does not recognize symlinks, and because of this building InstallBin will fail. A workaround is to delete `awk.exe` from the cygwin installation and copy `gawk.exe` to `awk.exe`. Also note the cygwin/mingw ports of gawk 3.0.x were buggy, please upgrade to 3.1.x before attempting to use any gawk port.

- [Optional] zlib library (for MOD_DEFLATE)

  Zlib must be installed into a `srclib` subdirectory named `zlib`. This must be built in-place. Zlib can be obtained from http://www.zlib.net/ – the MOD_DEFLATE is confirmed to work correctly with version 1.2.3.

```
nmake -f win32\Makefile.msc
nmake -f win32\Makefile.msc test
```

- [Optional] OpenSSL libraries (for MOD_SSL and `ab.exe` with ssl support)

  ⟹ The OpenSSL library is cryptographic software. The country in which you currently reside may have restrictions on the import, possession, use, and/or re-export to another country, of encryption software. BEFORE using any encryption software, please check your country's laws, regulations and policies concerning the import, possession, or use, and re-export of encryption software, to see if this is permitted. See http://www.wassenaar.org/ for more information.

  Configuring and building OpenSSL requires perl to be installed.

  OpenSSL must be installed into a `srclib` subdirectory named `openssl`, obtained from http://www.openssl.org/source/, in order to compile MOD_SSL or the `abs.exe` project, which is ab.c with SSL support enabled. To prepare OpenSSL to be linked to Apache mod_ssl or abs.exe, and disable patent encumbered features in OpenSSL, you might use the following build commands:

```
perl Configure no-rc5 no-idea enable-mdc2 enable-zlib VC-WIN32
-Ipath/to/srclib/zlib -Lpath/to/srclib/zlib
ms\do_masm.bat
nmake -f ms\ntdll.mak
```

  ⟹ It is not advisable to use zlib-dynamic, as that transfers the cost of deflating SSL streams to the first request which must load the zlib dll. Note the suggested patch enables the -L flag to work with windows builds, corrects the name of zdll.lib and ensures .pdb files are generated for troubleshooting. If the assembler is not installed, you would add no-asm above and use ms\do_ms.bat instead of the ms\do_masm.bat script.

- [Optional] Database libraries (for MOD_DBD and MOD_AUTHN_DBM)

  The apr-util library exposes dbm (keyed database) and dbd (query oriented database) client functionality to the httpd server and its modules, such as authentication and authorization. The sdbm dbm and odbc dbd providers are compiled unconditionally.

  The dbd support includes the Oracle instantclient package, MySQL, PostgreSQL and sqlite. To build these all, for example, set up the LIB to include the library path, INCLUDE to include the headers path, and PATH to include the dll bin path of all four SDK's, and set the DBD_LIST environment variable to inform the build which client driver SDKs are installed correctly, e.g.;

```
set DBD_LIST=sqlite3 pgsql oracle mysql
```

  Similarly, the dbm support can be extended with DBM_LIST to build a Berkeley DB provider (db) and/or gdbm provider, by similarly configuring LIB, INCLUDE and PATH first to ensure the client library libs and headers are available.

```
set DBM_LIST=db gdbm
```

  ⟹ Depending on the choice of database distributions, it may be necessary to change the actual link target name (e.g. gdbm.lib vs. libgdb.lib) that are listed in the corresponding .dsp/.mak files within the directories srclib\apr-util\dbd or ...\dbm.

  See the README-win32.txt file for more hints on obtaining the various database driver SDKs.

Building from Unix sources

The policy of the Apache HTTP Server project is to only release Unix sources. Windows source packages made available for download have been supplied by volunteers and may not be available for every release. You can still build the server on Windows from the Unix source tarball with just a few additional steps.

1. Download and unpack the Unix source tarball for the latest version.
2. Download and unpack the Unix source tarball for latest version of APR, AR-Util and APR-Iconv, place these sources in directories httpd-2.x.x\srclib\apr, httpd-2.x.x\srclib\apr-util and httpd-2.x.x\srclib\apr-iconv
3. Open a Command Prompt and CD to the httpd-2.x.x folder
4. Run the line endings conversion utility at the prompt;

```
perl srclib\apr\build\lineends.pl
```

You can now build the server with the Visual Studio development environment using the IDE. Command-Line builds of the server are not possible from Unix sources unless you export .mak files as explained below.

Command-Line Build

`Makefile.win` is the top level Apache makefile. To compile Apache on Windows, simply use one of the following commands to build the `release` or `debug` flavor:

```
nmake /f Makefile.win _apacher
nmake /f Makefile.win _apached
```

Either command will compile Apache. The latter will disable optimization of the resulting files, making it easier to single step the code to find bugs and track down problems.

You can add your apr-util dbd and dbm provider choices with the additional make (environment) variables DBD_LIST and DBM_LIST, see the comments about [Optional] Database libraries, above. Review the initial comments in Makefile.win for additional options that can be provided when invoking the build.

Developer Studio Workspace IDE Build

Apache can also be compiled using VC++'s Visual Studio development environment. To simplify this process, a Visual Studio workspace, `Apache.dsw`, is provided. This workspace exposes the entire list of working `.dsp` projects that are required for the complete Apache binary release. It includes dependencies between the projects to assure that they are built in the appropriate order.

Open the `Apache.dsw` workspace, and select `InstallBin` (`Release` or `Debug` build, as desired) as the Active Project. `InstallBin` causes all related project to be built, and then invokes `Makefile.win` to move the compiled executables and dlls. You may personalize the `INSTDIR=` choice by changing `InstallBin`'s Settings, General tab, Build command line entry. `INSTDIR` defaults to the `/Apache2` directory. If you only want a test compile (without installing) you may build the `BuildBin` project instead.

The `.dsp` project files are distributed in Visual Studio 6.0 (98) format. Visual C++ 5.0 (97) will recognize them. Visual Studio 2002 (.NET) and later users must convert `Apache.dsw` plus the `.dsp` files into an `Apache.sln` plus `.msproj` files. Be sure you reconvert the `.msproj` file again if its source `.dsp` file changes! This is really trivial, just open `Apache.dsw` in the VC++ 7.0 IDE once again and reconvert.

⟹ There is a flaw in the .vcproj conversion of .dsp files. devenv.exe will mis-parse the /D flag for RC flags containing long quoted /D'efines which contain spaces. The command:

```
perl srclib\apr\build\cvtdsp.pl -2005
```

will convert the /D flags for RC flags to use an alternate, parseable syntax; unfortunately this syntax isn't supported by Visual Studio 97 or its exported .mak files. These /D flags are used to pass the long description of the mod_apachemodule.so files to the shared .rc resource version-identifier build.

Visual Studio 2002 (.NET) and later users should also use the Build menu, Configuration Manager dialog to uncheck both the `Debug` and `Release` Solution modules `abs`, MOD_DEFLATE and MOD_SSL components, as well as every component starting with `apr_db*`. These modules are built by invoking `nmake`, or the IDE directly with the `BinBuild` target, which builds those modules conditionally if the `srclib` directories `openssl` and/or `zlib` exist, and based on the setting of `DBD_LIST` and `DBM_LIST` environment variables.

Exporting command-line .mak files

Exported `.mak` files pose a greater hassle, but they are required for Visual C++ 5.0 users to build MOD_SSL, abs (`ab` with SSL support) and/or MOD_DEFLATE. The .mak files also support a broader range of C++ tool chain distributions, such as Visual Studio Express.

You must first build all projects in order to create all dynamic auto-generated targets, so that dependencies can be parsed correctly. Build the entire project from within the Visual Studio 6.0 (98) IDE, using the `BuildAll` target, then use the Project Menu Export for all makefiles (checking on "with dependencies".) Run the following command to correct absolute paths into relative paths so they will build anywhere:

```
perl srclib\apr\build\fixwin32mak.pl
```

You must type this command from the *top level* directory of the httpd source tree. Every `.mak` and `.dep` project file within the current directory and below will be corrected, and the timestamps adjusted to reflect the `.dsp`.

Always review the generated `.mak` and `.dep` files for Platform SDK or other local, machine specific file paths. The `DevStudio\Common\MSDev98\bin\` (VC6) directory contains a `sysincl.dat` file, which lists all exceptions. Update this file (including both forward and backslashed paths, such as both `sys/time.h` and `sys\time.h`) to ignore such newer dependencies. Including local-install paths in a distributed `.mak` file will cause the build to fail completely.

If you contribute back a patch that revises project files, we must commit project files in Visual Studio 6.0 format. Changes should be simple, with minimal compilation and linkage flags that can be recognized by all Visual Studio environments.

Installation

Once Apache has been compiled, it needs to be installed in its server root directory. The default is the `\Apache2` directory, of the same drive.

To build and install all the files into the desired folder *dir* automatically, use one of the following `nmake` commands:

```
nmake /f Makefile.win installr INSTDIR=dir
nmake /f Makefile.win installd INSTDIR=dir
```

The *dir* argument to `INSTDIR` provides the installation directory; it can be omitted if Apache is to be installed into `\Apache22` (of the current drive).

Warning about building Apache from the development tree

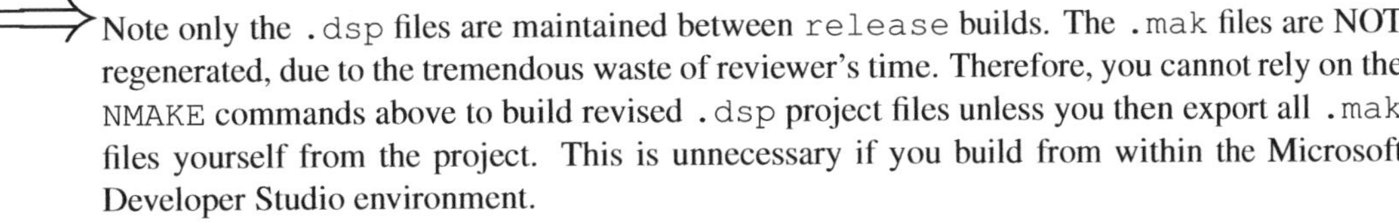

⟹ Note only the `.dsp` files are maintained between `release` builds. The `.mak` files are NOT regenerated, due to the tremendous waste of reviewer's time. Therefore, you cannot rely on the NMAKE commands above to build revised `.dsp` project files unless you then export all `.mak` files yourself from the project. This is unnecessary if you build from within the Microsoft Developer Studio environment.

Building httpd with cmake

The primary documentation for this build mechanism is in the `README.cmake` file in the source distribution. Refer to that file for detailed instructions.

Building httpd with cmake requires building APR and APR-util separately. Refer to their `README.cmake` files for instructions.

The primary limitations of the cmake-based build are inherited from the APR-util project, and are listed below because of their impact on httpd:

- No cmake build for the APR-iconv subproject is available, and the APR-util cmake build cannot consume an existing APR-iconv build. Thus, MOD_CHARSET_LITE and possibly some third-party modules cannot be used.
- The cmake build for the APR-util subproject does not support most of the optional DBM and DBD libraries supported by the included Visual Studio project files. This limits the database backends supported by a number of bundled and third-party modules.

7.4 Using Apache With RPM Based Systems (Redhat / CentOS / Fedora)

While many distributions make Apache httpd available as operating system supported packages, it can sometimes be desirable to install and use the canonical version of Apache httpd on these systems, replacing the natively provided versions of the packages.

While the Apache httpd project does not currently create binary RPMs for the various distributions out there, it is easy to build your own binary RPMs from the canonical Apache httpd tarball.

This document explains how to build, install, configure and run Apache httpd 2.4 under Unix systems supporting the RPM packaging format.

Creating a Source RPM

The Apache httpd source tarball can be converted into an SRPM as follows:

```
rpmbuild -ts httpd-2.4.x.tar.bz2
```

Building RPMs

RPMs can be built directly from the Apache httpd source tarballs using the following command:

```
rpmbuild -tb httpd-2.4.x.tar.bz2
```

Corresponding "-devel" packages will be required to be installed on your build system prior to building the RPMs, the `rpmbuild` command will automatically calculate what RPMs are required and will list any dependencies that are missing on your system. These "-devel" packages will not be required after the build is completed, and can be safely removed.

If successful, the following RPMs will be created:

httpd-2.4.x-1.i686.rpm The core server and basic module set.

httpd-debuginfo-2.4.x-1.i686.rpm Debugging symbols for the server and all modules.

httpd-devel-2.4.x-1.i686.rpm Headers and development files for the server.

httpd-manual-2.4.x-1.i686.rpm The webserver manual.

httpd-tools-2.4.x-1.i686.rpm Supporting tools for the webserver.

mod_authnz_ldap-2.4.x-1.i686.rpm MOD_LDAP and MOD_AUTHNZ_LDAP, with corresponding dependency on openldap.

mod_lua-2.4.x-1.i686.rpm MOD_LUA module, with corresponding dependency on lua.

mod_proxy_html-2.4.x-1.i686.rpm MOD_PROXY_HTML module, with corresponding dependency on libxml2.

mod_socache_dc-2.4.x-1.i686.rpm MOD_SOCACHE_DC module, with corresponding dependency on distcache.

mod_ssl-2.4.x-1.i686.rpm MOD_SSL module, with corresponding dependency on openssl.

Installing the Server

The `httpd` RPM is the only RPM necessary to get a basic server to run. Install it as follows:

```
rpm -U httpd-2.4.x-1.i686.rpm
```

Self contained modules are included with the server. Modules that depend on external libraries are provided as separate RPMs to install if needed.

Configuring the Default Instance of Apache httpd

The default configuration for the server is installed by default beneath the `/etc/httpd` directory, with logs written by default to `/var/log/httpd`. The environment for the webserver is set by default within the optional `/etc/sysconfig/httpd` file.

Start the server as follows:

```
service httpd restart
```

Configuring Additional Instances of Apache httpd on the Same Machine

It is possible to configure additional instances of the Apache httpd server running independently alongside each other on the same machine. These instances can have independent configurations, and can potentially run as separate users if so configured.

This was done by making the httpd startup script aware of its own name. This name is then used to find the environment file for the server, and in turn, the server root of the server instance.

To create an additional instance called `httpd-additional`, follow these steps:

- Create a symbolic link to the startup script for the additional server:

  ```
  ln -s /etc/rc.d/init.d/httpd /etc/rc.d/init.d/httpd-additional
  chkconfig --add httpd-additional
  ```

- Create an environment file for the server, using the `/etc/sysconfig/httpd` file as a template:

  ```
  # template from httpd
  cp /etc/sysconfig/httpd /etc/sysconfig/httpd-additional
  ```

  ```
  # blank template
  touch /etc/sysconfig/httpd-additional
  ```

  Edit `/etc/sysconfig/httpd-additional` and pass the server root of the new server instance within the `OPTIONS` environment variable.

  ```
  OPTIONS="-d /etc/httpd-additional -f conf/httpd-additional.conf"
  ```

- Edit the server configuration file `/etc/httpd-additional/conf/httpd-additional.conf` to ensure the correct ports and paths are configured.
- Start the server as follows:

```
service httpd-additional restart
```

- Repeat this process as required for each server instance.

7.5 Using Apache With Novell NetWare

This document explains how to install, configure and run Apache 2.0 under Novell NetWare 6.0 and above. If you find any bugs, or wish to contribute in other ways, please use our bug reporting page.[7]

The bug reporting page and dev-httpd mailing list are *not* provided to answer questions about configuration or running Apache. Before you submit a bug report or request, first consult this document, the Frequently Asked Questions[8] page and the other relevant documentation topics. If you still have a question or problem, post it to the novell.devsup.webserver[9] newsgroup, where many Apache users are more than willing to answer new and obscure questions about using Apache on NetWare.

Most of this document assumes that you are installing Apache from a binary distribution. If you want to compile Apache yourself (possibly to help with development, or to track down bugs), see the section on Compiling Apache for NetWare below.

Requirements

Apache 2.0 is designed to run on NetWare 6.0 service pack 3 and above. If you are running a service pack less than SP3, you must install the latest NetWare Libraries for C (LibC)[10].

NetWare service packs are available here[11].

Apache 2.0 for NetWare can also be run in a NetWare 5.1 environment as long as the latest service pack or the latest version of the NetWare Libraries for C (LibC)[12] has been installed . **WARNING:** Apache 2.0 for NetWare has not been targeted for or tested in this environment.

Downloading Apache for NetWare

Information on the latest version of Apache can be found on the Apache web server at http://www.apache.org/. This will list the current release, any more recent alpha or beta-test releases, together with details of mirror web and anonymous ftp sites. Binary builds of the latest releases of Apache 2.0 for NetWare can be downloaded from here[13].

Installing Apache for NetWare

There is no Apache install program for NetWare currently. If you are building Apache 2.0 for NetWare from source, you will need to copy the files over to the server manually.

Follow these steps to install Apache on NetWare from the binary download (assuming you will install to `sys:/apache2`):

- Unzip the binary download file to the root of the `SYS:` volume (may be installed to any volume)
- Edit the `httpd.conf` file setting SERVERROOT and SERVERNAME along with any file path values to reflect your correct server settings
- Add `SYS:/APACHE2` to the search path, for example:

```
SEARCH ADD SYS:\APACHE2
```

[7] http://httpd.apache.org/bug_report.html
[8] http://wiki.apache.org/httpd/FAQ
[9] news://developer-forums.novell.com/novell.devsup.webserver
[10] http://developer.novell.com/ndk/libc.htm
[11] http://support.novell.com/misc/patlst.htm#nw
[12] http://developer.novell.com/ndk/libc.htm
[13] http://www.apache.org/dist/httpd/binaries/netware

Follow these steps to install Apache on NetWare manually from your own build source (assuming you will install to `sys:/apache2`):

- Create a directory called `Apache2` on a NetWare volume
- Copy `APACHE2.NLM`, `APRLIB.NLM` to `SYS:/APACHE2`
- Create a directory under `SYS:/APACHE2` called `BIN`
- Copy `HTDIGEST.NLM`, `HTPASSWD.NLM`, `HTDBM.NLM`, `LOGRES.NLM`, `ROTLOGS.NLM` to `SYS:/APACHE2/BIN`
- Create a directory under `SYS:/APACHE2` called `CONF`
- Copy the `HTTPD-STD.CONF` file to the `SYS:/APACHE2/CONF` directory and rename to `HTTPD.CONF`
- Copy the `MIME.TYPES`, `CHARSET.CONV` and `MAGIC` files to `SYS:/APACHE2/CONF` directory
- Copy all files and subdirectories in `\HTTPD-2.0\DOCS\ICONS` to `SYS:/APACHE2/ICONS`
- Copy all files and subdirectories in `\HTTPD-2.0\DOCS\MANUAL` to `SYS:/APACHE2/MANUAL`
- Copy all files and subdirectories in `\HTTPD-2.0\DOCS\ERROR` to `SYS:/APACHE2/ERROR`
- Copy all files and subdirectories in `\HTTPD-2.0\DOCS\DOCROOT` to `SYS:/APACHE2/HTDOCS`
- Create the directory `SYS:/APACHE2/LOGS` on the server
- Create the directory `SYS:/APACHE2/CGI-BIN` on the server
- Create the directory `SYS:/APACHE2/MODULES` and copy all nlm modules into the `modules` directory
- Edit the `HTTPD.CONF` file searching for all `@@Value@@` markers and replacing them with the appropriate setting
- Add `SYS:/APACHE2` to the search path, for example:

```
SEARCH ADD SYS:\APACHE2
```

Apache may be installed to other volumes besides the default `SYS` volume.

During the build process, adding the keyword "install" to the makefile command line will automatically produce a complete distribution package under the subdirectory `DIST`. Install Apache by simply copying the distribution that was produced by the makfiles to the root of a NetWare volume (see: Compiling Apache for NetWare below).

Running Apache for NetWare

To start Apache just type `apache` at the console. This will load apache in the OS address space. If you prefer to load Apache in a protected address space you may specify the address space with the load statement as follows:

```
load address space = apache2 apache2
```

This will load Apache into an address space called apache2. Running multiple instances of Apache concurrently on NetWare is possible by loading each instance into its own protected address space.

After starting Apache, it will be listening to port 80 (unless you changed the LISTEN directive in the configuration files). To connect to the server and access the default page, launch a browser and enter the server's name or address. This should respond with a welcome page, and a link to the Apache manual. If nothing happens or you get an error, look in the `error_log` file in the `logs` directory.

Once your basic installation is working, you should configure it properly by editing the files in the `conf` directory.

To unload Apache running in the OS address space just type the following at the console:

```
unload apache2
```

or

```
apache2 shutdown
```

If apache is running in a protected address space specify the address space in the unload statement:

```
unload address space = apache2 apache2
```

When working with Apache it is important to know how it will find the configuration files. You can specify a configuration file on the command line in two ways:

- `-f` specifies a path to a particular configuration file

```
apache2 -f "vol:/my server/conf/my.conf"
```

```
apache -f test/test.conf
```

In these cases, the proper SERVERROOT should be set in the configuration file.

If you don't specify a configuration file name with `-f`, Apache will use the file name compiled into the server, usually `conf/httpd.conf`. Invoking Apache with the `-V` switch will display this value labeled as `SERVER_CONFIG_FILE`. Apache will then determine its SERVERROOT by trying the following, in this order:

- A `ServerRoot` directive via a `-C` switch.
- The `-d` switch on the command line.
- Current working directory
- The server root compiled into the server.

The server root compiled into the server is usually `sys:/apache2`. invoking apache with the `-V` switch will display this value labeled as `HTTPD_ROOT`.

Apache 2.0 for NetWare includes a set of command line directives that can be used to modify or display information about the running instance of the web server. These directives are only available while Apache is running. Each of these directives must be preceded by the keyword `APACHE2`.

RESTART Instructs Apache to terminate all running worker threads as they become idle, reread the configuration file and restart each worker thread based on the new configuration.

VERSION Displays version information about the currently running instance of Apache.

MODULES Displays a list of loaded modules both built-in and external.

DIRECTIVES Displays a list of all available directives.

SETTINGS Enables or disables the thread status display on the console. When enabled, the state of each running threads is displayed on the Apache console screen.

SHUTDOWN Terminates the running instance of the Apache web server.

HELP Describes each of the runtime directives.

By default these directives are issued against the instance of Apache running in the OS address space. To issue a directive against a specific instance running in a protected address space, include the -p parameter along with the name of the address space. For more information type "apache2 Help" on the command line.

Configuring Apache for NetWare

Apache is configured by reading configuration files usually stored in the `conf` directory. These are the same as files used to configure the Unix version, but there are a few different directives for Apache on NetWare. See the Apache module documentation (p. 1025) for all the available directives.

The main differences in Apache for NetWare are:

- Because Apache for NetWare is multithreaded, it does not use a separate process for each request, as Apache does on some Unix implementations. Instead there are only threads running: a parent thread, and multiple child or worker threads which handle the requests.

  Therefore the "process"-management directives are different:

  MAXCONNECTIONSPERCHILD - Like the Unix directive, this controls how many connections a worker thread will serve before exiting. The recommended default, `MaxConnectionsPerChild 0`, causes the thread to continue servicing request indefinitely. It is recommended on NetWare, unless there is some specific reason, that this directive always remain set to `0`.

  STARTTHREADS - This directive tells the server how many threads it should start initially. The recommended default is `StartThreads 50`.

  MINSPARETHREADS - This directive instructs the server to spawn additional worker threads if the number of idle threads ever falls below this value. The recommended default is `MinSpareThreads 10`.

  MAXSPARETHREADS - This directive instructs the server to begin terminating worker threads if the number of idle threads ever exceeds this value. The recommended default is `MaxSpareThreads 100`.

  MAXTHREADS - This directive limits the total number of work threads to a maximum value. The recommended default is `ThreadsPerChild 250`.

  THREADSTACKSIZE - This directive tells the server what size of stack to use for the individual worker thread. The recommended default is `ThreadStackSize 65536`.

- The directives that accept filenames as arguments must use NetWare filenames instead of Unix names. However, because Apache uses Unix-style names internally, forward slashes must be used rather than backslashes. It is recommended that all rooted file paths begin with a volume name. If omitted, Apache will assume the `SYS:` volume which may not be correct.

- Apache for NetWare has the ability to load modules at runtime, without recompiling the server. If Apache is compiled normally, it will install a number of optional modules in the `\Apache2\modules` directory. To activate these, or other modules, the LOADMODULE directive must be used. For example, to active the status module, use the following:

  ```
  LoadModule status_module modules/status.nlm
  ```

  Information on creating loadable modules (p. 845) is also available.

Additional NetWare specific directives:

- CGIMAPEXTENSION - This directive maps a CGI file extension to a script interpreter.

- SECURELISTEN - Enables SSL encryption for a specified port.

- NWSSLTRUSTEDCERTS - Adds trusted certificates that are used to create secure connections to proxied servers.

- NWSSLUPGRADEABLE - Allow a connection created on the specified address/port to be upgraded to an SSL connection.

Compiling Apache for NetWare

Compiling Apache requires MetroWerks CodeWarrior 6.x or higher. Once Apache has been built, it can be installed to the root of any NetWare volume. The default is the `sys:/Apache2` directory.

Before running the server you must fill out the `conf` directory. Copy the file `HTTPD-STD.CONF` from the distribution `conf` directory and rename it to `HTTPD.CONF`. Edit the `HTTPD.CONF` file searching for all `@@Value@@` markers and replacing them with the appropriate setting. Copy over the `conf/magic` and `conf/mime.types` files as well. Alternatively, a complete distribution can be built by including the keyword `install` when invoking the makefiles.

Requirements:

The following development tools are required to build Apache 2.0 for NetWare:

- Metrowerks CodeWarrior 6.0 or higher with the NetWare PDK 3.0[14] or higher.
- NetWare Libraries for C (LibC)[15]
- LDAP Libraries for C[16]
- ZLIB Compression Library source code[17]
- AWK utility (awk, gawk or similar). AWK can be downloaded from http://developer.novell.com/ndk/apache.htm. The utility must be found in your windows path and must be named `awk.exe`.
- To build using the makefiles, you will need GNU make version 3.78.1 (GMake) available at http://developer.novell.com/ndk/apache.htm.

Building Apache using the NetWare makefiles:

- Set the environment variable `NOVELLLIBC` to the location of the NetWare Libraries for C SDK, for example:

```
Set NOVELLLIBC=c:\novell\ndk\libc
```

- Set the environment variable `METROWERKS` to the location where you installed the Metrowerks CodeWarrior compiler, for example:

```
Set METROWERKS=C:\Program Files\Metrowerks\CodeWarrior
```

  If you installed to the default location `C:\Program Files\Metrowerks\CodeWarrior`, you don't need to set this.

- Set the environment variable `LDAPSDK` to the location where you installed the LDAP Libraries for C, for example:

```
Set LDAPSDK=c:\Novell\NDK\cldapsdk\NetWare\libc
```

- Set the environment variable `ZLIBSDK` to the location where you installed the source code for the ZLib Library, for example:

14 http://developer.novell.com/ndk/cwpdk.htm
15 http://developer.novell.com/ndk/libc.htm
16 http://developer.novell.com/ndk/cldap.htm
17 http://www.gzip.org/zlib/

```
Set ZLIBSDK=D:\NOVELL\zlib
```

- Set the environment variable PCRESDK to the location where you installed the source code for the PCRE Library, for example:

```
Set PCRESDK=D:\NOVELL\pcre
```

- Set the environment variable AP_WORK to the full path of the httpd source code directory.

```
Set AP_WORK=D:\httpd-2.0.x
```

- Set the environment variable APR_WORK to the full path of the apr source code directory. Typically \httpd\srclib\apr but the APR project can be outside of the httpd directory structure.

```
Set APR_WORK=D:\apr-1.x.x
```

- Set the environment variable APU_WORK to the full path of the apr-util source code directory. Typically \httpd\srclib\apr-util but the APR-UTIL project can be outside of the httpd directory structure.

```
Set APU_WORK=D:\apr-util-1.x.x
```

- Make sure that the path to the AWK utility and the GNU make utility (gmake.exe) have been included in the system's PATH environment variable.
- Download the source code and unzip to an appropriate directory on your workstation.
- Change directory to \httpd-2.0 and build the prebuild utilities by running "gmake -f nwgnumakefile prebuild". This target will create the directory \httpd-2.0\nwprebuild and copy each of the utilities to this location that are necessary to complete the following build steps.
- Copy the files \httpd-2.0\nwprebuild\GENCHARS.nlm and \httpd-2.0\nwprebuild\DFTABLES.nlm to the SYS: volume of a NetWare server and run them using the following commands:

```
SYS:\genchars > sys:\test_char.h
SYS:\dftables sys:\chartables.c
```

- Copy the files test_char.h and chartables.c to the directory \httpd-2.0\os\netware on the build machine.
- Change directory to \httpd-2.0 and build Apache by running "gmake -f nwgnumakefile". You can create a distribution directory by adding an install parameter to the command, for example:

```
gmake -f nwgnumakefile install
```

Additional make options

- `gmake -f nwgnumakefile`Builds release versions of all of the binaries and copies them to a `\release` destination directory.
- `gmake -f nwgnumakefile DEBUG=1`Builds debug versions of all of the binaries and copies them to a `\debug` destination directory.
- `gmake -f nwgnumakefile install`Creates a complete Apache distribution with binaries, docs and additional support files in a `\dist\Apache2` directory.
- `gmake -f nwgnumakefile prebuild`Builds all of the prebuild utilities and copies them to the `\nwprebuild` directory.
- `gmake -f nwgnumakefile installdev`Same as install but also creates a `\lib` and `\include` directory in the destination directory and copies headers and import files.
- `gmake -f nwgnumakefile clean`Cleans all object files and binaries from the `\release.o` or `\debug.o` build areas depending on whether `DEBUG` has been defined.
- `gmake -f nwgnumakefile clobber_all`Same as clean and also deletes the distribution directory if it exists.

Additional environment variable options

- To build all of the experimental modules, set the environment variable `EXPERIMENTAL`:

```
Set EXPERIMENTAL=1
```

- To build Apache using standard BSD style sockets rather than Winsock, set the environment variable `USE_STDSOCKETS`:

```
Set USE_STDSOCKETS=1
```

Building mod_ssl for the NetWare platform

By default Apache for NetWare uses the built-in module MOD_NW_SSL to provide SSL services. This module simply enables the native SSL services implemented in NetWare OS to handle all encryption for a given port. Alternatively, mod_ssl can also be used in the same manner as on other platforms.

Before mod_ssl can be built for the NetWare platform, the OpenSSL libraries must be provided. This can be done through the following steps:

- Download the recent OpenSSL 0.9.8 release source code from the OpenSSL Source[18] page (older 0.9.7 versions need to be patched and are therefore not recommended).
- Edit the file `NetWare/set_env.bat` and modify any tools and utilities paths so that they correspond to your build environment.
- From the root of the OpenSSL source directory, run the following scripts:

```
Netware\set_env netware-libc
Netware\build netware-libc
```

[18] http://www.openssl.org/source/

For performance reasons you should enable to build with ASM code. Download NASM from the SF site[19]. Then configure OpenSSL to use ASM code:

```
Netware\build netware-libc nw-nasm enable-mdc2 enable-md5
```

Warning: dont use the CodeWarrior Assembler - it produces broken code!

- Before building Apache, set the environment variable `OSSLSDK` to the full path to the root of the openssl source code directory, and set WITH_MOD_SSL to 1.

```
Set OSSLSDK=d:\openssl-0.9.8x
Set WITH_MOD_SSL=1
```

[19] http://nasm.sourceforge.net/

7.6 Running a High-Performance Web Server on HPUX

```
Date: Wed, 05 Nov 1997 16:59:34 -0800
From: Rick Jones <raj@cup.hp.com>
Reply-To: raj@cup.hp.com
Organization: Network Performance
Subject: HP-UX tuning tips
```

Here are some tuning tips for HP-UX to add to the tuning page.

For HP-UX 9.X: Upgrade to 10.20
For HP-UX 10.[00—01—10]: Upgrade to 10.20

For HP-UX 10.20:

Install the latest cumulative ARPA Transport Patch. This will allow you to configure the size of the TCP connection lookup hash table. The default is 256 buckets and must be set to a power of two. This is accomplished with adb against the *disc* image of the kernel. The variable name is `tcp_hash_size`. Notice that it's critically important that you use "W" to write a 32 bit quantity, not "w" to write a 16 bit value when patching the disc image because the `tcp_hash_size` variable is a 32 bit quantity.

How to pick the value? Examine the output of ftp://ftp.cup.hp.com/dist/networking/tools/connhist and see how many total TCP connections exist on the system. You probably want that number divided by the hash table size to be reasonably small, say less than 10. Folks can look at HP's SPECweb96 disclosures for some common settings. These can be found at http://www.specbench.org/. If an HP-UX system was performing at 1000 SPECweb96 connections per second, the `TIME_WAIT` time of 60 seconds would mean 60,000 TCP "connections" being tracked.

Folks can check their listen queue depths with ftp://ftp.cup.hp.com/dist/networking/misc/listenq.

If folks are running Apache on a PA-8000 based system, they should consider "chatr'ing" the Apache executable to have a large page size. This would be "`chatr +pi L <BINARY>`". The GID of the running executable must have `MLOCK` privileges. `Setprivgrp(1m)` should be consulted for assigning `MLOCK`. The change can be validated by running Glance and examining the memory regions of the server(s) to make sure that they show a non-trivial fraction of the text segment being locked.

If folks are running Apache on MP systems, they might consider writing a small program that uses `mpctl()` to bind processes to processors. A simple `pid % numcpu` algorithm is probably sufficient. This might even go into the source code.

If folks are concerned about the number of `FIN_WAIT_2` connections, they can use nettune to shrink the value of `tcp_keepstart`. However, they should be careful there - certainly do not make it less than oh two to four minutes. If `tcp_hash_size` has been set well, it is probably OK to let the `FIN_WAIT_2`'s take longer to timeout (perhaps even the default two hours) - they will not on average have a big impact on performance.

There are other things that could go into the code base, but that might be left for another email. Feel free to drop me a message if you or others are interested.

sincerely,

rick jones

http://www.netperf.org/netperf/

7.7 The Apache EBCDIC Port

! **Warning:** This document has not been updated to take into account changes made in the 2.0 version of the Apache HTTP Server. Some of the information may still be relevant, but please use it with care.

Overview of the Apache EBCDIC Port

Version 1.3 of the Apache HTTP Server was the first version which included a port to a (non-ASCII) mainframe machine which uses the EBCDIC character set as its native codeset.

(It is the SIEMENS family of mainframes running the BS2000/OSD operating system[20]. This mainframe OS nowadays features a SVR4-derived POSIX subsystem).

The port was started initially to

- prove the feasibility of porting the Apache HTTP server[21] to this platform
- find a "worthy and capable" successor for the venerable CERN-3.0[22] daemon (which was ported a couple of years ago), and to
- prove that Apache's preforking process model can on this platform easily outperform the accept-fork-serve model used by CERN by a factor of 5 or more.

This document serves as a rationale to describe some of the design decisions of the port to this machine.

Design Goals

One objective of the EBCDIC port was to maintain enough backwards compatibility with the (EBCDIC) CERN server to make the transition to the new server attractive and easy. This required the addition of a configurable method to define whether a HTML document was stored in ASCII (the only format accepted by the old server) or in EBCDIC (the native document format in the POSIX subsystem, and therefore the only realistic format in which the other POSIX tools like `grep` or `sed` could operate on the documents). The current solution to this is a "pseudo-MIME-format" which is intercepted and interpreted by the Apache server (see below). Future versions might solve the problem by defining an "ebcdic-handler" for all documents which must be converted.

Technical Solution

Since all Apache input and output is based upon the BUFF data type and its methods, the easiest solution was to add the conversion to the BUFF handling routines. The conversion must be settable at any time, so a BUFF flag was added which defines whether a BUFF object has currently enabled conversion or not. This flag is modified at several points in the HTTP protocol:

- **set** before a request is received (because the request and the request header lines are always in ASCII format)
- **set/unset** when the request body is received - depending on the content type of the request body (because the request body may contain ASCII text or a binary file)
- **set** before a reply header is sent (because the response header lines are always in ASCII format)
- **set/unset** when the response body is sent - depending on the content type of the response body (because the response body may contain text or a binary file)

[20] http://www.siemens.de/servers/bs2osd/osdbc_us.htm
[21] http://httpd.apache.org/
[22] http://www.w3.org/Daemon/

Porting Notes

1. The relevant changes in the source are `#ifdef`'ed into two categories:

   `#ifdef CHARSET_EBCDIC` Code which is needed for any EBCDIC based machine. This includes character translations, differences in contiguity of the two character sets, flags which indicate which part of the HTTP protocol has to be converted and which part doesn't *etc.*

   `#ifdef _OSD_POSIX` Code which is needed for the SIEMENS BS2000/OSD mainframe platform only. This deals with include file differences and socket implementation topics which are only required on the BS2000/OSD platform.

2. The possibility to translate between ASCII and EBCDIC at the socket level (on BS2000 POSIX, there is a socket option which supports this) was intentionally *not* chosen, because the byte stream at the HTTP protocol level consists of a mixture of protocol related strings and non-protocol related raw file data. HTTP protocol strings are always encoded in ASCII (the `GET` request, any Header: lines, the chunking information *etc.*) whereas the file transfer parts (*i.e.*, GIF images, CGI output *etc.*) should usually be just "passed through" by the server. This separation between "protocol string" and "raw data" is reflected in the server code by functions like `bgets()` or `rvputs()` for strings, and functions like `bwrite()` for binary data. A global translation of everything would therefore be inadequate.

   (In the case of text files of course, provisions must be made so that EBCDIC documents are always served in ASCII)

3. This port therefore features a built-in protocol level conversion for the server-internal strings (which the compiler translated to EBCDIC strings) and thus for all server-generated documents. The hard coded ASCII escapes `\012` and `\015` which are ubiquitous in the server code are an exception: they are already the binary encoding of the ASCII `\n` and `\r` and must not be converted to ASCII a second time. This exception is only relevant for server-generated strings; and *external* EBCDIC documents are not expected to contain ASCII newline characters.

4. By examining the call hierarchy for the BUFF management routines, I added an "ebcdic/ascii conversion layer" which would be crossed on every puts/write/get/gets, and a conversion flag which allowed enabling/disabling the conversions on-the-fly. Usually, a document crosses this layer twice from its origin source (a file or CGI output) to its destination (the requesting client): `file -> Apache`, and `Apache -> client`.

   The server can now read the header lines of a CGI-script output in EBCDIC format, and then find out that the remainder of the script's output is in ASCII (like in the case of the output of a WWW Counter program: the document body contains a GIF image). All header processing is done in the native EBCDIC format; the server then determines, based on the type of document being served, whether the document body (except for the chunking information, of course) is in ASCII already or must be converted from EBCDIC.

5. For Text documents (MIME types text/plain, text/html *etc.*), an implicit translation to ASCII can be used, or (if the users prefer to store some documents in raw ASCII form for faster serving, or because the files reside on a NFS-mounted directory tree) can be served without conversion.

   Example:

   to serve files with the suffix `.ahtml` as a raw ASCII `text/html` document without implicit conversion (and suffix `.ascii` as ASCII `text/plain`), use the directives:

   ```
   AddType text/x-ascii-html .ahtml
   AddType text/x-ascii-plain .ascii
   ```

   Similarly, any `text/foo` MIME type can be served as "raw ASCII" by configuring a MIME type "`text/x-ascii-foo`" for it using `AddType`.

6. Non-text documents are always served "binary" without conversion. This seems to be the most sensible choice for, *.e.g.*, GIF/ZIP/AU file types. This of course requires the user to copy them to the mainframe host using the "`rcp -b`" binary switch.

7. Server parsed files are always assumed to be in native (*i.e.*, EBCDIC) format as used on the machine, and are converted after processing.

8. For CGI output, the CGI script determines whether a conversion is needed or not: by setting the appropriate Content-Type, text files can be converted, or GIF output can be passed through unmodified. An example for the latter case is the wwwcount program which we ported as well.

Document Storage Notes

Binary Files

All files with a `Content-Type:` which does not start with `text/` are regarded as *binary files* by the server and are not subject to any conversion. Examples for binary files are GIF images, gzip-compressed files and the like.

When exchanging binary files between the mainframe host and a Unix machine or Windows PC, be sure to use the ftp `"binary"` (`TYPE I`) command, or use the `rcp -b` command from the mainframe host (the `-b` switch is not supported in unix `rcp`'s).

Text Documents

The default assumption of the server is that Text Files (*i.e.*, all files whose `Content-Type:` starts with `text/`) are stored in the native character set of the host, EBCDIC.

Server Side Included Documents

SSI documents must currently be stored in EBCDIC only. No provision is made to convert it from ASCII before processing.

Apache Modules' Status

Module	Status	Notes
CORE	+	
MOD_ACCESS	+	
MOD_ACTIONS	+	
MOD_ALIAS	+	
MOD_ASIS	+	
MOD_AUTH	+	
MOD_AUTHN_ANON	+	
MOD_AUTHN_DBM	?	with own `libdb.a`
MOD_AUTHZ_DBM	?	with own `libdb.a`
MOD_AUTOINDEX	+	
MOD_CERN_META	?	
MOD_CGI	+	
mod_digest	+	
MOD_DIR	+	
MOD_SO	-	no shared libs
MOD_ENV	+	
MOD_EXAMPLE	-	(test bed only)
MOD_EXPIRES	+	
MOD_HEADERS	+	

MOD_IMAGEMAP	+	
MOD_INCLUDE	+	
MOD_INFO	+	
mod_log_agent	+	
mod_log_config	+	
MOD_LOG_REFERER	+	
MOD_MIME	+	
MOD_MIME_MAGIC	?	not ported yet
MOD_NEGOTIATION	+	
MOD_PROXY	+	
MOD_REWRITE	+	untested
MOD_SETENVIF	+	
MOD_SPELING	+	
MOD_STATUS	+	
MOD_UNIQUE_ID	+	
MOD_USERDIR	+	
MOD_USERTRACK	?	untested

Third Party Modules' Status

Module	Status	Notes
mod_jserv[a] [a]http://java.apache.org/	-	JAVA still being ported.
mod_php3[a] [a]http://www.php.net/	+	mod_php3 runs fine, with LDAP and GD and FreeType libraries.
mod_put[a] [a]http://hpwww.ec-lyon.fr/~vincent/apache/mod_put.html	?	untested
mod_session[a] [a]ftp://hachiman.vidya.com/pub/apache/	-	untested

Chapter 8

Apache HTTP Server and Supporting Programs

8.1 Server and Supporting Programs

This page documents all the executable programs included with the Apache HTTP Server.

Index

`httpd` Apache hypertext transfer protocol server

`apachectl` Apache HTTP server control interface

`ab` Apache HTTP server benchmarking tool

`apxs` APache eXtenSion tool

`configure` Configure the source tree

`dbmmanage` Create and update user authentication files in DBM format for basic authentication

`fcgistarter` Start a FastCGI program

`htcacheclean` Clean up the disk cache

`htdigest` Create and update user authentication files for digest authentication

`htdbm` Manipulate DBM password databases.

`htpasswd` Create and update user authentication files for basic authentication

`httxt2dbm` Create dbm files for use with RewriteMap

`logresolve` Resolve hostnames for IP-addresses in Apache logfiles

`log_server_status` Periodically log the server's status

`rotatelogs` Rotate Apache logs without having to kill the server

`split-logfile` Split a multi-vhost logfile into per-host logfiles

`suexec` Switch User For Exec

8.2 httpd - Apache Hypertext Transfer Protocol Server

`httpd` is the Apache HyperText Transfer Protocol (HTTP) server program. It is designed to be run as a standalone daemon process. When used like this it will create a pool of child processes or threads to handle requests.

In general, `httpd` should not be invoked directly, but rather should be invoked via `apachectl` on Unix-based systems or as a service on Windows NT, 2000 and XP (p. 251) and as a console application on Windows 9x and ME (p. 251) .

See also

- Starting Apache httpd (p. 25)
- Stopping Apache httpd (p. 27)
- Configuration Files (p. 30)
- Platform-specific Documentation (p. 250)
- `apachectl`

Synopsis

httpd [**-d** *serverroot*] [**-f** *config*] [**-C** *directive*] [**-c** *directive*] [**-D** *parameter*] [**-e** *level*] [**-E** *file*] [**-k** start|restart|graceful|stop|graceful-stop] [**-R** *directory*] [**-h**] [**-l**] [**-L**] [**-S**] [**-t**] [**-v**] [**-V**] [**-X**] [**-M**] [**-T**]

On Windows systems (p. 251) , the following additional arguments are available:

httpd [**-k** install|config|uninstall] [**-n** *name*] [**-w**]

Options

-d *serverroot* Set the initial value for the SERVERROOT directive to *serverroot*. This can be overridden by the ServerRoot directive in the configuration file. The default is `/usr/local/apache2`.

-f *config* Uses the directives in the file *config* on startup. If *config* does not begin with a /, then it is taken to be a path relative to the SERVERROOT. The default is `conf/httpd.conf`.

-k start|restart|graceful|stop|graceful-stop Signals `httpd` to start, restart, or stop. See Stopping Apache httpd (p. 27) for more information.

-C *directive* Process the configuration *directive* before reading config files.

-c *directive* Process the configuration *directive* after reading config files.

-D *parameter* Sets a configuration *parameter* which can be used with <IFDEFINE> sections in the configuration files to conditionally skip or process commands at server startup and restart. Also can be used to set certain less-common startup parameters including `-DNO_DETACH` (prevent the parent from forking) and `-DFOREGROUND` (prevent the parent from calling `setsid()` et al).

-e *level* Sets the LOGLEVEL to *level* during server startup. This is useful for temporarily increasing the verbosity of the error messages to find problems during startup.

-E *file* Send error messages during server startup to *file*.

-h Output a short summary of available command line options.

-l Output a list of modules compiled into the server. This will **not** list dynamically loaded modules included using the LOADMODULE directive.

-L Output a list of directives provided by static modules, together with expected arguments and places where the directive is valid. Directives provided by shared modules are not listed.

-M Dump a list of loaded Static and Shared Modules.

-S Show the settings as parsed from the config file (currently only shows the virtualhost settings).

-T (Available in 2.3.8 and later) Skip document root check at startup/restart.

-t Run syntax tests for configuration files only. The program immediately exits after these syntax parsing tests with either a return code of 0 (Syntax OK) or return code not equal to 0 (Syntax Error). If -D *DUMP_VHOSTS* is also set, details of the virtual host configuration will be printed. If -D *DUMP_MODULES* is set, all loaded modules will be printed.

-v Print the version of `httpd`, and then exit.

-V Print the version and build parameters of `httpd`, and then exit.

-X Run httpd in debug mode. Only one worker will be started and the server will not detach from the console.

The following arguments are available only on the Windows platform (p. 251) :

-k install|config|uninstall Install Apache httpd as a Windows NT service; change startup options for the Apache httpd service; and uninstall the Apache httpd service.

-n *name* The *name* of the Apache httpd service to signal.

-w Keep the console window open on error so that the error message can be read.

8.3 ab - Apache HTTP server benchmarking tool

ab is a tool for benchmarking your Apache Hypertext Transfer Protocol (HTTP) server. It is designed to give you an impression of how your current Apache installation performs. This especially shows you how many requests per second your Apache installation is capable of serving.

See also

- httpd

Synopsis

ab [**-A** *auth-username:password*] [**-b** *windowsize*] [**-B** *local-address*] [**-c** *concurrency*] [**-C** *cookie-name=value*] [**-d**] [**-e** *csv-file*] [**-f** *protocol*] [**-g** *gnuplot-file*] [**-h**] [**-H** *custom-header*] [**-i**] [**-k**] [**-l**] [**-m** *HTTP-method*] [**-n** *requests*] [**-p** *POST-file*] [**-P** *proxy-auth-username:password*] [**-q**] [**-r**] [**-s** *timeout*] [**-S**] [**-t** *timelimit*] [**-T** *content-type*] [**-u** *PUT-file*] [**-v** *verbosity*] [**-V**] [**-w**] [**-x** *<table>-attributes*] [**-X** *proxy*[:*port*]] [**-y** *<tr>-attributes*] [**-z** *<td>-attributes*] [**-Z** *ciphersuite*] [http[s]://]*hostname*[:*port*]/*path*

Options

-A ***auth-username:password*** Supply BASIC Authentication credentials to the server. The username and password are separated by a single : and sent on the wire base64 encoded. The string is sent regardless of whether the server needs it (*i.e.*, has sent an 401 authentication needed).

-b ***windowsize*** Size of TCP send/receive buffer, in bytes.

-B ***local-address*** Address to bind to when making outgoing connections.

-c ***concurrency*** Number of multiple requests to perform at a time. Default is one request at a time.

-C ***cookie-name=value*** Add a Cookie: line to the request. The argument is typically in the form of a *name=value* pair. This field is repeatable.

-d Do not display the "percentage served within XX [ms] table". (legacy support).

-e ***csv-file*** Write a Comma separated value (CSV) file which contains for each percentage (from 1% to 100%) the time (in milliseconds) it took to serve that percentage of the requests. This is usually more useful than the 'gnuplot' file; as the results are already 'binned'.

-f ***protocol*** Specify SSL/TLS protocol (SSL2, SSL3, TLS1, TLS1.1, TLS1.2, or ALL). TLS1.1 and TLS1.2 support available in 2.4.4 and later.

-g ***gnuplot-file*** Write all measured values out as a 'gnuplot' or TSV (Tab separate values) file. This file can easily be imported into packages like Gnuplot, IDL, Mathematica, Igor or even Excel. The labels are on the first line of the file.

-h Display usage information.

-H ***custom-header*** Append extra headers to the request. The argument is typically in the form of a valid header line, containing a colon-separated field-value pair (*i.e.*, "Accept-Encoding: zip/zop;8bit").

-i Do HEAD requests instead of GET.

-k Enable the HTTP KeepAlive feature, *i.e.*, perform multiple requests within one HTTP session. Default is no KeepAlive.

-l Do not report errors if the length of the responses is not constant. This can be useful for dynamic pages. Available in 2.4.7 and later.

-m ***HTTP-method*** Custom HTTP method for the requests. Available in 2.4.10 and later.

-n ***requests*** Number of requests to perform for the benchmarking session. The default is to just perform a single request which usually leads to non-representative benchmarking results.

-p ***POST-file*** File containing data to POST. Remember to also set `-T`.

-P ***proxy-auth-username*:*password*** Supply BASIC Authentication credentials to a proxy en-route. The username and password are separated by a single `:` and sent on the wire base64 encoded. The string is sent regardless of whether the proxy needs it (*i.e.*, has sent an 407 proxy authentication needed).

-q When processing more than 150 requests, `ab` outputs a progress count on `stderr` every 10% or 100 requests or so. The `-q` flag will suppress these messages.

-r Don't exit on socket receive errors.

-s ***timeout*** Maximum number of seconds to wait before the socket times out. Default is 30 seconds. Available in 2.4.4 and later.

-S Do not display the median and standard deviation values, nor display the warning/error messages when the average and median are more than one or two times the standard deviation apart. And default to the min/avg/max values. (legacy support).

-t ***timelimit*** Maximum number of seconds to spend for benchmarking. This implies a `-n 50000` internally. Use this to benchmark the server within a fixed total amount of time. Per default there is no timelimit.

-T ***content-type*** Content-type header to use for POST/PUT data, eg. `application/x-www-form-urlencoded`. Default is `text/plain`.

-u ***PUT-file*** File containing data to PUT. Remember to also set `-T`.

-v ***verbosity*** Set verbosity level - `4` and above prints information on headers, `3` and above prints response codes (404, 200, etc.), `2` and above prints warnings and info.

-V Display version number and exit.

-w Print out results in HTML tables. Default table is two columns wide, with a white background.

-x ***<table>-attributes*** String to use as attributes for `<table>`. Attributes are inserted `<table` *here* `>`.

-X ***proxy*[:*port*]** Use a proxy server for the requests.

-y ***<tr>-attributes*** String to use as attributes for `<tr>`.

-z ***<td>-attributes*** String to use as attributes for `<td>`.

-Z ***ciphersuite*** Specify SSL/TLS cipher suite (See openssl ciphers)

Output

The following list describes the values returned by `ab`:

Server Software The value, if any, returned in the *server* HTTP header of the first successful response. This includes all characters in the header from beginning to the point a character with decimal value of 32 (most notably: a space or CR/LF) is detected.

Server Hostname The DNS or IP address given on the command line

Server Port The port to which ab is connecting. If no port is given on the command line, this will default to 80 for http and 443 for https.

SSL/TLS Protocol The protocol parameters negotiated between the client and server. This will only be printed if SSL is used.

Document Path The request URI parsed from the command line string.

Document Length This is the size in bytes of the first successfully returned document. If the document length changes during testing, the response is considered an error.

Concurrency Level The number of concurrent clients used during the test

Time taken for tests This is the time taken from the moment the first socket connection is created to the moment the last response is received

Complete requests The number of successful responses received

Failed requests The number of requests that were considered a failure. If the number is greater than zero, another line will be printed showing the number of requests that failed due to connecting, reading, incorrect content length, or exceptions.

Write errors The number of errors that failed during write (broken pipe).

Non-2xx responses The number of responses that were not in the 200 series of response codes. If all responses were 200, this field is not printed.

Keep-Alive requests The number of connections that resulted in Keep-Alive requests

Total body sent If configured to send data as part of the test, this is the total number of bytes sent during the tests. This field is omitted if the test did not include a body to send.

Total transferred The total number of bytes received from the server. This number is essentially the number of bytes sent over the wire.

HTML transferred The total number of document bytes received from the server. This number excludes bytes received in HTTP headers

Requests per second This is the number of requests per second. This value is the result of dividing the number of requests by the total time taken

Time per request The average time spent per request. The first value is calculated with the formula `concurrency * timetaken * 1000 / done` while the second value is calculated with the formula `timetaken * 1000 / done`

Transfer rate The rate of transfer as calculated by the formula `totalread / 1024 / timetaken`

Bugs

There are various statically declared buffers of fixed length. Combined with the lazy parsing of the command line arguments, the response headers from the server and other external inputs, this might bite you.

It does not implement HTTP/1.x fully; only accepts some 'expected' forms of responses. The rather heavy use of `strstr(3)` shows up top in profile, which might indicate a performance problem; *i.e.*, you would measure the `ab` performance rather than the server's.

8.4 apachectl - Apache HTTP Server Control Interface

apachectl is a front end to the Apache HyperText Transfer Protocol (HTTP) server. It is designed to help the administrator control the functioning of the Apache httpd daemon.

The apachectl script can operate in two modes. First, it can act as a simple front-end to the httpd command that simply sets any necessary environment variables and then invokes httpd, passing through any command line arguments. Second, apachectl can act as a SysV init script, taking simple one-word arguments like start, restart, and stop, and translating them into appropriate signals to httpd.

If your Apache installation uses non-standard paths, you will need to edit the apachectl script to set the appropriate paths to the httpd binary. You can also specify any necessary httpd command line arguments. See the comments in the script for details.

The apachectl script returns a 0 exit value on success, and >0 if an error occurs. For more details, view the comments in the script.

See also

- Starting Apache (p. 25)
- Stopping Apache (p. 27)
- Configuration Files (p. 30)
- Platform Docs (p. 250)

- httpd

Synopsis

When acting in pass-through mode, apachectl can take all the arguments available for the httpd binary.

apachectl [*httpd-argument*]

When acting in SysV init mode, apachectl takes simple, one-word commands, defined below.

apachectl *command*

Options

Only the SysV init-style options are defined here. Other arguments are defined on the httpd manual page.

start Start the Apache httpd daemon. Gives an error if it is already running. This is equivalent to apachectl -k start.

stop Stops the Apache httpd daemon. This is equivalent to apachectl -k stop.

restart Restarts the Apache httpd daemon. If the daemon is not running, it is started. This command automatically checks the configuration files as in configtest before initiating the restart to make sure the daemon doesn't die. This is equivalent to apachectl -k restart.

fullstatus Displays a full status report from MOD_STATUS. For this to work, you need to have MOD_STATUS enabled on your server and a text-based browser such as lynx available on your system. The URL used to access the status report can be set by editing the STATUSURL variable in the script.

status Displays a brief status report. Similar to the fullstatus option, except that the list of requests currently being served is omitted.

graceful Gracefully restarts the Apache httpd daemon. If the daemon is not running, it is started. This differs from a normal restart in that currently open connections are not aborted. A side effect is that old log files will not be closed immediately. This means that if used in a log rotation script, a substantial delay may be necessary to ensure that the old log files are closed before processing them. This command automatically checks the configuration files as in configtest before initiating the restart to make sure Apache doesn't die. This is equivalent to apachectl -k graceful.

graceful-stop Gracefully stops the Apache httpd daemon. This differs from a normal stop in that currently open connections are not aborted. A side effect is that old log files will not be closed immediately. This is equivalent to apachectl -k graceful-stop.

configtest Run a configuration file syntax test. It parses the configuration files and either reports Syntax Ok or detailed information about the particular syntax error. This is equivalent to apachectl -t.

The following option was available in earlier versions but has been removed.

startssl To start httpd with SSL support, you should edit your configuration file to include the relevant directives and then use the normal apachectl start.

8.5 apxs - APache eXtenSion tool

apxs is a tool for building and installing extension modules for the Apache HyperText Transfer Protocol (HTTP) server. This is achieved by building a dynamic shared object (DSO) from one or more source or object *files* which then can be loaded into the Apache server under runtime via the LOADMODULE directive from MOD_SO.

So to use this extension mechanism your platform has to support the DSO feature and your Apache httpd binary has to be built with the MOD_SO module. The apxs tool automatically complains if this is not the case. You can check this yourself by manually running the command

```
$ httpd -l
```

The module MOD_SO should be part of the displayed list. If these requirements are fulfilled you can easily extend your Apache server's functionality by installing your own modules with the DSO mechanism by the help of this apxs tool:

```
$ apxs -i -a -c mod_foo.c
gcc -fpic -DSHARED_MODULE -I/path/to/apache/include -c mod_foo.c
ld -Bshareable -o mod_foo.so mod_foo.o
cp mod_foo.so /path/to/apache/modules/mod_foo.so
chmod 755 /path/to/apache/modules/mod_foo.so
[activating module 'foo' in /path/to/apache/etc/httpd.conf]
$ apachectl restart
/path/to/apache/sbin/apachectl restart:  httpd not running, trying to
start
[Tue Mar 31 11:27:55 1998] [debug] mod_so.c(303):  loaded module
foo_module
/path/to/apache/sbin/apachectl restart:  httpd started
$ _
```

The arguments *files* can be any C source file (.c), a object file (.o) or even a library archive (.a). The apxs tool automatically recognizes these extensions and automatically used the C source files for compilation while just using the object and archive files for the linking phase. But when using such pre-compiled objects make sure they are compiled for position independent code (PIC) to be able to use them for a dynamically loaded shared object. For instance with GCC you always just have to use -fpic. For other C compilers consult its manual page or at watch for the flags apxs uses to compile the object files.

For more details about DSO support in Apache read the documentation of MOD_SO or perhaps even read the src/modules/standard/mod_so.c source file.

See also

- apachectl
- httpd

Synopsis

apxs -g [**-S** *name=value*] **-n** *modname*

apxs -q [**-v**] [**-S** *name=value*] *query* ...

apxs -c [**-S** *name=value*] [**-o** *dsofile*] [**-I** *incdir*] [**-D** *name=value*] [**-L** *libdir*] [**-l** *libname*] [**-Wc,***compiler-flags*] [**-Wl,***linker-flags*] *files* ...

apxs -i [**-S** *name=value*] [**-n** *modname*] [**-a**] [**-A**] *dso-file* ...

apxs -e [**-S** *name=value*] [**-n** *modname*] [**-a**] [**-A**] *dso-file* ...

Options

Common Options

-n *modname* This explicitly sets the module name for the -i (install) and -g (template generation) option. Use this to explicitly specify the module name. For option -g this is required, for option -i the apxs tool tries to determine the name from the source or (as a fallback) at least by guessing it from the filename.

Query Options

-q Performs a query for variables and environment settings used to build httpd. When invoked without *query* parameters, it prints all known variables and their values. The optional -v parameter formats the list output.

Use this to manually determine settings used to build the httpd that will load your module. For instance use

```
INC=-I`apxs -q INCLUDEDIR`
```

inside your own Makefiles if you need manual access to Apache's C header files.

Configuration Options

-S *name=value* This option changes the apxs settings described above.

Template Generation Options

-g This generates a subdirectory *name* (see option -n) and there two files: A sample module source file named mod_*name*.c which can be used as a template for creating your own modules or as a quick start for playing with the apxs mechanism. And a corresponding Makefile for even easier build and installing of this module.

DSO Compilation Options

-c This indicates the compilation operation. It first compiles the C source files (.c) of *files* into corresponding object files (.o) and then builds a dynamically shared object in *dsofile* by linking these object files plus the remaining object files (.o and .a) of *files*. If no -o option is specified the output file is guessed from the first filename in *files* and thus usually defaults to mod_*name*.so.

-o *dsofile* Explicitly specifies the filename of the created dynamically shared object. If not specified and the name cannot be guessed from the *files* list, the fallback name mod_unknown.so is used.

-D *name=value* This option is directly passed through to the compilation command(s). Use this to add your own defines to the build process.

-I *incdir* This option is directly passed through to the compilation command(s). Use this to add your own include directories to search to the build process.

-L *libdir* This option is directly passed through to the linker command. Use this to add your own library directories to search to the build process.

-l *libname* This option is directly passed through to the linker command. Use this to add your own libraries to search to the build process.

-Wc,*compiler-flags* This option passes *compiler-flags* as additional flags to the libtool --mode=compile command. Use this to add local compiler-specific options.

`-Wl, linker-flags` This option passes *linker-flags* as additional flags to the `libtool --mode=link` command. Use this to add local linker-specific options.

`-p` This option causes apxs to link against the apr/apr-util libraries. This is useful when compiling helper programs that use the apr/apr-util libraries.

DSO Installation and Configuration Options

`-i` This indicates the installation operation and installs one or more dynamically shared objects into the server's *modules* directory.

`-a` This activates the module by automatically adding a corresponding LOADMODULE line to Apache's `httpd.conf` configuration file, or by enabling it if it already exists.

`-A` Same as option `-a` but the created LOADMODULE directive is prefixed with a hash sign (#), *i.e.*, the module is just prepared for later activation but initially disabled.

`-e` This indicates the editing operation, which can be used with the `-a` and `-A` options similarly to the `-i` operation to edit Apache's `httpd.conf` configuration file without attempting to install the module.

Examples

Assume you have an Apache module named `mod_foo.c` available which should extend Apache's server functionality. To accomplish this you first have to compile the C source into a shared object suitable for loading into the Apache server under runtime via the following command:

```
$ apxs -c mod_foo.c
/path/to/libtool --mode=compile gcc ...  -c mod_foo.c
/path/to/libtool --mode=link gcc ...  -o mod_foo.la mod_foo.slo
$ _
```

Then you have to update the Apache configuration by making sure a LOADMODULE directive is present to load this shared object. To simplify this step `apxs` provides an automatic way to install the shared object in its "modules" directory and updating the `httpd.conf` file accordingly. This can be achieved by running:

```
$ apxs -i -a mod_foo.la
/path/to/instdso.sh mod_foo.la /path/to/apache/modules
/path/to/libtool --mode=install cp mod_foo.la /path/to/apache/modules
...  chmod 755 /path/to/apache/modules/mod_foo.so
[activating module 'foo' in /path/to/apache/conf/httpd.conf]
$ _
```

This way a line named

```
LoadModule foo_module modules/mod_foo.so
```

is added to the configuration file if still not present. If you want to have this disabled per default use the `-A` option, *i.e.*

```
$ apxs -i -A mod_foo.c
```

For a quick test of the apxs mechanism you can create a sample Apache module template plus a corresponding Makefile via:

```
$ apxs -g -n foo
Creating [DIR] foo
Creating [FILE] foo/Makefile
Creating [FILE] foo/modules.mk
Creating [FILE] foo/mod_foo.c
Creating [FILE] foo/.deps
$ _
```

Then you can immediately compile this sample module into a shared object and load it into the Apache server:

```
$ cd foo
$ make all reload
apxs -c mod_foo.c
/path/to/libtool --mode=compile gcc ...  -c mod_foo.c
/path/to/libtool --mode=link gcc ...  -o mod_foo.la mod_foo.slo
apxs -i -a -n "foo" mod_foo.la
/path/to/instdso.sh mod_foo.la /path/to/apache/modules
/path/to/libtool --mode=install cp mod_foo.la /path/to/apache/modules
...  chmod 755 /path/to/apache/modules/mod_foo.so
[activating module 'foo' in /path/to/apache/conf/httpd.conf]
apachectl restart
/path/to/apache/sbin/apachectl restart:  httpd not running, trying to
start
[Tue Mar 31 11:27:55 1998] [debug] mod_so.c(303):  loaded module
foo_module
/path/to/apache/sbin/apachectl restart:  httpd started
$ _
```

8.6 configure - Configure the source tree

The `configure` script configures the source tree for compiling and installing the Apache HTTP Server on your particular platform. Various options allow the compilation of a server corresponding to your personal requirements.

This script, included in the root directory of the source distribution, is for compilation on Unix and Unix-like systems only. For other platforms, see the platform (p. 250) documentation.

See also

- Compiling and Installing (p. 20)

Synopsis

You should call the `configure` script from within the root directory of the distribution.

`./configure` [*OPTION*]... [*VAR=VALUE*]...

To assign environment variables (e.g. `CC`, `CFLAGS` ...), specify them as *VAR=VALUE*. See below for descriptions of some of the useful variables.

Options

- Configuration options
- Installation directories
- System types
- Optional features
- Options for support programs

Configuration options

The following options influence the behavior of `configure` itself.

`-C`

`--config-cache` This is an alias for `--cache-file=config.cache`

`--cache-file=FILE` The test results will be cached in file *FILE*. This option is disabled by default.

`-h`

`--help [short|recursive]` Output the help and exit. With the argument `short` only options specific to this package will displayed. The argument `recursive` displays the short help of all the included packages.

`-n`

`--no-create` The `configure` script is run normally but does not create output files. This is useful to check the test results before generating makefiles for compilation.

`-q`

`--quiet` Do not print `checking ...` messages during the configure process.

`--srcdir=DIR` Defines directory *DIR* to be the source file directory. Default is the directory where `configure` is located, or the parent directory.

--silent Same as --quiet

-V

–version Display copyright information and exit.

Installation directories

These options define the installation directory. The installation tree depends on the selected layout.

--prefix=*PREFIX* Install architecture-independent files in *PREFIX*. By default the installation directory is set to /usr/local/apache2.

--exec-prefix=*EPREFIX* Install architecture-dependent files in *EPREFIX*. By default the installation directory is set to the *PREFIX* directory.

By default, make install will install all the files in /usr/local/apache2/bin, /usr/local/apache2/lib etc. You can specify an installation prefix other than /usr/local/apache2 using --prefix, for instance --prefix=$HOME.

Define a directory layout

--enable-layout=*LAYOUT* Configure the source code and build scripts to assume an installation tree based on the layout *LAYOUT*. This allows you to separately specify the locations for each type of file within the Apache HTTP Server installation. The config.layout file contains several example configurations, and you can also create your own custom configuration following the examples. The different layouts in this file are grouped into <Layout FOO>...</Layout> sections and referred to by name as in FOO. The default layout is Apache.

Fine tuning of the installation directories

For better control of the installation directories, use the options below. Please note that the directory defaults are set by autoconf and are overwritten by the corresponding layout setting.

--bindir=*DIR* Install user executables in *DIR*. The user executables are supporting programs like htpasswd, dbmmanage, etc. which are useful for site administrators. By default *DIR* is set to *EPREFIX*/bin.

--datadir=*DIR* Install read-only architecture-independent data in *DIR*. By default datadir is set to *PREFIX*/share. This option is offered by autoconf and currently unused.

--includedir=*DIR* Install C header files in *DIR*. By default includedir is set to *EPREFIX*/include.

--infodir=*DIR* Install info documentation in *DIR*. By default infodir is set to *PREFIX*/info. This option is currently unused.

--libdir=*DIR* Install object code libraries in *DIR*. By default libdir is set to *EPREFIX*/lib.

--libexecdir=*DIR* Install the program executables (i.e., shared modules) in *DIR*. By default libexecdir is set to *EPREFIX*/modules.

--localstatedir=*DIR* Install modifiable single-machine data in *DIR*. By default localstatedir is set to *PREFIX*/var. This option is offered by autoconf and currently unused.

--mandir=*DIR* Install the man documentation in *DIR*. By default mandir is set to *EPREFIX*/man.

--oldincludedir=*DIR* Install C header files for non-gcc in *DIR*. By default `oldincludedir` is set to `/usr/include`. This option is offered by `autoconf` and currently unused.

--sbindir=*DIR* Install the system administrator executables in *DIR*. Those are server programs like `httpd`, `apachectl`, `suexec`, etc. which are necessary to run the Apache HTTP Server. By default `sbindir` is set to *EPREFIX*/`sbin`.

--sharedstatedir=*DIR* Install modifiable architecture-independent data in *DIR*. By default `sharedstatedir` is set to *PREFIX*/`com`. This option is offered by `autoconf` and currently unused.

--sysconfdir=*DIR* Install read-only single-machine data like the server configuration files `httpd.conf`, `mime.types`, etc. in *DIR*. By default `sysconfdir` is set to *PREFIX*/`conf`.

System types

These options are used to cross-compile the Apache HTTP Server to run on another system. In normal cases, when building and running the server on the same system, these options are not used.

--build=*BUILD* Defines the system type of the system on which the tools are being built. It defaults to the result of the script `config.guess`.

--host=*HOST* Defines the system type of the system on which the server will run. *HOST* defaults to *BUILD*.

--target=*TARGET* Configure for building compilers for the system type *TARGET*. It defaults to *HOST*. This option is offered by `autoconf` and not necessary for the Apache HTTP Server.

Optional Features

These options are used to fine tune the features your HTTP server will have.

General syntax

Generally you can use the following syntax to enable or disable a feature:

--disable-*FEATURE* Do not include *FEATURE*. This is the same as `--enable-`*FEATURE*`=no`.

--enable-*FEATURE*[=*ARG*] Include *FEATURE*. The default value for *ARG* is `yes`.

--enable-*MODULE*=shared The corresponding module will be build as DSO module. By default enabled modules are linked dynamically.

--enable-*MODULE*=static The corresponding module will be linked statically.

**Note**

`configure` will not complain about `--enable-`*foo* even if *foo* doesn't exist, so you need to type carefully.

Choosing modules to compile

Most modules are compiled by default and have to be disabled explicitly or by using the keywords `few` or `none` (see `--enable-modules`, `--enable-mods-shared` and `--enable-mods-static` below for further explanation) to be removed.

Other modules are not compiled by default and have to be enabled explicitly or by using the keywords `all` or `reallyall` to be available.

To find out which modules are compiled by default, run `./configure -h` or `./configure --help` and look under `Optional Features`. Suppose you are interested in `mod_example1` and `mod_example2`, and you see this:

```
Optional Features:
  ...
  --disable-example1      example module 1
  --enable-example2       example module 2
  ...
```

Then `mod_example1` is enabled by default, and you would use `--disable-example1` to not compile it. `mod_example2` is disabled by default, and you would use `--enable-example2` to compile it.

Multi-Processing Modules

Multi-Processing Modules (p. 80) , or MPMs, implement the basic behavior of the server. A single MPM must be active in order for the server to function. The list of available MPMs appears on the module index page (p. 1025) .

MPMs can be built as DSOs for dynamic loading or statically linked with the server, and are enabled using the following options:

`--with-mpm=MPM` Choose the default MPM for your server. If MPMs are built as DSO modules (see `--enable-mpms-shared`), this directive selects the MPM which will be loaded in the default configuration file. Otherwise, this directive selects the only available MPM, which will be statically linked into the server.

If this option is omitted, the default MPM (p. 80) for your operating system will be used.

`--enable-mpms-shared=`*`MPM-LIST`* Enable a list of MPMs as dynamic shared modules. One of these modules must be loaded dynamically using the LOADMODULE directive.

MPM-LIST is a space-separated list of MPM names enclosed by quotation marks. For example:

```
--enable-mpms-shared='prefork worker'
```

Additionally you can use the special keyword `all`, which will select all MPMs which support dynamic loading on the current platform and build them as DSO modules. For example:

```
--enable-mpms-shared=all
```

Third-party modules

To add additional third-party modules use the following options:

--with-module=*module-type*:*module-file*[, *module-type*:*module-file*] Add one or more third-party modules to the list of statically linked modules. The module source file *module-file* will be searched in the modules/*module-type* subdirectory of your Apache HTTP server source tree. If it is not found there configure is considering *module-file* to be an absolute file path and tries to copy the source file into the *module-type* subdirectory. If the subdirectory doesn't exist it will be created and populated with a standard Makefile.in.

This option is useful to add small external modules consisting of one source file. For more complex modules you should read the vendor's documentation.

 **Note**

If you want to build a DSO module instead of a statically linked use apxs.

Cumulative and other options

--enable-maintainer-mode Turn on debugging and compile time warnings and load all compiled modules.

--enable-mods-shared=*MODULE-LIST* Defines a list of modules to be enabled and build as dynamic shared modules. This mean, these module have to be loaded dynamically by using the LOADMODULE directive.

MODULE-LIST is a space separated list of modulenames enclosed by quotation marks. The module names are given without the preceding mod_. For example:

```
--enable-mods-shared='headers rewrite dav'
```

Additionally you can use the special keywords reallyall, all, most, few and none. For example,

```
--enable-mods-shared=most
```

will compile most modules and build them as DSO modules,

```
--enable-mods-shared=few
```

will only compile a very basic set of modules.

The default set is most.

The LOADMODULE directives for the chosen modules will be automatically generated in the main configuration file. By default, all those directives will be commented out except for the modules that are either required or explicitly selected by a configure --enable-foo argument. You can change the set of loaded modules by activating or deactivating the LOADMODULE directives in httpd.conf. In addition the LOADMODULE directives for all built modules can be activated via the configure option --enable-load-all-modules.

--enable-mods-static=*MODULE-LIST* This option behaves similar to --enable-mods-shared, but will link the given modules statically. This mean, these modules will always be present while running httpd. They need not be loaded with LOADMODULE.

--enable-modules=*MODULE-LIST* This option behaves like to --enable-mods-shared, and will also link the given modules dynamically. The special keyword none disables the build of all modules.

--enable-v4-mapped Allow IPv6 sockets to handle IPv4 connections.

--with-port=*PORT* This defines the port on which httpd will listen. This port number is used when generating the configuration file httpd.conf. The default is 80.

--with-program-name Define an alternative executable name. The default is httpd.

Optional packages

These options are used to define optional packages.

General syntax

Generally you can use the following syntax to define an optional package:

--with-*PACKAGE*[=*ARG*] Use the package *PACKAGE*. The default value for *ARG* is `yes`.

--without-*PACKAGE* Do not use the package *PACKAGE*. This is the same as `--with-PACKAGE=no`. This option is provided by `autoconf` but not very useful for the Apache HTTP Server.

Specific packages

--with-apr=*DIR*|*FILE* The Apache Portable Runtime (APR) is part of the httpd source distribution and will automatically be build together with the HTTP server. If you want to use an already installed APR instead you have to tell `configure` the path to the `apr-config` script. You may set the absolute path and name or the directory to the installed APR. `apr-config` must exist within this directory or the subdirectory `bin`.

--with-apr-util=*DIR*|*FILE* The Apache Portable Runtime Utilities (APU) are part of the httpd source distribution and will automatically be build together with the HTTP server. If you want to use an already installed APU instead you have to tell `configure` the path to the `apu-config` script. You may set the absolute path and name or the directory to the installed APU. `apu-config` must exist within this directory or the subdirectory `bin`.

--with-ssl=*DIR* If MOD_SSL has been enabled `configure` searches for an installed OpenSSL. You can set the directory path to the SSL/TLS toolkit instead.

--with-z=*DIR* `configure` searches automatically for an installed `zlib` library if your source configuration requires one (e.g., when MOD_DEFLATE is enabled). You can set the directory path to the compression library instead.

Several features of the Apache HTTP Server, including MOD_AUTHN_DBM and MOD_REWRITE's DBM REWRITEMAP use simple key/value databases for quick lookups of information. SDBM is included in the APU, so this database is always available. If you would like to use other database types, use the following options to enable them:

--with-gdbm[=*path*] If no *path* is specified, `configure` will search for the include files and libraries of a GNU DBM installation in the usual search paths. An explicit *path* will cause `configure` to look in `path/lib` and `path/include` for the relevant files. Finally, the *path* may specify specific include and library paths separated by a colon.

--with-ndbm[=*path*] Like `--with-gdbm`, but searches for a New DBM installation.

--with-berkeley-db[=*path*] Like `--with-gdbm`, but searches for a Berkeley DB installation.

**Note**

The DBM options are provided by the APU and passed through to its configuration script. They are useless when using an already installed APU defined by `--with-apr-util`.
You may use more then one DBM implementation together with your HTTP server. The appropriated DBM type will be configured within the runtime configuration at each time.

Options for support programs

--enable-static-support Build a statically linked version of the support binaries. This means, a stand-alone executable will be built with all the necessary libraries integrated. Otherwise the support binaries are linked dynamically by default.

--enable-suexec Use this option to enable suexec, which allows you to set uid and gid for spawned processes. **Do not use this option unless you understand all the security implications of running a suid binary on your server.** Further options to configure suexec are described below.

It is possible to create a statically linked binary of a single support program by using the following options:

--enable-static-ab Build a statically linked version of ab.

--enable-static-checkgid Build a statically linked version of checkgid.

--enable-static-htdbm Build a statically linked version of htdbm.

--enable-static-htdigest Build a statically linked version of htdigest.

--enable-static-htpasswd Build a statically linked version of htpasswd.

--enable-static-logresolve Build a statically linked version of logresolve.

--enable-static-rotatelogs Build a statically linked version of rotatelogs.

suexec configuration options

The following options are used to fine tune the behavior of suexec. See Configuring and installing suEXEC (p. 322) for further information.

--with-suexec-bin This defines the path to suexec binary. Default is --sbindir (see Fine tuning of installation directories).

--with-suexec-caller This defines the user allowed to call suexec. It should be the same as the user under which httpd normally runs.

--with-suexec-docroot This defines the directory tree under which suexec access is allowed for executables. Default value is --datadir/htdocs.

--with-suexec-gidmin Define this as the lowest GID allowed to be a target user for suexec. The default value is 100.

--with-suexec-logfile This defines the filename of the suexec logfile. By default the logfile is named suexec_log and located in --logfiledir.

--with-suexec-safepath Define the value of the environment variable PATH to be set for processes started by suexec. Default value is /usr/local/bin:/usr/bin:/bin.

--with-suexec-userdir This defines the subdirectory under the user's directory that contains all executables for which suexec access is allowed. This setting is necessary when you want to use suexec together with user-specific directories (as provided by MOD_USERDIR). The default is public_html.

--with-suexec-uidmin Define this as the lowest UID allowed to be a target user for suexec. The default value is 100.

--with-suexec-umask Set umask for processes started by suexec. It defaults to your system settings.

Environment variables

There are some useful environment variables to override the choices made by `configure` or to help it to find libraries and programs with nonstandard names or locations.

CC Define the C compiler command to be used for compilation.

CFLAGS Set C compiler flags you want to use for compilation.

CPP Define the C preprocessor command to be used.

CPPFLAGS Set C/C++ preprocessor flags, e.g. `-I`*`includedir`* if you have headers in a nonstandard directory *includedir*.

LDFLAGS Set linker flags, e.g. `-L`*`libdir`* if you have libraries in a nonstandard directory *libdir*.

8.7 dbmmanage - Manage user authentication files in DBM format

`dbmmanage` is used to create and update the DBM format files used to store usernames and password for basic authentication of HTTP users via MOD_AUTHN_DBM. Resources available from the Apache HTTP server can be restricted to just the users listed in the files created by `dbmmanage`. This program can only be used when the usernames are stored in a DBM file. To use a flat-file database see `htpasswd`.

Another tool to maintain a DBM password database is `htdbm`.

This manual page only lists the command line arguments. For details of the directives necessary to configure user authentication in `httpd` see the httpd manual, which is part of the Apache distribution or can be found at http://httpd.apache.org/.

See also

- `httpd`
- `htdbm`
- MOD_AUTHN_DBM
- MOD_AUTHZ_DBM

Synopsis

dbmmanage [*encoding*] *filename* add|adduser|check|delete|update *username* [*encpasswd* [*group*[,*group*...] [*comment*]]]

dbmmanage *filename* view [*username*]

dbmmanage *filename* import

Options

filename The filename of the DBM format file. Usually without the extension `.db`, `.pag`, or `.dir`.

username The user for which the operations are performed. The *username* may not contain a colon (`:`).

encpasswd This is the already encrypted password to use for the `update` and `add` commands. You may use a hyphen (`-`) if you want to get prompted for the password, but fill in the fields afterwards. Additionally when using the `update` command, a period (`.`) keeps the original password untouched.

group A group, which the user is member of. A groupname may not contain a colon (`:`). You may use a hyphen (`-`) if you don't want to assign the user to a group, but fill in the comment field. Additionally when using the `update` command, a period (`.`) keeps the original groups untouched.

comment This is the place for your opaque comments about the user, like realname, mailaddress or such things. The server will ignore this field.

Encodings

-d crypt encryption (default, except on Win32, Netware)

-m MD5 encryption (default on Win32, Netware)

-s SHA1 encryption

-p plaintext (*not recommended*)

Commands

`add` Adds an entry for *username* to *filename* using the encrypted password *encpasswd*.

```
dbmmanage passwords.dat add rbowen foKntnEF3KSXA
```

`adduser` Asks for a password and then adds an entry for *username* to *filename*.

```
dbmmanage passwords.dat adduser krietz
```

`check` Asks for a password and then checks if *username* is in *filename* and if it's password matches the specified one.

```
dbmmanage passwords.dat check rbowen
```

`delete` Deletes the *username* entry from *filename*.

```
dbmmanage passwords.dat delete rbowen
```

`import` Reads *`username`*`:`*`password`* entries (one per line) from `STDIN` and adds them to *filename*. The passwords already have to be crypted.

`update` Same as the `adduser` command, except that it makes sure *username* already exists in *filename*.

```
dbmmanage passwords.dat update rbowen
```

`view` Just displays the contents of the DBM file. If you specify a *username*, it displays the particular record only.

```
dbmmanage passwords.dat view
```

Bugs

One should be aware that there are a number of different DBM file formats in existence, and with all likelihood, libraries for more than one format may exist on your system. The three primary examples are SDBM, NDBM, the GNU project's GDBM, and Berkeley DB 2. Unfortunately, all these libraries use different file formats, and you must make sure that the file format used by *filename* is the same format that `dbmmanage` expects to see. `dbmmanage` currently has no way of determining what type of DBM file it is looking at. If used against the wrong format, will simply return nothing, or may create a different DBM file with a different name, or at worst, it may corrupt the DBM file if you were attempting to write to it.

`dbmmanage` has a list of DBM format preferences, defined by the `@AnyDBM::ISA` array near the beginning of the program. Since we prefer the Berkeley DB 2 file format, the order in which `dbmmanage` will look for system libraries is Berkeley DB 2, then NDBM, then GDBM and then SDBM. The first library found will be the library `dbmmanage` will attempt to use for all DBM file transactions. This ordering is slightly different than the standard `@AnyDBM::ISA` ordering in Perl, as well as the ordering used by the simple `dbmopen()` call in Perl, so if you use any other utilities to manage your DBM files, they must also follow this preference ordering. Similar care must be taken if using programs in other languages, like C, to access these files.

One can usually use the `file` program supplied with most Unix systems to see what format a DBM file is in.

8.8 fcgistarter - Start a FastCGI program

See also

- MOD_PROXY_FCGI

Note

Currently only works on Unix systems.

Synopsis

fcgistarter -**c** *command* -**p** *port* [-**i** *interface*] -**N** *num*

Options

-c ***command*** FastCGI program

-p ***port*** Port which the program will listen on

-i ***interface*** Interface which the program will listen on

-N ***num*** Number of instances of the program

8.9 htcacheclean - Clean up the disk cache

`htcacheclean` is used to keep the size of MOD_CACHE_DISK's storage within a given size limit, or limit on inodes in use. This tool can run either manually or in daemon mode. When running in daemon mode, it sleeps in the background and checks the cache directory at regular intervals for cached content to be removed. You can stop the daemon cleanly by sending it a TERM or INT signal. When run manually, a once off check of the cache directory is made for cached content to be removed. If one or more URLs are specified, each URL will be deleted from the cache, if present.

See also

- MOD_CACHE_DISK

Synopsis

htcacheclean [**-D**] [**-v**] [**-t**] [**-r**] [**-n**] [**-R***round*] **-p***path* [**-l***limit*| **-L***limit*]

htcacheclean [**-n**] [**-t**] [**-i**] [**-P***pidfile*] [**-R***round*] **-d***interval* **-p***path* [**-l***limit*| **-L***limit*]

htcacheclean [**-v**] [**-R***round*] **-p***path* [**-a**] [**-A**]

htcacheclean [**-D**] [**-v**] [**-t**] [**-R***round*] **-p***path* *url*

Options

-d*interval* Daemonize and repeat cache cleaning every *interval* minutes. This option is mutually exclusive with the `-D`, `-v` and `-r` options. To shutdown the daemon cleanly, just send it a `SIGTERM` or `SIGINT`.

-D Do a dry run and don't delete anything. This option is mutually exclusive with the `-d` option. When doing a dry run and deleting directories with `-t`, the inodes reported deleted in the stats cannot take into account the directories deleted, and will be marked as an estimate.

-v Be verbose and print statistics. This option is mutually exclusive with the `-d` option.

-r Clean thoroughly. This assumes that the Apache web server is not running (otherwise you may get garbage in the cache). This option is mutually exclusive with the `-d` option and implies the `-t` option.

-n Be nice. This causes slower processing in favour of other processes. `htcacheclean` will sleep from time to time so that (a) the disk IO will be delayed and (b) the kernel can schedule other processes in the meantime.

-t Delete all empty directories. By default only cache files are removed, however with some configurations the large number of directories created may require attention. If your configuration requires a very large number of directories, to the point that inode or file allocation table exhaustion may become an issue, use of this option is advised.

-p*path* Specify *path* as the root directory of the disk cache. This should be the same value as specified with the CACHEROOT directive.

-P*pidfile* Specify *pidfile* as the name of the file to write the process ID to when daemonized.

-R*round* Specify *round* as the amount to round sizes up to, to compensate for disk block sizes. Set to the block size of the cache partition.

-l*limit* Specify *limit* as the total disk cache size limit. The value is expressed in bytes by default (or attaching `B` to the number). Attach `K` for Kbytes or `M` for MBytes.

-L*limit* Specify *limit* as the total disk cache inode limit.

-i Be intelligent and run only when there was a modification of the disk cache. This option is only possible together with the `-d` option.

-a List the URLs currently stored in the cache. Variants of the same URL will be listed once for each variant.

-A List the URLs currently stored in the cache, along with their attributes in the following order: url, header size, body size, status, entity version, date, expiry, request time, response time, body present, head request.

Deleting a specific URL

If `htcacheclean` is passed one or more URLs, each URL will be deleted from the cache. If multiple variants of an URL exists, all variants would be deleted.

When a reverse proxied URL is to be deleted, the effective URL is constructed from the **Host** header, the **port**, the **path** and the **query**. Note the '?' in the URL must always be specified explicitly, whether a query string is present or not. For example, an attempt to delete the path / from the server **localhost**, the URL to delete would be **http://localhost:80/?**.

Listing URLs in the Cache

By passing the `-a` or `-A` options to `htcacheclean`, the URLs within the cache will be listed as they are found, one URL per line. The `-A` option dumps the full cache entry after the URL, with fields in the following order:

url The URL of the entry.

header size The size of the header in bytes.

body size The size of the body in bytes.

status Status of the cached response.

entity version The number of times this entry has been revalidated without being deleted.

date Date of the response.

expiry Expiry date of the response.

request time Time of the start of the request.

response time Time of the end of the request.

body present If 0, no body is stored with this request, 1 otherwise.

head request If 1, the entry contains a cached HEAD request with no body, 0 otherwise.

Exit Status

`htcacheclean` returns a zero status ("true") if all operations were successful, `1` otherwise. If an URL is specified, and the URL was cached and successfully removed, `0` is returned, `2` otherwise. If an error occurred during URL removal, `1` is returned.

8.10 htdbm - Manipulate DBM password databases

htdbm is used to manipulate the DBM format files used to store usernames and password for basic authentication of HTTP users via MOD_AUTHN_DBM. See the dbmmanage documentation for more information about these DBM files.

See also

- httpd
- dbmmanage
- MOD_AUTHN_DBM

Synopsis

htdbm [**-T***DBTYPE*] [**-i**] [**-c**] [**-m** | **-B** | **-d** | **-s** | **-p**] [**-C** *cost*] [**-t**] [**-v**] *filename username*

htdbm -b [**-T***DBTYPE*] [**-c**] [**-m** | **-B** | **-d** | **-s** | **-p**] [**-C** *cost*] [**-t**] [**-v**] *filename username password*

htdbm -n [**-i**] [**-c**] [**-m** | **-B** | **-d** | **-s** | **-p**] [**-C** *cost*] [**-t**] [**-v**] *username*

htdbm -nb [**-c**] [**-m** | **-B** | **-d** | **-s** | **-p**] [**-C** *cost*] [**-t**] [**-v**] *username password*

htdbm -v [**-T***DBTYPE*] [**-i**] [**-c**] [**-m** | **-B** | **-d** | **-s** | **-p**] [**-C** *cost*] [**-t**] [**-v**] *filename username*

htdbm -vb [**-T***DBTYPE*] [**-c**] [**-m** | **-B** | **-d** | **-s** | **-p**] [**-C** *cost*] [**-t**] [**-v**] *filename username password*

htdbm -x [**-T***DBTYPE*] *filename username*

htdbm -l [**-T***DBTYPE*]

Options

-b Use batch mode; *i.e.*, get the password from the command line rather than prompting for it. This option should be used with extreme care, since **the password is clearly visible** on the command line. For script use see the -i option.

-i Read the password from stdin without verification (for script usage).

-c Create the *passwdfile*. If *passwdfile* already exists, it is rewritten and truncated. This option cannot be combined with the -n option.

-n Display the results on standard output rather than updating a database. This option changes the syntax of the command line, since the *passwdfile* argument (usually the first one) is omitted. It cannot be combined with the -c option.

-m Use MD5 encryption for passwords. On Windows and Netware, this is the default.

-B Use bcrypt encryption for passwords. This is currently considered to be very secure.

-C This flag is only allowed in combination with -B (bcrypt encryption). It sets the computing time used for the bcrypt algorithm (higher is more secure but slower, default: 5, valid: 4 to 31).

-d Use `crypt()` encryption for passwords. The default on all platforms but Windows and Netware. Though possibly supported by `htdbm` on all platforms, it is not supported by the `httpd` server on Windows and Netware. This algorithm is **insecure** by today's standards.

-s Use SHA encryption for passwords. Facilitates migration from/to Netscape servers using the LDAP Directory Interchange Format (ldif). This algorithm is **insecure** by today's standards.

-p Use plaintext passwords. Though `htdbm` will support creation on all platforms, the `httpd` daemon will only accept plain text passwords on Windows and Netware.

-l Print each of the usernames and comments from the database on stdout.

-v Verify the username and password. The program will print a message indicating whether the supplied password is valid. If the password is invalid, the program exits with error code 3.

-x Delete user. If the username exists in the specified DBM file, it will be deleted.

-t Interpret the final parameter as a comment. When this option is specified, an additional string can be appended to the command line; this string will be stored in the "Comment" field of the database, associated with the specified username.

filename The filename of the DBM format file. Usually without the extension `.db`, `.pag`, or `.dir`. If `-c` is given, the DBM file is created if it does not already exist, or updated if it does exist.

username The username to create or update in *passwdfile*. If *username* does not exist in this file, an entry is added. If it does exist, the password is changed.

password The plaintext password to be encrypted and stored in the DBM file. Used only with the `-b` flag.

-TDBTYPE Type of DBM file (SDBM, GDBM, DB, or "default").

Bugs

One should be aware that there are a number of different DBM file formats in existence, and with all likelihood, libraries for more than one format may exist on your system. The three primary examples are SDBM, NDBM, GNU GDBM, and Berkeley/Sleepycat DB 2/3/4. Unfortunately, all these libraries use different file formats, and you must make sure that the file format used by *filename* is the same format that `htdbm` expects to see. `htdbm` currently has no way of determining what type of DBM file it is looking at. If used against the wrong format, will simply return nothing, or may create a different DBM file with a different name, or at worst, it may corrupt the DBM file if you were attempting to write to it.

One can usually use the `file` program supplied with most Unix systems to see what format a DBM file is in.

Exit Status

`htdbm` returns a zero status ("true") if the username and password have been successfully added or updated in the DBM File. `htdbm` returns `1` if it encounters some problem accessing files, `2` if there was a syntax problem with the command line, `3` if the password was entered interactively and the verification entry didn't match, `4` if its operation was interrupted, `5` if a value is too long (username, filename, password, or final computed record), `6` if the username contains illegal characters (see the Restrictions section), and `7` if the file is not a valid DBM password file.

Examples

```
htdbm /usr/local/etc/apache/.htdbm-users jsmith
```

Adds or modifies the password for user `jsmith`. The user is prompted for the password. If executed on a Windows system, the password will be encrypted using the modified Apache MD5 algorithm; otherwise, the system's `crypt()` routine will be used. If the file does not exist, `htdbm` will do nothing except return an error.

```
htdbm -c /home/doe/public_html/.htdbm jane
```

Creates a new file and stores a record in it for user `jane`. The user is prompted for the password. If the file exists and cannot be read, or cannot be written, it is not altered and `htdbm` will display a message and return an error status.

```
htdbm -mb /usr/web/.htdbm-all jones Pwd4Steve
```

Encrypts the password from the command line (`Pwd4Steve`) using the MD5 algorithm, and stores it in the specified file.

Security Considerations

Web password files such as those managed by `htdbm` should *not* be within the Web server's URI space – that is, they should not be fetchable with a browser.

The use of the `-b` option is discouraged, since when it is used the unencrypted password appears on the command line.

When using the `crypt()` algorithm, note that only the first 8 characters of the password are used to form the password. If the supplied password is longer, the extra characters will be silently discarded.

The SHA encryption format does not use salting: for a given password, there is only one encrypted representation. The `crypt()` and MD5 formats permute the representation by prepending a random salt string, to make dictionary attacks against the passwords more difficult.

The SHA and `crypt()` formats are insecure by today's standards.

Restrictions

On the Windows platform, passwords encrypted with `htdbm` are limited to no more than `255` characters in length. Longer passwords will be truncated to 255 characters.

The MD5 algorithm used by `htdbm` is specific to the Apache software; passwords encrypted using it will not be usable with other Web servers.

Usernames are limited to `255` bytes and may not include the character `:`.

8.11 htdigest - manage user files for digest authentication

`htdigest` is used to create and update the flat-files used to store usernames, realm and password for digest authentication of HTTP users. Resources available from the Apache HTTP server can be restricted to just the users listed in the files created by `htdigest`.

This manual page only lists the command line arguments. For details of the directives necessary to configure digest authentication in `httpd` see the Apache manual, which is part of the Apache distribution or can be found at http://httpd.apache.org/.

See also

- `httpd`
- MOD_AUTH_DIGEST

Synopsis

`htdigest` `[` **`-c`** `]` *`passwdfile realm username`*

Options

`-c` Create the *passwdfile*. If *passwdfile* already exists, it is deleted first.

`passwdfile` Name of the file to contain the username, realm and password. If `-c` is given, this file is created if it does not already exist, or deleted and recreated if it does exist.

`realm` The realm name to which the user name belongs. See

http://tools.ietf.org/html/rfc2617#section-3.2.1[1] for more details.

`username` The user name to create or update in *passwdfile*. If *username* does not exist is this file, an entry is added. If it does exist, the password is changed.

Security Considerations

This program is not safe as a setuid executable. Do *not* make it setuid.

[1] http://tools.ietf.org/html/rfc2617#section-3.2.1

8.12 htpasswd - Manage user files for basic authentication

`htpasswd` is used to create and update the flat-files used to store usernames and password for basic authentication of HTTP users. If `htpasswd` cannot access a file, such as not being able to write to the output file or not being able to read the file in order to update it, it returns an error status and makes no changes.

Resources available from the Apache HTTP server can be restricted to just the users listed in the files created by `htpasswd`. This program can only manage usernames and passwords stored in a flat-file. It can encrypt and display password information for use in other types of data stores, though. To use a DBM database see `dbmmanage` or `htdbm`.

`htpasswd` encrypts passwords using either bcrypt, a version of MD5 modified for Apache, SHA1, or the system's `crypt()` routine. Files managed by `htpasswd` may contain a mixture of different encoding types of passwords; some user records may have bcrypt or MD5-encrypted passwords while others in the same file may have passwords encrypted with `crypt()`.

This manual page only lists the command line arguments. For details of the directives necessary to configure user authentication in `httpd` see the Apache manual, which is part of the Apache distribution or can be found at http://httpd.apache.org/[2].

See also

- `httpd`
- `htdbm`
- The scripts in support/SHA1 which come with the distribution.

Synopsis

htpasswd [**-c**] [**-i**] [**-m** | **-B** | **-d** | **-s** | **-p**] [**-C** *cost*] [**-D**] [**-v**] *passwdfile username*

htpasswd **-b** [**-c**] [**-m** | **-B** | **-d** | **-s** | **-p**] [**-C** *cost*] [**-D**] [**-v**] *passwdfile username password*

htpasswd **-n** [**-i**] [**-m** | **-B** | **-d** | **-s** | **-p**] [**-C** *cost*] *username*

htpasswd **-nb** [**-m** | **-B** | **-d** | **-s** | **-p**] [**-C** *cost*] *username password*

Options

-b Use batch mode; *i.e.*, get the password from the command line rather than prompting for it. This option should be used with extreme care, since **the password is clearly visible** on the command line. For script use see the `-i` option. Available in 2.4.4 and later.

-i Read the password from stdin without verification (for script usage).

-c Create the *passwdfile*. If *passwdfile* already exists, it is rewritten and truncated. This option cannot be combined with the `-n` option.

-n Display the results on standard output rather than updating a file. This is useful for generating password records acceptable to Apache for inclusion in non-text data stores. This option changes the syntax of the command line, since the *passwdfile* argument (usually the first one) is omitted. It cannot be combined with the `-c` option.

-m Use MD5 encryption for passwords. This is the default (since version 2.2.18).

[2] http://httpd.apache.org

-B Use bcrypt encryption for passwords. This is currently considered to be very secure.

-C This flag is only allowed in combination with `-B` (bcrypt encryption). It sets the computing time used for the bcrypt algorithm (higher is more secure but slower, default: 5, valid: 4 to 31).

-d Use `crypt()` encryption for passwords. This is not supported by the `httpd` server on Windows and Netware. This algorithm limits the password length to 8 characters. This algorithm is **insecure** by today's standards. It used to be the default algorithm until version 2.2.17.

-s Use SHA encryption for passwords. Facilitates migration from/to Netscape servers using the LDAP Directory Interchange Format (ldif). This algorithm is **insecure** by today's standards.

-p Use plaintext passwords. Though `htpasswd` will support creation on all platforms, the `httpd` daemon will only accept plain text passwords on Windows and Netware.

-D Delete user. If the username exists in the specified htpasswd file, it will be deleted.

-v Verify password. Verify that the given password matches the password of the user stored in the specified htpasswd file. Available in 2.4.5 and later.

passwdfile Name of the file to contain the user name and password. If `-c` is given, this file is created if it does not already exist, or rewritten and truncated if it does exist.

username The username to create or update in *passwdfile*. If *username* does not exist in this file, an entry is added. If it does exist, the password is changed.

password The plaintext password to be encrypted and stored in the file. Only used with the `-b` flag.

Exit Status

`htpasswd` returns a zero status ("true") if the username and password have been successfully added or updated in the *passwdfile*. `htpasswd` returns `1` if it encounters some problem accessing files, `2` if there was a syntax problem with the command line, `3` if the password was entered interactively and the verification entry didn't match, `4` if its operation was interrupted, `5` if a value is too long (username, filename, password, or final computed record), `6` if the username contains illegal characters (see the Restrictions section), and `7` if the file is not a valid password file.

Examples

```
htpasswd /usr/local/etc/apache/.htpasswd-users jsmith
```

Adds or modifies the password for user `jsmith`. The user is prompted for the password. The password will be encrypted using the modified Apache MD5 algorithm. If the file does not exist, `htpasswd` will do nothing except return an error.

```
htpasswd -c /home/doe/public_html/.htpasswd jane
```

Creates a new file and stores a record in it for user `jane`. The user is prompted for the password. If the file exists and cannot be read, or cannot be written, it is not altered and `htpasswd` will display a message and return an error status.

```
htpasswd -db /usr/web/.htpasswd-all jones Pwd4Steve
```

Encrypts the password from the command line (`Pwd4Steve`) using the `crypt()` algorithm, and stores it in the specified file.

Security Considerations

Web password files such as those managed by `htpasswd` should *not* be within the Web server's URI space – that is, they should not be fetchable with a browser.

This program is not safe as a setuid executable. Do *not* make it setuid.

The use of the `-b` option is discouraged, since when it is used the unencrypted password appears on the command line.

When using the `crypt()` algorithm, note that only the first 8 characters of the password are used to form the password. If the supplied password is longer, the extra characters will be silently discarded.

The SHA encryption format does not use salting: for a given password, there is only one encrypted representation. The `crypt()` and MD5 formats permute the representation by prepending a random salt string, to make dictionary attacks against the passwords more difficult.

The SHA and `crypt()` formats are insecure by today's standards.

Restrictions

On the Windows platform, passwords encrypted with `htpasswd` are limited to no more than `255` characters in length. Longer passwords will be truncated to 255 characters.

The MD5 algorithm used by `htpasswd` is specific to the Apache software; passwords encrypted using it will not be usable with other Web servers.

Usernames are limited to `255` bytes and may not include the character `:`.

8.13 httxt2dbm - Generate dbm files for use with RewriteMap

`httxt2dbm` is used to generate dbm files from text input, for use in REWRITEMAP with the `dbm` map type.

If the output file already exists, it will not be truncated. New keys will be added and existing keys will be updated.

See also

- `httpd`
- MOD_REWRITE

Synopsis

`httxt2dbm` `[ -v ] [ -f` *`DBM_TYPE`* `] -i` *`SOURCE_TXT`* `-o` *`OUTPUT_DBM`*

Options

`-v` More verbose output

`-f` ***`DBM_TYPE`*** Specify the DBM type to be used for the output. If not specified, will use the APR Default. Available types are: `GDBM` for GDBM files, `SDBM` for SDBM files, `DB` for berkeley DB files, `NDBM` for NDBM files, `default` for the default DBM type.

`-i` ***`SOURCE_TXT`*** Input file from which the dbm is to be created. The file should be formated with one record per line, of the form: `key value`. See the documentation for REWRITEMAP for further details of this file's format and meaning.

`-o` ***`OUTPUT_DBM`*** Name of the output dbm files.

Examples

```
httxt2dbm -i rewritemap.txt -o rewritemap.dbm
httxt2dbm -f SDBM -i rewritemap.txt -o rewritemap.dbm
```

8.14 logresolve - Resolve IP-addresses to hostnames in Apache log files

`logresolve` is a post-processing program to resolve IP-addresses in Apache's access logfiles. To minimize impact on your nameserver, logresolve has its very own internal hash-table cache. This means that each IP number will only be looked up the first time it is found in the log file.

Takes an Apache log file on standard input. The IP addresses must be the first thing on each line and must be separated from the remainder of the line by a space.

Synopsis

logresolve [**-s** *filename*] [**-c**] < *access_log* > *access_log.new*

Options

-s *filename* Specifies a filename to record statistics.

-c This causes `logresolve` to apply some DNS checks: after finding the hostname from the IP address, it looks up the IP addresses for the hostname and checks that one of these matches the original address.

8.15 log_server_status - Log periodic status summaries

This perl script is designed to be run at a frequent interval by something like cron. It connects to the server and downloads the status information. It reformats the information to a single line and logs it to a file. Adjust the variables at the top of the script to specify the location of the resulting logfile. MOD_STATUS will need to be loaded and configured in order for this script to do its job.

Usage

The script contains the following section.

```
my $wherelog = "/usr/local/apache2/logs/";  # Logs will be like "/usr/local/apache2/logs/1
my $server   = "localhost";          # Name of server, could be "www.foo.com"
my $port     = "80";                 # Port on server
my $request = "/server-status/?auto";     # Request to send
```

You'll need to ensure that these variables have the correct values, and you'll need to have the `/server-status` handler configured at the location specified, and the specified log location needs to be writable by the user which will run the script.

Run the script periodically via cron to produce a daily log file, which can then be used for statistical analysis.

8.16 rotatelogs - Piped logging program to rotate Apache logs

`rotatelogs` is a simple program for use in conjunction with Apache's piped logfile feature. It supports rotation based on a time interval or maximum size of the log.

Synopsis

rotatelogs [**-l**] [**-L** *linkname*] [**-p** *program*] [**-f**] [**-t**] [**-v**] [**-e**] [**-c**] [**-n** *number-of-files*] *logfile* *rotationtime*|*filesize*(B|K|M|G) [*offset*]

Options

-l Causes the use of local time rather than GMT as the base for the interval or for `strftime(3)` formatting with size-based rotation.

-L ***linkname*** Causes a hard link to be made from the current logfile to the specified link name. This can be used to watch the log continuously across rotations using a command like `tail -F linkname`.

-p ***program*** If given, `rotatelogs` will execute the specified program every time a new log file is opened. The filename of the newly opened file is passed as the first argument to the program. If executing after a rotation, the old log file is passed as the second argument. `rotatelogs` does not wait for the specified program to terminate before continuing to operate, and will not log any error code returned on termination. The spawned program uses the same stdin, stdout, and stderr as rotatelogs itself, and also inherits the environment.

-f Causes the logfile to be opened immediately, as soon as `rotatelogs` starts, instead of waiting for the first logfile entry to be read (for non-busy sites, there may be a substantial delay between when the server is started and when the first request is handled, meaning that the associated logfile does not "exist" until then, which causes problems from some automated logging tools)

-t Causes the logfile to be truncated instead of rotated. This is useful when a log is processed in real time by a command like tail, and there is no need for archived data. No suffix will be added to the filename, however format strings containing '%' characters will be respected.

-v Produce verbose output on STDERR. The output contains the result of the configuration parsing, and all file open and close actions.

-e Echo logs through to stdout. Useful when logs need to be further processed in real time by a further tool in the chain.

-c Create log file for each interval, even if empty.

-n ***number-of-files*** Use a circular list of filenames without timestamps. With -n 3, the series of log files opened would be "logfile", "logfile.1", "logfile.2", then overwriting "logfile". Available in 2.4.5 and later.

logfile The path plus basename of the logfile. If *logfile* includes any '%' characters, it is treated as a format string for `strftime(3)`. Otherwise, the suffix *.nnnnnnnnnn* is automatically added and is the time in seconds (unless the -t option is used). Both formats compute the start time from the beginning of the current period. For example, if a rotation time of 86400 is specified, the hour, minute, and second fields created from the `strftime(3)` format will all be zero, referring to the beginning of the current 24-hour period (midnight).

When using `strftime(3)` filename formatting, be sure the log file format has enough granularity to produce a different file name each time the logs are rotated. Otherwise rotation will overwrite the same file instead of starting a new one. For example, if *logfile* was `/var/log/errorlog.%Y-%m-%d` with log rotation at 5 megabytes, but 5 megabytes was reached twice in the same day, the same log file name would be produced and log rotation would keep writing to the same file.

rotationtime The time between log file rotations in seconds. The rotation occurs at the beginning of this interval. For example, if the rotation time is 3600, the log file will be rotated at the beginning of every hour; if the rotation time is 86400, the log file will be rotated every night at midnight. (If no data is logged during an interval, no file will be created.)

***filesize*(B|K|M|G)** The maximum file size in followed by exactly one of the letters `B` (Bytes), `K` (KBytes), `M` (MBytes) or `G` (GBytes).

When time and size are specified, the size must be given after the time. Rotation will occur whenever either time or size limits are reached.

offset The number of minutes offset from UTC. If omitted, zero is assumed and UTC is used. For example, to use local time in the zone UTC -5 hours, specify a value of `-300` for this argument. In most cases, `-l` should be used instead of specifying an offset.

Examples

```
CustomLog "|bin/rotatelogs /var/log/logfile 86400" common
```

This creates the files /var/log/logfile.nnnn where nnnn is the system time at which the log nominally starts (this time will always be a multiple of the rotation time, so you can synchronize cron scripts with it). At the end of each rotation time (here after 24 hours) a new log is started.

```
CustomLog "|bin/rotatelogs -l /var/log/logfile.%Y.%m.%d 86400" common
```

This creates the files /var/log/logfile.yyyy.mm.dd where yyyy is the year, mm is the month, and dd is the day of the month. Logging will switch to a new file every day at midnight, local time.

```
CustomLog "|bin/rotatelogs /var/log/logfile 5M" common
```

This configuration will rotate the logfile whenever it reaches a size of 5 megabytes.

```
ErrorLog "|bin/rotatelogs /var/log/errorlog.%Y-%m-%d-%H_%M_%S 5M"
```

This configuration will rotate the error logfile whenever it reaches a size of 5 megabytes, and the suffix to the logfile name will be created of the form `errorlog.YYYY-mm-dd-HH_MM_SS`.

```
CustomLog "|bin/rotatelogs -t /var/log/logfile 86400" common
```

This creates the file /var/log/logfile, truncating the file at startup and then truncating the file once per day. It is expected in this scenario that a separate process (such as tail) would process the file in real time.

Portability

The following logfile format string substitutions should be supported by all `strftime(3)` implementations, see the `strftime(3)` man page for library-specific extensions.

`%A`	full weekday name (localized)

%a	3-character weekday name (localized)
%B	full month name (localized)
%b	3-character month name (localized)
%c	date and time (localized)
%d	2-digit day of month
%H	2-digit hour (24 hour clock)
%I	2-digit hour (12 hour clock)
%j	3-digit day of year
%M	2-digit minute
%m	2-digit month
%p	am/pm of 12 hour clock (localized)
%S	2-digit second
%U	2-digit week of year (Sunday first day of week)
%W	2-digit week of year (Monday first day of week)
%w	1-digit weekday (Sunday first day of week)
%X	time (localized)
%x	date (localized)
%Y	4-digit year
%y	2-digit year
%Z	time zone name
%%	literal '%'

8.17 split-logfile - Split up multi-vhost logfiles

This perl script will take a combined Web server access log file and break its contents into separate files. It assumes that the first field of each line is the virtual host identity, put there using the "%v" variable in LOGFORMAT.

Usage

Create a log file with virtual host information in it:

```
LogFormat "%v %h %l %u %t \"%r\" %>s %b \"%{Referer}i\" \"%{User-agent}i\"" combined_plus_
CustomLog logs/access_log combined_plus_vhost
```

Log files will be created, in the directory where you run the script, for each virtual host name that appears in the combined log file. These logfiles will named after the hostname, with a .log file extension.

The combined log file is read from stdin. Records read will be appended to any existing log files.

```
split-logfile < access_log
```

8.18 suexec - Switch user before executing external programs

`suexec` is used by the Apache HTTP Server to switch to another user before executing CGI programs. In order to achieve this, it must run as `root`. Since the HTTP daemon normally doesn't run as `root`, the `suexec` executable needs the setuid bit set and must be owned by `root`. It should never be writable for any other person than `root`.

For further information about the concepts and the security model of suexec please refer to the suexec documentation (http://httpd.apache.org/docs/2.4/suexec.html).

Synopsis

suexec -V

Options

-V If you are `root`, this option displays the compile options of `suexec`. For security reasons all configuration options are changeable only at compile time.

8.19 Other Programs

This page used to contain documentation for programs which now have their own docs pages. Please update any links.

`log_server_status`

`split-logfile`

Chapter 9

Apache Miscellaneous Documentation

9.1 Apache Miscellaneous Documentation

Below is a list of additional documentation pages that apply to the Apache web server development project.

> **Warning**
> The documents below have not been fully updated to take into account changes made in the 2.1 version of the Apache HTTP Server. Some of the information may still be relevant, but please use it with care.

Performance Notes - Apache Tuning (p. 327) Notes about how to (run-time and compile-time) configure Apache for highest performance. Notes explaining why Apache does some things, and why it doesn't do other things (which make it slower/faster).

Security Tips (p. 338) Some "do"s - and "don't"s - for keeping your Apache web site secure.

Relevant Standards (p. 343) This document acts as a reference page for most of the relevant standards that Apache follows.

Password Encryption Formats (p. 345) Discussion of the various ciphers supported by Apache for authentication purposes.

9.2 Apache Performance Tuning

Apache 2.x is a general-purpose webserver, designed to provide a balance of flexibility, portability, and performance. Although it has not been designed specifically to set benchmark records, Apache 2.x is capable of high performance in many real-world situations.

Compared to Apache 1.3, release 2.x contains many additional optimizations to increase throughput and scalability. Most of these improvements are enabled by default. However, there are compile-time and run-time configuration choices that can significantly affect performance. This document describes the options that a server administrator can configure to tune the performance of an Apache 2.x installation. Some of these configuration options enable the httpd to better take advantage of the capabilities of the hardware and OS, while others allow the administrator to trade functionality for speed.

Hardware and Operating System Issues

The single biggest hardware issue affecting webserver performance is RAM. A webserver should never ever have to swap, as swapping increases the latency of each request beyond a point that users consider "fast enough". This causes users to hit stop and reload, further increasing the load. You can, and should, control the MAXREQUESTWORKERS setting so that your server does not spawn so many children that it starts swapping. The procedure for doing this is simple: determine the size of your average Apache process, by looking at your process list via a tool such as `top`, and divide this into your total available memory, leaving some room for other processes.

Beyond that the rest is mundane: get a fast enough CPU, a fast enough network card, and fast enough disks, where "fast enough" is something that needs to be determined by experimentation.

Operating system choice is largely a matter of local concerns. But some guidelines that have proven generally useful are:

- Run the latest stable release and patch level of the operating system that you choose. Many OS suppliers have introduced significant performance improvements to their TCP stacks and thread libraries in recent years.
- If your OS supports a `sendfile(2)` system call, make sure you install the release and/or patches needed to enable it. (With Linux, for example, this means using Linux 2.4 or later. For early releases of Solaris 8, you may need to apply a patch.) On systems where it is available, `sendfile` enables Apache 2 to deliver static content faster and with lower CPU utilization.

Run-Time Configuration Issues

Related Modules	Related Directives
MOD_DIR	ALLOWOVERRIDE
MPM_COMMON	DIRECTORYINDEX
MOD_STATUS	HOSTNAMELOOKUPS
	ENABLEMMAP
	ENABLESENDFILE
	KEEPALIVETIMEOUT
	MAXSPARESERVERS
	MINSPARESERVERS
	OPTIONS
	STARTSERVERS

HostnameLookups and other DNS considerations

Prior to Apache 1.3, HOSTNAMELOOKUPS defaulted to On. This adds latency to every request because it requires a DNS lookup to complete before the request is finished. In Apache 1.3 this setting defaults to Off. If you need to have addresses in your log files resolved to hostnames, use the logresolve program that comes with Apache, or one of the numerous log reporting packages which are available.

It is recommended that you do this sort of postprocessing of your log files on some machine other than the production web server machine, in order that this activity not adversely affect server performance.

If you use any ALLOW from domain or DENY from domain directives (i.e., using a hostname, or a domain name, rather than an IP address) then you will pay for two DNS lookups (a reverse, followed by a forward lookup to make sure that the reverse is not being spoofed). For best performance, therefore, use IP addresses, rather than names, when using these directives, if possible.

Note that it's possible to scope the directives, such as within a <Location "/server-status"> section. In this case the DNS lookups are only performed on requests matching the criteria. Here's an example which disables lookups except for .html and .cgi files:

```
HostnameLookups off
<Files ~ "\.(html|cgi)$">
  HostnameLookups on
</Files>
```

But even still, if you just need DNS names in some CGIs you could consider doing the gethostbyname call in the specific CGIs that need it.

FollowSymLinks and SymLinksIfOwnerMatch

Wherever in your URL-space you do not have an Options FollowSymLinks, or you do have an Options SymLinksIfOwnerMatch, Apache will need to issue extra system calls to check up on symlinks. (One extra call per filename component.) For example, if you had:

```
DocumentRoot "/www/htdocs"
<Directory "/">
  Options SymLinksIfOwnerMatch
</Directory>
```

and a request is made for the URI /index.html, then Apache will perform lstat(2) on /www, /www/htdocs, and /www/htdocs/index.html. The results of these lstats are never cached, so they will occur on every single request. If you really desire the symlinks security checking, you can do something like this:

```
DocumentRoot "/www/htdocs"
<Directory "/">
  Options FollowSymLinks
</Directory>

<Directory "/www/htdocs">
  Options -FollowSymLinks +SymLinksIfOwnerMatch
</Directory>
```

This at least avoids the extra checks for the DOCUMENTROOT path. Note that you'll need to add similar sections if you have any ALIAS or REWRITERULE paths outside of your document root. For highest performance, and no symlink protection, set FollowSymLinks everywhere, and never set SymLinksIfOwnerMatch.

AllowOverride

Wherever in your URL-space you allow overrides (typically `.htaccess` files), Apache will attempt to open `.htaccess` for each filename component. For example,

```
DocumentRoot "/www/htdocs"
<Directory "/">
  AllowOverride all
</Directory>
```

and a request is made for the URI `/index.html`. Then Apache will attempt to open `/.htaccess`, `/www/.htaccess`, and `/www/htdocs/.htaccess`. The solutions are similar to the previous case of `Options FollowSymLinks`. For highest performance use `AllowOverride None` everywhere in your filesystem.

Negotiation

If at all possible, avoid content negotiation if you're really interested in every last ounce of performance. In practice the benefits of negotiation outweigh the performance penalties. There's one case where you can speed up the server. Instead of using a wildcard such as:

```
DirectoryIndex index
```

Use a complete list of options:

```
DirectoryIndex index.cgi index.pl index.shtml index.html
```

where you list the most common choice first.

Also note that explicitly creating a `type-map` file provides better performance than using `MultiViews`, as the necessary information can be determined by reading this single file, rather than having to scan the directory for files.

If your site needs content negotiation, consider using `type-map` files, rather than the `Options MultiViews` directive to accomplish the negotiation. See the Content Negotiation (p. 68) documentation for a full discussion of the methods of negotiation, and instructions for creating `type-map` files.

Memory-mapping

In situations where Apache 2.x needs to look at the contents of a file being delivered–for example, when doing server-side-include processing–it normally memory-maps the file if the OS supports some form of `mmap(2)`.

On some platforms, this memory-mapping improves performance. However, there are cases where memory-mapping can hurt the performance or even the stability of the httpd:

- On some operating systems, `mmap` does not scale as well as `read(2)` when the number of CPUs increases. On multiprocessor Solaris servers, for example, Apache 2.x sometimes delivers server-parsed files faster when `mmap` is disabled.
- If you memory-map a file located on an NFS-mounted filesystem and a process on another NFS client machine deletes or truncates the file, your process may get a bus error the next time it tries to access the mapped file content.

For installations where either of these factors applies, you should use `EnableMMAP off` to disable the memory-mapping of delivered files. (Note: This directive can be overridden on a per-directory basis.)

Sendfile

In situations where Apache 2.x can ignore the contents of the file to be delivered – for example, when serving static file content – it normally uses the kernel sendfile support for the file if the OS supports the `sendfile(2)` operation.

On most platforms, using sendfile improves performance by eliminating separate read and send mechanics. However, there are cases where using sendfile can harm the stability of the httpd:

- Some platforms may have broken sendfile support that the build system did not detect, especially if the binaries were built on another box and moved to such a machine with broken sendfile support.
- With an NFS-mounted filesystem, the kernel may be unable to reliably serve the network file through its own cache.

For installations where either of these factors applies, you should use `EnableSendfile off` to disable sendfile delivery of file contents. (Note: This directive can be overridden on a per-directory basis.)

Process Creation

Prior to Apache 1.3 the MinSpareServers, MaxSpareServers, and StartServers settings all had drastic effects on benchmark results. In particular, Apache required a "ramp-up" period in order to reach a number of children sufficient to serve the load being applied. After the initial spawning of StartServers children, only one child per second would be created to satisfy the MinSpareServers setting. So a server being accessed by 100 simultaneous clients, using the default StartServers of `5` would take on the order of 95 seconds to spawn enough children to handle the load. This works fine in practice on real-life servers because they aren't restarted frequently. But it does really poorly on benchmarks which might only run for ten minutes.

The one-per-second rule was implemented in an effort to avoid swamping the machine with the startup of new children. If the machine is busy spawning children, it can't service requests. But it has such a drastic effect on the perceived performance of Apache that it had to be replaced. As of Apache 1.3, the code will relax the one-per-second rule. It will spawn one, wait a second, then spawn two, wait a second, then spawn four, and it will continue exponentially until it is spawning 32 children per second. It will stop whenever it satisfies the MinSpareServers setting.

This appears to be responsive enough that it's almost unnecessary to twiddle the MinSpareServers, MaxSpareServers and StartServers knobs. When more than 4 children are spawned per second, a message will be emitted to the ErrorLog. If you see a lot of these errors, then consider tuning these settings. Use the mod_status output as a guide.

Related to process creation is process death induced by the MaxConnectionsPerChild setting. By default this is `0`, which means that there is no limit to the number of connections handled per child. If your configuration currently has this set to some very low number, such as `30`, you may want to bump this up significantly. If you are running SunOS or an old version of Solaris, limit this to `10000` or so because of memory leaks.

When keep-alives are in use, children will be kept busy doing nothing waiting for more requests on the already open connection. The default KeepAliveTimeout of `5` seconds attempts to minimize this effect. The tradeoff here is between network bandwidth and server resources. In no event should you raise this above about `60` seconds, as most of the benefits are lost[1].

Compile-Time Configuration Issues

Choosing an MPM

Apache 2.x supports pluggable concurrency models, called Multi-Processing Modules (p. 80) (MPMs). When building Apache, you must choose an MPM to use. There are platform-specific MPMs for some platforms: mpm_netware,

[1] http://www.hpl.hp.com/techreports/Compaq-DEC/WRL-95-4.html

MPMT_OS2, and MPM_WINNT. For general Unix-type systems, there are several MPMs from which to choose. The choice of MPM can affect the speed and scalability of the httpd:

- The WORKER MPM uses multiple child processes with many threads each. Each thread handles one connection at a time. Worker generally is a good choice for high-traffic servers because it has a smaller memory footprint than the prefork MPM.
- The EVENT MPM is threaded like the Worker MPM, but is designed to allow more requests to be served simultaneously by passing off some processing work to supporting threads, freeing up the main threads to work on new requests.
- The PREFORK MPM uses multiple child processes with one thread each. Each process handles one connection at a time. On many systems, prefork is comparable in speed to worker, but it uses more memory. Prefork's threadless design has advantages over worker in some situations: it can be used with non-thread-safe third-party modules, and it is easier to debug on platforms with poor thread debugging support.

For more information on these and other MPMs, please see the MPM documentation (p. 80) .

Modules

Since memory usage is such an important consideration in performance, you should attempt to eliminate modules that you are not actually using. If you have built the modules as DSOs (p. 65) , eliminating modules is a simple matter of commenting out the associated LOADMODULE directive for that module. This allows you to experiment with removing modules and seeing if your site still functions in their absence.

If, on the other hand, you have modules statically linked into your Apache binary, you will need to recompile Apache in order to remove unwanted modules.

An associated question that arises here is, of course, what modules you need, and which ones you don't. The answer here will, of course, vary from one web site to another. However, the *minimal* list of modules which you can get by with tends to include MOD_MIME, MOD_DIR, and MOD_LOG_CONFIG. `mod_log_config` is, of course, optional, as you can run a web site without log files. This is, however, not recommended.

Atomic Operations

Some modules, such as MOD_CACHE and recent development builds of the worker MPM, use APR's atomic API. This API provides atomic operations that can be used for lightweight thread synchronization.

By default, APR implements these operations using the most efficient mechanism available on each target OS/CPU platform. Many modern CPUs, for example, have an instruction that does an atomic compare-and-swap (CAS) operation in hardware. On some platforms, however, APR defaults to a slower, mutex-based implementation of the atomic API in order to ensure compatibility with older CPU models that lack such instructions. If you are building Apache for one of these platforms, and you plan to run only on newer CPUs, you can select a faster atomic implementation at build time by configuring Apache with the `--enable-nonportable-atomics` option:

```
./buildconf
./configure --with-mpm=worker --enable-nonportable-atomics=yes
```

The `--enable-nonportable-atomics` option is relevant for the following platforms:

- Solaris on SPARC
  By default, APR uses mutex-based atomics on Solaris/SPARC. If you configure with `--enable-nonportable-atomics`, however, APR generates code that uses a SPARC v8plus opcode for fast hardware compare-and-swap. If you configure Apache with this option, the atomic operations

will be more efficient (allowing for lower CPU utilization and higher concurrency), but the resulting executable will run only on UltraSPARC chips.

- Linux on x86
  By default, APR uses mutex-based atomics on Linux. If you configure with `--enable-nonportable-atomics`, however, APR generates code that uses a 486 opcode for fast hardware compare-and-swap. This will result in more efficient atomic operations, but the resulting executable will run only on 486 and later chips (and not on 386).

mod_status and ExtendedStatus On

If you include MOD_STATUS and you also set `ExtendedStatus On` when building and running Apache, then on every request Apache will perform two calls to `gettimeofday(2)` (or `times(2)` depending on your operating system), and (pre-1.3) several extra calls to `time(2)`. This is all done so that the status report contains timing indications. For highest performance, set `ExtendedStatus off` (which is the default).

accept Serialization - Multiple Sockets

Warning:
This section has not been fully updated to take into account changes made in the 2.x version of the Apache HTTP Server. Some of the information may still be relevant, but please use it with care.

This discusses a shortcoming in the Unix socket API. Suppose your web server uses multiple LISTEN statements to listen on either multiple ports or multiple addresses. In order to test each socket to see if a connection is ready, Apache uses `select(2)`. `select(2)` indicates that a socket has *zero* or *at least one* connection waiting on it. Apache's model includes multiple children, and all the idle ones test for new connections at the same time. A naive implementation looks something like this (these examples do not match the code, they're contrived for pedagogical purposes):

```
for (;;) {
  for (;;) {
    fd_set accept_fds;

    FD_ZERO (&accept_fds);
    for (i = first_socket; i <= last_socket; ++i) {
      FD_SET (i, &accept_fds);
    }
    rc = select (last_socket+1, &accept_fds, NULL, NULL, NULL);
    if (rc < 1) continue;
    new_connection = -1;
    for (i = first_socket; i <= last_socket; ++i) {
      if (FD_ISSET (i, &accept_fds)) {
        new_connection = accept (i, NULL, NULL);
        if (new_connection != -1) break;
      }
    }
    if (new_connection != -1) break;
  }
  process_the(new_connection);
}
```

But this naive implementation has a serious starvation problem. Recall that multiple children execute this loop at the same time, and so multiple children will block at `select` when they are in between requests. All those blocked children will awaken and return from `select` when a single request appears on any socket. (The number of children which awaken varies depending on the operating system and timing issues.) They will all then fall down into the loop and try to `accept` the connection. But only one will succeed (assuming there's still only one connection ready). The rest will be *blocked* in `accept`. This effectively locks those children into serving requests from that one socket and no other sockets, and they'll be stuck there until enough new requests appear on that socket to wake them all up. This starvation problem was first documented in PR#467[2]. There are at least two solutions.

One solution is to make the sockets non-blocking. In this case the `accept` won't block the children, and they will be allowed to continue immediately. But this wastes CPU time. Suppose you have ten idle children in `select`, and one connection arrives. Then nine of those children will wake up, try to `accept` the connection, fail, and loop back into `select`, accomplishing nothing. Meanwhile none of those children are servicing requests that occurred on other sockets until they get back up to the `select` again. Overall this solution does not seem very fruitful unless you have as many idle CPUs (in a multiprocessor box) as you have idle children (not a very likely situation).

Another solution, the one used by Apache, is to serialize entry into the inner loop. The loop looks like this (differences highlighted):

```
for (;;) {
  accept_mutex_on ();
  for (;;) {
    fd_set accept_fds;

    FD_ZERO (&accept_fds);
    for (i = first_socket; i <= last_socket; ++i) {
      FD_SET (i, &accept_fds);
    }
    rc = select (last_socket+1, &accept_fds, NULL, NULL, NULL);
    if (rc < 1) continue;
    new_connection = -1;
    for (i = first_socket; i <= last_socket; ++i) {
      if (FD_ISSET (i, &accept_fds)) {
        new_connection = accept (i, NULL, NULL);
        if (new_connection != -1) break;
      }
    }
    if (new_connection != -1) break;
  }
  accept_mutex_off ();
  process the new_connection;
}
```

The functions `accept_mutex_on` and `accept_mutex_off` implement a mutual exclusion semaphore. Only one child can have the mutex at any time. There are several choices for implementing these mutexes. The choice is defined in `src/conf.h` (pre-1.3) or `src/include/ap_config.h` (1.3 or later). Some architectures do not have any locking choice made, on these architectures it is unsafe to use multiple LISTEN directives.

The MUTEX directive can be used to change the mutex implementation of the `mpm-accept` mutex at run-time. Special considerations for different mutex implementations are documented with that directive.

Another solution that has been considered but never implemented is to partially serialize the loop – that is, let in a certain number of processes. This would only be of interest on multiprocessor boxes where it's possible that multiple

[2] http://bugs.apache.org/index/full/467

children could run simultaneously, and the serialization actually doesn't take advantage of the full bandwidth. This is a possible area of future investigation, but priority remains low because highly parallel web servers are not the norm.

Ideally you should run servers without multiple LISTEN statements if you want the highest performance. But read on.

accept Serialization - Single Socket

The above is fine and dandy for multiple socket servers, but what about single socket servers? In theory they shouldn't experience any of these same problems because all the children can just block in `accept(2)` until a connection arrives, and no starvation results. In practice this hides almost the same "spinning" behavior discussed above in the non-blocking solution. The way that most TCP stacks are implemented, the kernel actually wakes up all processes blocked in `accept` when a single connection arrives. One of those processes gets the connection and returns to user-space. The rest spin in the kernel and go back to sleep when they discover there's no connection for them. This spinning is hidden from the user-land code, but it's there nonetheless. This can result in the same load-spiking wasteful behavior that a non-blocking solution to the multiple sockets case can.

For this reason we have found that many architectures behave more "nicely" if we serialize even the single socket case. So this is actually the default in almost all cases. Crude experiments under Linux (2.0.30 on a dual Pentium pro 166 w/128Mb RAM) have shown that the serialization of the single socket case causes less than a 3% decrease in requests per second over unserialized single-socket. But unserialized single-socket showed an extra 100ms latency on each request. This latency is probably a wash on long haul lines, and only an issue on LANs. If you want to override the single socket serialization, you can define `SINGLE_LISTEN_UNSERIALIZED_ACCEPT`, and then single-socket servers will not serialize at all.

Lingering Close

As discussed in draft-ietf-http-connection-00.txt[3] section 8, in order for an HTTP server to **reliably** implement the protocol, it needs to shut down each direction of the communication independently. (Recall that a TCP connection is bi-directional. Each half is independent of the other.)

When this feature was added to Apache, it caused a flurry of problems on various versions of Unix because of short-sightedness. The TCP specification does not state that the `FIN_WAIT_2` state has a timeout, but it doesn't prohibit it. On systems without the timeout, Apache 1.2 induces many sockets stuck forever in the `FIN_WAIT_2` state. In many cases this can be avoided by simply upgrading to the latest TCP/IP patches supplied by the vendor. In cases where the vendor has never released patches (*i.e.*, SunOS4 – although folks with a source license can patch it themselves), we have decided to disable this feature.

There are two ways to accomplish this. One is the socket option `SO_LINGER`. But as fate would have it, this has never been implemented properly in most TCP/IP stacks. Even on those stacks with a proper implementation (*i.e.*, Linux 2.0.31), this method proves to be more expensive (cputime) than the next solution.

For the most part, Apache implements this in a function called `lingering_close` (in `http_main.c`). The function looks roughly like this:

```
void lingering_close (int s)
{
  char junk_buffer[2048];

  /* shutdown the sending side */
  shutdown (s, 1);

  signal (SIGALRM, lingering_death);
  alarm (30);
```

[3] http://www.ics.uci.edu/pub/ietf/http/draft-ietf-http-connection-00.txt

```
    for (;;) {
      select (s for reading, 2 second timeout);
      if (error) break;
      if (s is ready for reading) {
        if (read (s, junk_buffer, sizeof (junk_buffer)) <= 0) {
          break;
        }
        /* just toss away whatever is here */
      }
    }

    close (s);
}
```

This naturally adds some expense at the end of a connection, but it is required for a reliable implementation. As HTTP/1.1 becomes more prevalent, and all connections are persistent, this expense will be amortized over more requests. If you want to play with fire and disable this feature, you can define `NO_LINGCLOSE`, but this is not recommended at all. In particular, as HTTP/1.1 pipelined persistent connections come into use, `lingering_close` is an absolute necessity (and pipelined connections are faster[4], so you want to support them).

Scoreboard File

Apache's parent and children communicate with each other through something called the scoreboard. Ideally this should be implemented in shared memory. For those operating systems that we either have access to, or have been given detailed ports for, it typically is implemented using shared memory. The rest default to using an on-disk file. The on-disk file is not only slow, but it is unreliable (and less featured). Peruse the `src/main/conf.h` file for your architecture, and look for either `USE_MMAP_SCOREBOARD` or `USE_SHMGET_SCOREBOARD`. Defining one of those two (as well as their companions `HAVE_MMAP` and `HAVE_SHMGET` respectively) enables the supplied shared memory code. If your system has another type of shared memory, edit the file `src/main/http_main.c` and add the hooks necessary to use it in Apache. (Send us back a patch too, please.)

⟹ Historical note: The Linux port of Apache didn't start to use shared memory until version 1.2 of Apache. This oversight resulted in really poor and unreliable behavior of earlier versions of Apache on Linux.

DYNAMIC_MODULE_LIMIT

If you have no intention of using dynamically loaded modules (you probably don't if you're reading this and tuning your server for every last ounce of performance), then you should add `-DDYNAMIC_MODULE_LIMIT=0` when building your server. This will save RAM that's allocated only for supporting dynamically loaded modules.

Appendix: Detailed Analysis of a Trace

Here is a system call trace of Apache 2.0.38 with the worker MPM on Solaris 8. This trace was collected using:

```
truss -l -p httpd_child_pid.
```

[4] http://www.w3.org/Protocols/HTTP/Performance/Pipeline.html

The `-l` option tells truss to log the ID of the LWP (lightweight process–Solaris' form of kernel-level thread) that invokes each system call.

Other systems may have different system call tracing utilities such as `strace`, `ktrace`, or `par`. They all produce similar output.

In this trace, a client has requested a 10KB static file from the httpd. Traces of non-static requests or requests with content negotiation look wildly different (and quite ugly in some cases).

```
/67:     accept(3, 0x00200BEC, 0x00200C0C, 1) (sleeping...)
/67:     accept(3, 0x00200BEC, 0x00200C0C, 1)           = 9
```

In this trace, the listener thread is running within LWP #67.

⟹ Note the lack of `accept(2)` serialization. On this particular platform, the worker MPM uses an unserialized accept by default unless it is listening on multiple ports.

```
/65:     lwp_park(0x00000000, 0)                        = 0
/67:     lwp_unpark(65, 1)                              = 0
```

Upon accepting the connection, the listener thread wakes up a worker thread to do the request processing. In this trace, the worker thread that handles the request is mapped to LWP #65.

```
/65:     getsockname(9, 0x00200BA4, 0x00200BC4, 1)      = 0
```

In order to implement virtual hosts, Apache needs to know the local socket address used to accept the connection. It is possible to eliminate this call in many situations (such as when there are no virtual hosts, or when LISTEN directives are used which do not have wildcard addresses). But no effort has yet been made to do these optimizations.

```
/65:     brk(0x002170E8)                                = 0
/65:     brk(0x002190E8)                                = 0
```

The `brk(2)` calls allocate memory from the heap. It is rare to see these in a system call trace, because the httpd uses custom memory allocators (`apr_pool` and `apr_bucket_alloc`) for most request processing. In this trace, the httpd has just been started, so it must call `malloc(3)` to get the blocks of raw memory with which to create the custom memory allocators.

```
/65:     fcntl(9, F_GETFL, 0x00000000)                  = 2
/65:     fstat64(9, 0xFAF7B818)                         = 0
/65:     getsockopt(9, 65535, 8192, 0xFAF7B918, 0xFAF7B910, 2190656) = 0
/65:     fstat64(9, 0xFAF7B818)                         = 0
/65:     getsockopt(9, 65535, 8192, 0xFAF7B918, 0xFAF7B914, 2190656) = 0
/65:     setsockopt(9, 65535, 8192, 0xFAF7B918, 4, 2190656) = 0
/65:     fcntl(9, F_SETFL, 0x00000082)                  = 0
```

Next, the worker thread puts the connection to the client (file descriptor 9) in non-blocking mode. The `setsockopt(2)` and `getsockopt(2)` calls are a side-effect of how Solaris' libc handles `fcntl(2)` on sockets.

```
/65:    read(9, " G E T   / 1 0 k . h t m".., 8000)     = 97
```

The worker thread reads the request from the client.

```
/65:    stat("/var/httpd/apache/httpd-8999/htdocs/10k.html", 0xFAF7B978) = 0
/65:    open("/var/httpd/apache/httpd-8999/htdocs/10k.html", O_RDONLY) = 10
```

This httpd has been configured with `Options FollowSymLinks` and `AllowOverride None`. Thus it doesn't need to `lstat(2)` each directory in the path leading up to the requested file, nor check for `.htaccess` files. It simply calls `stat(2)` to verify that the file: 1) exists, and 2) is a regular file, not a directory.

```
/65:    sendfilev(0, 9, 0x00200F90, 2, 0xFAF7B53C)      = 10269
```

In this example, the httpd is able to send the HTTP response header and the requested file with a single `sendfilev(2)` system call. Sendfile semantics vary among operating systems. On some other systems, it is necessary to do a `write(2)` or `writev(2)` call to send the headers before calling `sendfile(2)`.

```
/65:    write(4, " 1 2 7 . 0 . 0 . 1   -   ".., 78)      = 78
```

This `write(2)` call records the request in the access log. Note that one thing missing from this trace is a `time(2)` call. Unlike Apache 1.3, Apache 2.x uses `gettimeofday(3)` to look up the time. On some operating systems, like Linux or Solaris, `gettimeofday` has an optimized implementation that doesn't require as much overhead as a typical system call.

```
/65:    shutdown(9, 1, 1)                               = 0
/65:    poll(0xFAF7B980, 1, 2000)                       = 1
/65:    read(9, 0xFAF7BC20, 512)                        = 0
/65:    close(9)                                        = 0
```

The worker thread does a lingering close of the connection.

```
/65:    close(10)                                       = 0
/65:    lwp_park(0x00000000, 0)         (sleeping...)
```

Finally the worker thread closes the file that it has just delivered and blocks until the listener assigns it another connection.

```
/67:    accept(3, 0x001FEB74, 0x001FEB94, 1) (sleeping...)
```

Meanwhile, the listener thread is able to accept another connection as soon as it has dispatched this connection to a worker thread (subject to some flow-control logic in the worker MPM that throttles the listener if all the available workers are busy). Though it isn't apparent from this trace, the next `accept(2)` can (and usually does, under high load conditions) occur in parallel with the worker thread's handling of the just-accepted connection.

9.3 Security Tips

Some hints and tips on security issues in setting up a web server. Some of the suggestions will be general, others specific to Apache.

Keep up to Date

The Apache HTTP Server has a good record for security and a developer community highly concerned about security issues. But it is inevitable that some problems – small or large – will be discovered in software after it is released. For this reason, it is crucial to keep aware of updates to the software. If you have obtained your version of the HTTP Server directly from Apache, we highly recommend you subscribe to the Apache HTTP Server Announcements List[5] where you can keep informed of new releases and security updates. Similar services are available from most third-party distributors of Apache software.

Of course, most times that a web server is compromised, it is not because of problems in the HTTP Server code. Rather, it comes from problems in add-on code, CGI scripts, or the underlying Operating System. You must therefore stay aware of problems and updates with all the software on your system.

Denial of Service (DoS) attacks

All network servers can be subject to denial of service attacks that attempt to prevent responses to clients by tying up the resources of the server. It is not possible to prevent such attacks entirely, but you can do certain things to mitigate the problems that they create.

Often the most effective anti-DoS tool will be a firewall or other operating-system configurations. For example, most firewalls can be configured to restrict the number of simultaneous connections from any individual IP address or network, thus preventing a range of simple attacks. Of course this is no help against Distributed Denial of Service attacks (DDoS).

There are also certain Apache HTTP Server configuration settings that can help mitigate problems:

- The REQUESTREADTIMEOUT directive allows to limit the time a client may take to send the request.
- The TIMEOUT directive should be lowered on sites that are subject to DoS attacks. Setting this to as low as a few seconds may be appropriate. As TIMEOUT is currently used for several different operations, setting it to a low value introduces problems with long running CGI scripts.
- The KEEPALIVETIMEOUT directive may be also lowered on sites that are subject to DoS attacks. Some sites even turn off the keepalives completely via KEEPALIVE, which has of course other drawbacks on performance.
- The values of various timeout-related directives provided by other modules should be checked.
- The directives LIMITREQUESTBODY, LIMITREQUESTFIELDS, LIMITREQUESTFIELDSIZE, LIMITREQUEST-LINE, and LIMITXMLREQUESTBODY should be carefully configured to limit resource consumption triggered by client input.
- On operating systems that support it, make sure that you use the ACCEPTFILTER directive to offload part of the request processing to the operating system. This is active by default in Apache httpd, but may require reconfiguration of your kernel.
- Tune the MAXREQUESTWORKERS directive to allow the server to handle the maximum number of simultaneous connections without running out of resources. See also the performance tuning documentation (p. 327) .

[5] http://httpd.apache.org/lists.html#http-announce

- The use of a threaded mpm (p. 80) may allow you to handle more simultaneous connections, thereby mitigating DoS attacks. Further, the EVENT mpm uses asynchronous processing to avoid devoting a thread to each connection. Due to the nature of the OpenSSL library the EVENT mpm is currently incompatible with MOD_SSL and other input filters. In these cases it falls back to the behaviour of the WORKER mpm.
- There are a number of third-party modules available through http://modules.apache.org/ that can restrict certain client behaviors and thereby mitigate DoS problems.

Permissions on ServerRoot Directories

In typical operation, Apache is started by the root user, and it switches to the user defined by the USER directive to serve hits. As is the case with any command that root executes, you must take care that it is protected from modification by non-root users. Not only must the files themselves be writeable only by root, but so must the directories, and parents of all directories. For example, if you choose to place ServerRoot in `/usr/local/apache` then it is suggested that you create that directory as root, with commands like these:

```
mkdir /usr/local/apache
cd /usr/local/apache
mkdir bin conf logs
chown 0 .  bin conf logs
chgrp 0 .  bin conf logs
chmod 755 .  bin conf logs
```

It is assumed that `/`, `/usr`, and `/usr/local` are only modifiable by root. When you install the `httpd` executable, you should ensure that it is similarly protected:

```
cp httpd /usr/local/apache/bin
chown 0 /usr/local/apache/bin/httpd
chgrp 0 /usr/local/apache/bin/httpd
chmod 511 /usr/local/apache/bin/httpd
```

You can create an htdocs subdirectory which is modifiable by other users – since root never executes any files out of there, and shouldn't be creating files in there.

If you allow non-root users to modify any files that root either executes or writes on then you open your system to root compromises. For example, someone could replace the `httpd` binary so that the next time you start it, it will execute some arbitrary code. If the logs directory is writeable (by a non-root user), someone could replace a log file with a symlink to some other system file, and then root might overwrite that file with arbitrary data. If the log files themselves are writeable (by a non-root user), then someone may be able to overwrite the log itself with bogus data.

Server Side Includes

Server Side Includes (SSI) present a server administrator with several potential security risks.

The first risk is the increased load on the server. All SSI-enabled files have to be parsed by Apache, whether or not there are any SSI directives included within the files. While this load increase is minor, in a shared server environment it can become significant.

SSI files also pose the same risks that are associated with CGI scripts in general. Using the `exec cmd` element, SSI-enabled files can execute any CGI script or program under the permissions of the user and group Apache runs as, as configured in `httpd.conf`.

There are ways to enhance the security of SSI files while still taking advantage of the benefits they provide.

To isolate the damage a wayward SSI file can cause, a server administrator can enable suexec (p. 105) as described in the CGI in General section.

Enabling SSI for files with `.html` or `.htm` extensions can be dangerous. This is especially true in a shared, or high traffic, server environment. SSI-enabled files should have a separate extension, such as the conventional `.shtml`. This helps keep server load at a minimum and allows for easier management of risk.

Another solution is to disable the ability to run scripts and programs from SSI pages. To do this replace `Includes` with `IncludesNOEXEC` in the OPTIONS directive. Note that users may still use `<--#include virtual="..." -->` to execute CGI scripts if these scripts are in directories designated by a SCRIPTALIAS directive.

CGI in General

First of all, you always have to remember that you must trust the writers of the CGI scripts/programs or your ability to spot potential security holes in CGI, whether they were deliberate or accidental. CGI scripts can run essentially arbitrary commands on your system with the permissions of the web server user and can therefore be extremely dangerous if they are not carefully checked.

All the CGI scripts will run as the same user, so they have potential to conflict (accidentally or deliberately) with other scripts e.g. User A hates User B, so he writes a script to trash User B's CGI database. One program which can be used to allow scripts to run as different users is suEXEC (p. 105) which is included with Apache as of 1.2 and is called from special hooks in the Apache server code. Another popular way of doing this is with CGIWrap[6].

Non Script Aliased CGI

Allowing users to execute CGI scripts in any directory should only be considered if:

- You trust your users not to write scripts which will deliberately or accidentally expose your system to an attack.
- You consider security at your site to be so feeble in other areas, as to make one more potential hole irrelevant.
- You have no users, and nobody ever visits your server.

Script Aliased CGI

Limiting CGI to special directories gives the admin control over what goes into those directories. This is inevitably more secure than non script aliased CGI, but only if users with write access to the directories are trusted or the admin is willing to test each new CGI script/program for potential security holes.

Most sites choose this option over the non script aliased CGI approach.

Other sources of dynamic content

Embedded scripting options which run as part of the server itself, such as `mod_php`, `mod_perl`, `mod_tcl`, and `mod_python`, run under the identity of the server itself (see the USER directive), and therefore scripts executed by these engines potentially can access anything the server user can. Some scripting engines may provide restrictions, but it is better to be safe and assume not.

[6] http://cgiwrap.sourceforge.net/

Dynamic content security

When setting up dynamic content, such as `mod_php`, `mod_perl` or `mod_python`, many security considerations get out of the scope of `httpd` itself, and you need to consult documentation from those modules. For example, PHP lets you setup Safe Mode[7], which is most usually disabled by default. Another example is Suhosin[8], a PHP addon for more security. For more information about those, consult each project documentation.

At the Apache level, a module named mod_security[9] can be seen as a HTTP firewall and, provided you configure it finely enough, can help you enhance your dynamic content security.

Protecting System Settings

To run a really tight ship, you'll want to stop users from setting up `.htaccess` files which can override security features you've configured. Here's one way to do it.

In the server configuration file, put

```
<Directory "/">
    AllowOverride None
</Directory>
```

This prevents the use of `.htaccess` files in all directories apart from those specifically enabled.

Note that this setting is the default since Apache 2.3.9.

Protect Server Files by Default

One aspect of Apache which is occasionally misunderstood is the feature of default access. That is, unless you take steps to change it, if the server can find its way to a file through normal URL mapping rules, it can serve it to clients.

For instance, consider the following example:

```
# cd /; ln -s / public_html
Accessing http://localhost/~root/
```

This would allow clients to walk through the entire filesystem. To work around this, add the following block to your server's configuration:

```
<Directory "/">
    Require all denied
</Directory>
```

This will forbid default access to filesystem locations. Add appropriate DIRECTORY blocks to allow access only in those areas you wish. For example,

```
<Directory "/usr/users/*/public_html">
    Require all granted
</Directory>
<Directory "/usr/local/httpd">
    Require all granted
</Directory>
```

[7] http://www.php.net/manual/en/ini.sect.safe-mode.php
[8] http://www.hardened-php.net/suhosin/
[9] http://modsecurity.org/

Pay particular attention to the interactions of LOCATION and DIRECTORY directives; for instance, even if `<Directory "/">` denies access, a `<Location "/">` directive might overturn it.

Also be wary of playing games with the USERDIR directive; setting it to something like `./` would have the same effect, for root, as the first example above. We strongly recommend that you include the following line in your server configuration files:

```
UserDir disabled root
```

Watching Your Logs

To keep up-to-date with what is actually going on against your server you have to check the Log Files (p. 53) . Even though the log files only reports what has already happened, they will give you some understanding of what attacks is thrown against the server and allow you to check if the necessary level of security is present.

A couple of examples:

```
grep -c "/jsp/source.jsp?/jsp/ /jsp/source.jsp??" access_log
grep "client denied" error_log | tail -n 10
```

The first example will list the number of attacks trying to exploit the Apache Tomcat Source.JSP Malformed Request Information Disclosure Vulnerability[10], the second example will list the ten last denied clients, for example:

```
[Thu Jul 11 17:18:39 2002] [error] [client foo.example.com] client
denied by server configuration: /usr/local/apache/htdocs/.htpasswd
```

As you can see, the log files only report what already has happened, so if the client had been able to access the `.htpasswd` file you would have seen something similar to:

```
foo.example.com - - [12/Jul/2002:01:59:13 +0200] "GET /.htpasswd
HTTP/1.1"
```

in your Access Log (p. 53) . This means you probably commented out the following in your server configuration file:

```
<Files ".ht*">
    Require all denied
</Files>
```

Merging of configuration sections

The merging of configuration sections is complicated and sometimes directive specific. Always test your changes when creating dependencies on how directives are merged.

For modules that don't implement any merging logic, such as MOD_ACCESS_COMPAT, the behavior in later sections depends on whether the later section has any directives from the module. The configuration is inherited until a change is made, at which point the configuration is *replaced* and not merged.

[10] http://online.securityfocus.com/bid/4876/info/

9.4 Relevant Standards

This page documents all the relevant standards that the Apache HTTP Server follows, along with brief descriptions.

In addition to the information listed below, the following resources should be consulted:

- http://purl.org/NET/http-errata[11] - HTTP/1.1 Specification Errata
- http://www.rfc-editor.org/errata.php[12] - RFC Errata
- http://ftp.ics.uci.edu/pub/ietf/http/#RFC[13] - A pre-compiled list of HTTP related RFCs

Notice
This document is not yet complete.

HTTP Recommendations

Regardless of what modules are compiled and used, Apache as a basic web server complies with the following IETF recommendations:

RFC 1945[14] **(Informational)** The Hypertext Transfer Protocol (HTTP) is an application-level protocol with the lightness and speed necessary for distributed, collaborative, hypermedia information systems. This documents HTTP/1.0.

RFC 2616[15] **(Standards Track)** The Hypertext Transfer Protocol (HTTP) is an application-level protocol for distributed, collaborative, hypermedia information systems. This documents HTTP/1.1.

RFC 2396[16] **(Standards Track)** A Uniform Resource Identifier (URI) is a compact string of characters for identifying an abstract or physical resource.

RFC 4346[17] **(Standards Track)** The TLS protocol provides communications security over the Internet. It provides encryption, and is designed to prevent eavesdropping, tampering, and message forgery.

HTML Recommendations

Regarding the Hypertext Markup Language, Apache complies with the following IETF and W3C recommendations:

RFC 2854[18] **(Informational)** This document summarizes the history of HTML development, and defines the "text/html" MIME type by pointing to the relevant W3C recommendations.

HTML 4.01 Specification[19] **(Errata**[20]**)** This specification defines the HyperText Markup Language (HTML), the publishing language of the World Wide Web. This specification defines HTML 4.01, which is a subversion of HTML 4.

HTML 3.2 Reference Specification[21] The HyperText Markup Language (HTML) is a simple markup language used to create hypertext documents that are portable from one platform to another. HTML documents are SGML documents.

XHTML 1.1 - Module-based XHTML[22] **(Errata**[23]**)** This Recommendation defines a new XHTML document type that is based upon the module framework and modules defined in Modularization of XHTML.

---

[11] http://purl.org/NET/http-errata
[12] http://www.rfc-editor.org/errata.php
[13] http://ftp.ics.uci.edu/pub/ietf/http/#RFC

XHTML 1.0 The Extensible HyperText Markup Language (Second Edition)[24] (Errata[25]) This specification defines the Second Edition of XHTML 1.0, a reformulation of HTML 4 as an XML 1.0 application, and three DTDs corresponding to the ones defined by HTML 4.

Authentication

Concerning the different methods of authentication, Apache follows the following IETF recommendations:

RFC 2617[26] (Standards Track) "HTTP/1.0", includes the specification for a Basic Access Authentication scheme.

Language/Country Codes

The following links document ISO and other language and country code information:

ISO 639-2[27] ISO 639 provides two sets of language codes, one as a two-letter code set (639-1) and another as a three-letter code set (this part of ISO 639) for the representation of names of languages.

ISO 3166-1[28] These pages document the country names (official short names in English) in alphabetical order as given in ISO 3166-1 and the corresponding ISO 3166-1-alpha-2 code elements.

BCP 47[29] (Best Current Practice), RFC 3066[30] This document describes a language tag for use in cases where it is desired to indicate the language used in an information object, how to register values for use in this language tag, and a construct for matching such language tags.

RFC 3282[31] (Standards Track) This document defines a "Content-language:" header, for use in cases where one desires to indicate the language of something that has RFC 822-like headers, like MIME body parts or Web documents, and an "Accept-Language:" header for use in cases where one wishes to indicate one's preferences with regard to language.

9.5 Password Formats

Notes about the password encryption formats generated and understood by Apache.

Basic Authentication

There are five formats that Apache recognizes for basic-authentication passwords. Note that not all formats work on every platform:

bcrypt "$2y$" + the result of the crypt_blowfish algorithm. See the APR source file crypt_blowfish.c[32] for the details of the algorithm.

MD5 "$apr1$" + the result of an Apache-specific algorithm using an iterated (1,000 times) MD5 digest of various combinations of a random 32-bit salt and the password. See the APR source file apr_md5.c[33] for the details of the algorithm.

SHA1 "{SHA}" + Base64-encoded SHA-1 digest of the password. Insecure.

CRYPT Unix only. Uses the traditional Unix `crypt(3)` function with a randomly-generated 32-bit salt (only 12 bits used) and the first 8 characters of the password. Insecure.

PLAIN TEXT (i.e. *unencrypted*) Windows & Netware only. Insecure.

Generating values with htpasswd

bcrypt

```
$ htpasswd -nbB myName myPassword
myName:$2y$05$c4WoMPo3SXsafkva.HHa6uXQZWr7oboPiC2bT/r7q1BB8I2s0BRqC
```

MD5

```
$ htpasswd -nbm myName myPassword
myName:$apr1$r31.....$HqJZimcKQFAMYayBlzkrA/
```

SHA1

```
$ htpasswd -nbs myName myPassword
myName:{SHA}VBPuJHI7uixaa6LQGWx4s+5GKNE=
```

CRYPT

```
$ htpasswd -nbd myName myPassword
myName:rqXexS6ZhobKA
```

[32] http://svn.apache.org/viewvc/apr/apr/trunk/crypto/crypt_blowfish.c?view=markup

[33] http://svn.apache.org/viewvc/apr/apr/trunk/crypto/apr_md5.c?view=markup

Generating CRYPT and MD5 values with the OpenSSL command-line program

OpenSSL knows the Apache-specific MD5 algorithm.

MD5
```
$ openssl passwd -apr1 myPassword
$apr1$qHDFfhPC$nITSVHgYbDAK1Y0acGRnY0
```

CRYPT
```
openssl passwd -crypt myPassword
qQ5vTYO3c8dsU
```

Validating CRYPT or MD5 passwords with the OpenSSL command line program

The salt for a CRYPT password is the first two characters (converted to a binary value). To validate `myPassword` against `rqXexS6ZhobKA`

CRYPT
```
$ openssl passwd -crypt -salt rq myPassword
Warning: truncating password to 8 characters
rqXexS6ZhobKA
```

Note that using `myPasswo` instead of `myPassword` will produce the same result because only the first 8 characters of CRYPT passwords are considered.

The salt for an MD5 password is between `$apr1$` and the following `$` (as a Base64-encoded binary value - max 8 chars). To validate `myPassword` against `$apr1$r31.....$HqJZimcKQFAMYayBlzkrA/`

MD5
```
$ openssl passwd -apr1 -salt r31..... myPassword
$apr1$r31.....$HqJZimcKQFAMYayBlzkrA/
```

Database password fields for mod_dbd

The SHA1 variant is probably the most useful format for DBD authentication. Since the SHA1 and Base64 functions are commonly available, other software can populate a database with encrypted passwords that are usable by Apache basic authentication.

To create Apache SHA1-variant basic-authentication passwords in various languages:

PHP
```
'{SHA}' . base64_encode(sha1($password, TRUE))
```

Java
```
"{SHA}" + new
sun.misc.BASE64Encoder().encode(java.security.MessageDigest.getInstance("SHA1").digest(
```

ColdFusion
```
"{SHA}" & ToBase64(BinaryDecode(Hash(password, "SHA1"), "Hex"))
```

Ruby
```
require 'digest/sha1'
require 'base64'
'{SHA}' + Base64.encode64(Digest::SHA1.digest(password))
```

C or C++
```
Use the APR function:  apr_sha1_base64
```

PostgreSQL (with the contrib/pgcrypto functions installed)
```
'{SHA}'||encode(digest(password,'sha1'),'base64')
```

Digest Authentication

Apache recognizes one format for digest-authentication passwords - the MD5 hash of the string `user:realm:password` as a 32-character string of hexadecimal digits. `realm` is the Authorization Realm argument to the AUTHNAME directive in httpd.conf.

Database password fields for mod_dbd

Since the MD5 function is commonly available, other software can populate a database with encrypted passwords that are usable by Apache digest authentication.

To create Apache digest-authentication passwords in various languages:

PHP
```
md5($user . ':' . $realm . ':' .$password)
```

Java
```
byte b[] = java.security.MessageDigest.getInstance("MD5").digest(
(user + ":" + realm + ":" + password ).getBytes());
java.math.BigInteger bi = new java.math.BigInteger(1, b);
String s = bi.toString(16);
while (s.length() < 32)
    s = "0" + s;
// String s is the encrypted password
```

ColdFusion
```
LCase(Hash( (user & ":" & realm & ":" & password) , "MD5"))
```

Ruby

```
require 'digest/md5'
Digest::MD5.hexdigest(user + ':' + realm + ':' + password)
```

PostgreSQL (with the contrib/pgcrypto functions installed)

```
encode(digest( user || ':' || realm || ':' || password , 'md5'),
'hex')
```

Made in the USA
Middletown, DE
23 April 2018